T0304656

Multilatinas

The challenges faced by Latin American multinational companies, or multilatinas, often require unique strategies tailored to a demanding global environment. This book studies the strategies of internationalism exercised by large multilatinas, offering the first systematic, quantitative effort to examine the pattern of their international investments within the context of their competitive position in the domestic market. *Multilatinas* uncovers common strategies among sixty-two multilatinas from six countries, and emphasises the unique challenges they face, as well as the diversity of their organisational resources. It also brings the institutional environment of Latin American countries to the fore, assessing its role as an essential component in understanding internationalisation decisions. Finally, the book studies the role of non-market organisational resources such as bribes, negotiations and favours in business strategies. *Multilatinas* is an invaluable read for students, scholars, practitioners and executives studying Latin America's place in international business.

VENETA ANDONOVA is Associate Professor at the Universidad de los Andes, Colombia. The outcomes of her research are published in international journals such as the *Journal of Development Economics*, the *Journal of Development Studies*, the *Journal of Business Research*, *Telecommunications Policy* and others. Her research interests include business growth and entrepreneurship, crafting business strategies in poor business environments and successful internationalisation strategies for Latin American and East European companies.

MAURICIO LOSADA-OTÁLORA is a professor at the Universidad Externado de Colombia, Business School. His current research focuses primarily on services marketing and on the relationships between institutions, resources and internationalisation of emerging multinationals. His research has been published in the *European Business Review*, *Business Horizons*, *International Journal of Retail and Distribution Management* and the *Journal of Retailing and Consumer Services*.

Multilatinas

Strategies for Internationalisation

EDITED BY

VENETA ANDONOVA
Universidad de los Andes, Colombia

MAURICIO LOSADA-OTÁLORA
Universidad Externado de Colombia

Shaftesbury Road, Cambridge CB2 8EA, United Kingdom

One Liberty Plaza, 20th Floor, New York, NY 10006, USA

477 Williamstown Road, Port Melbourne, VIC 3207, Australia

314–321, 3rd Floor, Plot 3, Splendor Forum, Jasola District Centre, New Delhi – 110025, India

103 Penang Road, #05–06/07, Visioncrest Commercial, Singapore 238467

Cambridge University Press is part of Cambridge University Press & Assessment, a department of the University of Cambridge.

We share the University's mission to contribute to society through the pursuit of education, learning and research at the highest international levels of excellence.

www.cambridge.org
Information on this title: www.cambridge.org/9781107130043

DOI: 10.1017/9781316417706

First published 2018

A catalogue record for this publication is available from the British Library

ISBN   978-1-107-13004-3   Hardback

Contents

Contributors

VENETA ANDONOVA
Universidad de los Andes, School of Management

FERNANDA RIBEIRO CAHEN
University of FEI - Centro Universitário da FEI.

LOURDES CASANOVA
Samuel Curtis Johnson Graduate School of Management

ERNESTO CUÉLLAR-URBANO
Universidad de los Andes, School of Management

ANABELLA DAVILA
EGADE Business School

JUANA GARCÍA
Universidad de los Andes, School of Management

JULIAN KASSUM
International Chamber of Commerce

MAURICIO LOSADA-OTÁLORA
Universidad Externado de Colombia

MOACIR MIRANDA DE OLIVEIRA JR.
University of São Paulo

JORGE RAMÍREZ-VALLEJO
Universidad de los Andes, School of Management
Harvard Business School

Acknowledgements

We are indebted to many people who have contributed to this research effort over the years. We have been inspired by the pioneers who drew attention to the phenomenon of emerging country multinationals and those who started the research endeavour on multilatinas when there were only a few stories to be told. We are grateful for the opportunity to interact and learn from the greatest minds on the problems of economic development and competitiveness in the last two decades, who prompted us to look at a different part of the world and think deeper about our role as researchers and educators who could make a difference.

The story of multilatinas started to be written many years, even decades, ago, and we are lucky to live during a time when we can build on the arduous work of those before us as we start to see increasingly clear patterns, not just a few anecdotes. We admire the commitment and persistence of previous generations of researchers in the topic and we are grateful for their struggle to build analytical frameworks, develop in-depth cases studies and convince editors that multilatinas represent a fruitful and even important field for research. Without these pioneers, frontrunners and gifted analytical thinkers this book would not exist.

We owe a deep debt of gratitude to the sixty-two executives in multilatinas whom we approached and who agreed to share details about the internationalisation strategies of their businesses with us. Without their understanding and willingness to support our research effort this would have been a very different book, an important part of which is a synthesis of the patterns that emerged in these structured conversations.

The idea for this book came at a time when many people felt the need to develop the stock of knowledge about multilatinas and emerging country multinationals more generally. During the Strategic Management Society Meeting in Santiago (Chile) in 2015 we got together and presented the Emerging Multinationals Research Network (EMNRN), a collaboration project between the Samuel Curtis Johnson Graduate School of Management at Cornell, Universidad de los Andes School of Management, Universidad de Sao Paulo Business School (FEAUSP) and EGADE Business School in Monterrey, Mexico. Our aim was and remains to produce and accumulate knowledge to support the internationalisation of multinationals from emerging countries to facilitate their integration in the regional and global economy. Both individually and as a group of researchers we aspire to take advantage of the academic excellence in the educational institutions in emerging markets and create actionable knowledge for emerging multinationals, the public sector and local and global communities. We are indebted to our colleagues and friends from the EMNRN for their contributions to this book and for enriching the perspective on the factors that affect the global success of multilatinas. We appreciate the time they took away from high-impact, policy-influencing and academic activities to present their unique perspective on the most critical issues for today's multilatinas. We would like to thank Lourdes Casanova, Anabella Davila, Juana García, Fernanda Ribeiro Cahen, Moacir Miranda de Oliveira Jr., Jorge Ramírez, Enesto Cuéllar-Urbano and Julian Kassum, who engaged in active conversation with us and pushed their agendas to the limit to contribute to this book and satisfy the curiosity of our readers.

Much of the research effort represented here has been supported by the international business schools in which it began. First, the Universidad de los Andes School of Management was the cradle of the project and has remained its strongest supporter over the years. INSEAD opened its doors and generously hosted the project for six months, during which professors Javier Gimeno and Hubert Gatignon contributed actively to the process of survey instrument development. Professor Lourdes Casanova was an indispensable part of our discussions about how to define, select and approach the population of multilatinas whose internationalisation strategies we wanted to understand better. At that time our work conversations engaged us in a broader debate and linked us to a group of experts in such a way that our narrow research question turned into a group effort of unanticipated dimensions. Along the way doctoral students Claudia Patricia Arias and Santiago Cabra researched and provided timely updates on multilatinas' business strategies. Christian Medina managed the database and answered all our questions about secondary data sources. The American University in Bulgaria partly supported the data collection process. Mariya Krasteva and Darya Yanitskaya advised on the design for the book's cover. The School of Management at Universidad Externado actively supported the original manuscript preparation and provided funding for the final stage of text development. This research also received financial support from the European Commission through the Integrated Project CIT3-513420 and the Spanish Ministry of the Economy and Competitiveness, project ECO2008-01116 and project MINECO-ECO2011-29445.

We are especially indebted to all EMBA and MBA students at Universidad de los Andes School of Management who helped us by pre-testing the survey instrument and participated in multiple discussions about the internationalisation strategies of multilatinas; they represented one of our reality checks in the process of thinking about the internationalisation patterns described here. Their interest and enthusiasm kept us motivated to pursue this research agenda and focus on both its academic value and managerial implications.

We are grateful to Valerie Appleby, Stephen Acerra, Paula Parish and Rebecca Coe from Cambridge University Press, who were very supportive and responsive to our enquiries and requests. We thank Sally Simmons of Cambridge Editorial, who helped improve the text, and Alvaro Cuervo-Cazurra for his openness and collegial support. We thank Puntoaparte Bookvertising for preparing the infographics and Juan David Martinez who worked on the graph design.

We put part of our life in this project. Working on it and helping Latin American companies to make well-considered choices about internationalisation has been very satisfactory. We hope our readers find some of the answers to their questions in this book.

Introduction

VENETA ANDONOVA AND
MAURICIO LOSADA-OTÁLORA

Experts are fascinated by Latin American multinationals, or multilatinas, many of which have proved to be particularly resilient in times of economic crisis. In fact, their steady rise has made some observers wonder if established views about international business are applicable to this particular type of multinational enterprise. While the flow of foreign direct investment (FDI) from emerging multinationals has been dominated by Asian companies,[1] multilatinas have gradually obtained a considerable share and attracted increasing attention. The rise of these companies is not a recent phenomenon; by 2011 these firms already represented around 27% of total investments from emerging multinationals.[2] Yet despite their growing participation in global FDI flows, there have not been many comprehensive studies on the internationalisation of multilatinas. The most ambitious works are those of Casanova,[3] Cuervo-Cazurra,[4] Fleury and Fleury[5] and Santiso.[6] However, there is not much systematic evidence of the strategies multinatinas follow and the strategic decisions they make when undertaking FDI. The theoretical debate is served, but the answer to the question whether scholars and managers are well equipped to

---

[1] Sauvant, K., Maschek, W. & McAllister, G. (2010). *Foreign direct investments from emerging markets: The challenges ahead*. Palgrave Macmillan.

[2] UNCTAD (2012). www.unctad.org.

[3] Casanova, L. (2009). *From multilatinas to Global Latinas: The new Latin American multinationals (Compilation case studies)*. Interamerican Development Bank; Casanova, L. (2009). *Global Latinas: Latin America's emerging multinationals*. Palgrave Macmillan.

[4] Cuervo-Cazurra, A. (2008). The multinationalisation of developing country MNEs: The case of multilatinas. *Journal of International Management*, 14, 138–54.

[5] Fleury, A. & Fleury. M. T. (2011). *Brazilian multinationals: Competences for internationalisation*. Cambridge University Press.

[6] Santiso, J. (2014). *The decade of the multilatinas*. Cambridge University Press.

1

explain the growing role of multilatinas inevitably hinges on firm-level empirical evidence, which for the time being is scarce and almost entirely anecdotal.

In the following chapters we bring the story of the internationalisation of some of the largest multinationals in Latin America up to date, focusing on businesses from Argentina, Brazil, Chile, Colombia, Mexico and Peru, and describe the circumstances under which strategic business decisions were taken. The central theme of this book is the strategic behaviour of Latin American multinationals. This behaviour emerges as a consequence of specific and systematic choices made about the place, timing and entry mode of internationalisation, triggered by the degree of institutional uncertainty in the environment and the unique organisational resources and competences of the businesses, including available non-market resources. We present a pattern of behavioural characteristic of multilatinas that offers food for thought to a broader audience interested in understanding the phenomenon of emerging countries' multinationals.

To set the stage for the important questions raised in the last part of this book, we begin by presenting a succinct analysis of the macro environment from which the multilatinas studied here emerge and pay special attention to the environmental context at the time our firm-level data were collected. Next, we present a framework to examine the strategic behaviour behind the internationalisation of contemporary multilatinas. To devise this framework, we undertook an extensive survey of representatives of the executive teams of sixty-two very large multilatinas. Our respondents described the processes and decision-making phases related to their latest international investments. This was a rich source of data collected between August 2012 and April 2013, during the challenging post-crisis period. These data enabled us to construct a model of the behaviour of multilatinas and present a holistic picture of the decision to internationalise, combining internal organisational drivers and environmental forces. This aspect of our research is particularly valuable, given the patchy nature of existing data on multilatinas and the anecdotal and over-theoretical style of much of the existing literature. The data also allowed us to inspect more closely previously discussed ideas about decision-making around internationalisation and to propose some new ideas, advancing empirical testing and suggesting directions for theory improvement.

Our empirical strategy is to focus on Argentina, Brazil, Chile and Mexico, countries that have traditionally produced a large number of successful international businesses; and two newcomers to the multilatinas group, Colombia and Peru, which have shown strong growth but traditionally appear in the footnotes of studies of international business (if they appear at all). We discuss the business strategies followed in the latest international project undertaken by our sample, analysing in detail the organisational resources and institutional realities of the context. Explanations are founded on a deep understanding of the relationship between formal and informal institutions in Latin American countries and the sources of competitive advantage that firms in this region have developed, which together affect the internationalisation strategies of mutilatinas.

This book is also a celebration of the rise of multilatinas, which has been seriously oversimplified in the existing literature, as so many current researchers seem fixated on Mexican and Brazilian firms. We hope to show that other equally impressive multilatinas from Argentina, Chile, Colombia and Peru are worth the attention of scholars, and that the phenomenon of multilatinas is far richer and more persistent than it might at first appear. Our book both complements existing research and takes a step forward in advancing the understanding of multilatinas and to some extent the broader case of emerging countries' multinationals in the second decade of the twenty-first century.

The transformation of emerging countries' multinationals, including multilatinas, into global players in various industries around the world has engaged scholars in a lively debate. Can existing approaches and theories of business internationalisation be used to explain the emergence and growth of these companies, or do we need new models to explain their strategies and guide business decision-making in today's international context? Some authors suggest that new frameworks and theories are needed because existing insights on internationalisation grew out of studies of developed countries' multinationals, a very different context; others suggest that the behaviour of emerging multinationals can be understood using existing theoretical paradigms, despite the differences between the two types of multinationals.[7] The middle

---

[7] Dunning, J. H, Kim C. & Park D. 2008. Old wine in new bottles: A comparison of emerging-market TNCs today and developed-country TNCs thirty years ago. In *The Rise of Transnational Corporations from Emerging Markets: Threat or Opportunity?* Sauvant K. (ed). Edward Elgar.

ground in these debates is occupied by a stream of international business research in which authors suggest that emerging multinationals provide rich ground for analysis and that their study can help to extend existing theories and models of internationalisation.[8] This is the argument behind this book. We hope to enrich the debate with detailed empirical data that reveal the distinctive features of multilatinas, their patterns of behaviour, resources and the environment of their countries of origin.

We see institutional context as a major determinant of the internationalisation strategies of multilatinas. Much theoretical and empirical work shows a persistent relationship between the quality of the domestic institutional environment and the strategic behaviour of emerging multinationals.[9] In the chapters that follow we analyse the interplay between the home-country institutional environment and firms' resources to explain the internationalisation strategies and strategic decisions of emerging multinationals. We explore a set of predictions that link the institutional environment (of home and host countries), firm resources and the strategic actions undertaken during the process of internationalisation.

Our approach is to combine the resource-based view of the firm[10] with the institutional perspective, following a growing trend in studies of emerging multinationals.[11] While the resource-based view allows us to identify the key characteristics of resources, institutional theory provides a framework for explaining what, why and when market

---

[8] Ramamurti, R. (2012). What is really different about emerging market multinationals? *Global Strategy Journal*, 2, 41–47.

[9] Luo, Y. & Wang, S. (2012). Foreign direct investment strategies by Developing country multinationals: A diagnostic model for home Country effects. *Global Strategy Journal* 2(3), 244–61; Dau, L. (2012). Pro-market reforms and developing country multinational corporations. *Global Strategy Journal*, 2(3), 262–76; Tan, D. & Meyer, K. (2010). Business groups' outward FDI: A managerial resources perspective. *Journal of International Management*, 16, 154–64; Cuervo-Cazurra, A. (2012) Extending theory by analyzing developing country multinational companies: Solving the Goldilocks debate. *Global Strategy Journal*, 2(3), 153–67.

[10] Barney, J. (1991). Firm resources and sustained competitive advantage. *Journal of Management*, 17, 99–120.

[11] Peng, M. W., Wang, D. Y. L. & Jiang, Y. (2008). An institution-based view of international business strategy: A focus on emerging economies. *Journal of International Business Studies*, 39, 920–36; Meyer, K. E., Estrin, S., Bhaumik, S. K. & Peng, M. W. (2009). Institutions, resources, and entry strategies in emerging economies. *Strategic Management Journal*, 30, 61–80.

and non-market resources are involved in the internationalisation of multilatinas.

A departure point for the ideas explored here is that the relationship between the institutional environment of emerging countries and multilatinas' internationalisation depends on the characteristics of the resources on which multilatinas base their advantages at home. The existing evidence suggests that emerging multinationals have developed a wide range of resources which they use to create advantages at home and to expand their operations abroad. Some of these resources are highly redeployable and fungible, that is, they are usable across a variety of markets (countries) without the need for major modifications and adaptations. For example, some emerging multinationals exploit their technological resources across various markets because the value of the technology is not eroded when used in a different context from the one where it was created. In other cases emerging multinationals have created market advantages at home based on context-specific resources, such as strong brands, distribution networks or deep managerial knowledge of the market. Unlike technological resources, these kinds of resources are not fungible or transferable across markets, and the possibilities of creating value abroad by exploiting them are limited.

We follow previous classifications of market resources and distinguish between technological and context-specific resources. Technological resources allow firms to create superior products or gain efficiency in the production process irrespective of context. Context-specific resources, on the other hand, allow firms to gain efficiency by fitting better into their environment (e.g. business networks).

Technological and context-specific resources differ in a number of ways. First, while technological resources might be standardised on the basis of explicit knowledge, standardisation is difficult or even impossible in the case of context-specific resources, which are frequently intangible. Second, while legal mechanisms may be appropriate to protect technological resources (e.g. via patents), applying these mechanisms to protect context-specific resources is difficult.[12] Third,

---

[12] Bloodgood, J. M., Sapienza, H. J. & Almeida, J.G. (1996). The internationalisation of new high-potential U.S. ventures: Antecedents and outcomes. *Entrepreneurship Theory and Practice*, 20(4), 61–76; Vega-Jurado, J., Gutiérrez-Gracia, A., Fernandez-de-Lucio, I., Manjarrés-Henriquez (2008).

while technological resources are generally fungible across markets at a low cost,[13] context-specific resources have low fungibility because they are developed for specific contexts.[14]

These differences expose resources to a different set of challenges in the context of institutional uncertainty and arguably determine the internationalisation strategy of companies whose competitive advantage is built predominantly on one or other type of resource. For example, if managers perceive that their company could lose its technological advantages due to an infringement of property rights, they are under strong pressure to defend their technological resources. Holding resources that are vulnerable to the loss of their value when exposed to institutional uncertainty might influence the internationalisation decisions of emerging multinationals.

A complementary element of the link between institutional context and internationalisation strategies is captured by the relationship between the institutional environment and the use of non-market resources. Anecdotal evidence suggests that doing business in contexts with weak institutions is positively correlated to the use of non-market resources, especially favours, bargaining skills and bribes. In institutional environments with high uncertainty, non-market resources are expected (and found) to be a valuable source of international advantage because they provide an immediate fit with the context. By questioning managers about their perceptions of the role of non-market resources in the markets on which they compete we can assess directly the importance of these resources for multilatinas.

We follow the recommendation made by several authors to use larger samples and move away from case studies in order to provide a richer picture of the relationship between institutional context,

The effect of external and internal factors on firms' product innovation. *Research Policy*, 37, 616–32.

[13] Anand, J. & Delios, D. (1997b). Location specificity and the transferability of downstream assets to foreign subsidiaries. *Journal of International Business Studies*, 28(3) 579–603; Sapienza, H., Autio, E., George, G. & Zahra, Sh. (2006). A capabilities perspective on the effects of early internationalisation on firm survival and growth. *Academy of Management Review*, 31(4), 914–33; Zahra, S., Matherne, B. & Carleton, J. (2003). Technological resources leveraging and the internationalisation of new ventures. *Journal of International Entrepreneurship*, 163–86.

[14] Rugman, A. & Verbeke, A. (2001) Subsidiary-specific advantages in multinational enterprises. *Strategic Management Journal*, 22(3), 237–50.

organisational resources and the behaviour of emerging multinationals. Our findings are drawn from a sample size that allows testable and replicable results. Cross-regional validation of the framework and the empirical results enable us to resolve the limited and often contradictory results of previous studies on emerging multinationals.[15]

This is the first book that goes purposefully beyond anecdotes and case studies to look at the successful internationalisation of Latin American multinationals from a numbers perspective, using primary data about their internationalisation strategy. It presents an integrative and comprehensive approach to explain the internationalisation process of global players that manoeuvred relatively successfully through the most recent global economic crisis. More specifically, it contains exhaustive evidence that informs a discussion about how the combination of available firm resources and contextual realities drives the distinctive strategies adopted by Latin American multinationals. This book contributes to the knowledge of practitioners and researchers alike in analysing the behaviour of Latin American multinationals. While it focuses on Latin American multinationals, it makes a legitimate contribution to the broader literature on emerging market multinationals. The questions answered in this book, and the new questions it raises, are relevant to the international business and strategic management fields in the region and beyond, as they relate to two central theories in this field, the resource-based view and institutional theory.

The book is organised in four parts. The six chapters in Part I give a historical account of the process of recent economic development and internationalisation of six Latin American countries, analysing economic progress, institutional and regulatory specificities and natural resources in Argentina, Brazil, Chile, Colombia, Mexico and Peru. An infographic summary presents important data in an intuitive and comprehensive manner. Part II, which looks at the theoretical framework and key constructs, describes the contextual and organisational drivers of internationalisation, namely the institutional uncertainty of the environment, organisational resources and competences, the availability of non-market resources and reliance on business groups. Part III contains the empirical exploration and discussion of the conceptual behavioural model of multilatinas, our empirical approach

[15] Dau, L. (2012). Pro-market reforms and developing country multinational corporations. *Global Strategy Journal*, 2(3), 262–76, 262.

and the ways in which multilatinas have recently tackled the where, when and how of internationalisation. In Part IV, leading researchers expand current knowledge of multilatinas by outlining their role in human capital development, innovation, shared social value creation and political processes. This part of the book is an invitation to extend the research canvas on multilatinas further, to understand and better appreciate their current and future role in labour markets and skills building, socially responsible and technology-driven ventures and the all-important interaction with the political sphere.

PART I

1 | Multilatinas – where do we find them?

MAURICIO LOSADA-OTÁLORA
AND VENETA ANDONOVA

Multilatinas are companies of Latin American origin that engage in foreign direct investment (FDI). There is no single well-recognised and readily available source to facilitate an in-depth quantitative analysis of the internationalisation strategies of multilatinas. In fact, the difficulty in identifying this class of companies is probably the main reason why our current understanding of the internationalisation strategies of multilatinas is based predominantly on case studies. This chapter describes how we identified the multilatinas discussed in this book and uncovered their internationalisation strategies.

Identifying multilatinas

We relied on several existing rankings of Latin American companies to identify the location of the key decision-makers in the process of internationalisation, including: the 500 largest Latin American companies in 2009 and 2010; the most global Latin American multinationals (LAMNEs) in 2012; the 500 largest Chilean companies in 2011, selected by AméricaEconomía[1]; the 500 most important Mexican companies in 2011 from the CNN magazine Expansion; and the 1,000 largest Colombian companies in 2012 from Semana. Fundação Dom Cabral publishes a ranking of Brazilian multinationals; however, the majority of the companies appear in the AméricaEconomía ranking, so the added value of this source was only modest. AméricaEconomía also publishes a ranking of Peruvian companies, but an exhaustive review of this ranking in 2012 showed that the participation of Peruvian companies in FDI is very limited. All of these sources draw heavily on information available from the companies' websites, from the financial supervisory bodies of different Latin American countries and from surveys of executives.

---

[1] www.americaeconomia.com.

We inspected these pooled data to identify Latin American Multinational Enterprises. Our approach has an obvious bias towards identifying large multilatinas and does not include micro-multinationals and Latin American born-global companies. In fact, we excluded all companies with sales less than US$100 million. This threshold is significant because traditionally companies with sales volumes of this magnitude have the resources necessary to make direct investments in foreign markets.[2] Although it has recently been recognised that firms with small national markets have incentives to become international very fast, because of the small scale and lower domestic opportunities,[3] empirical evidence suggests that these firms do not engage in FDI but rely on specialised international networks instead.[4] For example, exporting and leveraging independent intermediaries helps Latin American born-global companies international operations become flexible without paying the cost of direct investments abroad. Therefore, we expect only a small number of multilatinas – that is, companies that use FDI in their overseas operations – to fall outside the selected pool of companies.

Our next step was to reject companies that were subsidiaries of firms from outside Latin America, companies that had only domestic operations and businesses in the insurance and banking industries, which are highly regulated and subject to considerable restrictions regarding internationalisation. We also discarded purely state-owned enterprises (SOEs) that were not publicly traded, on the assumption that their internationalisation process would obey not only a market but also and mainly a political logic. The behaviour of SOEs frequently responds to political pressures that make comparisons with the internationalisation strategies of other companies questionable. However, at this stage we retained Petrobras, Ecopetrol and Grupo ISA in our sample because they were publicly traded SOEs. The 2015 corruption scandal at Petrobras illustrates vividly the risks of this approach.

[2] Bloodgood, J. M., Sapienza, H. J. & Almeida, J. G. (1996). The internationalization of new high-potential U.S. ventures: Antecedents and outcomes. *Entrepreneurship Theory and Practice*, 20(4), 61–76.

[3] Knight, G. & Cavusgil, T. (2004). Innovation, organizational capabilities, and born-global firms. *Journal of International Business Studies*, 35, 124–41.

[4] Oviatt, B. & McDougall, P. (2005). Defining international entrepreneurship and modeling the speed of Internationalization. *Entrepreneurship Theory and Practice*, 29, 537–54.

The sophisticated scheme of interdependencies and transfers in which Petrobras was involved and which benefitted individuals and political parties, worsened the economic crisis in Brazil and undermined the international credibility of the country while stigmatising one of the champion multilatinas. As SOEs, the uniqueness of Petrobras, Ecopetrol and Grupo ISA stands out in many aspects of their operations, including their internationalisation strategy, so much so that their exclusion would have hampered our overall understanding of the internationalisation strategy of multilatinas. Ecopetrol was the only Colombian multinational company in the Fortune Global 500 list in 2015, in which Petrobras ranked twenty-eighth.

The resulting pool of companies was revised and double-counted entities were eliminated, to arrive at 247 firms. Because business groups are a pervasive organisational form in emerging economies,[5] we had to examine ownership relationships among these 247 multilatinas. Using Standard and Poor's (S&P) and Reuters' databases and the firms' websites, we identified 71 conglomerates or headquarters of business groups, 57 subsidiaries of other Latin American companies and 125 standalone enterprises. We classified firms as conglomerates if S&P or Reuters described their economic activity as 'business conglomerate or holding', they presented themselves as a business group on their website, or they had several clearly identifiable affiliate companies. Firms were classified as 'subsidiaries' if S&P and Reuters identified them as such or their website indicated that they were controlled by another Latin American company.

We subsequently eliminated fourteen conglomerate headquarters whose subsidiaries were already included in the list: CGE, Empresas COPEC, Femsa, Grupo Alfa, Grupo Bal, Grupo Camargo Correa, Grupo Carso, Grupo Casa Saba, Grupo Elektra, Grupo Salinas, Grupo Xignux, Norberto Odebrecht, Techint and Vale. This decision was made for two reasons: (1) a parent and a subsidiary share important features, especially resources; and (2) the international business literature suggests that subsidiaries' behaviour reflects the business group's

---

[5] Guillen, M. (2000). Business groups in emerging economies: A resource based view. *Academy of Management Journal*, 43(3), 362–80. Chang, S. J. & Hong, J. (2000). Economic performance of group-affiliated companies in Korea: Intragroup resource sharing and internal business transactions. *Academy of Management Journal*, 43(3), 429–48.

strategy;[6] and we therefore risked double-counting some companies as their strategic decision-making processes overlapped. We also omitted six conglomerate headquarters that were in essence pure holdings[7] and whose only economic activity, described by S&P, was to provide administrative and financial support to members of the group without being involved in strategic decision-making.

We expect the firms that are part of a conglomerate and the stand-alone firms in our sample to be largely comparable even when they have a distinct resource base. Conglomerates, like independent firms, are characterised by unitary management and administrative coordination. In independent firms, the unitary management is in the hands of the general manager, who defines strategies and supervises the different business activities of the company. In business groups, unitary management is possible because the responsibility for defining long-term strategies and control, in the form of monitoring and supervising any affiliated companies, are in the hands of the managers of the parent company or the owner in the case of a family group. Also, in a business group, the parent company coordinates the administrative function of any subsidiaries to achieve mutual adjustments and (ideally) synergies in planning and decision-making, standardise processes and procedures and exert direct supervision over subsidiaries – much like a general manager does in an independent firm.

The decisions made about internationalisation by stand-alone firms and business groups are also comparable in terms of their purpose and the role played by resources. Decisions about internationalisation are made to improve the position of the group as a whole as well as improving the competitive position of individual entities. As for resources, internationalisation decisions are comparable because for both firms and groups they are related to the resources that control viable business operations abroad or are required for creating them. That said, we acknowledge that business groups and their affiliates share resources that might not be available for standalone firms, such as internal capital markets, for example, which can provide the

[6] Cainelli, G. & Iacobucci, D. (2011). Business groups and the boundaries of the firm. *Management Decision*, 49(9), 1549–73.
[7] We are grateful to Lourdes Casanova for highlighting this aspect. The companies deleted were Carvajal Internacional, Quiñenco, CMPC Papeles y Cartones, Grupo Votorantim, Cencosud and Grupo Nutresa.

financial resources to invest abroad.[8] Table 1.1 summarises the process of identifying the companies for this study.

A group of nineteen firms included in the initial list of companies shared a parent company with other firms in the sample. In these cases, we decided to retain the firms if each subsidiary belonged to a different industry.[9] We made this decision because empirical evidence has shown that although firms share some resources within a business group, each also has a unique set of resources that it uses to achieve its business purposes.[10] These differences naturally tend to be larger when entities within a business group belong to unrelated industries. When the process of selection was complete, we had a list of 226 multilatinas, full details of which, including their industries and country of origin, are shown in Table 1.2.

Unit of analysis

Our unit of analysis is the most recent foreign investment project undertaken by the Latin American multinationals in a foreign country. We chose this unit of analysis because it is at the transaction level that internal organisational resources and competences and contextual variables, such as the interaction between home and host country institutional factors, shape firms' strategies abroad.[11] We purposefully and explicitly invited the executives surveyed for this study to answer questions about their most recent approach to internationalisation in relation to their companies' most recent project involving FDI.

By using this unit of analysis we aimed to diminish recall bias and rely on managers remembering recent experiences more vividly and

---

[8] Mahmood I. & Mitchell, W. (2004). Two faces: Effects of business groups on innovation in emerging economies. *Management Science*, 50(10), 1348–65.

[9] The only exceptions were Tenaris and Ternium, which had the same parent, Techint Group, and both competed in the siderurgical industry. In this case Tenaris was retained because its sales in 2010 were greater.

[10] Chang, S. & Hong, J. (2000). Economic performance of group-affiliated companies in Korea: Intragroup resource sharing and internal business transactions. *Academy of Management Journal*, 43(3), 429–48.

[11] Cho, D., Moon, H. & and Kim, M. (2008). Characterizing international competitiveness in international business research: A MASI approach to national competitiveness. *Research in International Business and Finance*, 22, 175–79.

Table 1.1 *Summary of the process of identification of multilatinas*

Ranking source of data	Firms in the ranking	Step 1	Step 2	Step 3	Step 4	Step 5	Steep 6	Step 7	Step 8	Final sample
500 largest LACs (2009 to 2010)	583	0	218	161	0	41	0	12	5	144
65 Most global Latin American companies (2012)	65	0	0	0	0	1	54	2	1	9
500 largest Mexican firms (2011)	500	0	219	131	76	1	49	0	0	24
500 largest Chilean firms (2011)	500	102	75	220	4	0	32	0	0	30
1,000 largest Colombian firms (2012)	1000	582	234	147		0	9	0	0	20
Final multilatina population										226

Table 1.2 *The population of multilatinas*

ID	Name	Origin country	Economic activity	Sales (2011)	Net income (2011)	Sample
1	Acegrasas	Colombia	Agroindustry	242,41	0,19	0
2	Acerias de Colombia	Colombia	Siderurgical	282,43	2,20	0
3	Agrosuper	Chile	Food	2.149,00	–	0
4	Agunsa (14)	Chile	Logistic and transport	572,70	23,80	0
5	Aje-Group	Peru	Beverages	1.719,00	–	0
6	Alfagres	Colombia	Construction	221,38	1,91	0
7	Alicorp	Peru	Food	1.578,00	120,00	0
8	All América Latina	Brazil	Logistic and transport	1.691,00	130,00	0
9	Alpargatas	Brazil	Footwear	1.372,00	163,00	0
10	Alpek	Mexico	Oil and gas	4.326,59	149,41	1
11	Alpina	Colombia	Food	851,09	16,29	1
12	Alsea	Mexico	Restaurants	690,54	8,34	0
13	Altos Hornos de México	Mexico	Siderurgical	2.928,00	140,00	1
14	Andrade Gutierrez	Brazil	Multisector	3.151,00	(96,00)	0
15	Antofagasta PLC	Chile	Mining	6.076,00	2.130,00	0
16	Arauco	Chile	Cellulose/paper	4.374,00	620,00	0
17	Arcor	Argentina	Food	3.100,00	–	1
18	Arcos Dorados	Argentina	Retailer	3.657,00	115,00	0
19	Artecola	Brazil	Chemical	238,30		0
20	Australis	Chile	Aquafarming	163,70	27,40	0

(continued)

Table 1.2 (*cont.*)

ID	Name	Origin country	Economic activity	Sales (2011)	Net income (2011)	Sample
21	Avianca–Taca	Colombia	Logistic and transport	3.566,00	102,00	1
22	Bematech	Brazil	Technology	158,40	(22,60)	1
23	Besalco	Chile	Construction	616,80	37,40	1
24	Bimbo	Mexico	Food	1.572,00	–	1
25	Biofilm	Colombia	Chemical	213,78	(26,09)	1
26	Biopappel	Mexico	Cellulose/paper	1.134,00	6,00	0
27	Braskem	Brazil	Oil and gas	17.686,00	(280,00)	1
28	BRF foods	Brazil	Food	13.704,00	729,00	1
29	Brightstar	Bolivia	Telecommunications	4.700,00	–	0
30	Brinsa	Colombia	Chemical	181,80	15,87	0
31	Camargo Corrêa Cimento	Brazil	Cement	1.247,00	117,00	0
32	CAP (Compañía Minera del Pacífico)	Chile	Siderurgical	2.787,00	441,00	0
33	Casa Luker	Colombia	Food	234,94	4,26	1
34	Cemento Polpaico	Chile	Cement	267,30	(5,00)	0
35	Cementos Argos	Colombia	Cement	1.852,00	186,00	0
36	Cemex	Mexico	Cement	13.546,00	(1.371,00)	0
37	Cía. Pesquera Camanchaca	Chile	Aquafarming	326,10	(22,40)	1
38	Cia.Brasileira de Metalurgia E Mineração	Brazil	Mining	7.528,00	–	0
39	Cicsa	Mexico	Construction	–	–	0

#	Company	Country	Sector			
40	Cinepolis	Mexico	Entertainment	705,24	–	1
41	CMPC Celulosa	Chile	Cellulose/paper	1.316,00	260,00	1
42	Coimex	Brazil	Retailer	1.400,00	251,00	0
43	Colombina	Colombia	Food	114,86	14,15	1
44	Compañía de Cervecerías Unidas – CCU	Chile	Beverages	20.931,00	(1.230,00)	0
45	Compañía Minera Autlán	Mexico	Mining	176,95	8,60	0
46	Const. E Comércio Camargo Corrêa	Brazil	Construction	2.418,00	–	0
47	Constructora Colpatria	Colombia	Construction	138,66	20,89	0
48	Construtora Norberto Odebrecht	Brazil	Construction	4.476,00	482,00	0
49	Construtora Queiroz Galvão	Brazil	Construction	1.654,00	27,00	0
50	Copa Airlines	Panama	Logistic and transport	1.830,00	310,00	0
51	Copec Combustibles	Chile	Oil and gas	7.969,00	–	0
52	Corp. Interamericana de entretenimiento (CIE)	Mexico	Entertainment	761,55	76,94	1
53	Corporación Durango	Mexico	Paper	827,28	127,69	0
54	Cosan	Brazil	Agroindustry	12.214,00	1.565,00	1
55	Coteminas	Brazil	Footwear	2.248,00	–	0
56	Cotia	Brazil	Retailer	1.766,00	46,00	0
57	Cruz Blanca Salud	Chile	Healthcare	326,10	(22,40)	1
58	CSAV	Chile	Shipping	5.151,90	(1.249,80)	0
59	CSN	Brazil	Siderurgical	8.806,00	1.975,00	0
60	Cyrela Realty	Brazil	Construction	3.266,00	265,00	0

(continued)

Table 1.2 (*cont.*)

ID	Name	Origin country	Economic activity	Sales (2011)	Net income (2011)	Sample
61	Detroit	Chile	Multisector	175,00	17,10	0
62	DHB Automotive	Brazil	Automotive	163,10	16,80	1
63	Duas Rodas	Brazil	Food	450,00		1
64	Duratex	Brazil	Manufacturing	1.583,00	199,00	0
65	Ecopetrol	Colombia	Oil and gas	33.194,00	7.801,00	1
66	Editorial Televisa	Mexico	Mass media	827,28	127,69	0
67	Elecmetal	Chile	Siderurgical	175,00	17,10	1
68	Elementia	Mexico	Construction	1.900,00	262,00	0
69	Embotelladora Andina	Chile	Beverages	1.884,00	186,00	0
70	Embotelladoras Arca	Argentina	Food	3.211,00	323,00	0
71	Embraer	Brazil	Aerospace	5.255,00	83,00	1
72	Empresas Banmédica	Chile	Healthcare	1.509,00	83,00	0
73	Empresas Iansa	Chile	Agroindustry	631,10	26,20	0
74	Empresas Ica	Mexico	Construction	3.066,00	106,00	0
75	Empresas Navieras	Chile	Logistic and transport	1.508,00	(23,00)	0
76	Enaex	Chile	Chemical	631,10	26,20	0
77	Enjoy	Chile	Retailer	255,00	2,20	0
78	Entel	Chile	Telecommunications	2.360,00	346,00	0
79	Falabella	Chile	Retailer	9,27	811,00	1
80	Ferreyros/Ferreycorp	Peru	Retailer	1.419,00	72,00	1
81	Ferromex	Mexico	Logistic and transport	1.419,00	72,00	0

#	Company	Country	Sector			
82	Fibria	Brazil	Cellulose/paper	3.121,00	(465,00)	0
83	Fomento Económico Mexicano	Mexico	Beverages	15.769,74	1.212,83	0
84	Forus	Chile	Retailer	273,00	54,50	0
85	Gasco	Chile	Oil and gas	1.785,00	63,00	1
86	Gerdau	Brazil	Siderurgical	18.875,00	1.069,00	0
87	Gicsa	Mexico	Construction	292,01	33,08	0
88	Gol	Brazil	Logistic and transport	4.019,00	(400,00)	1
89	Grupo Andre Maggi	Brazil	Agroindustry	4.133,00	377,00	0
90	Grupo Chedraui	Mexico	Retailer	4.133,00	377,00	0
91	Grupo Deacero	Mexico	Siderurgical	4.133,00	377,00	0
92	*Grupo Famsa*	Mexico	Retailer	4.133,00	377,00	1
93	Grupo Gloria	Peru	Retailer	4.133,00	377,00	0
95	Grupo Industrial Lala	Mexico	Food	4.133,00	377,00	0
96	Grupo Abril	Brazil	Mass media	1.680,00	99,00	0
97	Grupo Accel	Mexico	Logistic and transport	228,07	0,26	0
98	Grupo Bafar	Mexico	Food	420,65	12,95	0
99	Grupo Cementos De Chihuahua	Mexico	Cement	734,09	31,00	1
100	Grupo Clarín	Argentina	Mass media	2.257,00	120,00	0
101	Grupo Condumex	Mexico	Manufacturing	1.560,00	120,00	0
102	Grupo Coppel	Mexico	Retailer	4.206,00	532,00	0
103	Grupo Gigante	Mexico	Multisector	765,43	65,36	0
104	Grupo Herdez	Mexico	Food	6.599,35	60,00	0
107	Grupo Isa	Colombia	Energy	4.802,00	–	1

(continued)

Table 1.2 (*cont.*)

ID	Name	Origin country	Economic activity	Sales (2011)	Net income (2011)	Sample
108	Grupo Iusa	Mexico	Manufacturing	4.802,00	–	0
109	Grupo Kuo	Mexico	Multisector	1.916,00	9,00	1
110	Grupo La Moderna	Mexico	Food	479,37	40,79	0
111	Grupo Maseca	Mexico	Food	1.604,00	14,00	1
112	Grupo México	Mexico	Mining	9.296,00	2.098,00	0
113	Grupo Minsa	Mexico	Food	363,54	17,29	0
114	Grupo Modelo	Mexico	Beverages	6.539,00	856,00	0
115	Grupo Pochteca	Mexico	Chemical	254,02	4,54	0
116	Grupo Posadas	Mexico	Hospitality	5.792,45	21,10	0
117	Grupo Radio Centro	Mexico	Mass media	63,20	0,35	0
118	Grupo Sanborns	Mexico	Retailer	2.656,00	209,00	0
119	Grupo Senda	Mexico	Logistic and transport	2.496,73	27,65	0
120	Grupo Simec	Mexico	Siderurgical	2.098,00	205,00	0
121	Grupo Televisa	Mexico	Mass media	4.486,00	564,00	1
122	Grupo Villacero	Mexico	Siderurgical	1.116,00	–	1
123	Grupo Viz	Mexico	Food	1.565,00	27,00	0
124	Haceb	Colombia	Electronics	289,57	11,60	0
125	Hildebrando	Mexico	Computers	154,94	3,64	0
126	Homex	Mexico	Construction	1.566,00	112,00	0
127	Hortifrut	Chile	Agroindustry	180,00	13,10	1
128	Hypermarcas	Brazil	Pharmaceutical	1.772,00	(29,00)	0

#	Company	Country	Sector			
129	Imcopa	Brazil	Agroindustry	1.392,00	237,00	0
130	Impsa	Argentina	Energy	–	–	0
131	Indura Industria Y Comercio	Chile	Multisector	453,40	33,50	1
132	Industrias Bachoco	Mexico	Food	1.988,00	11,00	0
133	Industrias Ch	Mexico	Siderurgical	2.323,00	218,00	0
134	Industrias Unidas	Mexico	Manufacturing	–	–	0
135	Industrias Peñoles	Mexico	Mining	6.944,00	914,00	1
136	Ingenio Manuelita	Colombia	Food	609,17	48,56	1
137	Intasa	Chile	Manufacturing	100,30	1,60	0
138	Intercement	Brazil	Cement	1.325,30		0
140	Interoceánica	Chile	Shipping	879,90	(39,90)	0
141	Inversiones Alsacia	Chile	Logistic and transport	142,80	(18,80)	0
142	Iochpe-Maxion	Brazil	Automotive	1.548,00	119,00	1
143	Italcol	Colombia	Food	203,22	2,06	0
144	Itautec	Brazil	Electronics	3.652,00	784,00	0
145	JBS Friboi	Brazil	Agroindustry	32.944,00	(40,00)	1
146	Jumbo	Chile	Retailer	1.916,00	–	0
147	Klabin	Brazil	Cellulose/paper	2.073,00	97,00	1
148	Küpfer Hermanos	Chile	Multisector	142,80	(18,80)	0
149	La polar	Chile	Retailer	–	–	0
150	Laboratorios Andrómaco	Chile	Pharmaceutical	169,90	6,30	0
151	Laboratorios Bagò	Argentina	Pharmaceutical	2.555,00	472,00	1
152	Lan	Chile	Logistic and transport	5.585,00	320,00	0
153	Leonisa	Colombia	Footwear	160,57	13,46	0
154	Localiza	Brazil	Logistic and transport	1.555,00	155,00	0

(continued)

23

Table 1.2 (*cont.*)

ID	Name	Origin country	Economic activity	Sales (2011)	Net income (2011)	Sample
155	Lupatech	Brazil	Engineering	327,30	(92,90)	0
156	M. Dias Branco	Brazil	Food	1.551,00	195,00	0
157	Mabe	Mexico	Electronics	3.264,00	(125,00)	1
158	Madeco	Chile	Forestry	428,20	19,20	0
159	Magnesita	Brazil	Mining	1.236,00	52,00	0
160	Mall Plaza	Chile	Retailer	4.022,00	–	0
161	Marcopolo	Brazil	Automotive	1.796,00	182,00	1
162	Marfrig	Brazil	Agroindustry	11.667,00	(397,00)	0
163	Masisa	Chile	Manufacturing	1.251,00	68,00	0
164	Matriz Ideas (Casa & Ideas)	Chile	Retailer	121,00	(30,00)	0
165	Melón	Chile	Cement	359,20	8,10	0
166	Metalfrio	Brazil	Electronics	402,60	3,90	1
167	Metalsa	Mexico	Automotive	1.271,00	–	1
168	Mexichem	Mexico	Oil and gas	3.392,00	194,00	0
169	Minerva	Brazil	Agroindustry	2.120,00	24,00	1
170	Molinos Río De La Plata	Argentina	Agroindustry	3.106,00	64,00	1
171	Molymet	Chile	Siderurgical	1.330,00	103,00	0
172	Nalsani	Colombia	Multisector	136,25	5,44	1
173	Natura	Brazil	Pharmaceutical	2.980,00	443,00	1
174	Nemak	Mexico	Automotive	3.204,00	76,00	0
175	Oas Engenharia	Brazil	Construction	1.474,00	7,00	0

176	Odinsa	Colombia	Construction	145,93	70,50	0
177	Oi-Telemar	Brazil	Telecommunications	4.928,00	536,00	0
178	Olímpica	Colombia	Retailer	1.588,00	45,00	0
179	Organización Terpel	Colombia	Oil and gas	4.384,00	86,00	0
180	Oxiteno	Brazil	Oil and gas	1.284,00	–	0
181	Oxxo (Femsa)	Mexico	Retailer	5.313,00	337,00	0
182	P.I. Mabe	Mexico	Manufacturing	320,00	–	0
183	Paranapanema	Brazil	Mining	2.184,00	(25,00)	0
184	Paz del Rio	Colombia	Siderurgical	380,97	(43,26)	0
185	PDG Realty	Brazil	Construction	3.666,00	375,00	0
186	Petrobras	Brazil	Oil and gas	130.171,70	17.759,00	1
187	Pintuco	Colombia	Chemical	207,60	16,23	1
188	Pluspetrol	Argentina	Oil and gas	1.281,00	–	1
189	Pollo Campero	Guatemala	Food	400,00	–	0
190	Positivo Informática	Brazil	Electronics	1.109,00	(36,00)	0
191	Procaps	Colombia	Pharmaceutical	186,85	3,71	1
192	Promigas	Colombia	Oil and gas	721,54	100,98	1
193	Pucobre	Chile	Mining	267,10	62,30	0
194	Quala	Colombia	Food	276,53	8,39	0
195	Quintec	Chile	Software	184,30	(5,80)	0
196	Randon Participaciones	Brazil	Automotive	2.425,00	56,00	1
197	Recalcine	Chile	Pharmaceutical	490,90	91,10	0
198	Ripley	Chile	Retailer	1.215,00	128,00	0
195	Salfacorp	Chile	Construction	1.728,00	30,00	0
196	Sigdo koppers	Chile	Construction	2.127,00	285,00	0

(continued)

Table 1.2 (*cont.*)

ID	Name	Origin country	Economic activity	Sales (2011)	Net income (2011)	Sample
197	Sigma	Mexico	Food	2.945,00	59,00	0
198	Sintex	Chile	Chemical	490,90	91,10	0
199	Sipsa	Chile	Construction	305,50	(19,00)	0
200	Sodimac	Chile	Retailer	2.684,00	165,00	0
201	Sonda	Chile	Technology	1.136,00	77,00	0
202	Soquimich Comercial	Chile	Mining	305,50	(19,00)	0
203	Springs	Brazil	Footwear	2.222,00	213,00	0
204	SQM	Chile	Mining	2.145,00	545,00	0
205	Sudamericana de Vapores	Chile	Logistic and transport	5.151,00	(1.249,00)	0
206	Supermercados Unimarc	Chile	Retailer	1.834,00	–	0
207	Suzano Papel E Cellulose	Brazil	Cellulose/paper	2.584,00	15,00	0
208	Tam	Brazil	Logistic and transport	6.927,00	(178,00)	0
209	Tecnoquimicas	Colombia	Pharmaceutical	492,17	32,84	0
210	Telmex Internacional	Mexico	Telecommunications	7.057,00	267,00	0
211	Tenaris	Argentina	Siderurgical	9.972,00	1.331,00	0
212	Tiendas Elektra	Mexico	Retailer	1.812,00	–	0
213	Tigre-Tubos E Conexões	Brazil	Manufacturing	1.546,00	–	1
214	Torvs	Brazil	Technology	681,90	90,00	1
215	Tupy	Brazil	Automotive	1.165,00	108,00	0
216	Ultrapar	Brazil	Oil and gas	25.941,00	452,00	0
217	Usiminas	Brazil	Siderurgical	6.345,00	124,00	0

218	Viakable	Mexico	Electronics	1.412,00	–	0
219	Viña Concha Y Toro	Chile	Beverages	810,70	96,80	1
220	Viña San Pedro Tarapacá	Chile	Beverages	265,30	25,50	0
221	Vitro	Mexico	Manufacturing	1.412,00	–	1
222	Voltran	Mexico	Electric equipment	69,33	12,05	0
223	Votorantim Cimentos	Brazil	Cement	4.639,00	483,00	0
224	Votorantim Siderugia	Brazil	Siderurgical	–	–	0
225	Vulcabras	Brazil	Footwear	4.020,00	(276,00)	0
226	Weg	Brazil	Equipment	2.766,00	312,00	0

Note: 1 = participated in the survey; 0 = otherwise. Sales and Net income in million US$.

RESOURCE BASE   INTERNATIONALISATION   STRATEGIC DECISIONS
                              STRATEGY

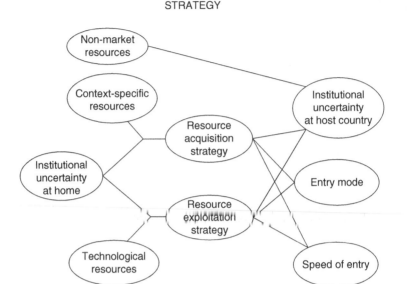

Figure 1.1 Conceptual model of strategic internationalisation decision-making.

easily than older ones.[12] We also aimed to reduce the confusion of respondents when responding to specific quantitative questions about the process of making foreign direct investments.

Strategising about internationalisation

We built a unique dataset to explore the conceptual model of strategic decision-making represented in Figure 1.1. According to this framework, the internationalisation strategy of multilatinas cannot be understood without identifying the most important resources on which their competitive position at home is built.

Resources

We adopted a wide definition of resources that includes all assets, capabilities, organisational processes, firm attributes, information,

[12] Bountempo, G. & Brockner, J. (2008) Emotional intelligence and the ease of recall judgment bias: The mediating effect of private self-focused attention. *Journal of Applied Social Psychology*, 38(1), 159–72.

knowledge, and so on, that a firm controls and that allow it to conceive and implement strategies in foreign markets.[13] Resources can be of two types: market or non-market.[14] Market resources are those that firms use to compete against each other in the market; they include efficient production facilities, brand names and product innovations. Non-market resources are the tangible and intangible assets firms develop that allow them to manage the formal and informal institutions that surround their business activities in the home country (for example, the exchange of favours and bribes).

Additionally, for the purposes of this research, we classified market resources as either technological or context-specific. Transferable technological resources are knowledge-intensive resources[15] that allow firms to create superior products, improve existing products and gain effectiveness and efficiency in production processes. Examples of these resources are R&D, patents and advanced production technologies. Context-specific resources, on the other hand, are developed by firms to fit their country-of-origin markets; their benefits, as a source of competitive advantage, are restricted to a specific country or a region.[16] Examples of these resources are business networks, brands and managerial market knowledge. The value of organisational resources is determined by the institutional environment in the home country, and this contextual element determines many of the differences between developed country multinationals and multilatinas.

[13] See, for example, Barney, J. (1991). Firm resources and sustained competitive advantage. *Journal of Management*, 17, 99–120; and Wernerfelt, B. (1984). A resource-based view of the firm. *Strategic Management Journal*, 5, 171–80.

[14] Cuervo-Cazurra, A. & Genc, M. (2011). Obligating, pressuring, and supporting dimensions of the environment and the nonmarket advantages of developing country multinational companies. *Journal of Management Studies*, 48(2), 441–55.

[15] Yiu, D. W., Lau, Ch. & Bruton, G. D. (2007). International venturing by emerging economy firms: The effects of firm, home country networks, and corporate entrepreneurship. *Journal of International Business Studies*, 38, 519–40.

[16] See, for example, Rugman, A. & Verbeke, A. (2001) Subsidiary-specific advantages in multinational enterprises. *Strategic Management Journal*, 22(3), 237–50; Sirmon, D., Hitt, M. & Ireland, D. (2007). Managing firm resources in dynamic environments to create value: Looking inside the black box. *Academy of Management Review*, 32(1), 273–92; and Anand, J. & Delios, D. (1997b). Location specificity and the transferability of downstream assets to foreign subsidiaries. *Journal of International Business Studies*, 28(3) 579–603.

Institutional uncertainty

We define institutions as the formal and informal rules of the game for doing business inside the borders of a specific country.[17] The institutional weakness of emerging countries, such as those in Latin America, is manifested in many characteristics of governance, including weak legal systems to protect intellectual property rights,[18] political instability,[19] risk of intervention by the home government through taxation, pricing, exchange rates, production and ownership requirements,[20] or corruption and abuse (or misuse) of public power for private benefit.[21] While these characteristics of a weak institutional context tend to be more or less acute in all emerging countries, the institutional uncertainty is particularly damaging for business transactions. These institutional weaknesses interact with the unique resources and core competences of multilatinas to shape their internationalisation strategies.

Strategies

By 'strategies' we mean firms' attempts to identify, protect and exploit their unique resources in order to gain a competitive advantage in the marketplace.[22] Following this definition, and considering the relationship between institutional uncertainty in the home country and firms' resources, we expect multilatinas to follow predominantly one of two generic internationalisation strategies: resource exploitation, which uses the firm's home-grown resources in its foreign markets

---

17 North, D. (1990). *Institutions, institutional change and economic performance. Cambridge*: Cambridge University Press.
18 Peng, M. (2003). Institutional transitions and strategic choices. *Academy of Management Review*, 28(2), 275–96.
19 Miller, K. D. (1992). A framework for integrated risk management in international business. *Journal of International Business Studies*, 23(2), 311–31.
20 Demirbag, M., McGuinness, M. & Altay H. (2010). Perceptions of institutional environment and entry mode: FDI from an emerging country. *Management International Review*, 50, 207–40.
21 See, for example, Bhardan, P. (1997). Corruption and development: A review of issues. *Journal of Economic Literature*, 18(2), 1–26; and Casanova, L. (2009b). *Global Latinas: Latin America's emerging multinationals*. Palgrave Macmillan.
22 Tallman, S. (1991). Strategic management models and resource-based strategies among MNEs in a host market. *Strategic Management Journal*, 12, 69–82.

to create competitive advantage;[23] and resource acquisition, which broadens the resource base of the firm through foreign investments in new resources and competences.[24] Each of these strategies gives rise to a specific set of strategic decisions that affect the where, when and how of internationalisation.

Strategic decisions

Internationalisation obliges firms to make at least three strategic decisions: choose a host market, select an entry mode, and determine the speed of investment.[25] Market choice refers to the selection of a foreign country in which to invest. Entry mode refers to the choice of greenfield investment, mergers, acquisitions or joint ventures as a contractual or organisational arrangement for operating abroad.[26] Speed of investment refers to how quickly organisations execute a plan for FDI, from initial consideration of alternatives to the commitment of resources abroad.[27]

Data collection

Data collection consisted of a telephone interview based on a structured questionnaire. All invited respondents fell into one of the following categories: vice-president of corporate planning, financial chief

---

[23] See, for example, Caves, R. E. (1971). International corporations: The industrial economics of foreign investment. *Economica*, 38, 1–27; Winter, S. & Szulanki, G. (2001). Replication as Strategy. *Organization Science*, 12(6), 730–43; and Makino, S., Lau, C. & Yeh, R. (2002). Asset-exploitation versus asset-seeking, Implications for location choice of foreign direct investment from newly industrialized economies. *Journal of International Business Studies*, 33, 403–21.

[24] See, for example, Dunning, J. H. (1993). *Multinational enterprises and the global economy*. Addison-Wesley; Dunning, J. H. (1988). The eclectic paradigm of international production: A restatement and some possible extensions. *Journal of International Business Studies*, 9(1), 1–31; and Deng, P. (2004). Outward investment by Chinese MNCs: Motivations and implications. *Business Horizons*, 47(3), 8–16.

[25] Hill, Ch. & Jones, G. (2008). *Strategic management theory: An integrated approach*. Houghton Mifflin.

[26] Meyer, K. E., Mudambi, R. & Narula, R. (2011). Multinational enterprises and local contexts: The opportunities and challenges of multiple embeddedness. *Journal of Management Studies*, 48, 235–52.

[27] Eisenhardt, K. (1989). Making fast strategic decisions in high-velocity environments. *Academy of Management Journal*, 32(3), 543–76.

or chief of international operations, and respondents were identified in specialised databases such as Standard & Poor's, Reuters and Bloomberg. A cover letter and questionnaire written in Spanish and Portuguese were sent via email to the key informants. In the following four months, market researchers, all Spanish and Portuguese native speakers, contacted the selected respondents or their assistants by phone and made appointments for the interviews. We received responses from sixty-two executives, one per company. The far-right column in Table 1.2 identifies the participating companies. In seven of the questionnaires returned, data relating to the speed of undertaking FDI were incomplete. These questionnaires noted only the year in which firms identified investment opportunities or started legal procedures in the host market to prepare for investment. In these cases, we took a conservative approach and assumed January as the month in which the opportunity was discovered or the legal procedures began. Additionally, some of the aspects about which we would ideally have liked information could not be fully explored because fewer than 60% of the respondents provided valid answers. Areas for which we could not access information with enough detail include aspects of ownership structure, drivers of perceived competition in the domestic market, business unit sales of the previous year and ownership participation in joint venture agreements.

Characteristics of the sample

Of the sixty-two participating multilatinas, forty-seven reported that they were entering a new host market. The participating companies belong to twenty-four industrial sectors, of which 30% are Brazilian multinationals, followed in frequency by Mexican, Colombian and Chilean. The sample consists of large multilatinas of which seven have more than 20,000 employees. Table 1.3 presents a detailed description of the data.

The subsequent chapters of Part I of this book present the most critical macroeconomic, social and institutional aspects of Argentina, Brazil, Chile, Colombia, Mexico and Peru, as these are seen as indispensable for understanding the internationalisation strategies of the multilatinas featured in the book. The contextual analysis in these chapters is focused almost entirely on the period of 2000 to 2015, a time period that allows us to examine the environmental context immediately before the FDI

Table 1.3 Characteristics of the multilatinas sample

	Frequency	%
a. Number of firms that invest in a new host country		
New	45	72.6
Old (reinvesting)	17	27.4
Total	62	100

b. Country of origin of firms in the sample		
Origen country	Frequency	%
Argentina	4	6.5
Brazil	19	30.6
Chile	10	16.1
Colombia	12	19.4
Mexico	15	24.2
Peru	2	3.2
Total	62	100

c. Age of the firms in the sample		
Age	Frequency	%
< 20 years	7	11.3
> 20 < 40	9	14.5
> 40 < 60	17	27.4
> 60 < 80	14	22.6
> 80 < 100	7	11.3
> 100 years	8	12.9
Total	62	100

d. Size of the firms in the sample		
Number of employees	Frequency	%
< 5,000	36	58.06
> 5,000 < 20,000	19	30.65
> 20,000	7	11.29
Total	62	100

(*continued*)

Table 1.3 (*cont.*)

e. Economic activities of the firms in the sample

Economic activity	Frequency
Aerospace	1
Agroindustry	5
Aqua farming	1
Automotive	5
Beverages	1
Cellulose/paper	2
Cement	1
Chemical	2
Construction	1
Electronics	2
Energy	1
Entertainment	2
Food	10
Healthcare	1
Logistic and transport	2
Manufacturing	2
Mass media	1
Mining	1
Multisector	3
Oil and gas	7
Pharmaceutical	3
Retailer	3
Siderurgical	3
Technology	2

process we studied and some years following it. The understanding of the macro environment is essential for the building of a holistic understanding of the internationalisation strategies of multilatinas. However, expanding the detailed description of the context beyond 2015 will introduce facts and forces that were not part of the decision-making consideration of multilatinas and will introduce a substantial cognitive bias in the interpretation of the results. The phone interviews, which revealed the internationalisation strategies of the multilatinas featured, took place between August 2012 and April 2013.

2 | Colombia – the new wave

JUANA GARCÍA AND VENETA ANDONOVA

Since it introduced a new constitution in 1991, Colombia has experienced tremendous changes: the country has put some rather difficult years behind it to emerge as an attractive economy that has room to expand. It has internationalised its economy and experienced significant growth in exports, imports and foreign direct investment (FDI). Colombian companies have ventured abroad, and a number of important trade agreements have been signed since 2002. In particular, economic indicators have improved considerably, turning the country into one of the most appealing investment destinations and the fourth-largest Latin American economy.

Politically, Colombia is a democracy and one of the most stable countries in the region. Governments since 1991 have worked on opening the economy and improving the country's global economic presence. The improvement in national security under the government of President Álvaro Uribe (2002–10) is one of the reasons for the country's growth and marks a turning point in international opinion.[1] Besides lower homicide and kidnapping rates, Colombia benefitted from new oil exploration at a time when international oil prices reached all-time heights in 2007.[2] Extractive industries have been the government's main source of income and the revenue windfall allowed an increase in public spending.

Social indexes in Colombia have undoubtedly improved. For example, there is easier access to health services, which translates into lower mortality rates and higher life expectancy. Assistance programmes, such as *Familias en Acción*, have helped reduce extreme poverty; the proportion of the population living below the poverty line

[1] *The Economist*, 17 April 2008. The Uribe temptation. Retrieved from: www.economist.com/node/11053186.
[2] OPEC. (n.a.). OPEC Basket Price. Retrieved from: www.opec.org/opec_web/en/data_graphs/40.htm.

35

fell from 49.7% in 2002 to 30.6% in 2013.[3] Additionally, national purchasing power continued to increase up to 2015, which improved the demand for goods and more sophisticated market offerings. As local demand grew stronger, unemployment decreased and more people obtained access to higher education.[4] However, growth has not reduced inequality and, compared to other emerging countries in the region, Colombia appears to need more ambitious social policies. In terms of the economy, Colombian companies still need to improve to help the country overcome the middle-income trap and produce more goods and services with increased added value rather than raw materials and simple manufacturing. Colombian businesses have to find a way to become part of the global chain of technological products that would increase the country's trade revenue.[5] This is also a major challenge for government policies, because shifting to a higher value added production basis requires better-educated employees and effective government policies to support it.

More recently, with the fall in oil prices, the value of Colombia's exports and imports has plummeted because of the country's dependence on its oil exports. Foreign investment has also slowed down because the extractive sector is less attractive for investors. Consequently, in 2015, the local currency depreciated by more than 40%, turning the strongest regional currency to one of the weakest.[6] It is a challenging time for Colombian businesses, and the strategies they decide to undertake are of critical importance for the country's competitiveness. It is also an opportunity to reorganise the local economy and make it stronger internationally. But even if confronted with hard

---

[3] See, for example, García, J. (2015). Development Partnerships in Middle-Income Countries (MICs) – Colombia as a beneficiary and a donor in international cooperation: managing hybridity? Paper presented at the CASID Conference, Ottawa, 2015; and World Bank. (2015). Data – Colombia. World Bank Data Bank. Retrieved from: http://data.worldbank.org/country/colombia.

[4] Euromonitor (2015). Consumer Lifestyles in Colombia. Euromonitor International. Retrieved from: www.euromonitor.com/consumer-lifestyles-in-colombia/report.

[5] Sanguinetti, P. & Villar, L. (2012). Patrones de desarrollo en América Latina: ¿Convergencia o caída en la trampa del ingreso medio? Bogotá: Fedesarrollo. Retrieved from: http://hdl.handle.net/11445/281.

[6] Jaramillo and Xie (2015). Colombia's Peso Weakens to record Low as crude oil prices tumble. Bloomberg Business. Retrieved from: www.bloomberg.com/news/articles/2015-08-13/colombia-s-peso-weakens-toward-record-low-as-crude-oil-tumbles.

challenges, Colombia can be expected to weather the current oil crisis with better results than most of its neighbours and the strength of its domestic market is undoubtedly a good sign.

After nearly seventy years of a four-sided civil war, an anticipated peace agreement offers a positive outlook for Colombia's economy. According to Francisco Rodríguez, director and senior Andean economist at Bank of America Merrill Lynch, the economy is not going to grow significantly, but there will be more confidence in it.[7] Opportunities for investment, for example, in infrastructure in rural areas, are expected to increase substantially. This is much needed for Colombia's development after so many decades of internal armed conflict and will arguably also boost the international competitiveness of Colombian businesses. One structurally important sector that is expected to enjoy stronger growth after the signing of peace agreements is tourism.

The macroeconomic environment

Over the past decade, Colombia's total GDP (Figure 2.1), GDP growth rate (Figure 2.2) and GDP per capita (Figure 2.3) have increased significantly. During the twenty-first century the total GDP has increased by 73%, and the GDP per capita by 67%.[8] In 2009, Colombia was the 'C' in CIVETS[9] – the acronym for the next wave of high-growth countries expected to overtake BRICS[10] in terms of growth.[11] The Colombian economy ranks thirty-first in the World Bank's GDP ranking and seventh-fourth in the GDP per capita ranking.[12] Figure 2.4 represents a considerable challenge because in order to avoid the middle-income trap into which many Latin American countries have fallen, Colombia

[7] Lafuente (2015), Colombia: una potencia emergente en América Latina. Diario El País. Retrieved from: http://economia.elpais.com/economia/2015/09/25/actualidad/1443187822_806022.html.

[8] World Bank. (2015). Data – Colombia. World Bank Data Bank. Retrieved from: http://data.worldbank.org/country/colombia.

[9] Colombia, Indonesia, Vietnam, Egypt, Turkey, South Africa.

[10] Brazil, Russia, India, China, South Africa.

[11] The Economist, 26 November 2009. The Word in 2010, BRICS and BICIS. Retrieved from: www.economist.com/blogs/theworldin2010/2009/11/acronyms_4.

[12] World Bank. (2015). Data – Colombia. World Bank Data Bank. Retrieved from: http://data.worldbank.org/country/colombia.

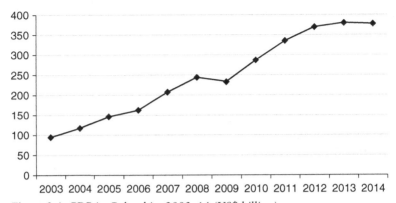

Figure 2.1 GDP in Colombia, 2003–14 (US$ billion).
Source: World Bank. (2015). World Development Indicators. Data Bank. Retrieved from: http://databank.worldbank.org/data/data﹖﹖﹖.aspx

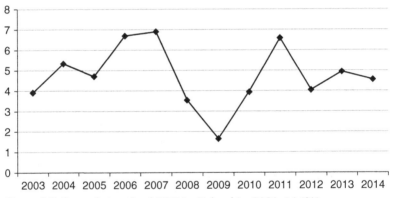

Figure 2.2 Rate of growth of GDP in Colombia, 2003–14 (%).
Source: World Bank. (2015). World Development Indicators. Data Bank. Retrieved from: http://databank.worldbank.org/data/databases.aspx.

will have to cross the US$12,000 GDP per capita barrier, as countries such as Chile have done. In its favour, Colombia has the third-largest population in the region, behind Brazil and Mexico, and can count on a demographic dividend, which increases its economic attractiveness for the near future if combined with the right macroeconomic policies and business strategies.

Furthermore, compared to other big economies in the region, such as Argentina and Venezuela, macroeconomic achievements such as stable

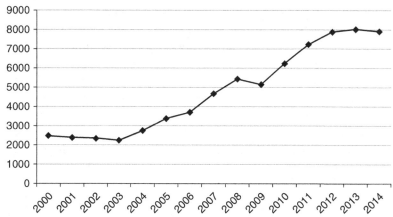

Figure 2.3 GDP per capita in Colombia, 2000–14 (US$).
Source: World Bank. (2015). World Development Indicators. Data Bank. Retrieved from: http://databank.worldbank.org/data/databases.aspx.

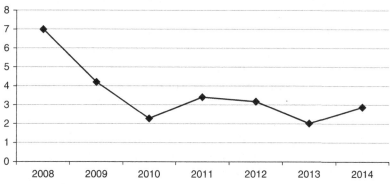

Figure 2.4 Inflation in Colombia (consumer prices, % annual).
Source: World Bank. (2015). World Development Indicators. Data Bank. Retrieved from: http://databank.worldbank.org/data/databases.aspx.

inflation, a decreasing unemployment rate and growing trade have strengthened the economy thanks to the implementation of sound policies. These include a framework for inflation targets and the control of capital inflows to manage international reserves.[13]

---

[13] IMF (2015), Colombia: Concluding Statement of the 2015 Article IV Mission. Referenced 20 October 2015. www.imf.org/external/np/ms/2015/032415.htm.

Colombia's GDP immediately after 2009 (see Figure 2.1), the year
of the global economic crisis, reveals a remarkable macroeconomic
stability that reduces its vulnerability to global economic shocks.
However, this is also a consequence of Colombia's low international
trade volumes compared to similar countries in the region. In 2014,
unemployment in Colombia reached a record low of 9.1% and the
inflation rate continued to be under control. Within the region, this
macroeconomic stability, combined with the government's political
priorities, attracts investment, maintains the positive growth outlook
and generates optimism among experts about the competitiveness of
local companies.

One of the biggest problems of the Colombian economy is the high
number of people employed in the grey economy or unemployed. The
government has made consistent efforts to reduce the unemployment
figure to a single digit but it still remains high compared to other countries in the region. (The most dramatic negative change is in Argentina,
which has experienced rapidly growing levels of unemployment.)

Nevertheless, income inequality in Colombia remains as high as
or higher than most other Latin American countries, as shown in
Figure 2.5. Even though the Gini index has decreased every year for
the past fourteen years, it still stands at 53.2,[14] making Colombia the
twelfth most unequal country in the world. There is no sign that this
may change any time soon. In reality, inequality and poverty have not
changed as expected in spite of the significant income growth rates in
the past decade. These dynamics have been linked to the high concentration in land ownership, where only a few owners can be productive
on a big scale.[15] Even if more people are employed, market wages in
Colombia, frequently below the minimal legal rate, are not enough to
reduce inequality substantially.

The most unequal countries among those studied are Colombia,
Brazil and Chile (see Figure 2.5). In the context of economic growth
in Colombia and Chile this issue should be assessed carefully, because
higher incomes can create higher social gaps that can take many years
to close. In Brazil, growing income inequality has contributed to

[14] World Bank. (2015). Data – Colombia. World Bank Data Bank. Retrieved
from: http://data.worldbank.org/country/colombia.
[15] Semana. (2011a). Tierra concentrada, modelo fracasado. Semana.com.
Retrieved from: www.semana.com/nacion/articulo/tierra-concentrada-modelo-
fracasado/247010-3.

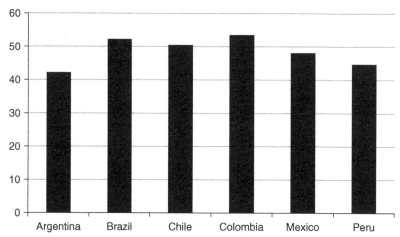

Figure 2.5 The Gini index for Latin America 2013 (max. 100).
Source: World Bank. (2015). World Development Indicators. Data Bank. Retrieved from: http://databank.worldbank.org/data/databases.aspx (NB: Mexico data for 2012).

economic depression and discontent, with the government making it more difficult to take the measures required to redirect the economy.

Trade

Figure 2.6 shows that Colombia's exports and imports increased almost yearly until 2014, with a peak in 2013, thanks to successive government policies that stimulated a more open economy. However, Colombia's trade balance has traditionally shown a deficit. The difference between imports and exports is important but between 2008 and 2013 and the average of net exports was 1.88% of the country's GDP.[16] This might be a consequence of the low value-added and price dependency of Colombia's exports, since commodities represent the lion's share of these. Figure 2.7 indicates that even if Colombia's trade grows along with its GDP, the share of trade in GDP has been almost constant since 2002.

During the first decade of the twenty-first century, high commodity prices, especially in extractive industries, had a huge impact on

---

[16] World Bank. (2015). Data – Colombia. World Bank Data Bank. Retrieved from: http://data.worldbank.org/country/colombia (authors' calculation).

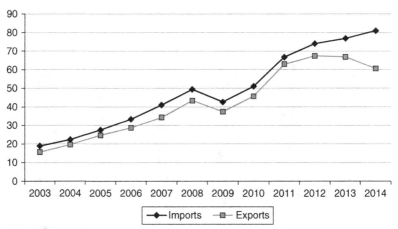

Figure 2.6 Colombia's import and export, 2003–14 (US$ billion).
Source: World Bank. (2015). World Development Indicators. Data Bank. Retrieved from: http://databank.worldbank.org/data/databases.aspx.

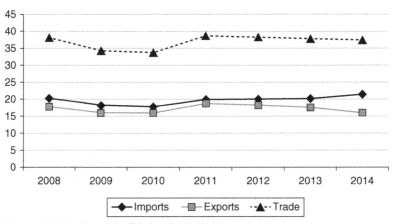

Figure 2.7 Trade as % of Colombia's GDP.
Source: World Bank. (2015). World Development Indicators. Data Bank. Retrieved from: http://databank.worldbank.org/data/databases.aspx.

Colombia's national economy. The increase in oil prices and the improved return on investment of mining ventures put Colombia in an attractive position for international business. However, increased exports were attributed mostly to higher oil prices rather than a significant increase in volumes exported. In contrast to countries like

Table 2.1 *Product exports share (%) in Colombia, 2015*

Product exported	Product exports share (%)
Mineral fuels, oils, distillation products, etc.	65.59
Coffee, tea, meat and spices	4.61
Pearls, precious stones, metals, coins, etc.	3.36
Plastics and plastic articles	2.95
Live trees, plants, bulbs, roots, cut flowers, etc.	2.53

Source: ITC (2015). Trade statistics for international business development. Retrieved from: www.trademap.org/Product_SelProductCountry.aspx.

Chile and Peru, Colombia's industrial exports have not played a more significant role in the economy. Although the need for risk diversification has been acknowledged, the country's dependence on commodity prices continues to dangle over it like a sword of Damocles.[17] Until 2013, the export share of mineral fuels increased continuously and at a higher rate than the share of most other products; in 2003 fuels represented 37.1% of exports. In 2014, mining and oil products accounted for 65.59% of exports while the second most important product categories, coffee and tea, represented only 4.61% of exports (see Table 2.1).[18] While the entire region has been affected by falling oil and commodity prices since 2014, Colombia is more vulnerable than other countries because it has no other products to help balance net exports.

Colombia has started diversifying its trade partners. The political crisis with neighbouring Venezuela, triggered by the U.S.-Colombia defence cooperation agreement,[19] significantly affected Colombian trade and exposed its dependence on a few countries. In 2007, Venezuela accounted for 17.37% of Colombia's total exports, which was particularly important because they were unrelated to oil or fuel[20]

[17] Hernández, M. (2012). Economic watch: Colombia. BBVA Research. Retrieved from: www.bbvaresearch.com/KETD/fbin/mult/120713_EcoWatch_Colombia_Markets_tcm348-341966.pdf?ts=3172012.
[18] ITC. (2015). Trade Map, Trade statistics for international business development. (Database). Retrieved from: www.trademap.org/Index.aspx.
[19] www.state.gov/r/pa/prs/ps/2009/aug/128021.htm.
[20] World Bank. (2015). Data – Colombia. World Bank Data Bank. Retrieved from: http://data.worldbank.org/country/colombia.

Table 2.2 *Colombia's top five export partners (2014)*

Partner	Partner share (%)
United States	26.41
China	10.5
Panama	6.6
Spain	5.96
India	5

Source: World Integrated Trade Solutions. (2015). Retrieved from the URL: http://wits.worldbank.org.

and consisted mainly of cars, manufacturing goods and agricultural products.[21] Exports to the United States have also decreased since 2012, although they were expected to grow when a free trade agreement came into force. In response, Colombia has found new partners to mitigate the effects of the Venezuelan crisis, as Venezuela saw the U.S.-Colombia agreement for defence cooperation as a security threat, and in 2015 trade with Venezuela was almost insignificant.[22] China has become the second most important Colombian partner for both imports and exports (see Tables 2.2 and 2.3). In 2006, Colombia's exports to China were only 1.86% of total exports while in 2014 they reached 10.50%.[23] However, trade with China remains low compared to Chinese trade with Chile, for example, and Colombia is still waiting for a free trade agreement to help catch up with the trade levels of other Latin American and emerging countries.[24] In fact, one important reason for Colombia to join the Pacific Alliance was to facilitate commercial ties with Asia with the help of its neighbouring countries, which already have trans-Pacific trade agreements.

[21] Concha, R. (2008). Consultorio de Comercio Exterior. ICESI. Retrieved from: www.icesi.edu.co/agenciadeprensa/contenido/pdfs/icecomex_7_mar.pdf.

[22] Universidad Nacional (2015). Bilateral trade between Colombia and China has increased 700 times in 35 years. Agencia de noticias. Retrieved from: http://agenciadenoticias.unal.edu.co/detalle/article/bilateral-trade-between-colombia-and-china-has-increased-700-times-in-35-years.html.

[23] World Bank. (2015). Data – Colombia. World Bank Data Bank. Retrieved from: http://data.worldbank.org/country/colombia.

[24] Semana (2014). El dragón que entró a Colombia. Semana.com. Retrieved from: www.semana.com/economia/articulo/el-dragon-que-entro-colombia/403420-3.

Table 2.3 *Colombia's top five import partners (2014)*

Partner	Partner share (%)
United States	28.51
China	18.41
Mexico	8.23
Germany	3.95
Brazil	3.95

Source: World Integrated Trade Solutions. (2015). Retrieved from the URL: http://wits.worldbank.org.

Trade agreements have been an important part of Colombia's strategy to internationalise its economy. Since 2002, seven new trade agreements have come into force (Table 2.4) and four more have been signed and are pending (Table 2.5). The reaction of businesses has been mixed: the strategy has support from the exporting sectors and opposition from sectors afraid of massive imports. In general, most Colombian businesses and highly vocal sectors, such as flower producers, are critical because this approach exposes them to international competition and forces them to become more productive. While some trade agreements do not necessarily generate significant value, their existence is a signal that increases the importance of Colombia in international trade. The main obstacle for Colombia to benefit fully from its trade agreements is the lack of diversity in its exports portfolio. Products with higher added value are more competitive without tariffs, while raw materials tariffs are hardly relevant as they are affected only by international prices. In fact, exports from the United States to Colombia have increased since the free trade agreement came into force but not the other way around. However, new imports (see Table 2.6), including machinery and technological equipment for local industries, are not necessarily a bad outcome even in the short run, if these are used to increase the productivity of Colombian firms.[25]

The most significant barrier for trade in Colombia is the country's deficient infrastructure. Even if local products have export potential, the internal costs of logistics and transportation push prices up,

[25] Reina, M. (2013). La verdad sobre el TLC. Portafolio. Retrieved from: www.portafolio.co/opinion/la-verdad-el-tlc.

Table 2.4 *Colombia's established trade agreements*

Multilateral agreements
World Trade Organisation

Customs unions
Andean Community

Free trade agreements	Year entered into force
Pacific Alliance	2015
European Union	2013
European Free Trade Association	2011
Canada	2011
Northern Triangle (El Salvador, Guatemala and Honduras)	2009 (Honduras), 2010
Chile	2009
United States of America	2012
Mexico	1995

Preferential trade agreements	Year entered into force
Venezuela	2012
MERCOSUR (Colombia, Ecuador, Venezuela)	2005
CARICOM	1995
Panama	1995
Costa Rica	
Nicaragua	1980

Table 2.5 *Colombian trade agreements (signed and pending)*

Free trade agreements
Israel
Panama
Costa Rica
Republic of Korea

Source: SICE OAS, (2015). Retrieved from the URL: www.sice.oas.org/ctyindex/COL/COLagreements_e.asp.

Table 2.6 *Product imports share (%) in Colombia, 2015*

Product imported	Product imports share (%)
Machinery, nuclear reactors, boilers, etc.	12.82
Mineral fuels, oils, distillation products, etc.	11.81
Electrical, electronic equipment	10.36
Vehicles other than railway and tramway	9.67
Plastics and plastic articles	4.22

Source: ITC. (2015). Trade Map, Trade statistics for international business development. (Database). Retrieved from: www.trademap .org/Index.aspx.

Table 2.7 *FDI inflow in Colombia, 2014 (% share by sector)*

Sector	Share (%)
Oil	31.53
Mining	22
Manufacturing	15.31
Financial and business services	9.91
Transportation, communications and storage	8.55

Source: Banco de la República (2015). Flujos de inversión directa – balanza de pagos. Banco de la República de Colombia. Retrieved from: www.banrep.gov.co/inversion-directa.

undermining the international competitiveness of local products. Additionally, Colombia still has to increase its participation in global production chains in order to take advantage of its trade agreements, a strategy that has been successfully applied by China and Mexico,[26] which have taken this approach as a way to shift economic activities from commodities to more sophisticated products and build strong local industries.

Foreign direct investment

Investment in Colombia has increased significantly over the past decade. Government incentives and improved security have stimulated

[26] Trujllo, E., Alvarez, M. and Rodríguez, M. (2014). *Inserción de Colombia en las cadenas globales de valor*. Ministerio de Comercio Exterior de Colombia.

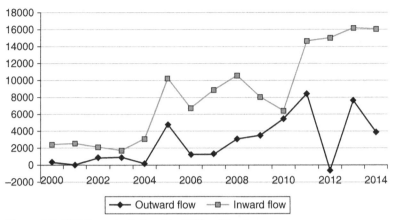

Figure 2.8 FDI flows in Colombia (US$ million).
Source: Foreign direct investment flows and stock. (2015). UNCTAD STAT. Retrieved from the URL: http://unctadstat.unctad.org/wds/ReportFolders/reportFolders.aspx

international investment, putting Colombia in fourth place in the region behind Brazil, Mexico and Chile in terms of FDI flows. Between 2008 and 2014, FDI inflows have doubled, maintaining constant growth.[27] In 2014, the sectors with highest growth in FDI were finance, transport and communications, while manufacturing saw year-to-year increases of 54%, 39% and 13%, respectively,[28] as shown in Figure 2.8. Moreover, in 2014 Colombia signed international investment agreements with Turkey and France providing stronger incentives to bilateral investment.

In 2014, FDI fell and the trend was expected to continue in 2015 Nevertheless, as in Chile, Colombia's FDI did not decrease as much as that of Brazil or Mexico.[29] Again, oil is very important for the dynamics of foreign investment in Colombia and high international prices were behind the rise of foreign investment in the past years.

[27] UNCTAD. (2014). World Investment Report 2014 – Overview. United Nations. Retrieved from: http://unctad.org/en/PublicationsLibrary/wir2014_overview_en.pdf.
[28] UNCTAD. (2014). World Investment Report 2014 – Overview. United Nations. Retrieved from: http://unctad.org/en/PublicationsLibrary/wir2014_overview_en.pdf.
[29] UNCTAD. (2014). World Investment Report 2014 – Overview. United Nations. Retrieved from: http://unctad.org/en/PublicationsLibrary/wir2014_overview_en.pdf.

Table 2.8 *Top five FDI inflows in Colombia,*
2014 (% share by country)

Country	Share (%)
Switzerland	17.46
Panama	14.94
United States	14.05
Spain	13.68
England	6.77

Source: Banco de la República (2015). Flujos de
inversión directa – balanza de pagos. Banco de
la República de Colombia. Retrieved from: www
.banrep.gov.co/inversion-directa.

Since 2006, oil investments have accounted, on average, for 32% of
yearly FDI inflows. In 2014 the second most attractive sector for foreign investment was mining, followed by manufacturing (22% and
15% of the FDI inflows, respectively).[30] The high concentration of FDI
flows in commodity industries is undoubtedly one of the reasons why
the government has been stimulating investment in other sectors, such
as tourism, to mitigate the impact of unfavourable commodity price
fluctuations. This shift might be succeeding: in 2014 FDI in extractive
industries declined by 21% on a yearly basis, while the overall FDI
decline was only 0.9%.

As for the origin of FDI inflows, the United States and the UK have
been in the top five for more than ten years, and in 2015 the largest
inflows came from Switzerland (see Table 2.8).[31] Occasional investments make an unusual country appear at the top of the list of the
biggest investors. For example, in 2012, Chile, which does not usually
feature among the top ten investors in Colombia, became the single
biggest investor thanks to the acquisition of Carrefour's operations in

[30] Banco de la República (2015). Flujos de inversión directa – balanza de pagos.
Banco de la República de Colombia. Retrieved from: www.banrep.gov
.co/inversion-directa.
[31] Banco de la República (2015). Flujos de inversión directa – balanza de pagos.
Banco de la República de Colombia. Retrieved from: www.banrep.gov
.co/inversion-directa.

Colombia by Cencosud.[32] The fact that a single business deal can have such a dramatic impact on the panorama of FDI inflows indicates that Colombia is still a small player in terms of FDI.

Importantly, in 2014 Colombia ranked third among Latin American countries in terms of FDI outflows. However, its numbers are very small compared to Chile, in top position, whose outward investment flows triple those of Colombia.[33]

Taxes

Taxes and tax exemptions are policy levers that significantly impact investment flows in Colombia. For example, hotels built between 2003 and 2017 are exempt from income tax for a period of thirty years, and software and technology companies approved by Colciencias, an agency promoting scientific advancement, have a five-year tax exemption.[34] However, local companies have been adversely affected by the latest tax reforms.

In 2013 and 2014, the government announced new tax reforms to cover the fiscal deficit and the consequent increases affected businesses rather than private citizens. This was a controversial decision: the average corporate tax rate in South America was 55.4% but in Colombia the total corporate tax rate could be as high as 75.4%. This figure can be broken down to 19.9% income tax, 26.9% labour taxes and 28.6% other taxes.[35] Colombia's industrial association (ANDI) claims that these tax reforms are hitting companies' operations very hard and threaten the country's competitiveness, as there are few incentives to produce locally. Consequently, local companies are moving their

---

[32] Banco de la República (2015). Flujos de inversión directa – balanza de pagos. Banco de la República de Colombia. Retrieved from: www.banrep.gov .co/inversion-directa.

[33] UNCTAD. (2015). Global FDI Flows Declined in 2014. China becomes the world's top FDI recipient. United Nations. Retrieved from: http://unctad.org/ en/PublicationsLibrary/webdiaeia2015d1_en.pdf.

[34] Procolombia (2014). Investment Incentives in Colombia. Ministerio de Relaciones Exteriores Colombia. Retrieved from: www.investincolombia .com.co/investment-incentives.html.

[35] PriceWaterhouseCoopers. (1 June 2015). Colombia, corporate taxes on corporate income. World Tax Summaries. Retrieved from: http://taxsummaries.pwc.com/uk/taxsummaries/wwts.nsf/ID/ Colombia-Corporate-Taxes-on-corporate-income.

production elsewhere to take advantage of free trade agreements and import their products for local consumers.[36] This translates into lower tax revenues, at a time when revenue from the extractive industries is down, damaging the government's ambitions to stimulate the long-overdue investments in infrastructure and education.

Labour taxes are also blamed for the high rate of employment in the grey economy. It is very expensive for companies to hire full-time employees; at the same time, employees do not receive competitive salaries.[37] The 2014 tax changes included a 'tax on wealth', levied on companies' liquid equity, which might equally apply to international companies. The CREE, a national tax on business earnings to benefit employees, has also increased: the CREE is progressive and is calculated on the basis of a company's revenue at the end of the year.[38] It should be noted that tax collection in Colombia is very low compared to other countries with similar levels of GDP.[39] While Colombia has fewer taxes than other countries,[40] the level of tax evasion is high. This is partly a consequence of the decisions of successive governments to maintain taxes that were intended to be temporary or emergency measures. Tax earnings could therefore be improved significantly with measures that make collection more efficient, rather than by creating new taxes or increasing existing ones.

Colombian multilatinas

Colombian multilatinas are companies that have actively sought the internationalisation of their business, mainly in the Latin American

[36] Dinero. (2015). ¿Pagan muchos impuestos las empresas en Colombia?. Referenced 18 September 2015 www.dinero.com/edicion-impresa/pais/articulo/pagan-muchos-impuestos-empresas-colombia/209869.

[37] Consejo Privado de Competitividad. (2015). Informe Nacional de Competitividad 2015-2016. Bogotá: Consejo Privado de Competitividad.

[38] KPMG. (2013). Doing Business in Colombia. Bogotá: KPMG Impuestos y Servicios Legales LTDA. Retrieved from: www.kpmg.com/CO/es/IssuesAndInsights/ArticlesPublications/Documents/DOING%20BUSINESS%20IN%20COLOMBIA%202013.pdf.

[39] Consejo Privado de Competitividad. (2015). Informe Nacional de Competitividad 2015-2016. Bogotá: Consejo Privado de Competitividad.

[40] PriceWaterhouseCoopers. (1 June 2015). Colombia, corporate taxes on corporate income. World Tax Summaries. Retrieved from: http://taxsummaries.pwc.com/uk/taxsummaries/wwts.nsf/ID/Colombia-Corporate-Taxes-on-corporate-income.

region. They have decided to expand their operations abroad, motivated by the need to find new markets, the desire to acquire valuable overseas assets or as a defensive strategy against potential competitors. In 2014, there were approximately 200 Colombian multilatinas in Latin America.[41] The expansion of these firms can be explained by domestic factors, including the abundance of cheap funds, difficulties associated with excessive internal regulation and increasing regional economic integration. Despite rapid growth in the number of Colombian multilatinas, Colombia seems to be lagging behind compared to other Latin American countries, such as Brazil and Mexico. In 2014, of 100 multilatinas, 9 were Colombian, 16 Chilean, 26 Mexican and 34 Brazilian, the rest coming from other Latin American countries. On the other hand, Colombian firms have managed the consequences of the global economic crisis that began in 2008 more effectively than other Latin American firms. Colombian companies took advantage of the opportunities created when their American and European competitors chose to withdraw from the region. For example, in the financial sector, Grupo Sura and Grupo Aval acquired assets sold by several weakened competitors and in this way enlarged their portfolio of international holdings. In the public services sector larger firms had a similar experience. Interconexión Eléctrica (ISA) is one of the biggest energy providers in Latin America, with operations in Brazil, Chile, Ecuador, Panama, Peru and Venezuela; in 2014 it was twenty-eighth in the ranking of biggest multilatinas compiled by AméricaEconomía thanks to aggressive expansion through M&As and greenfield investments that led the company to diversify into a wide range of industries, including transportation and telecommunications.[42] Other private capital firms have shown improvement in the ranking as well and are recognised at international level: Grupo Nutresa is a fast-growing company that was thirty-fourth in the 2014 ranking. Nutresa is present in fifteen countries and is the sixth-largest food company in Latin America.

[41] Dinero (2014). *Expansión, clave en la estrategia de las empresas*. Retrieved from the URL: www.dinero.com/empresas/articulo/expansion-empresas-colombianas-america-latina/202455.

[42] Poveda Garcés, Ana-María (2011). Outward FDI from Colombia and its policy context. VALE Columbia Center on Sustainable International Investment. Available at http://ccsi.columbia.edu/files/2014/03/Colombia_OFDI_-_1_Sept_2011_-_FINAL_-_REV_2.pdf.

Grupo Argos, the biggest Colombian holding, well positioned in the cement industry, has had a successful strategy of internationalisation and growth. As a result, in 2015 the firm had operations in fifteen countries. Diversification and investment in fast-growing sectors such as construction also helped to boost Grupo Argos. The pharmaceutical laboratory Tecnoquímicas followed a similar economic logic, simultaneously investing in international markets and diversifying its lines of business.

One of the most aggressive firms taking advantage of the growth opportunities generated by the latest world economic crisis is Grupo Éxito. This company acquired 50% of the voting rights of Grupo Pão de Açúcar (GPA) in Brazil and 100% of Libertad in Argentina and in 2015 came under the control of the French retail giant Casino. Its operations are financed by loans from Citibank, Bancolombia, Grupo Aval and Davivienda. The final three banks have themselves been active on the international M&A market.

Davivienda acquired the operations of HSBC in Costa Rica, Honduras and El Salvador and in 2015 had more than 800,000 clients outside Colombia.[43] Bancolombia bought HSBC's operations in Panama; this step into the Central American market meant it would benefit from the possibilities offered by the fastest-growing country in the region. However, the leading Colombian investor in Central America is Banco de Bogotá, which bought the multinational financial group BAC Credomatic in 2010 and, in 2013, Grupo Financiero Reformador in Guatemala and BVBA in Panama. In 2015, Banco de Bogotá was the leader in loans and deposits in the Central American region.[44]

Colombian multilatinas face some unique challenges, including long-lasting armed conflict and a negative country image, together with acute social inequality and a deficient educational system. Nevertheless, their internationalisation strategies seem to be very similar to those of other multilatinas. Colombian firms invest in countries with similar levels of institutional and economic development, on the

[43] Dinero. (2015). ¿Pagan muchos impuestos las empresas en Colombia?. Referenced 18 September 2015 www.dinero.com/edicion-impresa/pais/articulo/pagan-muchos-impuestos-empresas-colombia/209869.
[44] Dinero, 2015, Banco de Bogota: Pionero Costa Afuera. Referenced 18 September 2015 www.dinero.com/edicion-impresa/caratula/articulo/banco-de-bogota-pionero-costa-afuera/211538.

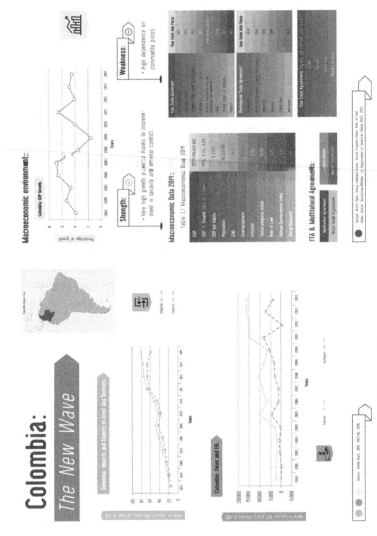

Infographic 2.1 Colombia in numbers.

basis that the experience and know-how gained in the home market will be useful in similar foreign environments. Their preferred mode of entry in international markets is acquisition, a strategy that guarantees fast growth and facilitates economic value creation from local opportunities.

The goal of Bancóldex, the state-owned import-export bank, is to increase the number of strong Colombian multilatinas from 70 to 2,000.[45] With strong leadership and the support of domestic institutions and public policies, this goal seems more realistic than optimistic. However, the accelerated process of internationalisation generates some concerns among institutional investors. For example, pension funds associate an aggressive internationalisation strategy with increased risk. But Colombian citizens also have something to be worried about, especially if the internationalisation strategy generates an increase in risk for large Colombian firms, particularly in the financial sector. In cases of bankruptcy, the government is likely to rescue big businesses and the bill for that will eventually be footed by the taxpayer.

[45] América economía (2014) Colombia tendrá en diez años 200 empresas multilatinas, según Bancoldex. Retrieved on September 20, 2015. www.americaeconomia.com/negocios-industrias/multilatinas/colombia-tendra-en-diez-anos-200-empresas-multilatinas-segun-bancol.

3 | Peru – the future

JUANA GARCÍA AND VENETA ANDONOVA

Peru is one of the countries with the greatest projected growth within Latin America. In fact, it has been recognised as one of the ten new emerging markets in Latin America by the French consulting firm Coface.[1] Peru's consistently high growth rates since the turn of the millennium were interrupted by the global financial crisis of 2008. However, after a modest 1% GDP growth rate in 2009, its economy soared, reaching 8.5% the following year (Figure 3.1). Since that point, it has decelerated gradually, but in the midst of the financial crisis, its growth rate remained above that of most countries in the region. The growth rate of GDP showed a trend towards stabilisation between 2011 and 2013, but fell more than three percentage points (from 5.8% to 2.4%) in 2014 as a result of a slowdown in private investment and a sudden decrease in the prices of minerals. The Minister of Finance and the Economy, Alonso Segura, pointed out in January 2014 that despite changes in the global environment the Peruvian economy was expected to grow at a 'reasonable' yearly rate of 5%. In support of this positive outlook, an economic study by CEPAL in June 2015 declared that 3.6% growth was expected for 2015 'as a consequence of the increase in the mining of gold and copper, the strengthening of private consumption supported by an expansive monetary policy, and the increase in public expenditure, in the context of greater incentives announced by the government at the end of 2014'.[2]

The macroeconomic environment

This stable and positive outlook contrasts with the predominant patterns of economic growth exhibited by the countries in the region (Figure 3.2). Brazil and Argentina in particular have experienced huge

---

[1] www.coface.com/News-Publications/News/Latin-America-Growth-picking-up-for-Pacific-countries. Accessed 7 April 2016.
[2] CEPAL. (2015). Estudio económico de América Latina y el Caribe (p. 5). Retrieved from: http://repositorio.cepal.org/bitstream/handle/11362/38713/S1500733_es.pdf?sequence=106.

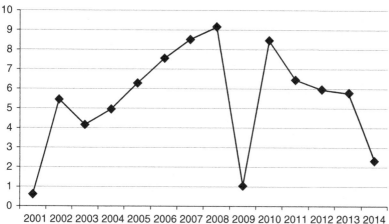

Figure 3.1 GDP growth in Peru, 2000–15 (%).
Source: World Bank. (2015). World Development Indicators. Data Bank. Retrieved from: http://databank.worldbank.org/data/databases.aspx.

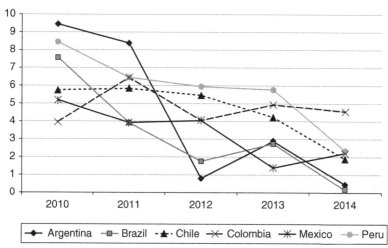

Figure 3.2 Growth rate of GDP in Latin America by country, 2010–14 (%).
Source: World Bank Group & Price Waterhouse Coopers. (2015). Paying Taxes 2015. Retrieved from: www.pwc.com/gx/en/services/tax/paying-taxes/about-the-report .html.

declines in their economic growth rates since 2010, while all countries have suffered the effects of the recent devaluation and decline in oil prices. The general expectation is that Peru will experience the highest GDP growth in the region in the years to come.

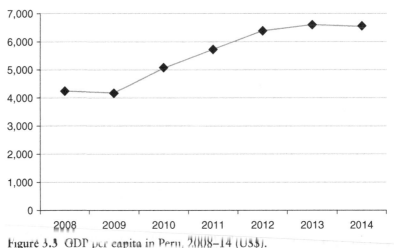

Figure 3.3 GDP per capita in Peru, 2008–14 (US$).
Source: World Bank. (2015). World Development Indicators. Data Bank. Retrieved from: http://data.worldbank.org/country/peru.

With a population close to 31 million and a GDP of US$203 billion, Peru has enviable macroeconomic indicators that confirm its status as one of the fastest-growing economies in the region. As Figure 3.3 shows, in 2014, its per capita GDP was US$6,541, a small decline from the previous year (US$6,662). Peruvian growth has flourished in a context of low and controlled inflation, which confirms the importance of the achievement: between 2002 and 2013, Peru registered an average inflation of 2.6%, one of the lowest in Latin America (Figure 3.4). In addition, a steady growth in the number of jobs has fuelled the country's prosperity, vastly reducing the poverty rate. Unemployment in Peru has remained below 5% in recent years, and a 3.9% unemployment rate was reported in 2013 (Figure 3.5). This resulted in a reduction of more than 50% in poverty rates between 2005 and 2013, a period in which poverty fell from 55.6% to 22.7% of the population. Additionally, the proportion of the population living below the absolute poverty line fell from 15.8% to 4.7% in the same period. Several social indicators show remarkable improvement and deliver the proof that progress in Peru is not limited to macroeconomic indicators, but also has an impact on the country's social context (Table 3.1). In 2014, the Peruvian Human Development Index (HDI) of 0.737 was very similar to that of Brazil (0.74), which is now one of the global powers, and the Social Progress Index (SPI) rose to 66.29. Meanwhile, the

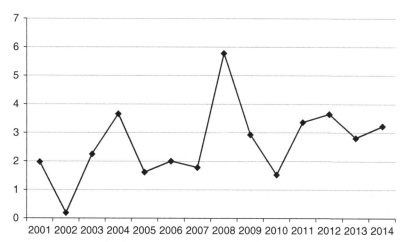

Figure 3.4 Rate of inflation in Peru, 2001–14 (%).
Source: World Bank. (2015). World Development Indicators. Data Bank. Retrieved from: http://databank.worldbank.org/data/databases.aspx.

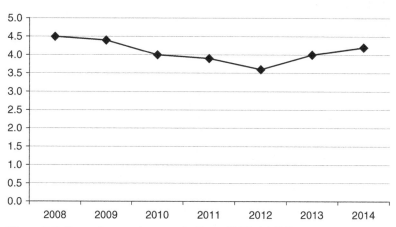

Figure 3.5 Rate of unemployment in Peru, 2008–14 (%).
Source: World Bank. (2015). World Development Indicators. Data Bank. Retrieved from: http://databank.worldbank.org/data/databases.aspx.

Gini coefficient for 2012 stood at 45.3, down from 49.3 in 2005. It is important to highlight that Peru is not the only country in the region that has achieved some social progress (see Figure 3.6). Most countries have implemented economic policies to improve international confidence in their economies. Favouring foreign investment and signing new trade agreements run in parallel with social welfare and cash

Table 3.1 *Peru's trade agreements*

Multilateral agreements World Trade Organisation	
Customs union Andean Community	
Free trade agreements	**Year entered into force**
Pacific Alliance	2015
European Union	2013
Japan	2012
Costa Rica	2013
Panama	2012
Mexico	2012
South Korea	2011
European Free Trade Association	2011
China	2010
Canada	2009
Singapore	2009
Chile	2009
United States of America	2009
MERCOSUR	2005
Thailand	2011
Agreements signed but not yet in force	
Free trade Agreements	
Trans-Pacific Partnership Agreements Honduras Guatemala	
Preferential trade agreements Venezuela	

Source: Foreign Trade Information System OAS, 2015. Retrieved from the URL: www.sice.oas.org/ctyindex/PER/PERagreements_e.asp.

transfer programmes to transmit welfare improvement and economic growth directly to Latin America's most disadvantaged citizens.

Trade

At the end of the 1980s, Peruvian exports began to increase at a significant rate and the country opened up its market to be able to import

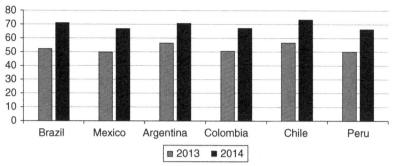

Figure 3.6 Social Progress Index (Latin America).
Source: Social Progress Imperative. (2015). *Social Progress Index 2015*. Retrieved from the URL: http://13i8vn49fibl3go3i12f59gh.wpengine.netdna-cdn.com/wp-content/uploads/2016/05/2015-SOCIAL-PROGRESS-INDEX_FINAL.pdf.

the lower-cost raw materials, technology and equipment needed to improve the competitiveness of its businesses. Peru began to export using trade preference systems offered by partners such as the United States and the European Union (EU). Although these systems represented tangible benefits, they proved inadequate owing to the uncertainty linked to their continuity. This prevented Peru from undertaking more ambitious and long-term export initiatives. With free trade agreements (FTAs), benefits related to export activities would no longer be temporary or limited.

By 2015, Peru had entered into seventeen FTAs with the Pacific Alliance and MERCOSUR, fifteen of which have come into force, and bilateral agreements with China, the EU and the United States. Peru also maintains a multilateral agreement as a member country of the World Trade Organisation (WTO), a customs union with the Andean Community and a preferential trade agreement with Venezuela. Although some of these FTAs were concluded in the late 1990s, most of them entered into force or were signed in the first decade of the new century (Table 3.1).

One of Peru's distinctive characteristics had been its positive trade balance. For a decade (2002–12), exports were consistently higher than imports. However, since 2013, Peru has presented a trade balance deficit and for the first semester of 2014, the Central Reserve Bank of Peru reported a deficit of US$1.949 billion (Figure 3.7). On the other hand, the share of trade in its GDP (the sum of exports and imports as a percentage of GDP) was high compared to other countries in

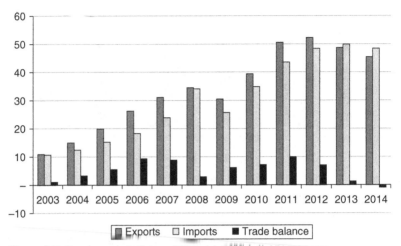

Figure 3.7 Peru's trade balance, 2003–14 (US$ billion).
Source: World Bank. (2015). World Development Indicators. Data Bank. Retrieved from:
http://databank.worldbank.org/data/reports.aspx?source=world-development-indicators.

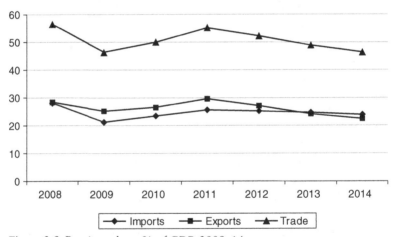

Figure 3.8 Peru's trade as % of GDP, 2008–14.
Source: World Bank. (2015). World Development Indicators. Data Bank. Retrieved from:
http://databank.worldbank.org/data/reports.aspx?source=world-development-indicators.

the region, reaching an average of 50.48% between 2009 and 2013
(Figure 3.8).[3]

---

[3] World Integrated Trade Solution. (2015). Country Profile: Peru. World Bank.
 Retrieved from: http://wits.worldbank.org/CountryProfile/Country/PER/Year/
 2013/Summary.

Table 3.2 *Peru's top five export partners (2014)*

Partner	Partner share (%)
China	18.27
United States	16.21
Switzerland	6.87
Canada	6.63
Brazil	4.14

Source: World Integrated Trade Solution. (2015). Country Profile: Peru. World Bank. Retrieved from: http://wits.worldbank .org/CountryProfile/Country/PER/Year/2013/Summary.

Table 3.3 *Peru's top five import partners (2014)*

Partner	Partner share (%)
China	21.15
United States	20.86
Brazil	4.73
Mexico	4.56
Ecuador	4.2

Source: World Integrated Trade Solution. (2015). Country Profile: Peru. World Bank. Retrieved from: http://wits .worldbank.org/CountryProfile/Country/PER/Year/2013/ Summary.

The bulk of Peruvian exports consists of minerals, stones and precious metals, mineral fuels, distillate products and copper and its derivatives. China and the United States are Peru's major trading partners, by a wide margin. In 2014, 18.27% of Peruvian exports were destined for the Asian giant, while 16.21% were sent to the United States. Other export markets worth mentioning are Switzerland (6.87% of total exports), Canada (6.63%), Brazil (4.14%) and Japan (4.12%) (Table 3.2). Concerning imports, 21.15% of the total came from China, followed by the United States with 20.86%. Brazil, Mexico and Ecuador trailed behind with 4.73%, 4.56% and 4.2%, respectively (Table 3.3). Most Peruvian imports consist of machinery, mineral fuels, oils, distillate products, electrical goods, electronic equipment and vehicles. In terms of products traded, the Peruvian economy relies

Table 3.4 *Main product exports and imports share (%) in Peru, 2015*

Category	Product exports share (%)
Ores, slag and ash	29.82
Pearls, precious stones, metals, coins, etc.	18.05
Mineral fuels, oils, distillation products, etc.	7.25
Copper and copper articles	5.79
Edible fruit, nuts, citrus fruit peel, melons	5.39

Category	Product imports share (%)
Machinery, nuclear reactors and boilers	14.37
Electrical, electronic equipment	11.68
Mineral fuels, oils, distillation products	10.33
Vehicles other than railway and tramway	9.56
Plastics and plastic articles	5.2

Source: ITC, 2015. Retrieved from www.intracen.org.

heavily on basic products, mining, precious stones and fruits. Like most countries in the region, the most important imports are machinery, fuels and electrical equipment (Table 3.4).

In Peru there is a noticeable change in the composition of exports with edible fruit, nuts, citrus fruit peel and melons making a substantial contribution in 2015.

Finally, the economies of Peru and Chile exhibit high geographical concentration and dependence on their capital cities. The same can be said for Colombia but there the dependence is not that marked. Bogota contributes about 25% of the country's GDP, whereas Lima and Santiago contribute roughly 48% of their countries' wealth. This fact is related to one of the most controversial impacts of FTAs on Peruvian society, namely the exacerbation of rural poverty. While the overall benefits of free trade are not questioned, the relative disadvantage at which the rural poor find themselves, in terms of their income from agricultural and farm-related activities, is expected to reduce their spending on education and healthcare unless powerful and effective compensatory measures are taken.[4]

Tourism, a form of international trade, is another sector whose positive development has given additional dynamism to the

[4] Mendoza Bellido, W. 2008. Trade Policy and Poverty in Peru How do free trade agreements (FTA) impact rural poverty? http://r4d.dfid.gov.uk/PDF/Outputs/COPLA/CIES-COPLA-ingles.pdf.

internationalisation of the Peruvian economy. In 2015, the competitiveness of Peru's travel and tourism industry saw it rise fifteen places compared to the previous year, to rank fifty-eighth in the world.[5] The international appeal of Peru's adventure and cultural tourism is building a momentum and contributing to strengthening Peru's country brand: in 2015 Peru went up three places to fifty-second in Bloom Consulting's Country Rank Branding for tourism.[6]

Foreign direct investment

Between 2010 and 2012, inbound foreign direct investment (FDI) flows in Peru showed an upward trend, but since 2012 they have shown a considerable decrease. The flow of inbound FDI dropped from US$12.240 million in 2012 to US$10.172 million in 2013 and US$7.607 million in 2014.[7] In contrast, outbound FDI has remained at very low levels, with a considerably lower rate of growth and a continuous decrease between 2008 and 2012.

In 2014 the flow of FDI in Peru reached US$7.607 million, which represented an 18% drop from 2013 and a 36% drop compared to 2012, as reported by the Economic Commission for Latin America.[8]

It is important to put this in context because in recent years the level of FDI in Peru has been very high compared to earlier trends and the size of its economy (Figure 3.9). The main reason for the downward turn in 2013 and 2014 was a significant fall in domestic and foreign investments in mining, estimated at 11%. Remarkably, FDI has increased over the past decade in Peru's service sector, but given the deceleration in GDP growth, investment in the domestic market is expected to lose some of its attractiveness.[9] While in 2014, the most

[5] World Economic Forum 2015, Travel and Tourism report www3 .weforum.org/docs/TT15/WEF_Global_Travel&Tourism_Report_2015.pdf.

[6] www.bloom-consulting.com/pdf/rankings/Bloom_Consulting_Country_Brand_ Ranking_Tourism.pdf.

[7] CEPAL. (2015). Estudio económico de América Latina y el Caribe. Retrieved from: http://repositorio.cepal.org/bitstream/handle/11362/38713/S1500733_ es.pdf?sequence=106.

[8] CEPAL. (2015). Estudio económico de América Latina y el Caribe. Retrieved from: http://repositorio.cepal.org/bitstream/handle/11362/38713/S1500733_ es.pdf?sequence=106.

[9] CEPAL. (2015). Estudio económico de América Latina y el Caribe. Retrieved from: http://repositorio.cepal.org/bitstream/handle/11362/38713/S1500733_ es.pdf?sequence=106.

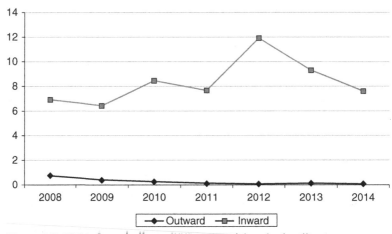

Figure 3.9 FDI inflows in Peru, 2008–13 (US$ hundred million)
Source: Foreign Direct Investment flows and stock. (2015). UNCTAD STAT. Retrieved from: http://unctadstat.unctad.org/wds/ReportFolders/reportFolders.aspx.

recent year for which the World Bank reports data, the net inflows of FDI represented about 4% of Peruvian GDP, the net outflows were negligible.[10]

Taxes

According to a 2014 study by the American consulting firm Deloitte,[11] Peru has established a clear and attractive legal framework that promotes local and foreign private investment. Conditions guarantee equal treatment for foreign investors and facilitate capital inflow to local companies. The tax regime in Peru mainly comprises income tax, VAT, customs, municipal taxes, social and labour contributions and a tax on financial transactions. Important tax agreements in force promote the growth of the Peruvian economy and the bulk of these prerogatives concerns the mining sector. All mining-related investments fall under a special tax regime known as 'Contract and Guarantee

[10] World Bank. (2015). World Development Indicators. Data Bank. Retrieved from: http://databank.worldbank.org/data/reports.aspx?source=world-development-indicators.

[11] Deloitte. (March 2014). Tax Guide, Peru 2014. Deloitte Touche Tohmatsu. Retrieved from: www2.deloitte.com/content/dam/Deloitte/pe/Documents/tax/tax_guide%202014-rev.pdf.

Measures to Promote Mining Investment'. The main advantage of this provision is legal stability: all taxpayers in the mining industry are guaranteed the same tax burden during the entire duration of a particular contract. Moreover, the Peruvian government has signed a series of international agreements with Brazil, Canada, Chile and Mexico based on the Organization for Economic Cooperation and Development 's (OECD) Model Tax Convention on Income and Capital in order to alleviate Peru's tax burden. Similar approved agreements with Spain, Switzerland, South Korea and Portugal have also been signed. As a member of the Andean Community, Peru also has agreements with Colombia, Bolivia and Ecuador to avoid double taxation.

A joint study of 189 countries by PricewaterhouseCoopers and the World Bank[12] concludes that, as a region, South America has the world's most time-consuming tax systems (greater *Total Tax Time*). The region's tax burden, calculated as the *Total Tax Rate*, has also increased continuously since 2009. However, in 2016 Peru ranks fiftieth among the countries, with a *Total Tax Rate* of 36%. The *Total Tax Rate* is defined as 'the measure of tax cost, the measure of all taxes born as a percentage of commercial profit'.[13] Peru's *Total Tax Rate* compares favourably to the South American average of 55%. In Peru, the number of tax payments is nine. The three main taxes – corporate income tax, labour taxes and consumption taxes – require a total of 260 hours to prepare, file and pay versus the average of 615 hours in South America. Although the Peruvian performance is second only to Chile among the South American countries, there is room for improvement.

Peruvian multilatinas

Given Peru's projected high growth rate, it is expected that a larger number of local companies will begin internationalisation processes. Currently, Peru has five well-established multilatinas and, according to

---

[12] World Bank Group & Price Waterhouse Coopers. (2015). Paying Taxes 2015. PWC. Retrieved from: www.pwc.com/gx/en/services/tax/paying-taxes/about-the-report.html.

[13] PricewaterhouseCoopers Paying Taxes 2016 report. http://read.pwc.com/i/601095-paying-taxes-2016.

a study by Deloitte,[14] their companies only account for 5% of business activity in the region. Peru's leading multinational companies, according to the ranking by multinationals magazine *AméricaEconomía*, are in the food industry (Ajegroup, Alicorp and Gloria Group). Other companies with international presence, such as Belcorp and Ferreyros, are part of the chemical and industrial machinery sectors.

Among the countries studied in this book, Peru has the fewest multinationals. A logical explanation for this state of affairs is grounded in the nature of Peruvian economic activity. Peru has been an interesting investment destination for extractive industries and regional businesses looking to internationalise using a standardised process or an easily replicated product. However, the internal growth of the country over the past fifteen years, as well as improvements in infrastructure and technology, have laid the foundation for regional business expansion and enabled a process of continuous acquisition. Recently, Peruvian companies have shown greater interest in companies abroad. In general, Peruvian multinationals' investments in the region are driven by the need to cut costs, find new customers, acquire the knowledge to build a competitive edge and obtain more attractive financing in more efficient markets.[15] This is a relatively recent development; out of the five well-established Peruvian multilatinas only Belcorp was a multinational before the 1990s.

According to a report published in March 2015,[16] almost all Peru's leading multinationals have opted to purchase other companies to shorten time to internationalisation. The exception is Ajegroup, which is already considered a global company and has preferred to develop greenfield projects in each of its international markets. Mergers and acquisitions (M&As) have been a key part of the corporate strategy of these companies and the number of M&As already exceeded ninety in 2015.

[14] Deloitte. (2014, March). Tax Guide, Peru 2014. Deloitte Touche Tohmatsu. Retrieved from: www2.deloitte.com/content/dam/Deloitte/pe/Documents/tax/tax_guide%202014-rev.pdf.

[15] El Comercio. (2015). *La ruta de la expansión mundial de las multilatinas peruanas* http://elcomercio.pe/economia/peru/ruta-expansion-mundial-multilatinas-peruanas-noticia-1797823.

[16] El Comercio. (2015). *La expansión de las multilatinas peruanas.* In KPMG (2015). *KPMG en medios.* Retrieved from www.kpmg.com/PE/es/IssuesAndInsights/sala-de-prensa/kpmg-medios/Documents/16-03-2015-expansion-de-multilatinas-peruanas.pdf.

The expansion of Peruvian multilatinas has focused on two partner countries through the Pacific Alliance, Chile and Colombia. The three countries have maintained similar political and economic models and an open market policy that provides a platform for the internationalisation of their companies.

Ajegroup

Ajegroup (AJE) is one of the largest Peruvian multinationals in the alcoholic and non-alcoholic beverages industry. It is present in more than twenty countries in Latin America, Asia and Africa and has 15,000 direct and indirect employees.[17] According to the company's website, AJE is the tenth-largest soft drinks company in the world in terms of sales volume and the world's fourth-largest producer of soft drinks.

AJE began as a family business in the Ayacucho region in 1988. Since the mid-1990s, the company has focused on entering emerging markets with the appropriate climate for soft drink consumption, either by building its own plants or in some cases through exports. AJE's internationalisation process has been gradual (see Table 3.5).

The company uses its export operations to learn about a potentially interesting host market; these volumes reflect acceptance of their products in different countries. After assessing the operating advantages and economic terms, decisions about greenfield investments are taken. Ajegroup's expansion began with countries in Latin America; in 2016, it was the only Peruvian multinational with a global presence in Europe and Asia.

Belcorp/Yanbal

Yanbal and Belcorp, founded in 1967 and 1968, respectively, by the Belmont Anderson brothers (Juan Fernando and Eduardo), are Peruvian cosmetics companies whose brands L'Bel, Ésika and Cyzone are recognised regionally. Their business model is based on direct sales and relies primarily on female 'beauty consultants' who operate their own small businesses. Through this business model, 8,000 people are employed across the Americas.

---

[17] www.ajegroup.com.

Table 3.5 *Ajegroup: Internationalisation*

Year	Country
1999	Venezuela
2000	Ecuador
2004	Costa Rica
2005	Guatemala, Honduras, Nicaragua
2006	Spain (corporate office)
2007	Colombia
2009	Panama
2010	India, Indonesia, Vietnam
2011	Brazil
2013	Bolivia

Table 3.6 *Yanbal (Juan Fernando Belmont Anderson): Internationalisation*

Year	Country
1976	United States
1977	Ecuador
1979	Bolivia, Colombia
1982	Mexico
Post-1982	Guatemala, Italy, Spain, Venezuela

The Belmont Anderson brothers were the first Peruvians who dared to undertake an ambitious international expansion strategy for their companies (Tables 3.6 and 3.7).

Yanbal currently has plants in Ecuador, Peru and Colombia. Belcorp has become the Peruvian cosmetics company with the greatest international reach through its rapid expansion into fifteen countries. The company has plants in Colombia, Ecuador and Mexico. Eduardo Belmont has declared his goal is for Belmont to become the number one cosmetic business in the region by 2020.

The internationalisation strategy of Belcorp/Yanbal differs considerably from the approach of the other Peruvian multinationals, given the specificities of their business model. The critical asset is a proper sales force in the host countries. Decisions about building a proprietary plant that enables cost reduction and decentralisation of production

Table 3.7 *Belcorp (Eduardo Belmont Anderson):*
Internationalisation

Year	Country
1988	Colombia, Chile
1995	Mexico
1997	Venezuela
2002	El Salvador, Guatemala, Puerto Rico
2003	Dominican Republic, Ecuador
2004	Costa Rica
2005	United States
2008	Panama
2010	Bolivia
2011	Brazil

are based on demand and margin. With this approach, Belcorp/Yanbal ventured into other countries nearly twenty years earlier than any other company of Peruvian origin.

Ferreyros

Ferreyros, established in 1922, is the largest provider of capital goods and their associated services in Peru. It is also the largest distributor of Caterpillar in Peru. The company was reorganised into a holding under the name Ferreycorp in order to align better with its international growth and the broad portfolio of brands or machines and equipment it represents.

The group's preferred entry mode in the international market is by mergers and acquisitions. Table 3.8 contains the international operations for Ferreyros. The development of the group closely follows the growth of the mining and construction sectors. In 2016, in the midst of the free fall of commodity prices and bleak expectations for the global mining and construction industry that punished Caterpillar's stock price, Peru's sales stood strong thanks to several new mining projects.

Alicorp

Alicorp, is a Peruvian consumer goods company founded in 1971, has its own investments and operations in Argentina, Brazil, Chile,

Table 3.8 *Ferreycorp: Internationalisation*

Year	Country
2009	Guatemala
2009	Belize
2009	El Salvador
2013	Nicaragua
2014	Chile
2014	Colombia
2014	Ecuador

Colombia and Ecuador. Its products are sold in more than twenty-three countries and the company has recently focused on animal nutrition and agriculture businesses. It has been known as Alicorp since 1997 after merging with flour and pasta producers Nicolini Hermanos SA and Molinera del Peru SA.

Alicorp laid the foundation for its internationalisation process through multiple local mergers and acquisitions. Its growth was driven by increasing local demand, served by eighteen plants in Peru. Its growth spurt began in 1991 under the leadership of Leslie Pierce, who increased the company's efficiency through factory closures and the acquisition of advanced technology equipment.[18]

Alicorp has grown internationally through acquisitions that fit its existing business strategy and have local market know-how. These operations have enabled the company to achieve economies of scale and to diversify its portfolio, while relying on local procurement. Table 3.9 shows the international spread of its acquisitions; Mexico is the company's next target for the future.[19]

Gloria Group

The Gloria Group is an industrial conglomerate with a Peruvian capital and is present in Bolivia, Colombia, Ecuador, Argentina and Puerto

---

[18] Semanaeconomica.com (2011). *ALICORP: Estrategia de internacionalización.* Retrieved from the URL: http://semanaeconomica.com/escala-global/2011/12/06/alicorp-estrategia-de-internacionalizacion/.

[19] *El Comercio*, 2014, http://elcomercio.pe/economia/negocios/empresas-peruanas-que-se-atrevieron-ir-al-exterior-noticia-1748120?ref=flujo_tags_520723&ft=nota_22&e=titulo.

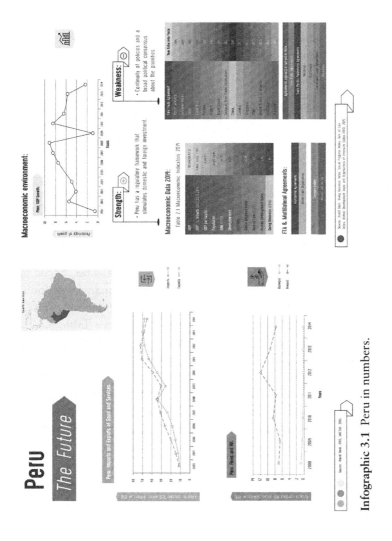

Infographic 3.1 Peru in numbers.

Table 3.9 *Alicorp: Acquisitions*

Year	Company and country
2007	Eskimo (ice cream), Ecuador
2008	TVB Propersa, Argentina and Colombia
2010	Okebon and Italo Macera Group, Argentina
2012	Salmofood, Chile
2013	Pastificio Santa Amalia (PSA), Brazil

Table 3.10 *Gloria Group: International investment*

Country	Company
Puerto Rico	Quina Dairy Fruit, Switzerland
Bolivia	Pil Andina
Argentina	Regional Dairy Company
Colombia	Algarra
Ecuador	Lechera Andina

Rico. It operates in a variety of sectors, including food, paper, agribusiness, cement and transport services. The company was founded in 1941 and its internationalisation strategy predominantly has been business acquisitions in neighbouring countries (see Table 3.10). Its expansion has focused on the food industry, especially dairy products.

The Gloria Group has been actively internationalising its operations since 2000 and currently serves customers in thirty-nine countries. After Alicorp, it is the second Peruvian multilatina with the most mergers and acquisitions (nineteen). These have enabled the group to diversify its product portfolio, expand its reach and increase profitability.

4 | *Chile – the disciplined*

JUANA GARCÍA AND VENETA ANDONOVA

Chile is currently one of Latin America's showcase countries, a status it has earned thanks to its open and stable economic model, which has favoured foreign investment and created the opportunity to expand its traditional businesses. According to the World Bank, Chile has had one of the highest rates of economic growth among Latin American economies in recent years.[1]

Chile was Latin America's fastest-growing economy in the 1990s and has weathered recent regional economic instability. However, it faces the challenges of having to diversify its copper-dependent economy – it is the world's largest producer of copper (see Table 4.4) – and addressing uneven wealth distribution. Remarkably, the fiscal discipline with which Chilean governments navigated the copper boom of 2003–08 and saved about 12% of GDP in the sovereign wealth fund, allowed for sizeable fiscal easing, and since 2008, public spending has increased. In 2009, the president, Michelle Bachelet, registered the highest approval rating of any president since the return of democracy, a result of her government's responsible fiscal management.[2]

Among the countries studied in this book, Chile has the smallest population and a comparatively small internal market. In 2012, its GDP growth was 5.35%, which declined to 4.7% in 2014, largely because of the lower price of copper, reduced investment in the mining sector (Chile's biggest export industry) and a slowdown in domestic consumption. Despite the strength and extent of development of its economy, there is a high degree of income inequality in Chile.

---

[1] World Bank, 2015. Chile overview, available at www.worldbank.org/en/country/chile/overview.
[2] Jeffrey Frankel's Blog. (2010). *Achieving Long-Term Fiscal Discipline: A Lesion from Chile*. Blog entry retrieved from the URL: www.jeffrey-frankel.com/2010/01/31/achieving-long-term-fiscal-discipline-a-lesson-from-chile/.

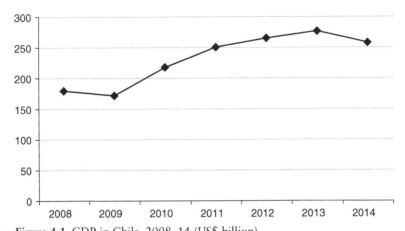

Figure 4.1 GDP in Chile, 2008–14 (US$ billion).
Source: World Bank, 2015. Chile Panorama General. Retrieved from: www
.bancomundial.org/es/country/chile/overview.

The Macroeconomic Environment

In 2009, Chile's GDP declined, triggered by the global financial crisis (Figure 4.1), but the disciplined fiscal policy of the government allowed for sizeable public spending in the subsequent years, moderating the effects of the downturn. After 2009 the growth rate remained more or less constant until 2013. In 2014, GDP increased by only 1.9%, which was significantly lower than the increase of 4.2% in the previous year.[3] The depreciation of the Chilean peso, however, led to a decline in the value of the GDP expressed in current U.S. dollars. Since 2009, there has been a marked slowdown in growth, with noticeable decreasing yearly growth rates (Figure 4.2).

Chile's economic growth is expected to pick up again in 2017 because of business development policies geared to boosting private investment and expected new tax revenue. Chile is also expected to see the fruit of monetary policies intended to gain the confidence of investors and spur recovery despite weak domestic demand.[4]

[3] ECLAC, 2015. *La Inversión Extranjera Directa en América Latina y el Caribe 2015.* Retrieved from: www.cepal.org/sites/default/files/presentation/files/150526_lie_2015_ppt_esp_v4.pdf.
[4] World Bank. (2015). World Development Indicators. Data Bank. Retrieved from: http://databank.worldbank.org/data/reports.aspx?source=world-development-indicators.

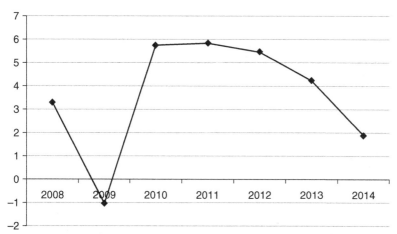

Figure 4.2 Rate of growth in GDP in Chile, 2008–14 (%).
Source: World Bank. (2015). World Development Indicators. Data Bank. Retrieved from:
http://databank.worldbank.org/data/reports.aspx?source=world-development-indicators.

The country's per capita income is high by regional standards (US$23,000 in 2014) but it still does not reach the OECD average of US$38,660 (Figure 4.3). The Gini coefficient (2009) for Chile is 52.1 while the OECD average is 32 (see Figure 4.4). Mexico and Chile have the highest rate of income inequality among OECD member countries.[5]

Despite income inequality, GDP growth is associated with relatively low unemployment; the unemployment figure hit historic lows in 2013 (see Figure 4.5). However, unemployment rose as a result of the general economic slowdown to an average of 6.4% in 2014.[6] Between January 2012 and October 2013 the central bank held the nominal inflation rate at 5% and then decided to bring it down to 3% by October 2014 (see Figure 4.6). The end of the commodities boom complicated the task of the central bank to maintain a low rate of inflation while sticking to a floating exchange-rate policy, as the cumulative depreciation

---

[5] OECD (2015). Prioridades de políticas para un crecimiento más fuerte y equitativo. CHILE. Serie 'Mejores Políticas'. Retrieved from: www.oecd .org/fr/chili/chile-prioridades-de-politicas-para-un-crecimiento-mas-fuerte-y-equitativo.pdf.

[6] ECLAC. (2014). *Preliminary Overview of the Economies of Latin America and the Caribbean*. http://repositorio.cepal.org/bitstream/handle/11362/37345/ Chile_en.pdf?sequence=35.

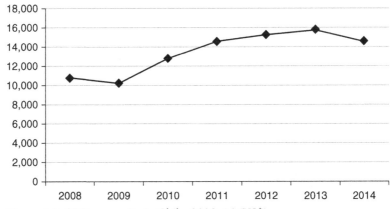

Figure 4.3 GDP per capita in Chile, 2008–14 (US$).
Source: World Bank (2015) World Development Indicators. Data Bank. Retrieved from:
http://databank.worldbank.org/data/reports.aspx?source=world-development-indicators

Country	Gini coefficient
Chile (2011)	0.503
Mexico (2012)	0.482
Turkey (2011)	0.412
United States (2012)	0.389
Israel (2011)	0.377

Figure 4.4 Top five Gini coefficient OECD members.
Source: OECD, income distribution database. Retrieved from the URL: http://oe.cd/idd.

of the peso with respect to the U.S. dollar between October 2013 and October 2014 was 17.8%.[7] The simultaneous occurrence of increasing inflation and decelerating economic growth is very challenging.

Nevertheless, Chile continues to generate a lot of optimism, as 'relative poverty has declined at a faster rate than in any other OECD country, and performance indicators in health and education have greatly improved'.[8] Higher education reform that would make university

[7] ECLAC. (2014). *Preliminary Overview of the Economies of Latin America and the Caribbean.* http://repositorio.cepal.org/bitstream/handle/11362/37345/Chile_en.pdf?sequence=35.
[8] OECD. (2015). *Prioridades de políticas para un crecimiento más fuerte y equitativo. Chile. Serie 'Mejores Políticas'.* Retrieved from the URL: www.oecd.org/fr/chili/chile-prioridades-de-politicas-para-un-crecimiento-mas-fuerte-y-equitativo.pdf.

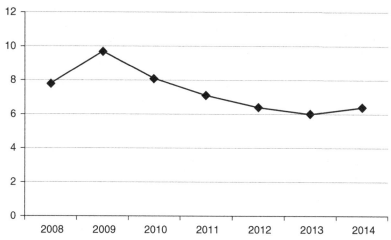

Figure 4.5 Unemployment in Chile, 2008–14 (% of working-age population).
Source: World Bank. (2015). World Development Indicators. Data Bank. Retrieved from:
http://databank.worldbank.org/data/reports.aspx?source=world-development-indicators.

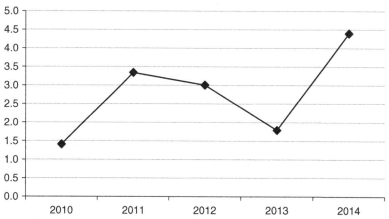

Figure 4.6 Inflation in Chile, 2010–14 (annual consumer prices %).
Source: World Bank. (2015). World Development Indicators. Data Bank. Retrieved from:
http://databank.worldbank.org/data/reports.aspx?source=world-development-indicators.

education free is seen as one of the means to improve educational outcomes, improve long-term economic perspectives and reduce the differences between rich and poor.[9]

[9] Bloomberg. (2015). *Chile's Education dream turns sour as teachers shut schools. Retrieved from the URL:* www.bloomberg.com/news/articles/2015-07-20/chile-s-education-dream-turns-sour-as-teachers-shut-down-schools.

Table 4.1 *Macroeconomic indicators, Chile 2014*

GDP	US$258,061,522,886.53
GDP growth (2012, 2013, 2014)	5.46%, 4.23%, 1.89%
GDP per capita	US$14,528.33
Population	17,762,647
GINI (2013)	50.45
Unemployment	6.40%
Inflation	4.40%
Social Progress Index	73.3
Rule of Law Index (2015)	0.68
Human Development Index	0.76
Doing Business (2016)	48

Source: World Bank (2015) World Development Indicators. Data Bank. Retrieved from: http://databank.worldbank.org/data/reports.aspx?source=world-development-indicators; Social Progress Imperative. (2015). *Social Progress Index 2015*. Retrieved from the URL: http://13i8vn49fibl3go3i12f59gh.wpengine.netdna-cdn.com/wp-content/uploads/2016/05/2015-SOCIAL-PROGRESS-INDEX_FINAL.pdf; The World Justice Project. (2015). *WJP Rule of Law*; United Nations Development Program. (2014). *Human Development Index*. Retrieved from the URL: http://hdr.undp.org/en/content/human-development-index-hdi; World Bank (2014). Doing Business 2015: Going beyond efficiency: comparing business regulations for domestic firms in 189 economies: A World Bank Group flagship report. Washington: World Bank Publications. Retrieved from: www.doingbusiness.org/~/media/GIAWB/Doing%20Business/Documents/Annual-Reports/English/DB15-Chapters/DB15-Report-Overview.pdf.

The country's main challenge is the sustainability of investors' confidence, which may be adversely affected in the present global context by the divergence between Chile's rate of economic growth and the levels of equality and quality of life in the country (Table 4.1).

Trade

Chile has a market-oriented economy characterised by a high level of foreign trade and a reputation for strong financial institutions and sound policy that have given it the strongest sovereign bond rating in South America. Exports of goods and services account for approximately one-third of GDP, with commodities making up some 60% of total exports. Copper alone provides 20% of government revenue.

Chile is the world's largest exporter of copper and its second-largest exporter of salmon.

Chile deepened its longstanding commitment to trade liberalisation with the signing of a free trade agreement with the United States that took effect on 1 January 2004. Chile has twenty-two trade agreements covering sixty countries, including agreements with the European Union, MERCOSUR, China, India, South Korea and Mexico. In May 2010, Chile signed the OECD Convention, becoming the first South American country to join the OECD. In October 2015, Chile joined the United States and ten other countries and concluded negotiations on the Trans-Pacific Partnership trade agreement. The agreement has to be ratified by the Chilean legislature.

Chile's trade balance remained positive until 2014, thanks to the expansion of external demand for its exports, which allowed Chile to increase its industrial mining exports (raw materials) significantly. However, in 2014 Chile presented almost no growth in its exports, because of unfavourable fluctuations in the international markets; this was accompanied by unchanged domestic consumption and investment. Despite an expansion policy and an open market, foreign investment in the country could not be maintained at the same levels, while domestic policies aimed to increase government revenue and tax benefit.

In the recent past, Chile has presented a steady growth in exports and imports, and in the crisis year of 2009 its trade balance showed a surplus (Figure 4.7). These achievements made the country a regional example in terms of market and trade policies in the context of an upcoming economic recovery (see Figure 4.8). This recovery, however, is probably not going to be the same as the previous era of high growth rates because the medium-term output growth is estimated to be about 3.5% for the next ten years or so.[10] As for other commodity exporters, the new era of economic growth will probably be driven more by internal factors, such as productivity gains, rather than by sustained long-term increases of international commodity prices.

The main importers of Chilean products outside Latin America are China (24.57%), the United States (12.17%), South Korea (6.23%) and Japan (10.01%), while Brazil and Argentina are the leading

[10] Rodrigo Vergara, Governor, Central Bank of Chile; 28 April 2016. Chile's growth opportunities and challenges to development. Keynote speech given at the Latin American Cities Conference 'Chile's Economy within a Global Context', organised by the Council of the Americas in Santiago, Chile.

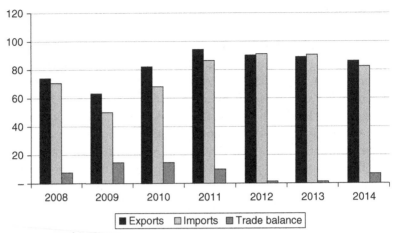

Figure 4.7 Chile's trade balance, 2008–14 (US$ million).
Source: World Bank. (2015). World Development Indicators, Data Bank. Retrieved from: http://databank.worldbank.org/data/reports.aspx?source=world-development-indicators

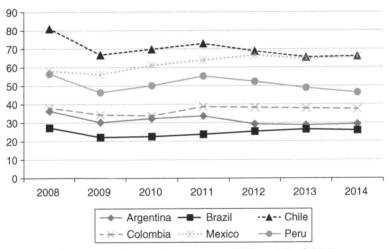

Figure 4.8 Total trade for the six countries, 2008–14 (% of GDP).
Source: World Bank. (2015). World Development Indicators. Data Bank. Retrieved from: http://databank.worldbank.org/data/reports.aspx?source=world-development-indicators.

regional importers (Table 4.2). In foreign exports, the leading countries of origin are China (20.88%) and the United States (19.77%); Brazil and Argentina are the main Latin American exporters to Chile (Table 4.3).

Table 4.2 *Chile's top five export partners, 2014*

Partner	Partner share (%)
China	24.57
United States	12.17
Japan	10.01
South Korea	6.23
Brazil	5.38

Source: World Integrated Trade Solutions. (2015). Retrieved from the URL: http://wits.worldbank.org.

Table 4.3 *Chile's top five import partners, 2014*

Partner	Partner share (%)
China	20.88
United States	19.77
Brazil	7.84
Argentina	4.03

Source: World Integrated Trade Solutions. (2015). Retrieved from: http://wits.worldbank.org.

Chile has maintained a trade balance with its most significant business partners. China and the United States are the countries with the highest percentage of exports to Chile but they are also the main import destinations, a trade balance (see Figure 4.7) that is exceptional in Latin America. In this context, the country managed to maintain a trade surplus until 2014 and skilfully mitigated international fluctuations, but with a dependence on primary goods (Table 4.4).

Chile is expected to diversify into production with high value added products or become well integrated in global production chains. Basic manufacturing would not be the way to diversify the economy in Chile, because the average income is high and the size of the domestic market does not provide sufficient scale. Moreover, a notable weakness in Chile's case is the sizeable share of intermediary goods currently imported.[11]

---

[11] OECD. (2015). *Strengthening Chile's investment promotion strategy. Retrieved from the URL:* www.oecd.org/daf/inv/investment-policy/Chile-investment-promotion-strategy-2015.pdf.

Table 4.4 *Main product exports and imports share (%)*
in Chile, 2015

Category	Product exports share (%)
Copper and copper articles	27.23
Ores, slag and ash	25.09
Edible fruit, nuts, citrus fruit peel, melons	8.9
Fish, crustaceans, molluscs, aquatic invertebrates	6.32
Wood pulp, fibrous cellulosic material, waste	4.06

Category	Product imports share (%)
Mineral fuels, oils, distillation products	14.16
Machinery, nuclear reactors and boilers	13.38
Vehicles other than railway and tramway	11.36
Electrical, electronic equipment	10.97
Mineral fuels, oils, distillation products	14.16
Machinery, nuclear reactors and boilers	13.38
Vehicles other than railway and tramway	11.36
Electrical, electronic equipment	10.97
Plastics and plastic articles	3.71

Source: ITC. (2015). Trade statistics for international business development. Retrieved from: www.trademap.org/Product_SelProductCountry.aspx.

A key lever to boost macroeconomic performance is improvement in education. This is seen as one of the most essential drivers of future economic growth, even more than the increasing participation of women in the Chilean labour force.[12] A positive example of successful diversification is provided by natural resource-based activities, such as fish and fruit farming (see Table 4.4), in which Chile has successfully upgraded from mere resource extraction to activities with substantial value added.[13]

---

[12] Rodrigo Vergara, Governor, Central Bank of Chile; 28 April 2016
   Chile's growth opportunities and challenges to development. Keynote speech given at the Latin American Cities Conference 'Chile's Economy within a Global Context', organised by the Council of the Americas in Santiago, Chile.

[13] OECD. (2015). *Strengthening Chile's investment promotion strategy. Retrieved from the URL:* www.oecd.org/daf/inv/investment-policy/Chile-investment-promotion-strategy-2015.pdf.

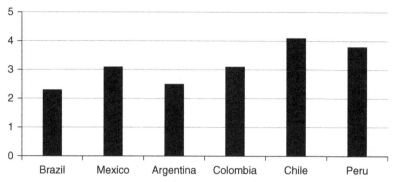

Figure 4.9 The Open Market Index for Chile, 2014.
Source: International Chamber of Commerce. (2015). *ICC Open Markets Index (3rd ed.)*. Retrieved from the URL: www.iccwbo.org/global-influence/g20/reports-and-products/open-markets-index/.

Chile depends strongly on exports of minerals such as copper and its derivatives. These represent more than 50% of the country's total exports value. While Chile achieves balanced trade flows with the United States and China, and maintains a positive trade balance, the country is highly dependent on raw materials, which is its main challenge. After a period of historically high prices for raw materials, there has been a sharp drop since 2012. As a consequence, investments in mining have diminished considerably and future projections are bleak. In response, government efforts have shifted towards stimulating domestic demand, with the aim of promoting sectors that are not dependent on commodities.

Figure 4.9 gives a comparison of the Open Market Index among the six Latin American countries studied, and shows that Chile is the most open country in the region. The Open Market Index was developed by the International Chamber of Commerce (ICC) to measure government efforts to create an open market and promote free trade and freedom of capital movement. The fact that Chile has the highest number of free trade agreements in this group (see Table 4.5) demonstrates its high degree of market liberalisation.

Foreign direct investment

In 2013, foreign direct investment (FDI) flows in Chile fell considerably because of their dependence on the mining industry, which was affected by the fall in copper prices. Chile has the second-largest FDI inflow among

Table 4.5 *Chile's trade agreements*

Multilateral agreements	Year entered into force
World Trade Organisation	1995

Agreement partners	Year entered into force
Pacific Alliance	2015
Hong Kong, China	2014
Vietnam	2014
Malaysia	2012
Turkey	2011
Australia	2009
Japan	2007
Colombia	2009
Peru	2009
Panama	2008
China	2006
New Zealand, Singapore and Brunei Darussalam	–
European Free Trade Association (EFTA)	2004
United States	2004
Republic of Korea	2004
European Union (UE)	2003
Central America (Costa Rica, El Salvador, Guatemala, Honduras and Nicaragua)	–
Mexico	1999
Canada	1997
MERCOSUR	1996

Preferential trade agreements	Year entered into force
Ecuador	2010
India	2007
Bolivia	1993
Venezuela	1993
Argentina	1991

Agreements signed but not yet in force	Year entered into force
Thailand	2013

Source: SICE OAS. (2015). Retrieved from the URL: www.sice.oas.org/ctyindex/ CHL/CHLagreements_e.asp.

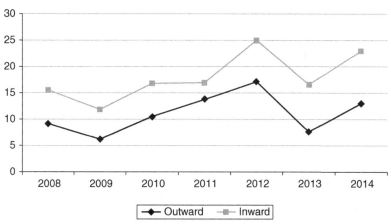

Figure 4.10 FDI flows in Chile, 2008–14 (US$ billion).
Source: Foreign direct investment flows and stock. (2015). UNCTAD STAT. Retrieved from the URL: http://unctadstat.unctad.org/wds/ReportFolders/reportFolders.aspx.

Latin American countries – after Brazil – with values close to US$23 billion in 2014 and the largest FDI outflow, at around US$13 billion (Figure 4.10).[14] In 2015, the FDI inflow fell by 46% compared to its lowest level since 2006. Generally, Chile's track record of both FDI flows and stocks is remarkable given the size of the country's population and economy. Between 2008 and 2014 FDI inflows never represented less than 6.5% of Chile's GDP while the total FDI stock in 2013 was 73% of GDP.

From a sector perspective, mining represents almost 40% of Chile's FDI stock, followed by financial intermediation, gas, electricity and water, and transport, storage and communication (Figure 4.11).

Services contribute more than 60% to the Chilean GDP and their contribution is increasing. Of the total number of employed, 67.1% work in services and contribute 61.5% to the value added in Chile's GDP. Agriculture, on the other hand, employs 9.2% of workers and generates 3.3% of the value added, supplying only half of current domestic agricultural needs.[15]

[14] UNCTAD (2015). World Investment Report 2015: *Reforming International Investment Governance*. Retrieved from: http://unctad.org/en/PublicationsLibrary/wir2015_en.pdf.
[15] Santander Trade Portal at en.portal.santandertrade.com/analyse-markets/chile/economic-political-outline.

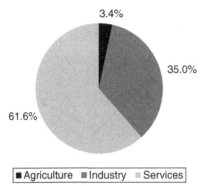

3.4%

35.0%

61.6%

◼ Agriculture ◼ Industry ▨ Services

Figure 4.11 GDP composition in Chile by sector (%).
Source: World Bank. (2015). World Development Indicators. Data Bank. Retrieved from:
http://databank.worldbank.org/data/reports.aspx?source=world-development-indicators.

Taxes

In 2014, Chile implemented reforms that were expected to increase
the country's tax revenue, boost its energy production and reduce its
dependence on copper. The priorities were to finance additional spending on education, reduce tax evasion and correct the fiscal deficit. The
receipts from the National Copper Corporation of Chile (CODELCO)
fell sharply from 0.9% of GDP in 2014 to 0.5% in 2015, together
with a drop in tax revenues from private-sector mining firms. Tax
reform that included a rise in the rate of corporate tax partially offset
this effect, as receipts from non-mining taxpayers rose from 15.7% to
16.3%. In 2016 the full effect of the tax reform is expected to be felt,
as Value Added Tax receipts are also expected to increase; tax evasion
will be addressed with more effective enforcement mechanisms.[16]

An essential element of tax reform is the increase of corporate
income taxes from 20% to 25% or 27%. A tax credit scheme allowing
companies to defer tax payments on profits for future investments was
eliminated. At the same time, the personal income tax allowance was
lowered from 40% to 35% and savings incentives schemes for small
and medium-sized businesses were created.[17] The ultimate goal of

[16] www.oecd.org/daf/inv/investment-policy/Chile-investment-promotion-
strategy-2015.pdf .http://repositorio.cepal.org/bitstream/handle/11362/39559/
1501279BPI_Chile_en.pdf;jsessionid=9F497E1A38284712FF4C900CD69561
AB?sequence=71

[17] www.oecd.org/daf/inv/investment-policy/Chile-investment-promotion-strategy-
2015.pdf.

this tax redesign is to finance the ambitious educational reforms that are expected to fuel the Chilean economy with more advanced skills sets that are 'critical to further expand the services sector, including strategic R&D and innovation activities, as well as high-end manufacturing of equipment for the mining sector'. The key directions for the future in Chile are renewable energy and the development of industry clusters for high-value integration in global value chains. Further developments in these directions demand deep economic and educational reforms.[18]

In general, together with its generally good macroeconomic indicators, Chile remains a political reference for Latin American countries because of the effectiveness of its governance institutions and its creative and ambitious policies.

Chilean multilatinas

Historically the Chilean mining industry has excelled in contributing to the country's GDP. However, since the global crisis of 2009, Chile has had to change its trade policies, driven by its high dependence on this sector and fluctuations in copper prices. Simultaneously, the retail and wine industries experienced a major upturn in terms of profitability and market penetration and gave a significant boost to some of their signature multilatinas. Companies like Arauco and CMPC are admired for their ability to adapt to different political environments, especially in other Latin American countries, such as Argentina, Peru and Colombia. Additionally, in the retail sector, Cencosud relies on both product and market diversification and has made successful efforts to achieve brand recognition. Finally, in the wine industry, Chile has managed to implement export policies that make efficient and sustainable contributions to the production and marketing of their own regional and geographical advantages.

Besides the macroeconomic and trade policies that have facilitated the competitiveness and internationalisation of Chilean businesses, its multilatinas have benefitted from valuable natural resources, privileged positions and market share in the relatively small domestic market. This situation has made it possible for many to export their

---

[18] www.oecd.org/daf/inv/investment-policy/Chile-investment-promotion-strategy-2015.pdf.

successful domestic business models directly without major host market adaptations. The wood product companies CMPC and Arauco expanded by implanting their domestic model of vertical integration of forest management with the production of wooden products to neighbouring Brazil, Argentina and Uruguay.[19]

In general, internationalisation in Chile has taken advantage of the global business environment to leverage the country's internal resources; some of the most prominent multilatinas are companies that rely on raw materials and have translated them into opportunities for significant expansion. However, in recent years Chile has experienced economic deceleration because of its dependence on commodities such as copper, which has suffered a drop in price worldwide, a fact that has greatly affected the performance of the country's main export-oriented industry. This situation has forced a debate about diversification and has led to the development of comprehensive contingency plans to mitigate the impact of market fluctuations.

The preferred market entry mode of Chilean multilatinas is acquisition, which has proved to be a speedy and successful strategy. Companies like LAN have also developed integrated business models and alliances that have allowed them to reach regional and global markets. Retail companies are the most asset-intensive multinationals and their international strategy relies on serving the same customer base they serve at home. Greenfield investments are the most common in this industry. In general, Chilean mutinationals focus on reaping economic benefits from investment in new markets, as in the case of retail (Cencosud) and from the country's geographical advantages, as in the case of wine production (Concha y Toro). The most significant international markets for many Chilean multinationals are still in Latin America, mainly Argentina, Brazil, Peru and Colombia, where they have acquired established traditional companies, achieved market recognition and continue to grow.

Arauco

Founded in 1968, Arauco is one of the largest forestry companies in the world. In 2016 it occupied third place in the global wood

---

[19] Pérez Ludeña, M. 2011. The top 20 multinationals in Chile in 2010: Retail, forestry and transport lead the international expansion, Serie Desarrollo Productivo 192, CEPAL document.

products industry. Arauco produces, manages and sells renewable forest resources. Since its foundation in 1976, it has focused on developing sustainable products and is now present in more than eighty countries worldwide. Arauco has thirty production plants in Chile, Argentina, Brazil, Uruguay, the United States and Canada, and maintains commercial operations in many more.

CMPC

Founded in 1920, CMPC is a forestry company and Chile's largest paper and tissue producer. In 1995 the company adopted a holding structure, dividing its business into subsidiaries and is now a highly diversified business across both product categories and markets. Its products are sold in more than forty-five countries. CMPC exports 90% of its domestic production to markets in the United States, Europe, Asia and Oceania. Its main strength has been the extensive logistics network it has built worldwide, and it has been successfully using this business model to commercialise forestry and pulp material. CMPC has stationery production facilities in Argentina and Peru and produces tissue in Argentina, Peru, Mexico, Uruguay and Colombia.

LAN

Founded in 1929, LAN is one of the largest airlines in South America. The increased flow of passengers in the region has brought LAN one of the highest operational incomes among air carriers in Latin America. LAN began growing its market share in the Chilean domestic market and currently controls about 74% of all air services consumption. A member of the international One World alliance, and well diversified in cargo operations, LAN has created beneficial alliances that have facilitated its expansion to Peru, Ecuador, Colombia and Argentina, flying to global destinations in the Americas, the Caribbean, Oceania and Europe.

Cencosud

Cencosud, which was founded in 1976, is considered to be the most important retail company in both Chile and Latin America. Its businesses include supermarket chains, home improvement outlets,

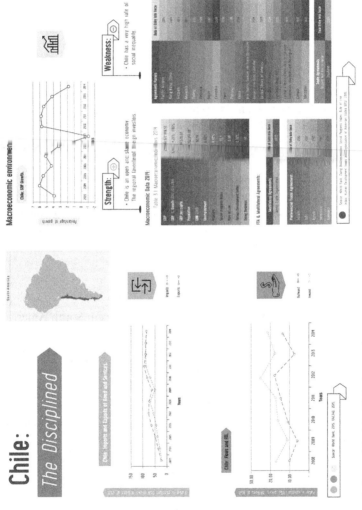

Infographic 4.1 Chile in numbers.

financial services, insurance products and family entertainment. This range of products and services makes Cencosud one of the most diversified Chilean companies with operations in Argentina, Brazil, Chile, Peru and Colombia.

Concha y Toro

Concha y Toro is a wine producer with operations in Chile and Argentina. The company owns vineyards, wine plants and bottling facilities and operates a distribution network. Concha y Toro produces premium, varietal and sparkling wines, which it exports worldwide, grows fruit and bottles mineral water. It has subsidiaries in South America and maintains joint venture arrangements with French vineyards, which have enabled it to enter important European markets such as the UK and Netherlands as well as countries in Asia and Oceania.

5 | *Argentina – the precursor*

JUANA GARCÍA AND VENETA ANDONOVA

A century ago, Argentina was a prosperous country that was poised to become the first developed country in Latin America and one of the world's most powerful economies. The country attracted Europeans looking for a new future during and after the two World Wars and its agricultural products were exported worldwide. Although Argentina's development has slowed down, in 2015 it was still the third-largest economy in Latin America and ranked twenty-fourth in the world for total GDP.[1] The economic crisis at the turn of the century hit the country very hard and subsequent government policies have failed to help the country regain its sustainable growth trajectory. In fact, since the 1990s Argentina has been losing its relative position in overall Latin American GDP. Also, statistics about the state of the Argentine economy cannot be fully trusted as measurement methodologies have changed and numbers are arbitrarily altered. For instance, the government underreported inflation statistics and increased deficit spending on politically sensitive energy subsidies ahead of the 2015 presidential elections.[2]

Throughout its history, Argentina has suffered from economic instability. During the 1990s, liberal macroeconomic policies were designed to increase the openness of the economy and take advantage of the global position Argentina enjoyed at the time. Later, during the government of President Nestor Kirchner (2003–07), the country embraced protectionism in an attempt to save the economy from the effects of the 2001 economic recession and redistribute wealth more equally.[3] With the extension of protectionist policies until 2015,

[1] World Bank. (2015). World Development Indicators. Data Bank. Retrieved from: http://databank.worldbank.org/data/reports.aspx?source=world-development-indicators.

[2] The Heritage Foundation. (2016). *2016 Index of Economic Freedom*. Retrieved from: www.heritage.org/index/country/argentina.

[3] The Economist, 15 February 2014. *A century of decline*. Retrieved from: www.economist.com/news/briefing/21596582-one-hundred-years-ago-argentina-was-future-what-went-wrong-century-decline.

Argentina grew more distant from global markets, limited the number of its trade partners, grew increasingly dependent on MERCOSUR (the Southern Common Market) and experienced difficulties with its debt. The presidential election of 2015 generated some optimism and new economic policies were expected to improve the country's competitiveness in the global economy. Argentina's recovery will require time and economic stability; the country's low dependence on commodities might be beneficial in the current regional context and enable it to catch up with its neighbours.

The macroeconomic environment

Compared to other countries in Latin America, Argentina has been more vulnerable to external shocks. For example, the 2008 global economic crisis hit the country harder than most; unemployment rose almost 1% and the GDP grew by only 0.05%, as shown in Figure 5.1.[4] This happened despite the relatively closed state of Argentina's economy and the extended policy of protectionism, designed to shield Argentina from global economic downturns. Even though the economy recovered in 2010 and 2011, recovery did not last long. In 2012, businesses were deterred by short-termism measures, such as increasing interest rates to address inflation, and the fear of nationalisation.[5] Productivity decreased, currency discrepancy affected the market and few new investments were made, leaving the economy with no means to grow.

Currency fluctuations have seriously affected Argentina's economy. The local currency has been steadily depreciating since 2010 and has hit its lowest level in recent history. In 2015, the growing strength of the U.S. dollar put Argentina in a precarious situation, with inflation already out of control. Its currency was over-valued, while its value on the black market fell by 32% with respect to the U.S. dollar.[6] This situation

[4] World Bank. (2015). World Development Indicators. Data Bank. Retrieved from: http://databank.worldbank.org/data/reports.aspx?source=world-development-indicators.

[5] The Economist. 23 January 2014. *First decline, now fall*. Retrieved from: www.economist.com/blogs/americasview/2014/01/argentinas-peso.

[6] Russo, C. (18 March 2015). Argentine Peso Forwards at Record Show Devaluation Bet for 2016. Bloomberg Business. Retrieved from: www.bloomberg.com/news/articles/2015-03-18/argentine-peso-forwards-at-record-show-devaluation-bet-for-2016.

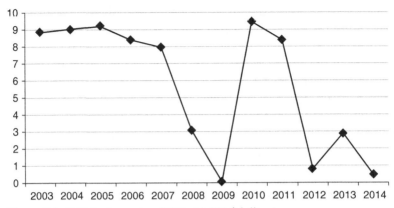

Figure 5.1 GDP in Argentina, 2003–14 (US $ billion).
Source: World Bank, (2015). World Development Indicators. Data Bank. Retrieved from:
http://databank.worldbank.org/data/reports.aspx?source=world-development-indicators.

occurred because of the exchange rate measures implemented by the government of President Cristina Fernández (2007–15) in 2011, when U.S. dollar flows were put under strict control.[7] The lack of U.S. dollars in the Argentine economy has been problematic for the country's debt and brought international tensions because the national government threatened to default. Inflation has also caused alarm in Argentina (see Figure 5.2) and reached a record rate of 40.5% in April 2016.[8]

As the Argentine economy has gradually slowed down, productive companies have had a hard time accessing supplies and consumer demand has fallen in response to rapidly increasing prices. There are no signs that the macroeconomic environment is going to change in the short term, unless new policies, steering away from recent government trends, are implemented.[9] Both investors and local consumers are interested that the new government prioritises getting the double-digit inflation under control.[10]

[7] Russo, C. (18 March 2015). Argentine Peso Forwards at
   Record Show Devaluation Bet for 2016. Bloomberg Business.
   Retrieved from: www.bloomberg.com/news/articles/2015-03-18/
   argentine-peso-forwards-at-record-show-devaluation-bet-for-2016
[8] www.tradingeconomics.com/argentina/inflation-cpi.
[9] Deloitte. (2015, March). Latin America Economic Outlook. Retrieved
   from: www2.deloitte.com/content/dam/Deloitte/global/Documents/About-
   Deloitte/gx-latin-america-economic-outlook-march-2015.pdf.
[10] Fast FT. (2015, February). Argentine peso devaluation matter
   of 'when'. Retrieved from: www.ft.com/intl/fastft/281663/
   devaluation-of-argentina-peso-matter-of.

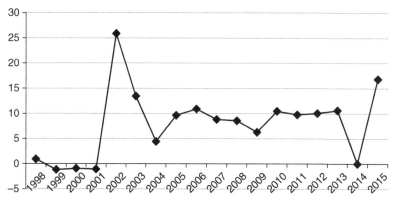

Figure 5.2 Inflation in Argentina (consumer prices, % annual).
Source: International Monetary Fund. (2015). *Inflation, average consumer prices.*
Retrieved from: www.imf.org/external/pubs/ft/weo/2016/01/weodata/weorept.aspx
?sy=1997&ey=2016&scsm=1&ssd=1&sort=country&ds=.&br=1&pr1.x=71&pr1
.y=8&c=213&s=PCPI&grp=0&a=. NB: there were no data for 2016.

Figure 5.3 is a comparative graph showing the differences in inflation between the six countries studied. The unparalleled inflation rate
in the Argentine economy is the biggest factor influencing the economic instability of the country. Unfortunately, the government has
only a limited set of feasible instruments with which to tackle this
problem owing to the persistent issue of external debt. Most other
Latin American countries (with the exception of Venezuela) apply relatively strict controls on inflation as they strive to build trust among
investors. Nevertheless, some increase in the inflation level in most
economies in the region is expected owing to devaluation against the
U.S. dollar.

Even with these setbacks, Argentina's GDP per capita (see Figure 5.4)
is still the second highest in the region, behind that of Chile, and
according to this indicator the country occupies the fifty-sixth position worldwide.[11] However, GDP per capita has decreased by almost
US$2000 dollars since 2013 and this trend is expected to continue.
This is another sign that Argentina needs economic reforms to stop
losing purchasing power and maintain its leading position in Latin
America in terms of GDP per capita. However, inequality is not as high

[11] World Bank. (2015). World Development Indicators. Data Bank.
Retrieved from: http://databank.worldbank.org/data/reports
.aspx?source=world-development-indicators.

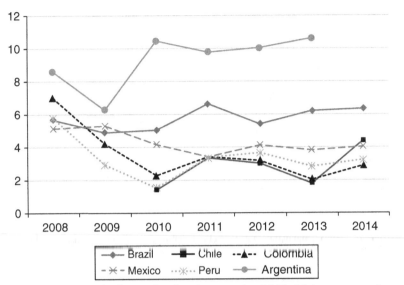

Figure 5.3 Rate of inflation for the six countries, 2008–14 (consumer prices, % annual).

Source: World Bank. (2015). World Development Indicators. Data Bank. Retrieved from: http://databank.worldbank.org/data/reports.aspx?source=world-development-indicators and International Monetary Fund. (2015). *Inflation, average consumer prices*. Retrieved from: www.imf.org/external/pubs/ft/weo/2016/01/weodata/weorept.aspx?sy=1997&ey=2016&scsm=1&ssd=1&sort=country&ds=.&br=1&pr1.x=71&pr1.y=8&c=213&s=PCPI&grp=0&a=.

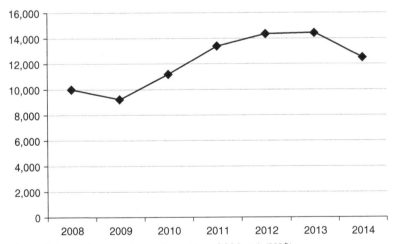

Figure 5.4 GDP per capita in Argentina, 2008–14 (US$).

Source: World Bank. (2015). World Development Indicators. Data Bank. Retrieved from: http://databank.worldbank.org/data/reports.aspx?source=world-development-indicators.

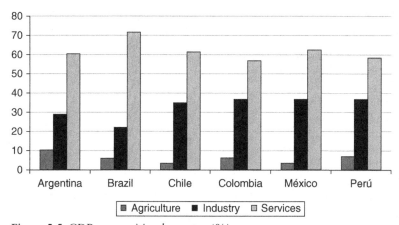

Figure 5.5 GDP composition by sector (%).
Source: World Bank. (2015). World Development Indicators. Data Bank. Retrieved from:
http://databank.worldbank.org/data/reports.aspx?source=world-development-indicators.

as it is in some of Argentina's neighbours, with inequality indexes close
to those of economically developed countries.

The GDP of many Latin American countries shows similar sectoral
composition, with a heavy reliance on primary goods. Colombia and Peru
still have a great deal of potential to grow their service sector, one in which
Argentina is more advanced, but still represents 60% of the economy
compared to about 70% in Brazil (Figure 5.5). Key institutional, economic and social indicators for Argentina are summarised in Table 5.1.

Trade

Since 2011, Argentina's imports and exports have been decreasing yearly as a consequence of the import restriction policies implemented by the government (see Figure 5.6). Although trade increased
yearly from 2001, it did not grow as much as it could have done and
Argentina lost its leading position as exporter of some products. For
example, in 2006 Argentina was the world's fourth-largest exporter
of wheat; in 2014 it was the eighth.[12] However, in 2015 Argentina
was still the number one exporter of soy oil, number three for cot-
tonseed oil and four for corn (see Table 5.2), which put it in a better

[12] Index mundi. (2014). [Graph illustration the Soybean oil exports by country]
Data from the United States Department of Agriculture. Retrieved from:
www.indexmundi.com/agriculture/?commodity=soybean-oil&graph=exports.

Table 5.1 *Macroeconomic indicators, Argentina 2014*

GDP (2014)	US$537,659,972,702,092
GDP % growth (2012, 2013, 2014)	0.8%, 2.89%, 0.45%
GDP per capita (2014)	US$12,509
Population (2014)	42,980,026
Gini (2013)	42.28
Unemployment (2014)	8.2%
Inflation (2014)	37.6%
Social Progress Index (2015)[a]	73.08
Rule of Law Index (2015)[b]	0.52
Human Development Index (2014)[c]	0.836
Doing Business (2014)[d]	124

[a] Social Progress Imperative. (2015). *Social Progress Index 2015.* Retrieved from: http://13i8vn49fibl3go3i12f59gh.wpengine.netdna-cdn.com/wp content/uploads/2016/05/2015-SOCIAL-PROGRESS-INDEX_FINAL.pdf.

[b] The World Justice Project. (2015). *WJP Rule of Law Index 2015.* Retrieved from: http://data.worldjusticeproject.org.

[c] United Nations Development Program. (2014). *Human Development Index.* Retrieved from: http://hdr.undp.org/en/content/human-development-index-hdi.

[d] World Bank (2014). Doing Business 2015: Going beyond efficiency: Comparing business regulations for domestic firms in 189 economies: a World Bank Group flagship report. Washington: World Bank Publications. Retrieved from: www.doingbusiness.org/~/media/GIAWB/Doing%20 Business/Documents/Annual-Reports/English/DB15-Chapters/DB15-Report-Overview.pdf.

Source: World Bank. (2015). World Development Indicators. Data Bank. Retrieved from: http://databank.worldbank.org/data/reports.aspx?source= world-development-indicators; Social Progress Imperative. (2015). *Social Progress Index 2015.* Retrieved from: http://13i8vn49fibl3go3i12f59gh .wpengine.netdna-cdn.com/wp-content/uploads/2016/05/2015-SOCIAL-PROGRESS-INDEX_FINAL.pdf; The World Justice Project. (2015). *WJP Rule of Law*; United Nations Development Program. (2014). *Human Development Index.* Retrieved from: http://hdr.undp.org/en/content/human-development-index-hdi; World Bank (2014). Doing Business 2015: Going beyond efficiency: Comparing business regulations for domestic firms in 189 economies: A World Bank Group flagship report. Washington: World Bank Publications. Retrieved from: www.doingbusiness.org/~/media/GIAWB/ Doing%20Business/Documents/Annual-Reports/English/DB15-Chapters/ DB15-Report-Overview.pdf.

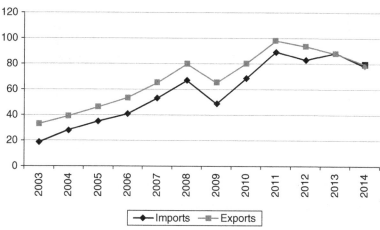

Figure 5.6 Argentina's imports and exports, 2003–14 (US$ billion).
Source: World Bank. (2015). World Development Indicators. Data Bank. Retrieved from:
http://databank.worldbank.org/data/reports.aspx?source=world-development-indicators.

position than most Latin American countries in international trade.[13]
Argentina's economy is heavily reliant on fossil fuels and the country
has been a net importer of oil and gas since 2011, with natural gas
responsible for 55% of its energy supply (see Table 5.3).[14] Despite all
its political and social troubles, Argentina has been able to maintain a
positive trade balance. However, while exports in 2011 reached a peak
of 24% of GDP, in 2015 they fell to a mere 12.26% (Figure 5.7).[15]
Trade has been losing importance as a share of Argentina's GDP and
falling short of the international benchmark, while the country is no
longer considered to be an emerging economy.

Overall, Argentina's export products are more diversified than the
products of most other countries in the region, which has made it
relatively easier for the economy to survive the current oil price crisis.

[13] Index mundi, 2016 [Graph illustration the Soybean oil exports by
country. Estimation for 2016] Data from the United States Department
of Agriculture. Retrieved from: www.indexmundi.com/agriculture/
?commodity=soybean-oil&graph=exports.
[14] GeoCurrents. The Peoples, Places and Languages Shaping Currents Events.
(2015). *Argentina's controversial energy policies.* www.geocurrents.info/
environmental-geography/argentinas-controversial-energy-policies.
[15] World Bank. (2015). World Development Indicators. Data Bank.
Retrieved from: http://databank.worldbank.org/data/reports
.aspx?source=world-development-indicators.

Table 5.2 *Product exports share (%) in Argentina, 2014*

Category	Product exports share (%)
Residues, waste from food industry, animal fodder	18.79
Vehicles other than railway and tramway	12.19
Cereals	7.66
Animal, vegetable fats and oils, cleavage products, etc.	6.32
Oil seed, oleagic fruits, grain, seed, fruit, etc.	6.16

Source: ITC. (2015). Trade statistics for international business development. Retrieved from: www.trademap.org/Product_SelProductCountry.aspx. NB: there were no data available for 2015.

Table 5.3 *Product imports share (%) in Argentina, 2014*

Category	Product imports share (%)
Mineral fuels, oils, distillation products, etc.	16.87
Machinery, nuclear reactors, boilers, etc.	14.68
Vehicles other than railway and tramway	13.41
Electrical, electronic equipment	11.03
Organic chemicals	4.61

Source: ITC. (2015). Trade statistics for international business development. Retrieved from: www.trademap.org/Product_SelProduct Country.aspx. NB: there were no data available for 2015.

It is important to note, however, Argentina's dependence on Brazil, its main trade partner (Tables 5.4 and 5.5). Brazil's difficulties might push Argentina to look for new partners to avoid a bigger fall in trade. However, Argentina also heavily relies on MERCOSUR for its trade and new partners might be difficult to find. Because the country has had a tendency to prioritise trade with its neighbours, it might be harder to diversify destinations since the entire region is facing economic challenges.

Besides the fact that China and the United States have lost some of their importance as trade partners, Argentina's trade agreements (see Tables 5.6 and 5.7) are an example of the regional preference for trade in goods and services. Argentina currently has trade agreements with

Table 5.4 *Argentina's top five export partners, 2014*

Partner	Partner share (%)
Brazil	20.31
China	6.53
United States	5.91
Chile	4.09
Venezuela	2.90

Source: World Integrated Trade Solutions. (2015). Retrieved from: http://wits.worldbank.org.

Table 5.5 *Argentina's top five import partners, 2014*

Partner	Partner share (%)
Brazil	21.75
China	16.39
United States	13.52
Germany	5.38
Bolivia	4.2

Source: World Integrated Trade Solutions. (2015). Retrieved from: http://wits.worldbank.org.

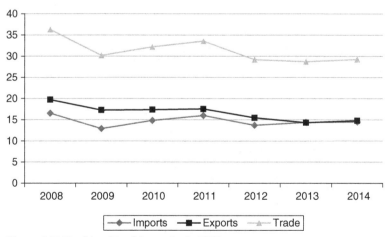

Figure 5.7 Trade as % of Argentina's GDP.
Source: World Bank. (2015). World Development Indicators. Data Bank. Retrieved from: http://databank.worldbank.org/data/reports.aspx?source=world-development-indicators.

Table 5.6 *Argentina's trade agreements*

Multilateral agreements	Year entered into force
World Trade Organisation	1995

Customs unions	Year entered into force
MERCOSUR	1991

Free trade agreements	Year entered into force
MERCOSUR Israel	2011
MERCOSUR Peru	2005
MERCOSUR Bolivia	1997
MERCOSUR Chile	1996

Framework agreements	Year entered into force
MERCOSUR Morocco	2010
MERCOSUR Mexico	2006

Preferential trade agreements	Year entered into force
Mexico	2012
MERCOSUR Colombia, Ecuador, Venezuela	2005
MERCOSUR India	2009
Uruguay (auto sector)	2003
Paraguay	1992
Chile	1991
Brazil	1990

Table 5.7 *Argentine trade agreements (signed and pending)*

Free trade agreements
MERCOSUR Egypt

Preferential trade agreements
MERCOSUR Southern African customs union

Source: SICE OAS. (2015). Retrieved from: www
.sice.oas.org/ctyindex/CHL/CHLagreements_e.asp.

only three non-Latin American countries through MERCOSUR: India, Israel and Morocco. This approach is very different from that followed by countries like Colombia, Peru and Chile, which have signed new trade agreements with numerous emerging and developed economies.

Notably, Argentina has been building stronger ties with China, which is the largest consumer of Argentine agricultural products. Indeed, Argentina might turn to China to compensate for the weak economic outlook for Latin America in 2015 and subsequent years.

The limited volume of trade between the United States and Argentina came as a result of a 'duty war' between the two countries in 2012, when Argentina violated a trade agreement and was expected to pay an arbitration award to U.S. investors. Instead of compensating the investors, the Argentine government made trade with the United States more difficult and in response the U.S. government reinstated duties on Argentine imports.

After the commodity boom that hit all the Latin American countries featured in this book, Argentina faced a number of particularly difficult challenges. Unlike the more institutionally mature Chile and to some degree Mexico, institution-building in Argentina was described as 'very quick and clientilist redistribution'.[16] This perception cuts across all types of government policies, including international deals and state taxes. These institutional weaknesses need to be remedied before Argentina's vast agricultural potential can be fully developed. Moreover, Argentina has the second-largest reserves of shale gas and the fourth-largest reserves of shale oil in the world and experts rank the potential importance of Argentine developments at number three, after the United States and China.

Foreign direct investment

Economic instability and political decisions have had a noticeable effect on FDI in Argentina, as shown in Figure 5.8. In 2014, investments fell 41%, mainly in extractive industries; this was partly a regional phenomenon, however. Argentina's substantial fall in FDI was largely because of the nationalisation of Repsol, a Spanish oil company, in 2012,[17] a decision that alienated foreign investors. After that,

---

[16] A Century of Decline; the Tragedy of Argentina. (2014, 15 February). *The Economist (US)*. Retrieved from: www.economist.com/news/briefing/ 21596582-one-hundred-years-ago-argentina-was-future-what-went-wrong-century-decline.

[17] UNCTAD. (2012, February). Investment Country Profiles, Argentina. United Nations. Retrieved from: http://unctad.org/en/PublicationsLibrary/ webdiaeia2012d5_en.pdf.

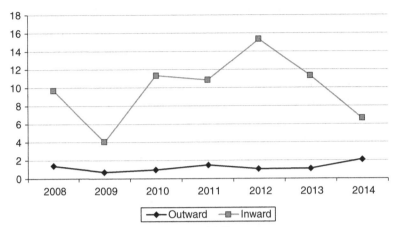

Figure 5.8 FDI flows in Argentina (US$ billion).
Source: Foreign Direct Investment flows and stock (2015), UNCTAD STAT. Retrieved from: http://unctadstat.unctad.org/wds/ReportFolders/reportFolders.aspx.

FDI plunged in 2014 and this trend is expected to continue until new government policies related to FDI are adopted.

Inflation and an unstable exchange rate are also constraining Argentina's business activity, which is not increasing as rapidly as prices, making financial forecasting extremely difficult. For example, in 2012 the Brazilian mining company Vale decided to end operations in Argentina when it failed to double its investment, as expected, because of local macroeconomic conditions.[18] Moreover, the Argentine government's ruling that companies could not return dividends and profits to the country of origin, depending on the economic sector in which they operate,[19] made companies less interested in investing in Argentina. Consumer goods companies that import their products have also left the country because of restrictions imposed to protect local producers.[20]

[18] Knowledge at Wharton. (2013, 29 May). Argentina's uncertain economic climate takes a toll on investments. School of Wharton, University of Pennsylvania. Retrieved from: http://knowledge.wharton.upenn.edu/article/argentinas-uncertain-economic-climate-takes-a-toll-on-investments/.

[19] Price, L. & Orihuela, R. (2011, 27 October). YPF gets dividend 'wake-up call' on Argentine decree, Itau says. Bloomberg Business. Retrieved from: www.bloomberg.com/news/articles/2011-10-27/ypf-gets-dividend-wake-up-call-on-argentine-decree-itau-says.

[20] Helft, D. (2012, 19 September). Luxury brands leave Argentina in droves. Fortune. Retrieved from: http://fortune.com/2012/09/19/luxury-brands-leave-argentina-in-droves/.

As Argentina's political direction changes, recovering investor trust will be one of the new president's main challenges, following his election in August 2015.

Until 2012, the countries with the largest FDI inflows in Argentina were the United States, Canada, Chile and the Netherlands. The primary sectors attracting investment were mining and other extractive industries, followed by manufacturing, services and financial institutions.[21] This is very similar to other Latin American countries, which is a problem for Argentina because it does not have a unique sector that investors might want to hold on to when the economic environment improves. The necessary diversification of the economy is hard to achieve without, among other things, ambitious judicial reform (to deal with scores of incompetent and corrupt judges) as well as reform of highly politicised lower courts. This is a critical prerequisite to guarantee the institutional protection of property rights.[22]

Contrary to FDI inflows, FDI outflows have remained more or less stable in Argentina (see Figure 5.8). They have not increased significantly since 2003 and are unlikely to do so, given the existing restrictions. In the short term, like most countries in the region, Argentina is a rather weak investor. When restrictions are lifted, Argentinean companies might adopt internationalisation as a strategy to keep up with regional competitors. Economic sectors that represent approximately one-third of the Argentinian economy, such as tourism, engineering services, commodity industries and wine production, are seen as internationally competitive, while the other two-thirds of the Argentinian economy experience competitiveness challenges.[23]

---

[21] UNCTAD. (2012, February). Investment Country Profiles, Argentina. United Nations. Retrieved from: http://unctad.org/en/PublicationsLibrary/webdiaeia2012d5_en.pdf.

[22] See, for example, The Heritage Foundation. (2016). 2016 Index of Economic Freedom. Retrieved from: www.heritage.org/index/country/argentina; and Transparency International. (2013). *Argentina and the Judiciary: Subverting the rule of law*. Retrieved from: www.transparency.org/news/feature/argentina_and_the_judiciary_subverting_the_rule_of_law.

[23] The Economist, 15 February 2014. *A century of decline*. Retrieved from: www.economist.com/news/briefing/21596582-one-hundred-years-ago-argentina-was-future-what-went-wrong-century-decline.

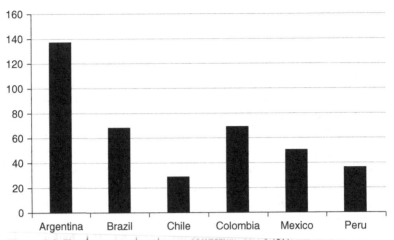

Figure 5.9 Total tax rate for the six countries, 2015 (%).
Source: World Bank. (2015). World Development Indicators. Data Bank. Retrieved from: http://databank.worldbank.org/data/reports.aspx?source=world-development-indicators; Paying Taxes, 2016. The World Bank Group, PwC. Retrieved from: www.pwc.com/gx/en/paying-taxes-2016/paying-taxes-2016.pdf.

Taxes

Argentine taxes are a big concern for companies, which have to pay close to 138% tax if labour contributions are included.[24] Argentina has the highest tax rates in Latin America, as the government's priority is to redistribute income and reduce inequality, and along with Brazil, has the highest tax rates of the G20 countries.[25] The latest corporate tax increase in Argentina was on turnover. This is a disincentive for production, as prices are already extremely high because of inflation. However, many companies do not actually pay income tax because they are losing money.[26] To some degree, the high tax rate is unavoidable in a context of debt repayment and fiscal readjustment. As Figure 5.9 shows, Argentina has the highest rate in taxes compared with the other five countries studied.

[24] Paying Taxes, 2016. The World Bank Group, PwC. Retrieved from: www.pwc.com/gx/en/paying-taxes-2016/paying-taxes-2016.pdf, p. 133, table A3.2: Total Tax Rate.

[25] Paying Taxes, 2015. The World Bank Group, PwC. Retrieved from: www.pwc.com/gx/en/paying-taxes/pdf/pwc-paying-taxes-2015-high-resolution.pdf.

[26] Paying Taxes, 2015. The World Bank Group, PwC. Retrieved from: www.pwc.com/gx/en/paying-taxes/pdf/pwc-paying-taxes-2015-high-resolution.pdf.

Since 2011, the number of tax payments has decreased thanks to the adoption of online filing and payment systems.[27] This advantage, however, is cancelled out by the number of hours (405) needed to comply with the tax regulations in Argentina (2014).

In 2016, tax incentives were available for mining, forestry, software production, biotechnology and biofuel production both at national and provincial levels.[28]

Argentine multilatinas

The extension of protectionist policies until 2015 distanced Argentine businesses from global markets, limiting the number of their partners and making the country increasingly dependent on MERCOSUR. In this context, Argentine multilatinas provide a perfect example of persistence in the internationalisation of their business, despite the regulatory setup and the economic performance of the country, which has not been the best home environment for ambitious companies. The economic crisis in 2001 hit the country very hard and government policies since then have not managed to return the country to a sustainable growth trajectory. Therefore, the expansion of these companies can be attributed to the need to find new markets and more institutionally certain contexts.

One example of the strength of Argentine business is Arcos Dorados, the largest Latin American franchise in the world. Founded in 1960, the company has extended its business through franchising investment activities. In 2007, Arcos Dorados increased its presence in Latin America with the acquisition of the license to franchise McDonalds in nineteen countries. The company is present in Argentina, Aruba, Colombia, Costa Rica, Curaçao, Ecuador, French Guyana, Guadeloupe, Martinique, Mexico, Panama, Peru, Puerto Rico, St Croix, St Thomas, Trinidad and Tobago, Uruguay and Venezuela.

Despite Argentina's economic instability over the past twenty years, several outstanding companies – almost all of which have grown out of family businesses – have maintained their key role in their respective industries through the implementation of thoughtful strategies and quick adaptation to the international context.

---

[27] www.pwc.com/gx/en/paying-taxes/assets/pwc-paying-taxes-2014.pdf.
[28] www2.deloitte.com/content/dam/Deloitte/global/Documents/Tax/dttl-tax-argentinaguide-2016.pdf.

Arcor

Arcor is the largest food company in Argentina. Founded in 1951, it is now the world's leading confectionery manufacturer and exporter. Today Arcor is consolidated in the international market and its brands are present in more than 120 countries. Arcor has forty industrial plants in Latin America and eleven commercial offices around the world. It has the largest number of active markets of any group in Argentina and has developed strategic alliances with leading companies such as Danone, Bimbo and Coca-Cola. Bagley Latinoamérica SA, a joint venture between Arcor and Danone, is one of the major biscuit and cracker companies in South America.

Laboratorios Bagó

Laboratorios Bagó was founded in 1934 and like Arcor is a family business. The company adheres to the highest-quality pharmaceutical standards, has invested heavily in R&D and relies on top-level multi-disciplinary scientists. The company has created its own subsidiaries around Latin America to distribute and manufacture its products. Bagó maintains commercial agreements and joint ventures with several leading companies, including Astellas, AstraZeneca, Boehringer Ingelheim, Eli Lilly, Ferrer, Ferozsons, Fidia, MSD, Novartis, Pfizer and UCB. The company has eighty-five patents.

Impsa

The energy company Impsa focuses on solutions for the generation of electric energy based on renewable resources. It was founded in 1965 and is currently present in thirteen countries. It has developed various projects in thirty countries in the Americas, Europe, Africa and Asia and has one of the largest greenfield investments among Argentine companies.

Molinos Río de la Plata

Molinos Río de la Plata is one of the oldest family business conglomerates. Founded in 1902, it is now one of the leading companies in the food industry, specialising in food for home consumption. It has a

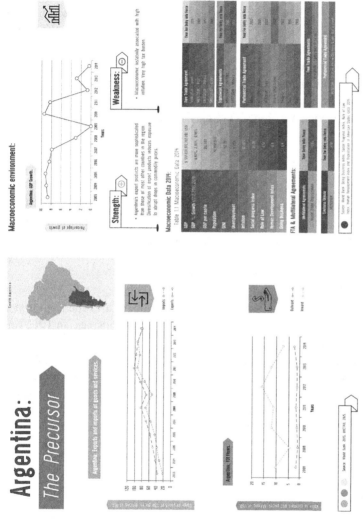

Infographic 5.1 Argentina in numbers.

111

wide distributional network in Argentina and its products are the top one or two in each product category.

Pluspetrol

Pluspetrol is a private oil and gas exploration and production company that was founded in 1977. Although it was hit by the fall in oil prices, it is the largest oil producer in Peru and one of the most important producers in Argentina. Pluspetrol's main operations are in Argentina but it also operates in Peru, Bolivia, Venezuela, Chile and Angola. Pluspetrol has a regional integration policy and maintains strategic participation in CEG and CEG Rio (Brazil) and TGP (Peru).

Tenaris

Tenaris is a successful multilatina and a public company. It was founded in 1954 to supply pipes for the oil and gas industry. In 2015 it was present in sixteen countries in North and South America, Europe, Asia and Oceania and operated five R&D units.

Ternium Siderar

Ternium Siderar is well positioned in its industry and the largest steel producer in Argentina. It was created as a family business in 1960 and is now a publicly traded company. Ternium has invested in production facilities around Latin America and its platforms are strategically located in MERCOSUR and North American Free Trade Association (NAFTA) countries. It aspires to become the leading steel company in Latin America.

6 | *Mexico – the lighthouse*

JUANA GARCÍA AND VENETA ANDONOVA

Mexico is the world's fifteenth-largest economy and the second-largest in Latin America.[1] Along with Chile, Mexico is one of the two Latin American members of the OECD (since May 1994) and it is one of the countries with the greatest number of free trade agreements (FTAs) in the WTO. Closely connected with the U.S. economy, mainly through the NAFTA agreement, Mexico maintains a relationship with the United States on four fronts: trade, remittances, investment and finance. Mexico is a federal republic. Over recent decades, the country has transformed from a highly protected economy to a more regionalised market-based economy, encouraging investment from foreign firms. Much of the country's economy today is driven by competition and export opportunities that arise from its various trade partnerships and FTAs.[2]

Despite its continued economic strength, Mexico's vulnerability to external economic shocks has taken its toll. Following the worldwide economic crisis in 2008–09, Mexico's GDP fell by 4.7%, after which it recovered slowly as the country expanded its productive capacity. By 2012, the economy had slowed down significantly, exhibiting a 1.2% growth in GDP. Although growth reached 2.4% in 2014, it is expected to be rather low in the years to come for many reasons, primarily the collapse of oil prices and a fall in FDI (see Figure 6.1).[3] Unemployment in Mexico is low by Latin American standards, but the country has a vast casual workforce and high income inequality; 46%

[1] World Bank. (2015). World Development Indicators. Data Bank. Retrieved from: http://databank.worldbank.org/data/reports.aspx?source=world-development-indicators.

[2] Santander Trade Portal. (2015). 'Mexico; Politics and Economics'. Market Analysis. Retrieved from: https://es.santandertrade.com/analizar-mercados/mexico/politica-y-economia.

[3] IMF. (2015). World Economic Outlook Database. Retrieved from: www.imf.org/external/pubs/ft/weo/2015/01/weodata/index.aspx.

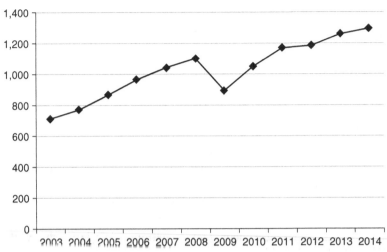

Figure 6.1 Rate of growth of GDP in Mexico, 2003–14 (%).
Source: World Bank Database, 2014, 2015.

of the population live in poverty. Public spending schedules have been halted by lower revenues, mainly because of the slump in oil prices and a conservative policy of economic growth that aims to limit fiscal deficit and external debt.

Under the leadership of President Enrique Peña Nieto the Mexican government has launched a series of structural reforms expected to stimulate growth, productivity and competitiveness. In 2014 and 2015, the focus was on the implementation of these reforms, targeted at employment, education, competitive policy, banking, telecommunications and legislation for the energy sector. While government reforms might succeed in improving competitiveness, Mexico still faces the enormous challenges posed by the much-reported violence in the country. The president himself has faced accusations of corruption linked to the awarding of public contracts. Mexico's tense social atmosphere could well be a threat to its economic development.

The macroeconomic environment

In 2014, Mexico's GDP totalled US$1.283 trillion (see Figure 6.2), with a GDP per capita of US$10,326.65, as shown in Figure 6.3. In terms of economic growth, Mexico has increased its productive capacity since 2009. However, GDP growth has not been consistent,

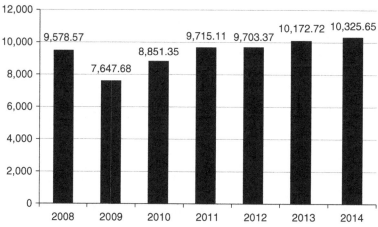

Figure 6.2 GDP in Mexico, 2003–14 (US$ billion).
Source: World Bank Database, 2014, 2015.

with a significant 4.7% fall in 2009 that coincided with the global financial crisis. By 2010, the economy was in recovery, signalled by 5.1% growth, although this has been less impressive in subsequent years. Mexico's economic growth in 2013 averaged 1.3% and, despite an increase in 2014 to 2.1%, remained below 2.5%. Double-digit growth levels in the manufacturing of auto parts have led the country's economy, while an evident lag in domestic demand, as a result of lower confidence levels and low salaries, had a negative effect on growth.

Growth perspectives for the country are mixed. However, these types of forecasts are frequently adjusted in response to changing conditions. The strengthening economy of the United States, Mexico's main commercial partner, has been a pull factor in the export sector. The growth of this sector is expected to build consumer confidence. The global oil crisis has caused a cut in the national budget of around 0.7% of the country's GDP, and additional public spending cuts in 2016 are expected to have a decelerating effect on economic growth in the years to come.[4]

Mexico has announced an official inflation target to be met by the country's central bank. Inflation targeting is a monetary policy designed

[4] OECD: Mexico: Economic Forecasts Summary. (2015, November). Economic outlook analysis and forecasts. Retrieved from: www.oecd.org/economy/mexico-economic-forecast-summary.htm.

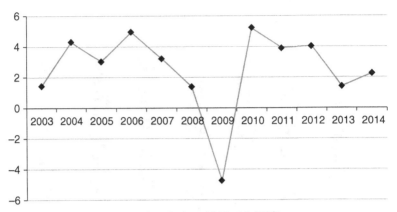

Figure 6.3 GDP per capita in Mexico, 2008–14 (US$).
Source: World Bank Database, 2014, 2015.

to guarantee transparency and allow rapid response to inflationary shocks. As Figure 6.4 shows, Mexico has successfully maintained a low and stable rate of inflation over the past five years, which has benefitted investment in the country. Although the inflation rate was 4% in 2014, lower rates followed in the two subsequent years when weak economic growth tamed inflationary pressures. Nevertheless, the central bank was still expected to raise interest rates as the Federal Reserve's rates increased, in order to prevent substantial depreciation of the peso.

Mexico's population in 2014 was 123,799,215 and growth has been constant at 1.2% in recent years (2008–14). The country has a Gini index of 48.8. Although this is lower than the average Gini for the Latin American economies, it is still alarming and indicates the polarisation between rich and poor in Mexico. Unemployment, however, is the lowest in the region, running at less than 5% for several years. Notwithstanding this, the country has so far failed to reach its target unemployment rate of 3.5%, most recently attained in 2008. While unemployment rates are very low in Mexico, there is a high rate of casual labour, as well as widespread unease owing to low wages. In periods when economic growth may be steadily increasing, this is not matched by improvements in equality and wealth. Significantly, the economy has not been able to absorb the growing workforce, driven by more women working outside the home and shifts in the country's demographic.

While the Social Progress Index (SPI) shows significant improvement, moving from 49.7 in 2012 to 66.9 in 2014, Mexico still faces

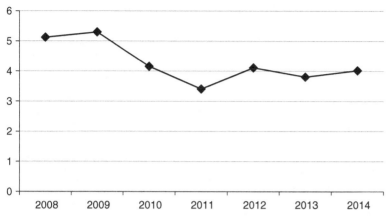

Figure 6.4 Inflation in Mexico (consumer prices, % annual).
Source: World Bank. (2015). World Development Indicators. Data Bank. Retrieved from: http://databank.worldbank.org/data/reports.aspx?source=world-development-indicators.

challenges in the form of law enforcement, criminal justice and corruption, captured in the Rule of Law Index of 0.45 in 2014 and 0.47 in 2015. The country's main macroeconomic, social and institutional indicators are shown in Table 6.1.

Trade

Mexico's economy is driven by international trade, as the country has taken advantage of its strategic position in the American continent. When imports and exports are aggregated, the proportion of trade as a percentage of Mexico's GDP is significant, reaching 65% in 2014 (see Figure 6.5).

Mexico's main exports are vehicle-related products, with a 23.79% share in the country's total exports value, followed by machinery (15.46%), mineral fuels, oils and other distillation products (5.98%) (see Table 6.2). Leading exporting companies include Tubos de Acero de Mexico (casing, tubing, pipes, iron and steel), Manufacturas Lee de Mexico (clothing and accessories), Autotek Mexico (vehicles and automotive parts) and Sitwell SA (chairs and seating).[5] The most significant import categories include electronic equipment, machinery and vehicles, which represent about half of the value of all Mexican imports (see Table 6.3).

[5] ZEPOL, Global Trade Intelligence. *Country Profile: Mexico*. Consulted 14 September 2015.

Table 6.1 *Macroeconomic indicators, Mexico 2014*

GDP	US$1.294 trillion
GDP growth (annual)	2.23%
GDP per capita	US$10,325.65
Inflation (consumer prices, annual)	4.02%
Population	125.385.833
Unemployment (% of total labour force, modelled ILO estimate, 2013)	4.9%
Gini (World Bank Estimate, 2013)	48.07
Social Progress Index	66.9
Rule of Law Index (2015)	0.47
Doing Business (2016)	38

Source: The World Justice Project. (2014), *Rule of Law Index 2014: Mexico*. Retrieved from: http://worldjusticeproject.org/sites/default/files/files/wjp_rule_of_law_index_2014_report.pdf; World Bank. (2015). World Development Indicators. Data Bank. Retrieved from: http://databank.worldbank.org/data/reports.aspx?source=world-development-indicators; Social Progress Imperative. (2015). *Social Progress Index 2015*. Retrieved: http://13i8vn49fibl3go3i12f59gh.wpengine.netdna-cdn.com/wp-content/uploads/2016/05/2015-SOCIAL-PROGRESS-INDEX_FINAL.pdf; The World Justice Project. (2015). *WJP Rule of Law*; United Nations Development Program. (2014). *Human Development Index*. Retrieved from: http://hdr.undp.org/en/content/human-development-index-hdi; World Bank (2014). Doing Business 2015: Going beyond efficiency: Comparing business regulations for domestic firms in 189 economies: a World Bank Group flagship report. Washington: World Bank Publications. Retrieved from: www.doingbusiness.org/~/media/GIAWB/Doing%20Business/Documents/Annual-Reports/English/DB15-Chapters/DB15-Report-Overview.pdf.

The United States is Mexico's largest trading partner, mainly because of its geographical proximity and the North American Free Trade Agreement (NAFTA) between Mexico, the United States and Canada. In fact, the United States and Canada are Mexico's top export partners, taking more than 80% of the value of exports (see Table 6.4), while the United States and China, Mexico's top import partners, account for two-thirds of the import value (see Table 6.5). According to the Organisation of American States, besides NAFTA, Mexico is engaged in ten FTAs with forty-five countries and thirty-nine commercial agreements, nine of which have limited scope and the rest reciprocal promotion and protection for investments (see Table 6.6). Such trade agreements have been fundamental in gaining the country

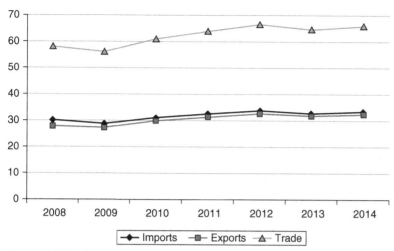

Figure 6.5 Trade as % Mexico's GDP.
Source: World Bank. (2015). World Development Indicators. Data Bank. Retrieved from: http://databank.worldbank.org/data/databases.aspx.

Table 6.2 *Product exports share (%) in Mexico, 2015*

Product exported	Product exports share (%)
Vehicles other than railway and tramway	23.73
Electrical, electronic equipment	21.33
Machinery, nuclear reactors, boilers, etc.	15.46
Mineral fuels, oils, distillation products, etc.	5.98
Optical, photographic, technical, medical and similar apparatus	3.68

Source: ITC. (2015). Trade statistics for international business development. Retrieved from: www.trademap.org/Product_SelProductCountry.aspx.

preferential rates in the import of goods. Mexico is also a member of the World Trade Organisation (WTO), which has eliminated most export limitations and substantially reduced export taxes and direct export subsidies. Mexico's main FTAs and commercial partnerships, with dates they entered into force, are summarised in Table 6.6.[6]

[6] SICE: Foreign Trade Information System. (2015). Information on Mexico. *Trade Agreements in force*. Organisation of American States. Retrieved from: www.sice.oas.org/ctyindex/MEX/MEXAgreements_e.asp.

Table 6.3 *Product imports share (%) in Mexico, 2015*

Product imported	Product imports share (%)
Electrical, electronic equipment	21.61
Machinery, nuclear reactors, boilers, etc.	17.12
Vehicles other than railway and tramway.	9.42
Mineral fuels, oils, distillation products, etc.	6.69
Plastics and plastic articles	5.64

Source: ITC. (2015). Trade statistics for international business development. Retrieved from: www.trademap.org/Product_SelProductCountry.aspx.

Table 6.4 *Mexico's top five export partners (2014)*

Partner	Partner share (%)
United States	80.3
Canada	2.68
China	1.5
Spain	1.5
Brazil	1.19

Source: World Integrated Trade Solutions. (2015). Retrieved from: http://wits.worldbank.org.

Table 6.5 *Mexico's top five import partners (2014)*

Partner	Partner share (%)
United States	48.97
China	16.56
Japan	4.39
South Korea	3.44
Germany	3.44

Source: World Integrated Trade Solutions. (2015). Retrieved from: http://wits.worldbank.org.

It is important to note that Mexico's balance of trade has maintained a deficit since 2003, as shown in Figure 6.6. The only exception was 2012, when there was a surplus. Since 2009, the deficit has been decreasing, from US$4.93 million in 2008 to US$2.57

Table 6.6 *Mexico's trade agreements*

Free trade agreements	Year entered into force
NAFTA	1994
Colombia	1994
European Union	2000
Chile)	1999
Israel	2001
European Free Trade Association (EFTA)	2001
Uruguay	2004
Japan	2005
Bolivia	2010
Peru	2012
Central America (Costa Rica, El Salvador, Guatemala, Honduras, Nicaragua)	2011
Pacific Alliance	2015
Panama	2015
Framework agreements	**Year entered into force**
MERCOSUR	2006
Preferential trade agreements	**Year entered into force**
Panama	1986
Ecuador	1993
Paraguay	1994
Brazil	2003
MERCOSUR (auto sector agreement)	2002
Argentina	2007

Source: Authors' elaboration with data from the Organisation of American States' Foreign trade Information Systems (SICE). SICE: Foreign Trade Information System. (2015). Information on Mexico. *Trade Agreements in force.* Organisation of American States. Retrieved from: www.sice.oas.org/ctyindex/MEX/MEXAgreements_e.asp.

million in 2014. Mexico's balance of trade in 2014 was negative with the European Union, China and India and positive with the United States. In terms of its neighbouring countries, the balance of trade is positive with Guatemala, Honduras, El Salvador and Nicaragua and negative with Panama and Costa Rica. Mexico trades with diverse partners, including India, China, Europe and its

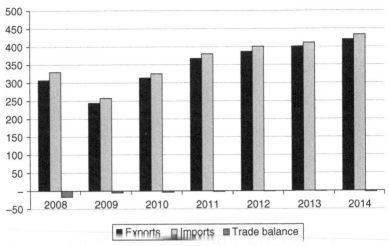

Figure 6.6 Mexico's trade balance, 2008–14 (US$ million).
Source: World Bank. (2015). World Development Indicators. Data Bank. Retrieved from:
http://databank.worldbank.org/data/reports.aspx?source=world-development-indicators.

Central American neighbours; however, the United States is its most
significant commercial partner, with a positive balance of trade for
2015.[7]

Mexico has a number of export incentivising programmes in place
that become particularly important during periods when the country's growth stalls. Legislation supports the *maquiladoras*, manufacturing operations where materials and equipment are imported duty
free and processed for export. This makes Mexico extremely attractive as an outsourcing destination for manufacturing goods. Mexico
City is the locus of most economic activity, while the country's six
northern border states are home to most of the manufacturing sector,
particularly the *maquiladoras*. The government has also implemented
sector promotion programmes (PROSEC), which allow preferential
duty rates for goods used by Mexican producers in the manufacturing process.

Since NAFTA came into force, Mexico has become a global leader in
manufacturing and a preferred destination for investors. Nonetheless,
economic growth continues to disappoint and there is no appreciable

---

[7] Trade Map. Trade statistics for international business development. Retrieved
from the URL: www.trademap.org/Bilateral_TS.aspx.

rise in living standards. The root cause of the situation is a deep-seated productivity gap that stems from the two-speed nature of the economy.[8] On the one hand, globally competitive multinational corporations and cutting-edge manufacturing facilities have led to rapid growth; on the other hand, a broad spectrum of Mexican companies is still moving in the opposite direction, plagued by slow growth and reduced productivity. More than thirty years of market-promoting measures have not translated into the anticipated spectacular growth and Mexico is facing an impending need to transform its traditional low-productivity sectors.

A clear example is the auto parts industry, which is largely responsible for Mexico's economic growth. Approximately 80% of auto parts enterprises have fewer than ten employees and are dedicated to supplying assembled parts to one of the country's seven global auto manufacturers. However, these small factories enjoy only 10% of the productivity rate of the larger manufacturers. Another obstacle to growth is the tax system, which provides exemptions to small businesses, indirectly encouraging them to remain small, informal and unproductive. Mexico's rather inflexible labour laws also discourage full-time hiring and encourage casual labour.[9]

Foreign direct investment

Mexico has substantial FDI inflows and outflows, mainly because of the country's internationalisation policies. There are incentive programmes for trade-related activities, and innovation and technological development are promoted through fiscal measures, such as tax deductions and credit systems. Mexico's FDI inflows fell in 2013 and 2014, as shown in Figure 6.7. FDI inflows demonstrate the economic proximity of Mexico and the United States, which accounted for 59% of

[8] Bolio, E; Remes, J; Laipus, T; Maniyija, J; Ramírez, E. (2014, March). A tale of two Mexicos. Growth and prosperity in a two-speed economy, McKinsey Global Institute Report. Insights and Publications. Retrieved from: www .mckinsey.com/insights/americas/a_tale_of_two_mexicos.

[9] Bolio, E; Remes, J; Laipus, T; Maniyija, J; Ramírez, E. (2014, March). A tale of two Mexicos. Growth and prosperity in a two-speed economy, McKinsey Global Institute Report. Insights and Publications. Retrieved from: www .mckinsey.com/insights/americas/a_tale_of_two_mexicos.

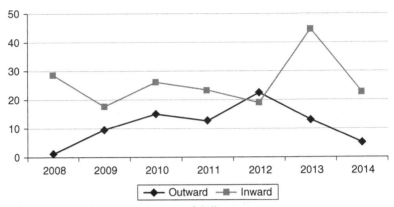

Figure 6.7 FDI flows in Mexico (US$ billion).
Source: Foreign Direct Investment flows and stock. (2015). UNCTAD STAT. Retrieved
from: http://unctadstat.unctad.org/wds/ReportFolders/reportFolders.aspx

the country's total FDI inflows in 2014. The EU occupies second place
(37%), while South American economies account for just 2%.

Mexican FDI outflows have been very variable. After a dramatic
increase from US$1.16 billion in 2008 to US$22.47 billion in 2012,
FDI outflows fell. In 2014, they amounted to US$5.2 billion, approxi-
mately 0.4% of the country's GDP.

The country's openness has helped position Mexico among the
world's top fifty places in which to do business, as well as making
it one of the most attractive foreign investment destinations worldwide. An additional attraction for companies willing to do business in
Mexico is ease of access to the world's largest economy. Investors are
also drawn to the country by its young and increasingly well-educated
population. More than 60% of Mexico's citizens are younger than
thirty-five years of age. As the country's industrial base has developed
important synergies, a significant surge in the automotive, aerospace
and electronics industries is expected.

Since 2013, the government has been developing a number of initiatives to stimulate FDI, including measures to streamline international
trade, tax concessions and investment in R&D. Specific policies include
the simplification of legislative requirements, less administrative bureaucracy, the elimination of licence requirements and reinforcement of intellectual property legislation. In Mexico, there are no significant restrictions
regarding the remittance of dividends or repatriation of capital.

Taxes

The main corporate taxes in Mexico are the federal corporate income tax, value added tax (VAT), tax on cash deposits, tax on real property and various social security contributions paid on behalf of employees. Some additional taxes are charged at the municipal level. The country offers double taxation relief for ordinary credit. There is tax pricing, thin capitalisation and controlled foreign company rules, as well as a tax integration regime. There is no capital gains tax or net wealth tax in Mexico, and payroll taxes are paid at state level.

Tax reforms in 2013 abolished some tax incentives, including the allowance of accelerated depreciation of fixed assets and land reductions for real estate developers. One of the main tax incentives is the *maquiladora* regime (IMMEX), designed to promote exports and encourage FDI. Under the *maquiladora* regime, duties, VAT and other tax exemptions are awarded, as well as income tax benefits.

Mexico has a solid tax treaty network with various countries worldwide. This is of utmost importance for investing in the country, as it provides relief from double taxation on all types of income, as well as protecting companies from discriminatory taxation.

Environmental taxes have become increasingly important in Mexico. In 2013, tax reforms introduced a novel tax on the import and sale of fossil fuels other than natural gas payable through carbon credits as defined and authorised by the Kyoto Protocol. A second environmental tax was applied to the sale of pesticides, with rates ranging between 6% and 9%, depending on the level of toxicity.[10]

Mexican multilatinas

Brazil and Mexico, the two largest economies in the region, also have the greatest number of multilatinas. Mexico's multilatinas come from diverse industrial sectors and have achieved notable expansion over a short length of time. Cemex's foreign acquisitions allowed it gradually

[10] Deloitte. (2014). Taxation and Investment in Mexico: Reach, Relevance and Reliability. Deloitte Touche Tohmatsu Limited. Retrieved from: www2.deloitte.com/content/dam/Deloitte/global/Documents/Tax/dttl-tax-mexicoguide-2014.pdf.

to start competing with the largest construction materials companies in the world, while América Móvil and Telmex developed in just a couple of years. The Alfa conglomerate has managed to establish societies and joint ventures with more than twenty companies in the United States, Japan, Europe and South Africa, while Grupo Bimbo has become a regional leader in the agro-industrial sector through numerous acquisitions. Here, the focus is on Cemex, América Móvil and Grupo Bimbo, the frontrunners of this phenomenon, to single out the factors that have contributed to the expansion of Mexican multilatinas.

Cemex

Cemex is a global construction materials company that offers high-quality products and reliable services to clients and communities in more than fifty countries around the world. The company also supplies cement, concrete and construction aggregates to more than 100 nations. Cemex has achieved international recognition as one of the world's largest cement producers and is a leader in the ready-mix concrete and aggregates sector, with close to 44,000 employees worldwide.[11]

The cement industry is highly capital-intensive, with significant economies of scale effects and high-cost distribution networks. As a result, there are high barriers to entry and exit and there are no close substitutes for cement or ready-mix concrete in the construction materials sector. This means that in most countries, the construction materials industry has an attractive oligopolistic structure with big global players such as Lafarge, Holcim, CRH, Cemex and HeidelbergCement enjoying strong market positions, pricing power and control, allowing also high levels of profitability of marginal local players. Under the leadership of Lorenzo Zambrano (1944–2014), Cemex initially had a double strategy. First, the conglomerate was dissolved and the diversified holdings divested in order to focus on cement, concrete and aggregates as the core businesses. Second, Cemex defended its domestic market position by focusing on acquisitions to secure market share, which is why Cementos Anahuac was acquired in 1987 and Cementos Tolteca in 1989.

---

[11] Cemex. *2014 Annual Report*. Available online in www.cemex.com/ InvestorCenter/Reports.aspx. Retrieved on 19 November 2015.

Cemex's acquisitions strategy focused on undervalued or underperforming assets that had the potential for better operational efficiency, targeting companies that were well-established players with high market share. Target companies had to be strong enough to incorporate the Cemex Way – standardised business processes, technology and organisational structure – although Cemex did not jettison the processes and practices of its new acquisitions. On the contrary, Cemex analysed their business model and organisational structure, adapting the strengths of the incoming companies to its own model.

América Móvil

América Móvil, a Mexican-based telecommunications company, is the leading wireless service provider in Latin America and the largest in the world in terms of equity subscribers. Although it was conceived as the mobile division of Mexico's privatised monopoly Telmex, controlled by Grupo Carso (of which Carlos Slim is the majority shareholder), it soon grew larger than its parent.[12]

While Telmex's opportunism was a major factor in the success of its internationalisation strategy, other factors also played a part in its rapid and successful expansion. The company is a classic example of an innovation-driven multilatina. Early in its expansion efforts, América Móvil recognised a distinctive characteristic in the Latin American mobile market: people were reluctant to engage in the lock-in contracts and post-paid services that were habitually offered by other telecom providers. América Móvil adopted the pre-paid model, which worked for low-income consumers who were not offered or couldn't afford the post-paid service. América Móvil also took advantage of the soaring popularity of GSM technology, using the same technological platform to expand across the region with its newly purchased assets. This proved to be a winning formula for the company to grow its subscribers and became one of the main competitive advantages that kept it ahead of the market. Realising that offering pre-paid services meant profits were driven by volume, América Móvil used aggressive sales tactics to maintain an otherwise churning customer base. Not only did it invest heavily in customer service and marketing, it also explored

---

[12] América Móvil. Annual Report 2014. Available online at www
.americamovil.com/amx/en/cm/investor/repY.html?p=29&s=41.

novel ways to increase its subscription base, mainly by subsidising the up-front costs of handsets.

As well as the infrastructure it shared with Telmex, América Móvil was able to achieve spectacular expansion, while maintaining a stable capital structure, by enlarging its asset portfolio through cheap purchases from distressed telecommunications companies. Outside Mexico, its growth was driven mainly through these acquisitions; while it was willing to expand through the creation of joint ventures (such as Telecom Américas), América Móvil ultimately sought control. Greenfield investments were made to reach the markets of Nicaragua, Uruguay and Brazil. Once América Móvil had consolidated its position in the South American market, it expanded towards Central America. Between 2003 and 2007, the company made acquisitions in Nicaragua, Honduras, Paraguay, the Dominican Republic, Puerto Rico and Jamaica. América Móvil's internationalisation process focused on market-seeking strategies, especially in geographically proximate countries whose shared language, cultural and institutional ties made marketing efforts less costly.[13]

Grupo Bimbo

Grupo Bimbo is a Mexican holding dedicated to the production, distribution and sales of bread, biscuits, confectionery, chocolates, snacks, tortillas and other processed foods. On the basis of brand positioning, production volume and sales, it is the largest baking company in the world and a market leader in Mexico, Latin America and the United States. Bimbo boasts a product portfolio of approximately 10,000 products under 100 brands. It operates 76 plants, 3 marketing companies, 980 distribution centres and nearly 34,600 delivery routes to service almost a million points of sale in more than 20 countries.[14]

Largely dependent on its own domestic market, and active in a sector characterised by low margins, Bimbo, like other Latin American multinationals, realised it needed to expand internationally, starting with neighbouring Latin American markets, with which it shared language

---

[13] Sharma, R. 2012. *Breakout nations: In pursuit of the next economic miracles.* Chapter 5: Mexico's Tycoon Economy. W. Norton & Co.

[14] Grupo Bimbo: Informe Anual Integrado 2014. Available online at www .grupobimbo.com/informe/Bimbo-Informe-Anual-2013/.

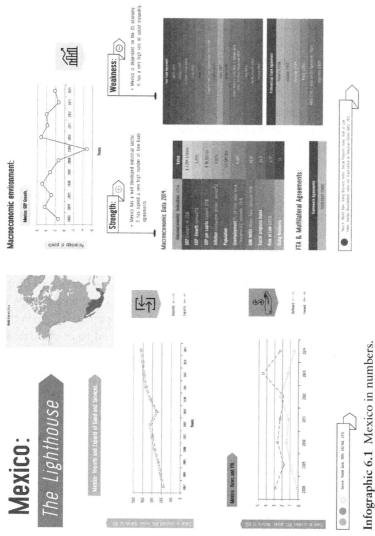

Infographic 6.1 Mexico in numbers.

and cultural ties. Bimbo sought to replicate its success in Mexico while deriving strength from the vertical integration of the production and distribution of baked products.[15] Its strategy was to target the largest players in each market and enter either through joint venture (with Noel in Colombia and Alicorp in Peru) or acquisition. Bimbo has also built greenfield facilities, for example, a plant in Argentina and a distribution centre in Honduras.

Bimbo's internationalisation strategy has mainly relied heavily on acquisition, in contrast to its growth in Mexico, which was much more organic. Traditionally, it has been financed by low levels of debt and high levels of reinvestment in its own operations. The company has also established a competitive advantage in its operations; it has pioneered packaging and just-in-time delivery to distribute to the markets in which it operates. In 2017, Bimbo is largely absent from Europe, only present in Park Lane Candy Distribution in the Czech Republic, but has begun to expand into the Asian market.

Bimbo's move into China signalled the company's attempt to become the first major Latin American firm in the Chinese market. In 2006, Bimbo bought Beijing Panrico Food Processing Centre, which, while a modest acquisition, was a major step towards the company's ambitions. Bimbo studied the Chinese market carefully before entry, hiring experts and using Chinese immigrants in Mexico as focus groups to adapt products to cater for local tastes. It also stepped up its marketing efforts. In the future Bimbo is likely to face the need to re-evaluate its market portfolio for non-Hispanic markets. Although seizing growth opportunities is part of Bimbo's internationalisation strategy, it has been very conservative about taking on debt.

---

[15] Casanova, L., Golstein, A., Almeida, A. et al. (2009). *From multilatinas to global latinas: The new Latin American multinationals.* IDB Vice Presidency For Sectors and Knowledge Integration and Trade Sector.

7 | Brazil – the heavyweight

JUANA GARCÍA AND VENETA ANDONOVA

From 2000 to 2010, when it became known as one of the BRIC countries, Brazil was one of the fastest-growing economies in both Latin America and the world but the country's boom seemed to slow down at the end of that period. Brazil's economic rise took place under the mandate of President Luiz Inácio Lula da Silva, referred to simply as 'Lula' (2003–11). After impressive growth of 7.5% in 2010, Brazil's GDP growth fell below 2% in subsequent years, and 2015 ended with the country in recession.

Demonstrations against the Brazilian government's economic policies and corruption scandals began to spread around the country in 2013. Despite facing fierce criticism for her economic policies, President Dilma Rousseff was narrowly re-elected for a second term in office on 26 October 2014. However, her popularity continued to decline, and in April 2016 the Brazilian parliament voted to impeach her on charges of manipulating government accounts to help ensure her 2014 re-election. The political crisis and the economic misfortunes of Brazil appear to be more intertwined than ever.

The largest country in Latin America, Brazil funnels approximately 40% of the FDI that reaches the region.[1] Brazil's territory is almost half the area of South America and the country is the seventh-largest economy in the world, in terms of GDP, and has the fifth-largest population. Notwithstanding these variables, in 2014 the country's per capita GDP placed it third among the six countries studied in this book, after Chile and Argentina.

The macroeconomic environment

Brazil has a favourable rate of unemployment (5.9% in 2013), which goes hand-in-hand with a high Human Development Index of 0.74

---

[1] CEPAL. (2015). La Inversión Extranjera Directa en América Latina y el Caribe 2015. Recuperado el 2015, de Cepal.org: www.cepal.org/sites/default/files/presentation/files/150526_lie_2015_ppt_esp_v4.pdf.

and a Social Progress Index of 70.89. However, the country still faces
critical challenges of inequality and corruption. With a Gini index
of 52.9, Brazil has failed significantly to improve income inequality
among its population of more than 202 million, a situation that is
aggravated by poor institutional quality reflected in a meagre Rule of
Law index of 0.54. Key macroeconomic, social and institutional indicators for Brazil are given in Table 7.1.

The problems ignited by the institutional weaknesses in Brazil
have fuelled a particularly acute political crisis in the country and the
approval rate of President Dilma Rousseff reached a historical low of
7.7% in 2015, partly because of corruption allegations.[2] The political
crisis coincided with a period of economic downturn in the country.
Its low rate of GDP growth (0.1% in 2014; see Figure 7.1) was a consequence of the economic slowdown of China, its top trade partner.
According to the IMF's World Economic Outlook update of July 2015,
Brazil's expected growth rate for that year was revised downwards to
−1.5%[3] but eventually it slipped into a recession.

GDP growth in Brazil slowed from an average of 4.5% in 2006–10
to 2.1% over the period 2011–14, reaching 0.1% in 2014. At the same
time, inflation began to climb, ending at 6.4% in 2014 (Figure 7.2).[4]
Brazil's medium-term outlook depends on the success of the adjustments announced by the government and the adoption of growth-
stimulating reforms, raising productivity and competitiveness. Despite
the economic slowdown and the challenges ahead, the country remains
among the ten largest economies in the world. GDP per capita is lower
(Figure 7.3), but Brazil continues to rank third among the six countries
studied in this book (Figure 7.4).

In 2014 Latin American countries had much lower than the median
income per capita for OECD members (about US$38.914). Moreover,
Argentina, Chile and Brazil showed a fall in the level of per capita
income as a result of the global economic crisis in 2008–09, while
Mexico, Colombia and Peru exhibited slow but persistent growth.

---

[2] Reuters, Brazil leader's popularity sinks in political crisis – poll. (2015, August
6). Retrieved 15 August 2015. http://uk.reuters.com/article/2015/08/06/
uk-brazil-rousseff-poll-idUKKCN0QB12K20150806.

[3] IMF. (2015, 9 July). World Economic Outlook Update. July 2015. Washington,
DC, USA.

[4] World Bank – Brazil Overview, 2015. Retrieved from www.worldbank
.org/en/country/brazil/overview.

Table 7.1 *Macroeconomic indicators, Brazil (2014)*

GDP	US$2,346,076,315,118.55
GDP % growth (2012, 2013, 2014)	1,76%, 2,74%, 0,14%
GDP per capita	US$11,384.42
Population	206,077,898
Gini (2013)	52.87
Unemployment	6.80%
Inflation	6.33%
Social Progress Index[a]	71
Rule of Law (2015)[b]	0.54
Human Development Index[c]	0.68
Doing Business (2016)[d]	116

[a] Social Progress Imperative. (2015). *Social Progress Index 2015*. Retrieved from: http://13i8vn49fibl3go3i12f59gh.wpengine.netdna-cdn.com/wp-content/uploads/2016/05/2015-SOCIAL-PROGRESS-INDEX_FINAL.pdf.

[b] The World Justice Project. (2015). *WJP Rule of Law Index 2015*. Retrieved from: http://data.worldjusticeproject.org.

[c] United Nations Development Program. (2014). *Human Development Index*. Retrieved from: http://hdr.undp.org/en/content/human-development-index-hdi.

[d] World Bank (2014). Doing Business 2015: Going beyond efficiency: Comparing business regulations for domestic firms in 189 economies: a World Bank Group flagship report. Washington: World Bank Publications. Retrieved from: www.doingbusiness.org/~/media/GIAWB/Doing%20Business/Documents/Annual-Reports/English/DB15-Chapters/DB15-Report-Overview.pdf.

Source: World Bank. (2015). World Development Indicators. Data Bank. Retrieved from: http://databank.worldbank.org/data/reports.aspx?source=world-development-indicators; Social Progress Imperative. (2015). *Social Progress Index 2015*. Retrieved from the URL: http://13i8vn49fibl3go3i12f59gh.wpengine.netdna-cdn.com/wp-content/uploads/2016/05/2015-SOCIAL-PROGRESS-INDEX_FINAL.pdf; The World Justice Project. (2015). *WJP Rule of Law*; United Nations Development Program. (2014). *Human Development Index*. Retrieved from the URL: http://hdr.undp.org/en/content/human-development-index-hdi; World Bank (2014). Doing Business 2015: Going beyond efficiency: Comparing business regulations for domestic firms in 189 economies: a World Bank Group flagship report. Washington: World Bank Publications. Retrieved from: www.doingbusiness.org/~/media/GIAWB/Doing%20Business/Documents/Annual-Reports/English/DB15-Chapters/DB15-Report-Overview.pdf.

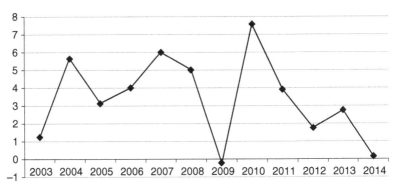

Figure 7.1 Rate of growth of GDP in Brazil, 2003–14 (%).
Source: World Bank. (2015). World Development Indicators. Data Bank. Retrieved
from: http://databank.worldbank.org/data/databases.aspx.

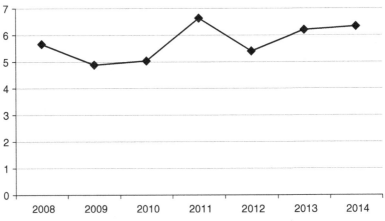

Figure 7.2 Inflation in Brazil (consumer prices, % annual).
Source: World Bank. (2015). World Development Indicators. Data Bank. Retrieved from:
http://databank.worldbank.org/data/reports.aspx?source=world-development-indicators.

Trade

Brazil's trade represented 25.8% of its GDP in 2014, as shown in
Figure 7.5, when imports exceeded exports by around US$66 billion,
resulting in a trade deficit (Figure 7.6). Traditionally, commodities have
been Brazil's main exports, representing about half of the total value
of trade (Table 7.2). Exports include ores, soybeans, petroleum, sugar
cane and meat. However, business services are becoming increasingly

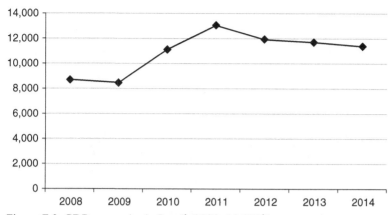

Figure 7.3 GDP per capita in Brazil, 2008–14 (US$).
Source: World Bank. (2015). World Development Indicators. Data Bank. Retrieved from: http://databank.worldbank.org/data/databases.aspx.

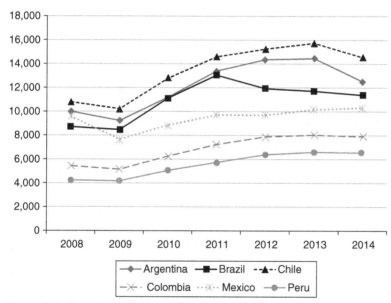

Figure 7.4 Growth of GDP per capita in Latin America by country, 2008–14.
Source: World Bank. (2015). World Development Indicators. Data Bank. Retrieved from: http://databank.worldbank.org/data/databases.aspx.

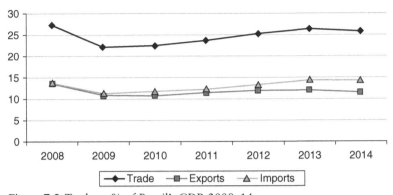

Figure 7.5 Trade as % of Brazil's GDP, 2008–14.
Source: World Bank. (2015). World Development Indicators. Data Bank. Retrieved
from: http://databank.worldbank.org/data/databases.aspx.

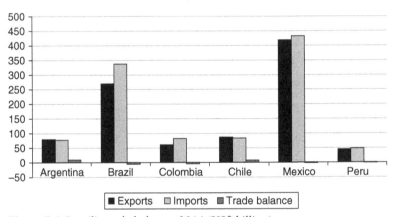

Figure 7.6 Brazil's trade balance, 2014 (US$ billion).
Source: World Bank. (2015). World Development Indicators. Data Bank. Retrieved
from: http://databank.worldbank.org/data/databases.aspx.

relevant, making 8% of total exports in 2014 (Table 7.3). Mineral
fuels, machinery, electronic components and vehicles make up the largest share of Brazil's imports. China stands out as the market for 18%
of Brazil's exports and is the source of 16% of the country's imports;
the United States is a close second, accounting for 12% of exports and
15% of imports and third is neighbouring Argentina, which accounts
for 6% of both exports and imports (Table 7.4).

Brazil, alongside Mexico, exhibits the highest trade volumes among
the countries in the region. Mexico's economy is more dependent on

Table 7.2 *Main product/services exports and imports share (%) in Brazil, 2014–15*

Product category	Product exports share (%) 2015
Oil seed, oleagic fruits, grain, seed, fruit, etc.	11.19
Ores, slag and ash	8.73
Mineral fuels, oils, distillation products, etc.	7.19
Meat and edible meat offal	6.84
Machinery, nuclear reactors, boilers	5.94

Product category	Product imports share (%) 2015
Mineral fuels, oils, distillation products, etc.	14.53
Machinery, nuclear reactors, boilers	14.47
Electrical, electronic equipment	11.88
Vehicles other than railway and tramway	7.91
Organic chemicals	5.41

Service category	Product exports share (%) 2014
Other business services	53.56
Travel	17.03
Transport	14.54
Telecommunications, computer and information services	3.60
Financial	2.92

Service category	Product imports share (%) 2014
Other business services	35.48
Travel	28.90
Transport	16.84
Charges for the use of intellectual property	6.69
Telecommunications, computer and information services	4.14

Source: International Trade Centre. (2015). Trade Map. Retrieved from: www.trademap.org/Service_SelCountry_TS.aspx?nvpm=1%7C076%7C%7C%7C%7C%7C%7CS00%7C1%7C3%7C1%7C2%7C2%7C1%7C%7C1%7C1.

Table 7.3 *Brazil's top five export partners (2014)*

Partner	Partner exports share (%)
China	18.04
United States	12.05
Argentina	6.34
Netherlands	5.79
Japan	2.98

Source: World Integrated Trade Solutions. (2015). Retrieved from: http://wits.worldbank.org.

Table 7.4 *Brazil's top five import partners (2014)*

Partner	Partner imports share (%)
China	16.30
USA	15.41
Argentina	6.17
Germany	6.04
Nigeria	4.15

Source: World Integrated Trade Solutions. (2015). Retrieved from: http://wits.worldbank.org.

trade: its trade history and links with the U.S. economy explain the importance of this sector. Notably, Brazil had the highest trade imbalance among our six countries in 2014, as shown in Figure 6.6. This was attributed to a bad economic context over several consecutive years and the cooling down of Chinese economic growth, as well as a sharp decline in commodity prices. Regional economic difficulties play a secondary role in this, as Brazil relies less on regional trade than most other Latin American economies.

Brazil has shown a particular reluctance to sign bilateral free trade agreements (FTAs) and presently has such agreements with only four partners: Chile, Bolivia, Peru and Israel.[5] Brazil is also part of MERCOSUR, the sub-regional trade bloc that includes Argentina,

[5] OAS. (2015). Information on Brazil – Trade Agreements. Recuperado el 10 de September de 2015, de Foreign Trade Information System: www.sice.oas .org/ctyindex/BRZ/BRZAgreements_e.asp.

Brazil, Paraguay, Uruguay and Venezuela (members in 2015). MERCOSUR forms a free trade area, and members not only harmonise their external tariffs, they also integrate into a political structure for cooperation between member and associated states. Brazil does not have any trade agreements with its two main trade partners, China and the United States. In fact, the country has maintained a comparatively protectionist tradition in its trade policy, safeguarding its top industries at the cost of freer trade flows. In the same vein, Brazil has shown a preference for manoeuvrability in trade conditions, apparent in several partial trade agreements, which may favour local businesses. Some of these agreements even overlap, for example, two preferential trade agreements and a framework agreement with Mexico and preferential trade agreements with Venezuela, Uruguay and Argentina, already members of MERCOSUR (Table 7.5). According to the WEF's *Global Competitiveness Report*, in 2014 Brazil had the sixth-biggest domestic market in the world, ranked at 5.7 out of 7, just behind these of the United States, China, India, Japan and Germany.[6]

Foreign direct investment

As the sixth-biggest recipient of FDI in the world, Brazil received US$62 billion in 2014, down by 2.3% compared to 2013, as shown in Figure 7.7. As the total FDI flows fell globally from US$1.47 trillion to US$1.23 trillion, Brazil moved up one place in the ranking in UNCTAD's *World Investment Report*. The decrease mostly affected the extractive industries, which received 58% less investment. On the other hand, secondary (manufacturing) and tertiary (services) sectors experienced an increase of 5% and 18%, respectively.[7] This reflected a trend towards more value-added activities that would attract more investor interest than extractive industries. The most attractive sectors for FDI industries in 2014 were commerce, telecommunications, oil and gas extraction and motor vehicle production. The biggest investors in Brazil in terms of FDI stock in 2015 were the United States, Luxembourg and the Netherlands, as shown in Figure 7.8.

[6] World Economic Forum. (2015). Competitiveness Rankings. World Economic Forum. Retrieved from: http://reports.weforum.org/global-competitiveness-report-2014-2015/rankings/#indicatorId=DOMMKTIDX.

[7] UNCTAD. (2015). World Investment Report 2015. Geneva, Switzerland: United Nations Publication.

Table 7.5 *Brazil's trade agreements*

Multilateral agreements World Trade Organisation	
Customs unions MERCOSUR	
Free trade agreements	**Year entered into force**
MERCOSUR – Israel	2011
MERCOSUR – Peru	2006
MERCOSUR – Bolivia	1997
MERCOSUR – Chile	1996
Framework agreements	**Year entered into force**
MERCOSUR – Morocco	2010
MERCOSUR – Mexico	2006
Preferential trade agreements	
Suriname	2006
MERCOSUR (Colombia, Ecuador, Venezuela)	2005
MERCOSUR – India	2009
MERCOSUR – Mexico	2003
MERCOSUR (Colombia, Ecuador, Venezuela)	2005
MERCOSUR – India	2009
MERCOSUR – Mexico	2003
Guyana	2004
Mexico	2003
Argentina	1990
Uruguay	1986
Trade agreements (signed and pending) Free trade agreements	
MERCOSUR – Egypt MERCOSUR – Southern African Customs Union	

Source: OAS. (2015). Information on Brazil – Trade Agreements. Recuperado el 10 de September de 2015, de Foreign Trade Information System: www .sice.oas.org/ctyindex/BRZ/BRZAgreements_e.asp.

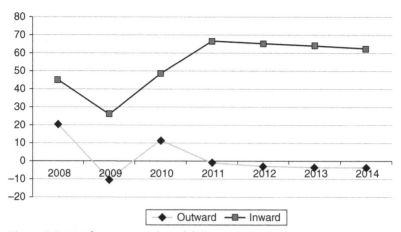

Figure 7.7 FDI flows in Brazil (US$ billion).
Source: Foreign Direct Investment flows and stock. (2015). UNCTAD STAT. Retrieved from: http://unctadstat.unctad.org/wds/ReportFolders/reportFolders.aspx.

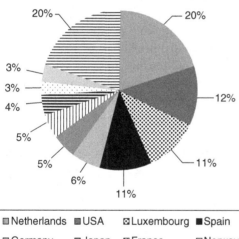

Figure 7.8 FDI in Brazil (by country of origin), 2015 (%).
Source: Deloitte, Doing Business. (2015). Retrieved from: www.deloitte.dbbrazil
.com.br/show.aspx?idCanal=Tap1ogfxsUipt3uYP2l7JA==.

Due to intra-company loans, Brazil is at the bottom of the region in terms of FDI outflow. Local companies in Brazil receive a significant number of loans from their foreign subsidiaries, resulting in negative net flows. The activities of the biggest multinational companies support this trend, as demonstrated by Petrobras's divestment of its Peruvian operations.

Taxes

Brazil has one of the most cumbersome tax regimes of the world,[8] mainly because of its high complexity, high variability and intense reporting. Various levels of government are authorised to impose taxes, which means that taxpayers are obliged to deal simultaneously with the requirements of the federal, state and municipal governments. The various levels of these taxes, the differences between geographical regions and the special cases associated with each of them make coping with tax obligations increasingly complex. Complexity is also added by constant changes in tax law, where amendments are adopted on almost a daily basis, making it difficult to keep up with the most recent regulation. Finally, Brazil has an aggressive tax collection policy, with authorities requesting constant reporting of accounting information, mainly through electronic means. However, the compliance process is also complicated, increasing the possibility of error, which in turn causes further questioning from the authorities.

Brazil also has the most time-consuming tax regime of the 189 economies studied by the World Bank,[9] requiring 2,600 hours to comply with all its rules. The total tax rate amounts to 68.9%, one of the highest in the world, which is divided into nine payments. This hinders Brazil's attractiveness for foreign capital, particularly from within the region. One particular example of the pressure this tax regime puts on manufacturers and importers is the 'tax substitution' procedure. Under this regime, all the taxes that are applied to a product throughout the different steps of a supply chain are paid in advance by the

---

[8] PwC & World Bank Group. (2015). Paying Taxes 2015. Retrieved from: www
.pwc.com/payingtaxes.
[9] PwC & World Bank Group. (2015). Paying Taxes 2015. Retrieved from: www
.pwc.com/payingtaxes.

first agent in the local market (manufacturer or importer). This model effectively concentrates tax collection, thus reducing evasion, but also puts enormous stress on the cash flow of the 'substitutes', and requires them to divert more resources to tax compliance.

Brazilian multilatinas

Brazil contributed 7 of the 12 Latin American companies in *Fortune* magazine's Global 500 ranking in 2015 and 46 of *AméricaEconomía*'s top 100 Latin American companies in 2014. Some of these companies were pioneers in the internationalisation process in the region, making their first FDI in the period between 1960 and 1980. Today, Brazilian companies stand out for the volume and range of their international investments, which are mainly concentrated in asset investments and mergers and acquisitions (M&As).

A special aspect of the biggest Brazilian companies featured in this chapter is that all of them are publicly traded in Brazil's securities exchange, BM&FBOVESPA. Although they differ in terms of their industry, age and ownership structure, these companies have all invested considerable resources to initiate and extend their internationalisation processes.

Petrobras

The largest company in Latin America, Petrobras is present in nineteen countries around the world, although its influence is greater in the vicinity of its headquarters; it is active in seven of the twelve countries of South America. Its operations stretch from the United States to Europe (two countries), Africa (four countries) and Asia (three countries). Petrobras focuses on the exploration, production and distribution of fossil fuels and lubricants and employs more than 80,000 workers. Founded in 1953, its internationalisation process started less than twenty years later when Petrobras began operating in Colombia, a neighbouring country with similar conditions for the fossil fuel market. Its two main strategies for extending its activities in foreign soil are greenfield investments and the acquisition of local operators' assets. Examples include the exploration and concession of oil fields, while buying out local companies' operations allows the company to expand throughout the supply chain.

The firm's strategic plan is based on the fundamental premise of a growth in oil production to 2020, aiming for an average of four million barrels per day. In order to fulfil this, Petrogras's international segment is expected to intensify its exploration and production operations in oil and natural gas in Latin America, Africa and the United States. Today, Petrobras has differentiated its operations and investments according to the geographic benefits of each location. Exploration and production activities are concentrated in the Americas and Africa where oil and gas deposits are most likely to be found. Labour costs and the regional and cultural proximity to Petrobras's headquarters in Brazil are also variables to be considered. Investment in fixed assets in these regions is intensive and the acquisition of local operations prevails.

Petrobras's activities in Asia and Europe concentrate on commercial objectives (reaching new clients and attracting foreign capital) and also host its R&D programmes. The UK and Japan are well-known education and innovation hubs and are natural sites for R&D facilities, which allow Petrobras to remain up to date in terms of efficiency and technological breakthroughs. Opening physical offices in global financial centres such as these also attracts foreign investors.

Itaú Unibanco

Resulting from the merger of two major Brazilian banks, Itaú and Unibanco, in 2008, Itaú Unibanco is one of the largest privately held banks in the southern hemisphere. With separate but similar stories, the original banks are examples of successful expansion by seizing acquisition opportunities in the local market, an ambition driven by the initiative of their controlling families. However, Itaú went beyond national boundaries and in 1979 simultaneously opened branches in Buenos Aires, New York and the Cayman Islands. Among these growth in Argentina was outstanding; in 1994, Itaú was granted permission to open thirty-two branches in the country and four years later its position was consolidated with the acquisition of Banco del Buen Ayre. In the first decade of the new century, the bank continued to expand through strategic investments and acquisitions in different financial subsectors. Itaú entered the European and Asian markets and strengthened its position in New York and South America, having bought BankBoston's operations in the subcontinent. In 2016, Itaú

Unibanco had around 96,000 employees and was present in twenty countries, generating revenues of BRL91.657 million.

Itaú Unibanco has international reach but aims for true global presence, seeking initially to consolidate as a regional order bank. This requires Itaú Unibanco to execute an aggressive but measured expansion strategy in the South American countries. Its main focus is retail banking, as it is already present in this segment in Argentina, Brazil, Chile, Paraguay and Uruguay. The next targets are Colombia, Mexico and Peru, where Itaú Unibanco has relatively small investments and is mostly limited to corporate and investment banking.

JBS

JBS Group is the world's leading meat-processing organisation, exporting animal protein to more than 150 countries. It was founded in 1953 as a beef-processing plant. The company expanded throughout the Brazilian market via greenfield investments and acquisitions until 2005, when it entered Argentina. JBS began its internationalisation process by acquiring the entire operation of Swift-Armour, the major beef-processing and beef-exporting company in Argentina. Subsequently, its growth strategy became more aggressive and ambitious. In 2007, JBS acquired Swift Company to enter the U.S. and Australian markets. Three years later it acquired the Belgian Toledo Group. With additional acquisitions within Brazil, it entered the pork, poultry and lamb markets. In 2016, JBS had 340 production units and more than 216,000 employees, direct investments in 24 countries on six continents, and revenues of US$47.468 million.

JBS Group comprises important brands such as Swift, Friboi, Maturatta, Cabaña Las Lilas, Pilgrim's, Gold Kist Farms, Pierce and 1855. With this diverse product portfolio, it serves more than 300,000 clients in more than 150 countries. Its internationalisation process has been driven by the search for new markets. Internationalisation has helped JBS increase its workforce by 30% and its daily production of chicken by 33% and pork by 30%.

JBS's internationalisation process is an example of an aggressive acquisition approach and has required considerable resources. Its first international investment move, in 2005, cost JBS approximately US$200 million. At that point the firm's revenues totalled about US$80 million. The company retained utilities and financed the project through loans. However, in May 2007 the company announced the acquisition of Swift Foods, the third-largest processor of beef and pork in the United States, for US$1.4 billion, a completely different scale of operation from its previous acquisition. Anticipating the size of the new project, JBS launched its IPO in March the same year and was able to raise approximately US$800 million, more than half the capital required. In order to complete the financing of the acquisition, the company relied once again on the capital markets and issued a total of US$600 million in corporate bonds.[10]

Banco do Brasil

In terms of assets, Banco do Brasil was the largest financial institution in Latin America in 2015. With almost complete coverage of Brazilian territory, Banco do Brasil is a financial conglomerate that acts as one of the principal agents for economic and social development in the country. As an organisation it seeks to reconcile return for its shareholders with the public interest. Founded in 1809 Banco do Brasil has been operating for more than two centuries and today it has a workforce of 111,000. State-related institutions hold 57.9% of the bank's shares, 29.3% represents the free float and 10.4% is held by the bank's employee retirement fund.

To remain as a benchmark for Brazilian companies with international operations, Banco do Brasil has extended its international reach with the intention of expanding the trade, investment and operations of Brazilian multinationals. Taking into account its public role, the bank executes sustainability activities throughout its different locations.

Banco do Brasil has forty-five proprietary units in twenty-four countries. It also extends its presence through alliances with other financial institutions, enabling the bank to offer services in 135 countries. Among its international activities, the most prominent are ownership of Banco Patagonia in Argentina, the operation of Banco do Brasil Americas in the United States, investments in Europe for the restructuring of platforms and the opening of a new branch in China.

Banco do Brasil is a commercial bank with consistent and growing revenues but as a state-owned company (the Brazilian government

---

[10] Rogerio Jelmayer, 2007, available at www.marketwatch.com/story/ brazils-jbs-buys-swift-foods-for-14-bln.

holds about 60% of its shares) and a public institution that issues currency, part of its initial internationalisation process was funded by public resources. As a result, despite being listed on BM&FBOVESPA, the resources channelled through the exchange have not been as significant as the bank's other sources of income. However, Banco do Brasil has been active in sustainability programmes sponsored by the Brazilian exchange, for example, as part of the Novo Mercado group of firms with the best corporate governance principles since 2006. Banco do Brasil is also listed in the Corporate Sustainability Index and Carbon Efficient Index.

Vale

Arising from an agreement between the governments of Brazil and the United States, Compañía Vale do Rio Doce was founded in 1942. One of the largest mining companies in the world, it is one of the main producers of iron ore and nickel. Vale underwent a privatisation process in 1997. Now diversified, Vale produces minerals and is also a logistics company. The firm has a workforce of 85,000 and generates gross revenue of US$26.047 billion.[11]

Since the 1950s, the company has used its positive cash flow to diversify its portfolio of investments. Vale bought companies in the natural resources sector and created joint ventures in its initial expansion process, while still a state-owned company. By the 1970s, Vale's operations included a robust distribution network (railways, ports and shipping lines), twelve subsidiaries and twelve joint ventures, the latter mainly used as way to explore the African continent. Because of adverse macroeconomic conditions, the expansion process halted between 1980 and 1997, when the privatisation process concluded and an internationalisation strategy was launched, increasing its range of products and geographical reach.

Vale is present in twenty-six countries on six continents, with a varying set of activities depending on the characteristics of each location, including mines, refineries, railways, hydroelectric plants and ports, reserves, R&D and teaching centres. Although Vale is listed on BM&FBOVESPA, NYSE, EURONEXT-NYSE-Paris and the Hong

---

[11] www.vale.com/EN/investors/information-market/Press-Releases/
ReleaseDocuments/vale_IFRs_USD_4t15i.pdf.

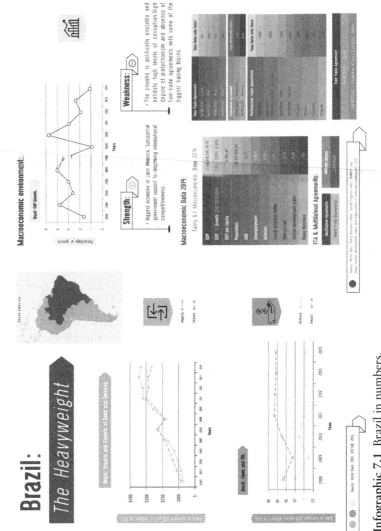

Infographic 7.1 Brazil in numbers.

Kong Stock Exchange, there is no clear evidence to link capital markets activity with the firm's internationalisation process. One of Vale's largest single investments was the acquisition of the Canadian company INCO; this purchase, which was made for US$17.4 billion in 2006, made Vale the largest producer of nickel in the world. The company regularly issues corporate bonds and makes acquisitions at a global level. In 2015 it had twelve corporate bond issuances worth more than US$14 billion, not surprising for a company that has made acquisitions worth more than US$9 billion in the past six years. Issuing debt is an alternative means to finance large acquisitions and investments, giving the issuer flexibility to define deadlines.

PART II

8 | Institutional uncertainty in Latin America

VENETA ANDONOVA AND
MAURICIO LOSADA-OTÁLORA

The role of market institutions is in part to reduce information and transaction costs and provide the predictability and certainty that market transactions require. Market imperfections are considered to be common in emerging economies[1] and therefore the institutional perspective is particularly useful for explaining firm behaviour in these contexts[2] in general and in the case of multilatinas in particular.

According to the economic historian and Nobel Prize winner Douglas North,[3] institutions are 'a set of rules, compliance procedures, and moral and ethical behavioural norms designed to constrain the behaviour of individuals in the interests of maximising the wealth or utility of principals'. Within the tradition of comparative institutional analysis, the 'depth',[4] permanence and durability of institutions are specifically emphasised.[5] This understanding of the aspects of institutions, however, stands in sharp contrast to the institutional measures used to perform much empirical analysis.

For example, variables listed in the International Country Risk Guide, such as law and order, bureaucratic quality, corruption, risk of expropriation by the government and risk of contract repudiation, appear to be highly volatile and lack the durability and permanence expected from institutional measures. Similarly, the World Bank index

---

[1] Khanna, Tarun & Palepu, Krishna. (28 April 2010). *Winning in emerging markets: A road map for strategy and execution.* Harvard Business Press. ISBN 978-1-4221-6695-6.

[2] Hoskisson, R., Eden, L., Lau, C. & Wright, M. 2000, Strategy in emerging economies. *Academy of Management Journal,* 43(3), 249–67.

[3] North, Douglass C. 1981. *Structure and change in economic history.* Norton & Co.

[4] Rodrik, D., Subramanian, A. & Trebbi, F. 2004. Institutions rule: The primacy of institutions over geography and integration in economic development. *Journal of Economic Growth,* 9(2), 131–65.

[5] Glaeser, E., Rafael La Porta, Florencio Lopez-de-Silanes & Andrei Shleifer. 2004. Do institutions cause growth? *Journal of Economic Growth,* 9(3), 271–303.

of government effectiveness[6] comprises subjective assessments of institutional quality and gives accounts of institutional outcomes instead of permanent rules, procedures and moral and ethical norms. This approach is also taken by the World Bank's Doing Business initiative[7] and by popular databases used by political scientists, Polity IV[8] and the POLCON index.[9] It seems that the variables that feature in these datasets can at best be interpreted as proxies for institutional outcomes, not institutions themselves. This important distinction, which is rarely taken into account, highlights the difficulty, if not the impossibility, of obtaining direct and faithful measurement of institutions.

Besides poor measurement, another major challenge to empirical institutional studies is endogeneity: most of the time it is hard to tell if institutions are the cause or the effect of some specific performance measure, such as GDP levels. While it is easy to recognise the positive correlation between favourable economic and institutional outcomes, demonstrating causality has proved difficult. A common strategy to tackle this problem is the use of instrumental variables, an applied statistics technique that is used to clarify the directionality of the relationship. The underlying question is usually whether better institutions, such as more predictable transaction rules, lead to higher levels of economic prosperity or whether rich countries with high GDP design better rules for market interaction. Unfortunately, it is not easy to find appropriate instrumental variables for institutions to prove the direction of causality. In the frequently cited work of Acemoglu, Johnson and Robinson,[10] for example, the authors explain

[6] Kaufmann, D., Kraay, D. & Mastruzzi, M. 2003. 'Governance matters III: Updated governance indicators for 1996-01', Working Paper Draft for comments. World Bank.

[7] www.doingbusiness.org.

[8] Jaggers, K. & Marshall, M. 2000. 'Polity IV project', *Center for International Development and Conflict Management*, University of Maryland.

[9] See, for example, Henisz, W. J. 2002. The institutional environment for infrastructure investment. *Industrial and Corporate Change*, 11(2), 355–89; and Henisz, Witold. 2005. POLCON 2005 release. www-management .wharton.upenn.edu/henisz/_vti_bin/shtml.dll/POLCON/ContactInfo.html.

[10] See, for example, Acemoglu, D., Jonson, S. & Robinson, J. 2001.The colonial origins of comparative development: An empirical investigation. *American Economic Review* 91(5), 1369–401; Acemoglu, D., Jonson, S. & Robinson, J. 2002. Reversal of fortune: Geography and development in the making of modern world income distribution. *Quarterly Journal of Economics*, 117(4), 1231–94; and Acemoglu, D. & Johnson, S. 2005. Unbundling institutions. *Journal of Political Economy*, 113(5), 949–95.

current economic development in terms of differences in institutions, taking as their instruments settler mortality in colonial times, indigenous population density and legal origin.[11] This empirical strategy does not guarantee success, however, because the instrumental variable can be weak, as has been argued about settlers' mortality.[12] Moreover, the interpretation of institutional outcomes as institutions is problematic. Thus, the methodological discussion in comparative institutional studies notes a need for better data and a clear distinction between institutions and institutional outcomes.[13] The approach taken in this book overcomes some of the shortcomings discussed here but is subject to others.

Self-reported perceptions of institutional outcomes are used to shed light on the largely under-studied internationalisation strategies of multilatinas. The specific internationalisation strategies of multilatinas are a result of both contextual and organisation-specific drivers. The self-reported perceptual data about the surrounding institutional context provide an opportunity to delve into strategists' minds and also raise the question of a possible self-report bias.[14] Managerial perceptions about the institutional context are treated here as antecedents of organisational strategic behaviour, an approach that resonates with research conducted within the field of strategic management.[15] Capturing some of the institutional drivers on multilatinas' internationalisation strategies is an ambitious endeavour. To simplify the task, a narrow focus was adopted and zoom in on the uncertainty that governments can bring to the business environment through two specific levers: price controls and the regime and enforcement of property rights.

---

[11] For a discussion about the role of legal origin, see Arruñada, B. & Andonova, V. 2005. 'Market institutions and judicial rulemaking'. In C. Menard & M. M. Shirley (eds). *Handbook of New Institutional Economics* (pp. 229–50). Springer.

[12] Murray. M. 2006. Avoiding invalid instruments and coping with weak instruments. *Journal of Economic Perspectives*, 20(4), 111–32.

[13] Rosenthal, H. & Voeten, E. 2007. Measuring legal systems. *Journal of Comparative Economics*, 35(4), 711–28.

[14] Donaldson, S. & Grant-Vallone, E. 2002. Understanding self-report bias in organisational behavior research. *Journal of Business and Psychology*, 17(2), Winter 2002.

[15] Özleblebici, Z. & Çetin, Ş. 2015. The role of managerial perception within strategic management: An exploratory overview of the literature. *Procedia – Social and Behavioral Sciences*, Volume 207, 20 October 2015, 296–305.

Why focus on institutional uncertainty? Comparative institutional studies generally support the view that there are no universally superior market-supporting institutions. For example, both common law countries, such as the UK, and civil law countries such as France support advanced market transactions and facilitate the creation of value in their economies and societies. Market-based societies can even be facilitated by state planning and intervention, as is the case in China. Because there are multiple institutional designs that lead to market-supporting economic and social configurations, we have to be cautious about making mechanical and simplistic institutional transplants. However, no matter what the specific institutional arrangement, frequent changes in the rules of the game – that is, institutional uncertainty – are disruptive and damaging for market-based transactions. For instance, when companies can foresee and estimate the cost of dealing with institutional voids they are able to tackle the problem with a varying degree of success by employing non-market resources such as exchange of favours or even bribes. When the institutional problem introduces uncertainty in the total cost of company operation, however, enterprises are unable to estimate the cost of operation in a given market. This process has been studied in the case of corruption in foreign markets,[16] where it has been found that the arbitrariness rather than pervasiveness of corruption imposes most cost on investors, implying that the uncertainty associated with the institutional context is more damaging to economic transactions than ineffective but stable institutional designs. Because of the damaging effect of uncertainty on business dealings, we focus on government price controls and deficiencies in property rights regime and enforcement, as these generate considerable levels of uncertainty in the business dealings of multilatinas.

As stated earlier, institutions are the formal and informal rules of the game for doing business inside the borders of a specific country.[17] Because the quality of national institutions affects the costs of

[16] Doh, J., Rodriguez, P., Uhlenbruck, K., Collins, C. & Eden, L. 2003. Coping with corruption in foreign markets. *Academy of Management Executive*, 17(3), 114–28.

[17] Chan, C., Isobe, T. & Makino, S. 2008. Which country matters? *Institutional Development and Foreign Affiliate Performance, Strategic Management Journal*, 29(11), 1179–205.

doing business, the relationship between institutions and emerging and developed country multinationals has been subjected to much attention.[18] When comparing emerging and developed contexts, both empirically and theoretically, authors have established that institutional characteristics such as political instability, corruption and arbitrary government interventions through taxation, pricing, exchange rates, production and ownership are much more prevalent governance characteristics in emerging markets.[19] Although most of these characteristics tend to be highly correlated, deficient property rights protection is probably the most basic and symptomatic of them all.[20] Well-defined property rights and their enforcement form the basis of all market transactions.

Unlike previous research that relies on secondary data to study the role of property rights and their protection by Latin American governments,[21] we rely on self-reported perceptions of institutional uncertainty related to both government price controls and property rights. For the purposes of our research we consider market-supporting institutions to be strong (i.e. predictable) if they provide appropriate conditions for doing business through the protection of property rights in general and the protection of intellectual property rights in particular (e.g. punishment of illegal imitation and non-infringement on intellectual property rights), as well as government abstention from using price controls. Weak market institutions are characterised by a high degree of uncertainty as they fail effectively to protect property rights

[18] See, for example, Witt, M. & Lewin, A. (2007). Outward foreign direct investment as escape response to home country institutional constraints. *Journal of International Business Studies*, 34, 579–94.

[19] See, for example, Demirbag, M., McGuinness, M. & Altay H. (2010). Perceptions of institutional environment and entry mode: FDI from an emerging country. *Management International Review*, 50, 207–40; and Rodriguez, P., Uhlenbruck, K. & Eden, L. (2005). Government corruption and the entry strategies of multinationals. *Academy of Management Review*, 30(2), 383–96.

[20] Haley, G. (2000). Intellectual property rights and foreign direct investment in emerging markets. *Marketing Intelligence & Planning*, 18(5), 273–80.

[21] See for example Cuervo-Cazurra, A. & Genc, M. (2011b). Obligating, pressuring, and supporting dimensions of the environment and the nonmarket advantages of developing country multinational companies. *Journal of Management Studies*, 48(2), 441–55 and their related work.

Table 8.1 *Managerial perceptions of key indicators of institutional uncertainty in home markets*

	Mean	Standard deviation
The government regulates the prices in your industry.	3.00	1.765
The risk of illegal imitation is high because of low protection of intellectual property rights.	2.45	1.522
The government enforces property rights in your industry.	2.50	1.098

against public and private infringement and introduce mechanisms for market interference through prices controls.[22]

Table 8.1 contains evidence of the perceptions of managers of sixty-two of the largest Latin-American multinationals about the degree of institutional uncertainty associated with price controls and property rights protection. Individual perceptions are measured with a Likert scale, in which 1 indicates the lowest and 7 the highest degree of institutional uncertainty associated with each statement. The descriptive analysis shows that on average there is no acute perceived institutional weakness associated with government enforcement of property rights and price controls in the Latin American countries. The mean values for each of the questions range between 2.45 and 3, pointing to a rather low degree of perceived institutional uncertainty. The standard deviation in the responses is high, indicating that the perceptions of the managers vary significantly, even though most of them do not report acute preoccupation with institutional uncertainty in any of the six countries in our study.

To grasp the degree of polarisation in the managers' perceptions, we perform cluster analysis and group the answers. We report the group average perception of the home country institutional uncertainty in Figure 8.1.

[22] Meyer, K. E., Estrin, S., Bhaumik, S. K. & Peng, M. W. (2009). Institutions, resources, and entry strategies in emerging economies. *Strategic Management Journal*, 30, 61–80.

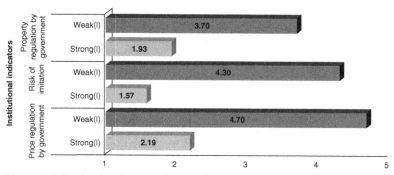

Figure 8.1 Institutional uncertainty in the home country.

The data indicate polarisation in the perceptions of managers regarding the protection of intellectual property rights (e.g. product imitation) and price controls. One group of managers reports low perceived institutional uncertainty (the strong institutions group in Figure 8.1) while the other expresses perceptions of high institutional uncertainty (the weak institutions group). Importantly, all managers have rather similar perceptions about the ability of their respective governments to enforce property rights and do not see this as a major source of institutional uncertainty.

Figure 8.1 shows that a much more significant source of institutional uncertainty is price intervention by Latin American governments. Price interventions clearly limit multilatinas' abilities to manoeuvre because government controls affect either the selling price of products or the input prices of resources like energy or raw materials. A number of Latin American governments directly or indirectly control the price of key resources in an attempt to limit inflation or secure the stability of public finances. Such interventions frequently hamper the ability of firms to allocate resources efficiently in their productive activities and introduce a lever through which governments can introduce huge disruptions in the operations of multilatinas. The main concern here is not price control per se, but the level of uncertainty that price control imposes on companies in the absence of credible government mechanisms to avoid abusing this lever for political reasons.

For a large number of multilatinas, product imitation represents an important source of concern and demonstrates government failure to deal effectively with the problem. Product categories that are especially vulnerable to imitation in Latin America are cement, alcohol,

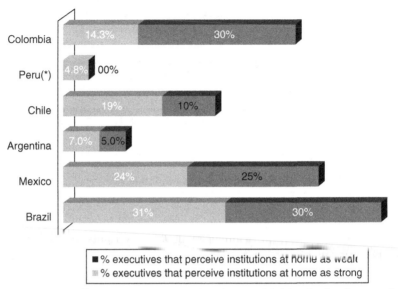

Figure 8.2 Differences across countries on perceived institutional strength at home.

soft drinks, clothes, lubricants and pharmaceuticals. Multilatinas have significant exposure to imitation and perceive it as a key factor of institutional uncertainty.

Because previous research shows that institutional uncertainty can vary significantly from one country to another, data on the cross-country differences in the managerial perceptions of institutional uncertainty provide valuable insights. We explore the prevalence of perceptions of weak market institutions (characterised by high institutional uncertainty) and strong market institutions (characterised by weak institutional uncertainty) for our six Latin American countries and present the results in Figure 8.2. The prevalence of perceptions of strong market institutions is clearly present in Colombia. This result might seem surprising as in 2013, when the data were collected: Colombia, Peru and Mexico featured in the fourth quartile of the Heritage Foundation Property Rights International Index,[23] a rather unfavourable position. In the 2015 data from the same index, Colombia showed a marked

[23] Heritage Foundation, 2013, International Property Rights Report 2013, available at www.micci.com/downloads/digests/eberita/2013/10/property.pdf.

improvement and fared better than Brazil in the country ranking of economic freedom. Arguably, the managerial perceptions of multilatinas and their managers' predominantly positive attitudes towards the level of institutional uncertainty in Colombia in 2013 were indicative of a deeper and significant change in the institutional context that was reflected in international country rankings several years later.

Chile, on the other hand, is frequently recognised as the undisputed regional frontrunner in supporting market-friendly institutions and the Heritage Foundation data on economic freedom confirm this. Our data collected in 2013, however, reveal that executives in Chilean multilatinas were remarkably sceptical about their government's ability to suppress institutional uncertainty; the majority of them identified Chile as a country with weak institutions, a surprising perception given Chile's status as a regional model with a working market economy. The executives' scepticism was reflected in subsequent declines in international rankings, and – in fact – since 2013 Chile has shown a slight but steady decline in the index of economic freedom.

In the case of Brazil and Mexico, the managers of the largest multilatinas are split equally between one group that perceives market institutions to be weak and a second that perceives them to be strong. In both countries this split appears to be a strong signal of a gradual decline of the quality of market-supporting institutions and both countries have experienced a decline in the Heritage Foundation economic freedom index.[24]

Our data on Peruvian and Argentinian multilatinas are somewhat limited and the results of our observations cannot serve as a base for a definite conclusion. Nevertheless, both Peruvian and Argentine executives express concern about institutional uncertainty. Ex-post, this appears to have been significantly more justified in the case of Argentina, which has seen a steady decline in economic freedom since 2011. The shift in political power at the end of 2015 and the election of a new president seems likely to change this, as numerous entrepreneurial and business personalities actively engaged in politics at that time.

A simple correlation between indicators of institutional uncertainty shows patterns of co-occurrence. In particular, perceptions of poor

---

[24] Heritage Foundation, 2015, Index of Economic Freedom, www.heritage.org/index/.

ability to prevent illegal imitation of products or services are accompanied by perceptions of strong price control and weakness in enforcing property rights (corr. = 0.68 and corr. = 0.73, p < 0.05, respectively). This result points to the complexity of the business environment for firms in Latin America, which under conditions of institutional uncertainty are pressed to respond simultaneously to challenges of a different nature that significantly limit their freedom and ability to generate economic benefits. This simultaneity of adverse institutional conditions also can be seen as evidence of the interconnected nature of institutional outcomes.

Our results also suggest that the executives in multilatinas do not share a common baseline against which to judge institutional uncertainty. As in previous research, we did not observe a strong correlation between the subjective perception of institutional uncertainty and the objective variable of market freedom.[25] For example, Colombian and Chilean executives clearly had different benchmarks, as most of them judged the Colombian institutional contexts to be strong and the Chilean weak, a judgement that does not correspond to the quality of the institutional environment of these countries when non-perceptual measures of quality are used.

More importantly, the data presented here suggest that the perceptions of multilatinas executives can help explain subsequent changes in the degree of institutional uncertainty in the region. Therefore, a systematic effort to collect data that are focused on these executives' perceptions can add a valuable perspective for decision-makers working on issues of national and regional competitiveness and complement existing approaches. Multilatinas executives' shared perceptions of the broader institutional environment are arguably good proxies for changes in institutional uncertainty because the connections between the economic and business elites in the countries of Latin America are particularly close, and frequently mediated by family ties. This puts the executives of multilatinas in a privileged position to notice and compare subtle differences between different institutional contexts and form well-informed opinions. For

[25] Wills-Herrera, E., Orozco, L., Forero-Pineda, C., Pardo, P. & Andonova, V. 2011. The relationship between perceptions of inequality, social capital and subjective well-being: Empirical evidences from areas of rural conflict in Colombia. *The Journal of Socio-Economics*, 40(1), 88–96.

example, a study of the interaction between the economic and political elites in Latin America provides a detailed account of the consequences of these interdependencies on tax initiatives, highlighting the extremely privileged position enjoyed by the Chilean business elite as opposed to the comparatively weaker position of that in Argentina.[26]

Any generalisation about institutions being similarly weak across Latin America is inappropriate. Chile still (2015) ranks seventh among the world's most free economies, according to the Heritage Foundation, and even though the region shares many important common factors, such as religion, colonial background and language (with the notable exception of Brazil), the institutional outcomes differ substantially and complicate the task of performing a simple, comprehensive analysis. The perceptions of multilatinas executives can provide an informative shortcut by capturing all available information about the shifting degree of institutional uncertainty, tapping into sources of formal, informal, explicit and tacit information. This approach is not flawless, but it does contribute key insights into the understanding of how institutional contexts interact with economic decision-making in Latin America and to what extent this interaction affects decisions related to the internationalisation of business operations.

What is clear is that companies operating in Latin America, including the multilatinas, do so under significant degrees of institutional uncertainty and that many of their resources are employed in dealing with this contextual flaw instead of being used to strengthen their competitive position through innovation, customer responsiveness or production enhancement. The toll that legal uncertainty can take even on powerful global multinationals, to say nothing of multilatinas, is illustrated by the fact that Unilever Brazil, a leader in fast-moving consumer goods, employs more staff in its tax and legal department than in its marketing department. In such contexts firms necessarily channel much of their efforts towards building competitive advantage and creating innovative solutions in the costly and uncertain process that characterises their interaction with the institutional environment. Eliminating this waste can free up substantial resources and talent in

---

[26] Fairfield, Tasha. 2015. *Private wealth and public revenue in Latin America: Business power and tax politics.* Cambridge University Press.

the companies of Latin America and boost their competitiveness by employing them in more productive ways. In Chapter 9 we discuss strategically relevant resources whose quality could be significantly upgraded if multilatinas did not have to pay the price of dealing with institutional uncertainty.

9 | Organisational resources and competences

VENETA ANDONOVA AND MAURICIO
LOSADA-OTÁLORA

Any research endeavour aimed at understanding the internationalisation strategies of multilatinas from a resource-based perspective requires information about the unique resources and core competences available in these organisations. One significant methodological feature of this chapter is that it uses a survey to gather this information, relying on the perceptions of top executives. This approach is advantageous because it provides direct perceptual measures[1] for a number of important constructs for which there are no available objective measures, such as the degree to which multilatinas rely on non-market resources such as bribes and favours to compete in a foreign market. Perceptual measures are especially appropriate in such cases because managerial perceptions shape firms' decision-making processes.[2] The use of perceptual measures also helps us to analyse the internationalisation of multilatinas by highlighting the priorities and challenges experienced by influential strategists, who might be considered key informants on the process of setting national competitiveness agendas in Latin America. Related to these, the resource base of multilatinas certainly reveals the realities faced by domestic competitors who do not pursue internationalisation strategies. After all, it is from this domestic base that multilatinas sprang into the international arena.

Following previous research,[3] a wide definition of resources was adopted to include all assets, capabilities, organisational processes,

---

[1] Agarwal, S. & Ramaswami, S. (1998). Choice of foreign market entry mode: Impact of ownership, location and internalisation factors. *Journal of International Business Studies*, 23, 1–27.

[2] Spanos, Y. & Lioukas, S. (2001). An examination into the causal logic of rent generation: Contrasting Porter's competitive strategy framework and the resource-based perspective. *Strategic Management Journal*, 22, 907–34; and Chattopadhyay, P., Glick, W., Millers. Ch. & Huber, G. (1999). Determinants of executive beliefs: Comparing functional conditioning and social influence. *Strategic Management Journal*, 20, 763–89.

[3] See, for example, Barney, J. (1991). Firm resources and sustained competitive advantage. *Journal of Management*, 17, 99–120; and Wernerfelt, B. (1984). A resource-based view of the firm. *Strategic Management Journal*, 5, 171–80.

firm attributes, information and knowledge controlled by a firm that allow it to conceive and undertake actions in foreign markets. Because multilatinas are studied, distinguishing between market and non-market resources is especially critical. Market resources are the resources firms use to out-compete rivals in the market; examples include efficient production facilities, brand names and product innovations. Market resources can be technological and context-specific. Technological resources are transferable, knowledge-intensive resources[4] that allow firms to create superior products, improve existing products and gain effectiveness and efficiency in production processes; examples of these are R&D, patents and advanced production technologies. Context-specific resources are the business networks, brands or managerial market knowledge firms develop to fit into the unique market realities of their country of origin. Context-specific resources deliver the greatest benefits as sources of competitive advantage in a specific country or regional area. They cannot be transferred abroad at a reasonable cost and if they are transferred their value is greatly diminished, as their value is largely determined by unique local solutions. Food brands are a good example. Generally speaking, the food and beverage industry is highly culturally sensitive; different cultures have very different gastronomic practices and preferences for ingredients, colours, textures and cooking methods. This specificity affects the challenges these companies face when expanding abroad and the management of brands is only one aspect of this complex process. No matter how strong Alpina's brands are in its home market in Colombia, there are serious questions about the market rationale of using the same brands in Ecuador, as consumers there have invested their trust in local brands for years and are largely unaware of the brands their Colombian neighbours buy from food retail outlets. In fact, the acquisition of local brands is one of the main reasons behind the successful internationalisation of Alpina in Ecuador. Choosing to use an existing local brand might not always be optimal but it certainly avoids building a new one from scratch, which is an extremely challenging endeavour in any internationalisation process.

---

[4] Yiu, D. W., Lau, Ch. & Bruton, G. D. (2007). International venturing by emerging economy firms: The effects of firm, home country networks, and corporate entrepreneurship. *Journal of International Business Studies*, 38, 519–40.

While technological and context-specific market resources equip multilatinas to win in the market place, non-market resources are the tangible and intangible assets that are deployed to facilitate market transactions by reducing the frictions that the formal and informal institutions surrounding their business activities might cause. Previous research shows convincingly that firms use both market and non-market resources to compete at home and in the global arena.[5] The role of non-market resources is expected to be prominent among multilatinas because the institutional challenges surrounding them, particularly the substantial degree of uncertainty surrounding rules and enforcement, prompt companies to invest in facilitating mechanisms such as favour exchanges and bribes. This chapter analyses the evidence about the use of market resources and the discussion of the use of non-market resources by multilatinas is presented in Chapter 10.

Technological and context-specific market resources differ in a number of ways. First, while technological resources might be standardised on the basis of explicit knowledge, such as protocols or technical manuals, similar standardisation is difficult or even impossible in the case of many intangible context-specific resources such as brands or supply networks. Second, while legal mechanisms may be appropriate to protect technological resources (using patents, for example[6]), applying the same mechanisms to protect context-specific resources, such as reputational capital, is difficult or even impossible. Present-day consumers and workers are highly informed and organised through social media, which have become venues where company boycotts are called on and off. In these circumstances company reputation is better protected by fast and effective public relations and media campaigns deeply embedded in the local context rather than by lengthy legal procedures. The case of leading Italian pasta producer Barilla is a dramatic illustration

---

[5] Cuervo-Cazurra, A. & Genc, M. (2011b). Obligating, pressuring, and supporting dimensions of the environment and the nonmarket advantages of developing country multinational companies. *Journal of Management Studies*, 48(2), 441–55.

[6] See, for example, Bloodgood, J. M., Sapienza, H. & Almeida, J. G. (1996). The internationalisation of new high-potential U.S. ventures: Antecedents and outcomes. *Entrepreneurship: Theory and Practice*, 20(4), 61–76; and Vega-Jurado, J., Gutiérrez-Gracia, A., Fernández-de-Lucio, I. & Manjarrés-Henríquez, L. (2008). The effect of external and internal factors on firms' product innovation. *Research Policy*, 37(4), 616–32. doi:10.1016/j.respol.2008.01.001.

of how a reputational issue can affect a global brand. In 2013, Guido Barilla stated publicly that he favours traditional families, triggering a boycott of the company's products by the lesbian, gay, bisexual and transgender (LGBT) community. In response, the company launched an effective media campaign that included an illustrated editorial in the *New York Times*.[7] The company was praised for the speed with which Guido Barilla apologised for his remarks. Barilla also moved on to create a diversity and inclusion board and contributed to LGBT causes.[8] This case vividly illustrates the means by which reputational capital is most effectively safeguarded. The Barilla story holds important lessons for multilatinas, firms whose competitive advantage is built in many cases on brand reputation.

Third, while technological resources are generally fungible across markets,[9] context specific resources have low fungibility[10] because they are developed for specific contexts. Fungibility is the property of assets to be equivalent at home and abroad. By design, context-specific assets lack this equivalence across different institutional environments.

Multilatinas that operate in comparable institutional environments but rely to a different degree on technology or context-specific resources face different costs of internationalisation and therefore follow a different strategic pattern. For example, if managers perceive that their company may lose its technological advantages because of the infringement of property rights, they have a strong incentive to defend the value of their asset as the property rights holders[11] by choosing

[7] www.advocate.com/politics/media/2014/03/17/new-york-times-feature-lets-barilla-hook-antigay-remarks.

[8] http://money.cnn.com/2014/11/19/news/companies/barilla-lgbt/.

[9] Anand, J. & Delios, A. (1997). Location specificity and the transferability of downstream assets to foreign subsidiaries. *Journal of International Business Studies*, 28(3), 579–603. doi:10.1057/palgrave.jibs.8490112; Sapienza, H. J., Autio, E., George, G. & Zahra, S. A. (2006). A capabilities perspective on the effects of early internationalisation on firm survival and growth. *The Academy of Management Review*, 31(4), 914–33; Zahra, S. A., Matherne, B. P. & Carleton, J. M. (2003). Technological resource leveraging and the internationalisation of new ventures. *Journal of International Entrepreneurship*, 1(2), 163–86. doi:10.1023/A:1023852201406.

[10] Rugman, A. M. & Verbeke, A. (2001). Subsidiary-specific advantages in multinational enterprises. *Strategic Management Journal*, 22(3), 237–50. doi:10.1002/smj.153.

[11] Bloodgood, J. M., Sapienza, H. & Almeida, J. G. (1996). The internationalisation of new high-potential U.S. ventures: Antecedents and outcomes. *Entrepreneurship: Theory and Practice*, 20(4), 61–76.

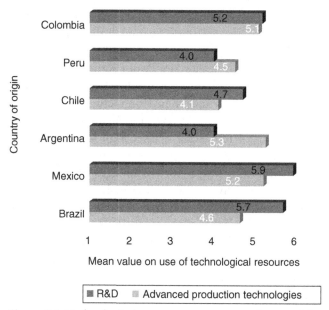

Figure 9.1 Technological resources as sources of competitive advantage for multilatinas.

Note: Mean values for technological resources as sources of competitive advantage in the full sample are M = 5.32 (S.D. = 1.99) for R&D and M = 4.81 (S.D. 1.77) for advanced production technologies.

a host country with sound legal enforcement. However, because the protection of property rights in emerging countries is relatively weak, multilatinas that rely mostly on technological resources and fear imitation have incentives to avoid similar settings.

Multilatinas benefit from both technological and context-specific resources as sources of competitive advantage. Figure 9.1 shows mean values of multilatinas' use of technological resources using a scale of 1–7, where the higher number indicates a stronger reliance on technological assets for building competitive advantage at home. The possession of advanced production technologies and own R&D units are the key technological resources under investigation here as these match best the technological sophistication of most multilatinas. Data for the period 1978–2001 show that out of a total of 2,636 Latin American patents, only 1,520 (56%) were owned by Latin American entities, the rest belonging to patent applicants outside Latin America, frequently multinationals from developed countries.[12] A remarkable exception here is Brazil with Embraco and Petrobras leading in the patent applications among multilatinas.

It is worth noting that the average score of our sample for possession of advanced production technologies and R&D is greater than 4.5, indicating a higher than average reliance on technological assets as a source of competitive advantage, given our scale of measurement (1 indicating low reliance, 4 indicating neither high nor low, and 7 indicating high reliance). The mean value for advanced production technologies is 4.81 and even higher for own R&D, at 5.7. While recognising that patenting activity is very low in Latin America, it is important to note that as a whole the group of large multilatinas has some degree of technological sophistication. This result could be interpreted as a pledge by most multilatinas to create new knowledge and use it in the products or services they offer to build a source of competitive advantage away from generic resources and reliance on commodities. The diversity of the sample naturally leads to sizeable standard deviations for both advanced production technologies and own R&D units, suggesting that there are important differences in the degree to which individual multilatinas rely on technological resources for their business success. These differences can also be deduced from the country comparisons in Figure 9.1. The strongest reliance on own R&D centres is consistent with the leadership positions of Brazil and Mexico in patenting activity. Between 1968 and 2001 Brazil and Mexico had, respectively, 1,715 and 1,783 patents granted, according to the U.S. Patents and Trademarks Office,[13] and were by far the most prolific inventor countries in Latin America. Although data for later years are not immediately comparable, owing to the specificity of the reporting method, they appear to confirm the leadership position of these two countries. However, Argentina's position is surprising. The country has had a strong tradition of invention activities, ahead of Venezuela but behind Mexico. It is possible that the prolonged period of political and economic uncertainty in Argentina since the turn of the century has reduced the reliance of

[12] Montobbio, F. 2007. Patenting Activity in Latin American and Caribbean Countries. Report for the project 'Technological Management and Intellectual Property' organised by the World Intellectual Property Organisation (WIPO) and Economic Commission for Latin America and The Caribbean (ECLAC).
[13] Ibid.

its multinationals on own R&D. The contrast between Brazilian and Argentine multilatinas may also be because of differences between the economic sectors to which they belong. In Argentina, manufacturing, processing and agriculture represent a huge volume of economic activity, while in Brazil the main economic sectors include mining and biotechnology, industries in which the development of new knowledge is instrumental for building competitive advantage. Colombian and Mexican multilatinas also report high reliance on advanced production technologies as a way to build competitive advantage at home.

In general, all multilatinas report high reliance on own R&D or advanced production technologies as sources of competitive advantage. In the sample there is a positive and statistically significant correlation for the use of both, which suggests that multilatinas possibly look for synergies in the parallel development and use of both.

Researchers have distinguished between two classes of context-specific resources: created and endowed.[14] The former are the product of human action and intimately linked to the business strategy of the organisation. Examples are brands, networks, market knowledge or managerial teams. Endowed resources are created by random, historical or social circumstances and examples are abundant labour or the availability of natural resources such as oil and coal. Although endowed natural resources are context-specific, they are completely fungible; for example, crude oil and precious metals found in one place are completely equivalent to those found in a different place. They become context-specific through site specificity, that is, when they are available only at a specific location and moveable only at great cost.[15]

Figure 9.2 reports top managers' perceptions of the degree to which their companies rely on created context-specific resources such as managerial knowledge, brands and supply chain networks for building competitive advantage at home. Deep managerial knowledge of market forces, strong brands based on idiosyncratic features of their home markets, such as cultural identity, and networks of local suppliers that

[14] Dunning, J. & Lundan, S. (2008). *Multinational enterprises and the global economy*. Edward Elgar.
[15] Williamson, O. E. Credible commitments: Using hostages to support exchange. *American Economic Review*, 1983, 519–38.

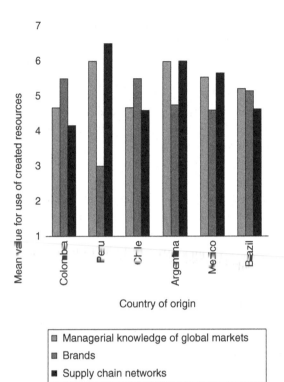

Figure 9.2 Created context-specific resources as sources of competitive advantage for multilatinas.

Note: Mean values for created-context-specific resources as sources of competitive advantage in the full sample are M = 5.16 (S.D. = 1.553) for Managerial knowledge; M = 4.82 (S.D. 2.33) for brands; and M = 4.94 (S.D. = 1.87) for supply chain networks.

provide access to key resources all make multilatinas deeply embedded in the local context. Managerial knowledge of this context sits at the top of the created context-specific resources used by multilatinas. It is paradoxical that strategists claim global managerial knowledge is important for domestic market competitiveness, as in many cases this knowledge does not go beyond the boundaries of relatively small elite circles. The inequality and stratification of Latin American societies, coupled with a deficient education system, reproduce relatively stable social strata from the top ranks of which managerial talent is recruited. This process builds in a structural distance between top managers, their employees and customers and possibly precludes more innovative business approaches in many industries. As Fernando

Fernandez, CEO of Unilever Brazil put it, 'My managers know their customers but they do not experience their lifestyle'.[16]

The use of brands as a tool to gain domestic market competitiveness merits special attention because it is along this dimension that multilatinas differ the most. Brands as unique strategic resources are especially popular among Colombian multinationals but much less popular in Peru and Chile, as Figure 9.2 shows. Take the case of Totto,[17] a Colombian firm that became known for its bags and backpacks and currently sells fashion products to the youth market. Totto's success can be attributed to managerial knowledge about the global market and a sophisticated network to assure access to raw materials. However, Totto's strongest asset is its brand and the associated fresh and youthful product design, which is sold in many countries in Latin America and Europe.

Not all counties' multilatinas rely so heavily on brands. For example, the approach of multilatinas in Mexico, Peru and Argentina is certainly conditioned by the industries in which they compete but they also have a strong strategic position in regional and global markets at a time when very large global brands and narrow niche brands have been putting pressure on middle-sized players, especially in fast-moving consumer goods. Multilatinas from these countries rely on managerial knowledge and supply chain networks rather than brands. In Chile and Brazil, reliance on all three types of created context-specific resources (brands, managerial knowledge and supply chain) seems to be balanced as their multilatinas do not show marked preference for one over the others.

Further analysis reveals a strong correlation between reliance on managerial knowledge and reliance on supply chain networks ($r = 0.772$; $p < 0.05$). This suggests that managers are able to integrate their market knowledge with their abilities to develop valuable local supply networks. The use of these context-specific assets appears to be an alternative to the use of brands as an essential strategic resource, an approach that certainly correlates with specific industries, such as mining, where brands have no relevance whatsoever. It is important to note that this reportedly high reliance on supplier networks comes

[16] Fernando Fernández, AIB-LAT, Sao Paulo Brazil, 19–20 February 2016, panel discussion.
[17] www.totto.com.

at a time when leading experts are concerned about supply chain risk in Latin America.[18] The riskiest industries from a supply chain perspective are mining, agro-commodities, manufacturing and construction and the riskiest countries Brazil, Mexico, Colombia and Peru. Coincidentally, these are the industries to which many large multilatinas from these countries belong. The biggest sources of supply chain risk are labour rights, working conditions and legislation that makes investors liable for the misbehaviour of subcontractors. Local content and offset requirements, reputational risks derived from companies' impacts on water reserves and biodiversity are central issues in the political agenda of many countries in the region. The most critically important issue, however, is still the capricious, uncertain and politically motivated enforcement of rules that impinge on the supply chain, creating institutional uncertainty, as discussed in Chapter 8.

The role of endowed resources is explored in Figure 9.3. The most remarkable aspect of the data is that managers of multilatinas report the least reliance on endowed resources for domestic competitiveness at a time when most observers would not see much merit in their operations if it were not for their access to labour or minerals. The crises in commodity prices[19] certainly hit the biggest multilatinas hard but it is far from proven that their competitiveness, both domestic and international, is solely derived from their privileged access to raw materials. As the data imply, multilatinas can access a rich and diverse resource base, something that has not been widely acknowledged.

Figure 9.3 shows the cross-country differences in reliance on endowed resources as a source of advantage by large multilatinas. Mexican multinationals seem to be well diversified, relying to the same degree on oil and minerals and abundant and inexpensive labour. This level of diversification is not common in any other multilatina. Brazilian multinationals, for example, rely extensively on natural resources as a source of competitive advantage. Brazil is the homeland of Petrobras and Vale, which are two of the biggest global competitors in mining and oil.

In the majority of cases, low-cost labour appears to be a weak source of advantage domestically. However, this fact cannot be assessed

---

[18] www.sedexglobal.com/wp-content/uploads/2014/01/Sedex-Briefing-Latin-America-January-2014.pdf.

[19] http://money.cnn.com/2015/12/09/investing/oil-prices-metals-crash-crisis-levels/.

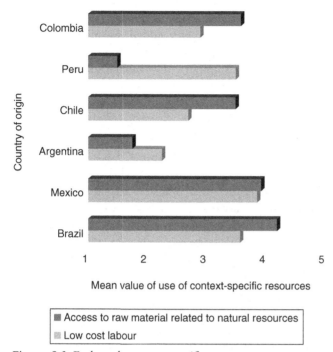

Figure 9.3 Endowed context-specific resources as sources of competitive advantage.

Note: Mean values for endowed context-specific resources as sources of competitive advantage in the full sample are M = 3.29 (S.D. = 1.46) for low-cost labour; and M = 4.66 (S.D. 2.31) for access to raw materials.

without taking regional labour productivity into account as well. When these two factors are considered, labour costs also emerge as a weak source of global advantage.[20] According to a 2015 report by the Global Economic Governance Initiative at Boston University, manufacturing goods from Latin America face fierce direct competition from China. From 2008 to 2013, 75% of Latin American manufactured exports were directly threatened by Chinese manufactured products, compared to 83% between 2003 and 2008. According to the report, this 12% decline in the threat from Chinese manufactured exports could not be attributed to better labour productivity in the Latin American manufacturing sector, because China's labour productivity

[20] Ray, R. & Gallagher, K. China–Latin America Economic Bulletin 2015 Edition www.bu.edu/pardeeschool/files/2015/02/Economic-Bulletin-2015.pdf.

outperformed it between 2000 and 2011. Moreover, specific country sectors, especially those with higher value added, sustained a serious blow in terms of international competitiveness.[21] Mexico's household and office electronics sector (computers, televisions, radios and telecom equipment) contributed 14% of Mexico's exports between 2008 and 2013, a fall from 22% between 2003 and 2008. Argentina's vehicles sector – comprising cars, trucks, motorcycles, aircraft and ships – fell from 23% to 8% during the same periods, and Peru's clothing sector decreased from 47% to 33% of its exports.[22]

In fact, the sizeable Chinese demand for natural resources in Latin America over this period is the most plausible explanation for the declining trend in the direct threat Latin American exports face from Chinese goods. Latin American exports to China are almost entirely concentrated in agriculture and extractive industries (China imports only 2% of Latin American manufacturing exports). Because Chinese imports from Latin America represent 15% of the region's agricultural and extractive exports, they also generate fewer jobs in the local economy and have a greater environmental footprint than other exports with higher local value added. These facts are frequently discussed in conjunction with regional regulatory policies on minimum wages, which all six countries studied here have. Despite these regulations, countries such as Mexico where, according to our data, the domestic competitive advantage is significantly reliant on low labour costs, exhibit only low wage increases.[23]

The competitiveness issue raised by the data on Latin American exports and multinationals' key resources should be discussed in conjunction with viable and actionable measures, such as industrial policies.[24] Industrial policies are interventions that pursue objectives unattainable by reliance on pure market forces; they often establish goals, such as increase in competitiveness, growth and productivity, supporting them through innovation, employment or the production of high value-added goods. There is no broad agreement on whether

---

[21] Ibid.

[22] Ibid.

[23] World of Work 2014: Developing with Jobs, International Labour Organization, www.ilo.org/wcmsp5/groups/public/--dgreports/--dcomm/documents/publication/wcms_243961.pdf.

[24] Rodrik, Dani, 2008. 'Normalising Industrial Policy'. Commission on Growth and Development, Working Paper 3.

industrial policies achieve their goals[25] but the implementation of even the best-intentioned industrial restructuring appears to be challenging. Also, softer industrial policies, such as free trade zones, industrial clusters and infrastructure upscaling, are significantly less controversial than tariffs and domestic content requirements.[26]

According to the perceptions of the decision-makers of sixty-two of the biggest multilatinas, they are self-reportedly reliant on a sophisticated resource base, which includes both technological resources, such as own R&D centres, and context-specific resources, such as brands and supplier networks. Some of these resources have been established through substantial and continuous government intervention in the form of state-subsidised R&D; this, for example, was instrumental in the rise of the Brazilian aircraft manufacturer Embraer to become the third-biggest player in an industry that generally receives large government subsidies. In 2016 Embraer fared extremely well in the commercial aircraft industry, behind Boeing and Airbus but ahead of Canadian, Chinese and Russian competitors, extending its reach with final-stage assembly facilities in the United States and China. The 2015–16 context, with record-low commodity prices and deep currency devaluations (with possible overshooting in Brazil and Colombia) inevitably puts competitiveness very high on national agendas. Multilatinas have a special role to play in this process as they are the front-runners and are best positioned to mobilise their existing resources and competences. Understanding the reasons behind the consolidated competitive advantage of multilatinas, which arises in conditions of sometimes significant institutional deficiencies, informs the agenda of industrial policy formulated in Latin America.

[25] Rodrik, Dani, 2004. 'Industrial Policy for the Twenty-First Century'. *Discussion Paper Series* No. 4767; Pack, Howard & Saggi, Kamal, 2005. 'Is there a case for industrial policy?' A critical survey. *Oxford Journals*, 21, 267–97.

[26] Newfarmer, R. 2011. 'What is "smart" industrial policy? Can it be done successfuly? Can it be replicated?', Trade, Investment and Climate Change, Searching for progress on key issues, www.youtube.com/watch?v=ywGHl3VMlFs.

10 Non-market resources and business groups

VENETA ANDONOVA AND
MAURICIO LOSADA-OTÁLORA

Non-market resources

The success of multilatinas in domestic and foreign environments does not depend solely on the market forces to which they are exposed. Because multilatinas have to deal with a substantial degree of institutional uncertainty at home, they develop capabilities and build resources that help them deal effectively with the non-market environmental forces shaped by the social, political and legal factors in emerging contexts.[1] In more institutionally mature environments, non-market forces operate in a highly structured and stable way and some are subject to explicit rules, for instance, lobbying activities. In emerging markets, however, these forces are highly uncertain and unstable and where there are rules they apply in environments where law enforcement is generally deficient. The uncertainty and unpredictability of these contextual non-market factors make it more difficult to do business in emerging than in developed markets[2] and force companies to equip themselves with a sophisticated set of resources, competences and general organisational solutions that their counterparts from more stable institutional environments might find unnecessary. This chapter focuses on the use of non-market resources and competences such as the ability to bargain with public officials, pay bribes and exchange favours and highlight the importance of belonging to a business group. There is no attempt to judge the morality or legality of the activities undertaken by the multilatinas and their competitors but to characterise the resource base on which their business success is constructed.

Because all classes of emerging multinationals face volatile environments at home, they have developed or learnt to use specialised

---

[1] Baron, D. (1995). The nonmarket strategy system. *Sloan Management Review*, 37(1), 73–85.
[2] Khanna, T., Palepu, K. & Sinha, J. (2005, June). Strategies that fit in emerging markets. *Harvard Business Review*, 63–75.

non-market resources to survive and prosper.[3] Non-market resources are intangible assets (e.g. the ability to bargain, pay bribes or ask for favours from influential people) that firms develop to deal with the external forces that surround their business activities.[4] These resources are the result of a deep understanding of the non-market setup at home, and of careful identification of the appropriate mechanisms to manage the social, political or legal pressures that act on them.

Non-market resources facilitate the international expansion of multilatinas because they bring a number of advantages to firms. First, their use might avoid institutional deficiencies in host countries. For example, by exchanging favours or bargaining, some firms avoid or reduce the amount paid in bribes to private entities or public officials.[5] These resources may also help firms obtain cheaper funding in countries where financial markets are underdeveloped, give timely access to policy-related information and manage their dependence on external agents like government officials and regulators.[6] In Latin America, for example, the prominence of big business groups is explained in part by the close personal ties between their owners and public policy makers.[7] These ease the international expansion of multilatinas because they offer resources unavailable to stand-alone firms.

Second, multilatinas maximise their growth opportunities by using non-market resources. For example, multilatinas use favours to secure bureaucratic preference in obtaining contracts, physical goods, business permits and introductions to potential customers, suppliers and partners.[8] Favours or bribes reduce the liability of foreignness in a

---

[3] Puffer, Sh., McCarthy, D., Jaeger, A. & Dunlap, D. (2012). The use of favors by emerging market managers: Facilitator or inhibitor of international expansion? *Asia Pacific Journal of Management*, 30(2), 327–49.

[4] Cuervo-Cazurra, A. & Genc, M. (2011). Obligating, pressuring, and supporting dimensions of the environment and the nonmarket advantages of developing country multinational companies. *Journal of Management Studies*, 48(2), 441–55.

[5] Chavis, L. (2013). Social networks and bribery: The case of entrepreneurs in Eastern Europe. *Journal of Comparative Economics*, 41, 279–93.

[6] Zhou, J. & Peng, M. W. (2012). Does bribery help or hurt firm growth around the world? *Asia Pacific Journal Management*, 29, 907–21.

[7] Hogenboom, B. & Fernández, A. (2012). Neo-liberalism, big business and the evolution of interest group activity in Latin America. *Journal of Public Affairs*, 14(3–4), 283–95.

[8] See, for example, Puffer, Sh., McCarty, D. & Peng, M. W. (2013). Managing favors in a global economy. *Asia Pacific Journal of Management*, 30, 321–26;

new market (that is, the disadvantage of being non-local); arguably multilatinas use them to gain advantages over firms from developed countries that do not have experience competing in developing markets.[9] Petrobras, for example, used the 'political friendship' between the Brazilian government and the governments of other developing countries, such as Iraq and Angola, to establish its operations in these countries, while other oil companies were not given permission to operate.[10]

Third, non-market resources can reduce uncertainty about changes in public policy and the reaction of key stakeholders and interest groups to firms' activities. Bribes and favours are a speedy way of obtaining reliable and timely information to forecast the behaviour of the policy-makers and interest groups that determine the business rules that affect multilatinas' interests. In essence, these non-market resources allow multilatinas to shape their environment.[11] For instance, during the waves of privatisation in the 1980s and 1990s in several Latin American countries, strong ties with government officials allowed local business groups to receive privileged treatment in the form of subsidies, the availability of public funds and special government loans.[12] Non-market resources have also allowed multilatinas to learn about new policies sooner than their competitors and to take advantage of political changes during social upheavals.

There are two main explanations for the use of non-market resources by multilatinas. First, for purposes of synergy and efficiency, multilatinas apparently exploit across countries the business practices that reflect their superior knowledge about markets in specific institutional environments, in this case their ability to deal with high levels of uncertainty at home.[13] Thus, multilatinas can use their deep

and Mudambi, R., Navarra, P. & Delios, A. (2013). Government regulation, corruption, and FDI. *Asia Pacific Journal of Management*, 30, 487–511.

9 Cuervo-Cazurra, A. (2006). Who cares about corruption? *Journal of International Business Studies*, 37, 807–22.

10 Goldstein, A. (2010). The emergence of multilatinas: The Petrobras experience. *Universia Business Review*, 98–111.

11 Baron, D. (1995b). Integrated strategy: Market and nonmarket components. *California Management Review*, 37(2), 47–65.

12 Hogenboom, B. & Fernández, A. (2012). Neo-liberalism, big business and the evolution of interest group activity in Latin America. *Journal of Public Affairs*, 14(3–4), 283–95.

13 Kostova, T. (1999). Transnational transfer of strategic organisational practices: A contextual perspective. *Academy of Management Review*, 24(2), 308–24.

understanding of the tacit and complex rules of the game that govern business activities in other equally uncertain emerging contexts. Multilatinas that use non-market resources are likely to be familiar with bargaining, favours and bribes as institutionalised social norms of running a business in their home context.[14]

Second, the use of non-market resources could be motivated by the excessive regulation of foreign direct investments (FDIs) that multilatinas face in some of the countries in which they operate, especially other countries in the region. Mexico and Brazil, for example, have scores of restrictive norms that govern FDI, much more than the average in OECD countries. Restrictions imposed on foreign investment are reflected in laws and regulations that affect ownership or impede flows of capital across markets.[15] The more rules there are, the more confusing the institutional framework for foreign investment becomes[16] and the greater the chances that the rules will be contradictory, which reduces effective enforcement, gives regulators greater discretion in interpreting and applying them and increases the likelihood that bribes, bargaining and favours will be used to get preferential terms.[17] The following sections describe the rationale behind companies' use of three types of non-market resources: negotiation with public officials, exchanging favours and bribes.

Negotiating with public officials

When the discretion of public officials is high, businesses face a greater risk that the rules that affect their activities will change frequently and unpredictably. In these circumstances uncertainty creates difficulties in assessing accurately the advantages and disadvantages associated with crucial managerial decisions, such as those affecting the volume

---

[14] Puffer, McCarty & Peng, 2013.
[15] World Bank (2010). *Investing across borders: Indicators of foreign direct investment regulation in 87 economies.* The World Bank Group.
[16] Tanzi, V. (1998). Corruption around the world: Causes, consequences, scope and cures. IMF Staff Papers, 45(4).
[17] Mudambi, Navarra & Delios, 2013.

of investment.[18] Negotiation skills are critical for influencing the business-friendliness of the context.[19]

Favours

Favours are exchanges of outcomes between individuals who typically have a relationship or are embedded in a network of relationships (e.g. family, friends and business partnerships). Business people are usually involved in multiple networks that give them access to policy makers and private or public regulators. These influential decision-makers are able to facilitate or hinder the activities of companies by slackening or tightening the formal rules of doing business. Through favours, one party in a relationship uses its status, influence or connections to help the other party to get round or even flout formal regulations and processes that impede business activities.[20]

Bribes

Finally, bribery is an informal payment that induces someone to act in favour of the money giver.[21] Private or public regulators are bribed to encourage them break the rules and facilitate the business activities of the briber. In the context of international business, bribery enables firms entering a foreign country to compensate for the connections they lack in this new host market.[22]

Table 10.1 shows perceived competitors' reliance on non-market resources for sixty-two large multilatinas on a scale of 1 to 5, where 1 indicates that competitors never make use of non-market resources

---

[18] Henisz, W. & Delios, A. (2004). Information or influence? The benefits of experience for managing political uncertainty. *Strategic Organisation*, 2(4), 389–421.

[19] See, for example, Baron, D. (1995). The nonmarket strategy system. *Sloan Management Review*, 37(1), 73–85; and Zhou & Peng, 2012.

[20] McCarthy, D., Puffer, S., Dunlap, D. & Jaeger, M. (2012). A stakeholder approach to the ethicality of BRIC-firm managers' use of favors. *Journal of Business Ethics*, 109, 27–38.

[21] Tian, Q. (2008). Perception of business bribery in China: The impact of moral philosophy. *Journal of Business Ethics*, 80, 437–45.

[22] Chavis, 2013.

Table 10.1 *Perceived reliance on non-market resources (62 large multilatinas)*

Non-market resources	Mean (1= never; 5 = very frequently)	Standard deviation
Request favours from influential decision-makers	2.40	1.42
Engage in negotiations with regulatory agencies to obtain favourable conditions for business	3.89	1.943
Offer money to government employees or regulators to obtain favourable conditions for business	2.68	1.566

to facilitate business in the most recent host country they invested in and 5 that competitors use non-market resources very frequently. It was not feasible to ask respondents directly about their use of non-market resources, as these practices present important ethical dilemmas and are subject to prosecution. Therefore, the results reported are probably a very distant measure of the use of non-market resources; however, they certainly reflect the rules of the game in the markets in which multilatinas choose to operate. It is highly unlikely that multilatinas will engage successfully in business activities in countries where non-market resources are important for competitors without using similar mechanisms to reduce the institutional uncertainty they face in the same market. Our results show that the most common non-market resource is the ability to negotiate with the regulatory authorities in host countries; negotiations are critical for Mexican, Brazilian and Argentine multilatinas but less important for those in Colombia, Chile and Peru. In all countries, decision-makers recognise the use of favours as non-market resources, most frequently in Mexico, Brazil and Colombia. Bribery is reportedly more frequent among competitors of Brazilian, Mexican and Argentine multilatinas.

The need to develop and use non-market resources hinges on the degree and nature of institutional uncertainty in the host market. If a multilatina invests in a country with high institutional uncertainty, it might use negotiation, bribes or favours to compensate for the weakness of host country institutions. Conversely, if a multilatina invests in a country with low institutional uncertainty the need to use non-market resources diminishes; what's more, they might threaten the legitimacy required to compete successfully in the host market. The reported perceptions of multilatinas' managers about the drivers of institutional uncertainty in their host market are used to explore simple correlations between these three types of non-market resources and the main drivers of institutional uncertainty described in Chapter 8, this time related to the host market.

Our correlation analysis reveals some patterns and common circumstances under which multilatinas use specific kinds of non-market resources to respond to institutional uncertainty in host countries. The data reveal that favours correlate strongly with a higher risk of product imitation ($r = 0.60$; $p < 0.05$) and government price controls ($r = 0.391$; $p < 0.05$) in host countries. If formal institutions and enforcement cannot provide protection against illicit product imitation or safeguard against politically motivated price controls, favours enable firms to circumvent formal controls or informal threats to protect the viability of their business. A significant positive correlation between favours and bribery suggests that bribes possibly play a key role in safeguarding the effectiveness of favours. Negotiation, on the other hand, appears to be strongly related to poor property rights protection by governments in host countries ($r = 0.656$; $p < 0.05$). This suggests that under conditions of deficient property rights protection, multilatinas tend to engage in negotiating more favourable terms for doing business in host countries. A strong and significant correlation between the use of negotiation and bribery ($r = 0.629$; $p < 0.005$) suggests a possible additional channel to circumvent poor definition and enforcement of property rights.

Business groups in Latin America

Business groups are some of the largest businesses in Latin America and among the largest multilatinas. Business groups are a collection of firms linked through both formal and informal ties.[23] They are seen as a solution to market failures in emerging economies, where firms seek to internalise transactions that cannot be carried out in

---

[23] Granovetter, M. (1995). Coase revisited: Business groups in the modern economy. *Industrial and Corporate Change*, 4, 93–130.

competitive markets outside the boundaries of the firm. From a socio-logical perspective, business groups are also a reflection of vertically structured social and authority relationships, where clusters of firms operate under the authority of a single entrepreneur.[24] Business groups are also seen as a form of privileging private interests over those of the state, enabling a few individuals with special interests to obtain rents across various industries.[25] From a resource-based perspec-tive, business groups are advantageous organisational arrangements where only some domestic entrepreneurs have access to valuable domestic and foreign resources simultaneously, which can give rise to capabilities that become key success factors in multiple industries.[26] For example, the key competitive capability in developing countries is sometimes identified as the capability to leverage contacts and match foreign technology to local markets. This capability is more valuable than any other in developing countries, where business suc-cess is explained by different technological and organisational cap-abilities from those responsible for business success in industrialised economies.[27] Business groups are also expected to enjoy economies of scope related, for example, to human capital, finance, technology and innovation.

In Latin America, a few dominant shareholders or families often exercise tight control over business groups, whose competitive advan-tage is explained by their dominance over domestic distribution chan-nels and risk management through industry diversification.[28] Owners see industry diversification as an effective risk-reducing strategy in highly volatile environments. In particular, the simultaneous diversi-fication in pro-cyclical and counter-cyclical industries – even in indus-tries that share no resource or technological base – can be seen as a strategy for survival in conditions of high environmental uncertainty.

[24] Guillen, M. (2000). Business groups in emerging economies: A resource based view. *Academy of Management Journal*, 43(3), 362–80.

[25] Evans, P. (1979). *Dependent development*. Princeton University Press.

[26] Guillen, 2000.

[27] Kock, C. & Guillen, M. (2001). Strategy and structure in developing countries: Business groups as an evolutionary response to opportunities for unrelated diversification. *Industrial and Corporate Change*, 10(1), 77–113.

[28] Grosse, R. (2007). The role of economic groups in Latin America. in R. Grosse & L. Mesquita (eds). *Can Latom American firms compete?* Oxford University Press.

Table 10.2 *The prevalence of business groups among 62 multilatinas*

Survey question		
Does the company belong to a business group?	Number of firms	%
No	29	46.8
Yes	33	53.2

Macroeconomic and political volatility in Latin America has been proved to be 'high and enduring'.[29]

Besides the use of non-market resources, multilatinas can expand the resource pool to which they have access by forming business groups, which studies have shown are pervasive in many emerging markets.[30] Of the firms in our sample, 53% are part of a business group (see Table 10.2). Figure 10.1 may be explained by the historical presence of business groups in the economic activity of the region's countries and by the close personal ties between big business owners and public policy-makers, who have traditionally favoured local champions. For instance, during the privatisation waves in the 1980s and the 1990s, the strong ties local firms had with Latin American governments meant that they received privileged treatment that eased the acquisition and consolidation of groups of enterprises across a number of industries. Subsequent benefits, such as subsidies, public funding and special government loans, facilitated the consolidation of their economic power by participating in regional markets.[31]

From this perspective, the affiliation of a multilatina to a business group certainly shapes its strategic behaviour during the internationalisation process. Privileged access to resources controlled by a conglomerate may enhance firms' international performance. Additionally, the social ties that characterise business groups enable affiliated firms to identify and exploit business opportunities in foreign

---

[29] Schneider, B. 2008. Economic liberalisation and corporate governance: The resilience of business groups in Latin America, *Comparative Politics*, 40(4), 379–97.

[30] Khanna, T. & Palepu, K. (2000.). The future of business groups in emerging markets: Long-run evidence from Chile. *Academy of Management Journal*, 43(3), 268–85.

[31] Hogenboom & Fernández, 2012.

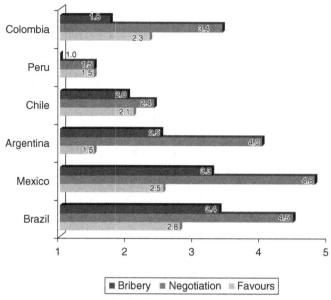

Figure 10.1 Perceived use of non-market resources by country of origin.

markets that are not available to stand-alone firms, giving them, for example, the financial muscle and confidence to benefit from fleeting business opportunities. As a result, affiliated firms may start new business ventures abroad at a lower cost than stand-alone companies, taking advantage of the capability of the business group to combine resources and to reduce transaction costs.[32] Moreover, business groups act as internal markets for affiliated firms.[33] These internal markets could offer affiliated firms enough tangible (e.g. finance, talent) and intangible (e.g. social ties, R&D) resources to perform acquisitions or undertake greenfield investment in foreign markets. Entering countries where a business group has established operations puts a set of context-specific tangible and intangible assets within the reach of an entering firm; these can help a firm overcome the liability of foreignness much more rapidly.

[32] Guillen, 2000.
[33] Ibid. and Chang, S. & Hong, J. (2000). Economic performance of group-affiliated companies in Korea: Intragroup resource sharing and internal business transactions. *Academy of Management Journal*, 43(3), 429–48.

Market integration and political factors present important challenges to business groups.[34] For example, some see political corruption as a result of differences in political systems, which incentivise business groups to bribe parties and politicians to vote for regulatory arrangements that provide private economic benefits for them.[35] Political instability can work to the advantage of Latin American business groups, although multiple factors also work against them and challenge their survival. These include the globalisation of product markets, which magnifies the benefits of specialisation, reliance on U.S. financial markets and the dominance of U.S.-style management training. Political changes, such as the rise of socialist parties, are also expected to put a check on the power of business groups. Nevertheless, their resilience has been remarkable and has been attributed to the economic logic of relying simultaneously on concentrated block-holding, family control and multisectoral diversification.[36] By taking this approach, Latin American business groups have enjoyed privileged access to capital, to information about the local economy and to policy-making, against which stand-alone companies cannot compete. These advantages are especially relevant in the context of high institutional uncertainty and the macroeconomic volatility that has characterised many of these countries.

Finally, while the number of companies in our study that belong to a business group is smaller than previous studies have shown, it is not surprising that it still comes to more than half. This organisational form offers substantial advantages, mostly to do with the importance of scale in securing access to low-cost capital, as well as information and political leverage. Risk-diversification for family-controlled businesses is also a prominent factor in the prevalence of business groups in Latin America, unlike the United States or Canada. The development of capital markets and the quality of property rights protection

---

[34] Schneider, 2008.
[35] Yadav, V. 2011. *Political parties, business groups and corruption in developing countries*, Oxford University Press.
[36] Schneider, 2008.

appear to be the critical variables that explain the resilience of business groups. Greater capital market liquidity and macroeconomic and political certainly are therefore expected to put Latin American business groups at a disadvantage compared to stand-alone companies that can reap greater advantages of specialisation. For the moment this appears to be a distant scenario for most Latin American companies and business groups, which continue to offer a generous mix of valuable resources to boost multilatinas' competitiveness.

PART III

11 Resource-dependent strategies of internationalisation: the where, when and how of going abroad

MAURICIO LOSADA-OTÁLORA AND
VENETA ANDONOVA

Internationalisation can have six economic effects on the competitive advantage of any firm: adding volume and growth, reducing cost, differentiating and increasing willingness to pay, increasing industry attractiveness, normalising risk and generating knowledge and other resources.[1]

Adding volume and growth is one of the key drivers of competitive advantage and most multinational organisations cite this as the main reason behind their internationalisation. EMBRAER's expansion into China, for example, was driven by optimistic expectations of the growth in regional and business air transport in the region. In 2015, as many as 130 planes were forecast to leave EMRAER's Chinese factory; however, only 2 were delivered and EMRAER was rumoured to be considering shutting down its Chinese operations, after the dramatic slump in Chinese business aviation that followed the government's crackdown on corporate corruption.[2] Cost reduction was the driver behind Marcopolo's expansion into Egypt; the Brazilian bus body manufacturer made the move to lower the cost of serving its markets in North Africa, the Middle East and Europe.[3] The Brazilian cosmetics company Natura boosted its differentiation and customers' willingness to pay by opening a flagship store in Paris, trading its

---

[1] Ghemawat, P. (2007). Grobal value creation: The ADDING value scorecard. In *Redefining global strategy: Crossing borders in a world where differences still matter*. Harvard Business School Press.

[2] www.bloomberg.com/news/articles/2015-06-10/
embraer-said-to-consider-closing-business-jet-factory-in-china-iaq2juy8.

[3] da Rocha, A., Arkader, R. & Barreto de Goes, B. (2015). International expansión of Marcopolo (B): Manufacturing in 'the other side of the world'. *Journal of Business Research*, 68, 241–54.

traditional direct sales model off against the reputational benefit of having a store in the world capital of cosmetics. Competitive advantage can also be derived from increased industry attractiveness. The Mexican company CEMEX exploited this masterfully when internationalising in Colombia and Venezuela, where it captured more than 70% of the installed market capacity. By internationalising, CEMEX also normalised its risk, as the construction industry that drives the cement business is characterised by uncorrelated national cycles. The company also benefitted from the development of new knowledge and integrated it into the 'CEMEX way'.

These six drivers of internationalisation give rise to the distinct strategies that multinationals use to mobilise their resources to create economic value. It is important to understand how the nature of home-based resources conditions the implementation of resource exploitation and resource acquisition strategies In an environment characterised by general institutional uncertainty, which is focused on as the most significant structural factor in the region. From this resource-based perspective, resource exploitation and resource acquisition are the two generic approaches to internationalisation and their desirability depends on the characteristics of the resources that lead to the consolidation of the competitive advantage at home.

In essence, the varying degrees of reliance on technological and context-specific resources in domestic environments with significant institutional uncertainty create dissimilar opportunities for multilatinas and influence the choices they make during the internationalisation process.

For firms whose domestic competitive advantage is predominantly reliant on technological resources, which are more easily transferred across borders, political instability and government intervention in their home market might stimulate the process of internationalisation to countries with a lower level of institutional uncertainty. Faced with challenges or deteriorating conditions of institutional uncertainty at home, these multilatinas can take the opportunity to move abroad to exploit their domestic technological resources in products and processes similar to those used in the home market. This gives them the potential to benefit from enhanced profitability,[4] increased economies

---

[4] Porter, M. (1990). *The competitive advantage of nations.* Free Press.

of scale[5] and possibly fewer competitive pressures,[6] besides the normalisation of risk. Exploitation of their strategically important domestic resources is feasible because technological resources are highly redeployable and their value is preserved or even increased across markets.[7]

On the other hand, multilatinas that compete domestically, relying predominantly on context-specific resources, such as brands and supplier networks, find it impossible to redeploy their assets as these are non-fungible and embedded in the context. Of course, under the pressure of institutional uncertainty, all business operations face greater risk, whatever the nature of their assets. This risk has to be taken into account when analysing the process of internationalisation of all kinds of emerging country multinationals.[8] For example, if firms base their competitive advantage at home on strong relations with local communities, as is the case of many oil and gas companies in Latin America, they might lose their competitiveness if national institutions intervene to alter the balance in these relationships. The temptation for different government institutions to shift the division of gains between indigenous groups and oil and gas companies, as in Colombia in 2016, substantially increases the risk of doing business in these contexts; companies are exposed to short- and long-term incentives, which ultimately lead to an even more adverse business environment. In the short run, and given the sunk-cost nature of the investment, companies

[5] Hitt, M., Hosskisson, R. E. & Kim, H. (1997). International diversification: Effects on innovation and firm performance in product-diversified firms. *Academy of Management Journal*, 40, 767–98.

[6] Aulakh, P. S. (2007). Special issue on emerging multinationals from developing economies: Motivations, paths, and performance. *Journal of International Management*, 13, 235–402.

[7] See for example, Bloodgood, J. M., Sapienza, H. J. & Almeida, J. G. (1996). The internationalization of new high-potential U.S. ventures: Antecedents and outcomes. *Entrepreneurship Theory and Practice*, 20(4), 61–76; Anand, J. & Kogut, B. (1997a). Technological capabilities of countries, firm rivalry and foreign direct investment. *Journal of International Business Studies*, 28(3), 445–65; Rugman, A. & Verbeke, A. (2001) Subsidiary-specific advantages in multinational enterprises. *Strategic Management Journal*, 22(3), 237–50; Zahra, S., Matherne, B. & Carleton, J. (2003). Technological resources leveraging and the internationalization of new ventures. *Journal of International Entrepreneurship*, 1(2), 163–86.

[8] Lu, J., Liu, X. & Wang, H. (2010). Motives for outward FDI of Chinese private firms: Firm resources, industry dynamics, and government policies. *Management and Organization Review*, 7, 223–48.

have an incentive to compensate local communities above and beyond the level initially agreed. In the long run, however, this can lead to the exponential escalation of ex-post rent-seeking by communities that were not even part of the initial negotiations with the oil and gas companies, triggering a bandwagon effect. This ultimately reduces the attractiveness of the local environment and creates incentives for companies to find alternative locations abroad. Knowledge that is useful for dealing with specific but critical institutional details cannot usually be reapplied within other institutional frameworks without substantial adaptation[9] and learning. For this reason, multilatinas, whose competitiveness is based on context-specific resources at home, invest abroad following a resources acquisition strategy in the host country,[10] unable to benefit from much of the home market advantages they have built.

Resource acquisition strategy increases firms' resources through investments abroad.[11] The rationale of this strategy is that resources that are new for the firm are acquired abroad to substitute for the internal development of resources or capabilities. Multilatinas that compete at home on the basis of context-specific resources need to acquire additional new resources when engaging in foreign direct investment (FDI) because of the non-fungibility of context-specific resources.[12]

A local supplier network that has been useful for a firm building advantages at home has low added value abroad because it represents a resource that was developed for and with a specific group of partners that are embedded in the home market. To compete successfully

[9] Tan, D. & Meyer, K. (2010). Business groups' outward FDI: A managerial resources perspective. *Journal of International Management*, 16,154–64, p. 158.

[10] Meyer, K. E., Estrin, S., Bhaumik, S. K. & Peng, M. W. (2009). Institutions, resources, and entry strategies in emerging economies. *Strategic Management Journal*, 30, 61–80.

[11] See, for example Makino, S., Lau, C. & Yeh, R. (2002). Asset-exploitation versus asset-seeking: Implications for location choice of foreign direct investment from newly industrialized economies. *Journal of International Business Studies*, 33, 403–21; Deng, P. (2004). Outward investment by Chinese MNCs: Motivations and implications. *Business Horizons*, 47(3), 8–16; Dunning, J. H. (2009). Location and the multinational enterprise: A neglected factor? *Journal of International Business Studies*, 40, 5–19.

[12] Tan & Meyer, 2010.

abroad, this firm would need to develop new networks with a different group of stakeholders in the host markets. These examples, and current research, suggest that context-specific resources might lose their value or even create disadvantages when deployed across contexts.[13] Therefore, multilatinas that compete successfully at home by relying on context-specific resources developed under conditions of institutional uncertainty take a resource acquisition approach to FDI.

Internationalisation strategies and strategic decisions

The strategic decisions related to the where, when and how of internationalisation are contingent on following a strategy of resource exploitation or resource acquisition. Technological resources that are essential to competitiveness at home are redeployable, so firms should not face significant delays when taking them abroad. For these firms, the time elapsing between discovering an investment opportunity and establishing operations abroad will be relatively short.[14] Faster speed of investment also allows multilatinas to escape from increasing institutional threats in their home market and reduces the risk of losing their advantage there. Even though contexts with a low degree of institutional uncertainty are more business-friendly and effectively protect technological resources, multilatinas might face late-entrant disadvantages in them. The redeployability of technological resources makes the prospect of initiating business operations in conditions of higher institutional uncertainty feasible, despite the fact that they are likely to offer fewer risk reduction opportunities.

In essence, countries with strong formal institutions, where the rules of the game are stable and predictable, are attractive for multilatinas that aim to exploit their technological resources by obtaining exclusive, enforceable rights to them, but this frequently comes with the disadvantages of serious competition and late entry.

---

[13] Cuervo-Cazurra, A., Maloney, M. & Manrakhan, S. (2007). Causes of the difficulties in iinternationalization. *Journal of International Business Studies*, 38, 709–25.

[14] See, for example Oviatt, B. & McDougall, P. (2005). Defining international entrepreneurship and modeling the speed of internationalization. *Entrepreneurship Theory and Practice*, 29, 537–54; Forbes, D. (2005). Managerial determinants of decision speed in new ventures. *Strategic Management Journal*, 26, 355–66.

Nevertheless, even institutionally uncertain host environments can be opportunistic choices, as the redeployability of technological resources allows them to be transferred away at a relatively low cost if necessary.[15]

Resource exploiters can benefit from a variety of entry formats. Greenfield investment is the most efficient way to transfer valuable resources between countries while minimising negotiation costs[16] and benefitting from economies of scale. Resource exploiters seek to replicate abroad the combination of core technological resources and competences they have used successfully in their home markets and usually need only complementary (non-essential) resources in the host country.[17] These emerging multinationals do not have a strong incentive to pay a premium price for a firm already positioned in the host market as they expect to be able to compete there successfully using their own resources. Compared to joint ventures and acquisitions, greenfield investments allow multilatinas to retain full ownership of the resources that are sources of advantage.[18] However, greenfield projects have an important disadvantage when it comes to speed of execution. If multilatinas pick host markets on the basis of the redeployability of their critical resources, the speed of relocation is likely to be an important decision variable. In this case, acquisitions have the advantage of faster execution, besides offering a more attractive market structure by eliminating a local competitor. The choice

---

[15] The redeployability of assets in mobile telephony versus the site-specificity of assets in fixed-line telephony have been used to explain the development of mobile phone networks in developing countries and the deficient state of development of fixed telephone infrastructure in environments with high institutional uncertainty. See Andonova, V. (2006). Mobile phones. The Internet and the institutional environment. *Telecommunications Policy*, 30(1), 29–45.

[16] See, for example Hennart J. & Park, Y. (1993). Greenfield vs. acquisition: The strategy of Japanese investors in the United States. *Management Science*, 39, 1054–70; Dunning, J. H. (1993). *Multinational Enterprises and the Global Economy*. Addison-Wesley.

[17] Meyer, Estrin, Bhaumik & Peng, 2009.

[18] See, for example, Anderson, E. & Gatignon H. (1986). Modes of foreign entry: A transaction costs analysis and propositions. *Journal of International Business Studies*, 17(3), 1–26; and Gatignon H & Anderson E. (1988). The multinational corporation's degree of control over foreign subsidiaries: An empirical test of a transaction cost explanation. *Journal of Law, Economics and Organization*, 4(2), 305–36.

between greenfield investment and acquisition as entry strategies is a choice between tighter control of key competitive assets and speed of relocation. This represents an important trade-off. In light of the evidence that the internationalisation of emerging multinationals is an opportunity-driven, time-sensitive process, speed is seen as the decisive advantage of acquisition as an entry strategy for resource exploiting multilatinas. This choice of entry mode is analysed with data in Chapter 12.

In short, the resource exploitation strategy is, conceptually, positively related to investments in countries with low institutional uncertainty (where), speedy FDI (when) and choice of greenfield as an entry mode (how), as it provides the most control over the valuable resources but is the least expeditious mode of international entry.

The strategic decisions of firms that base their home advantage on context-specific resources are different from those of firms that base their advantage on technological resources.[19] The former have to build them up from scratch in every host market. As a result, firms that rely on context-specific resources at home draw their advantage not so much from the home-based resources themselves but from their experience of having built them in an uncertain institutional environment. Therefore, multilatinas in the process of building context-specific resources abroad might actually enjoy an advantage from investing in countries with similarly uncertain institutional environments. By selecting host markets with high levels of institutional uncertainty multilatinas reduce the cost of learning how to do business in the host country because they can take advantage of the similarities across institutional settings between the home and host country.[20] Because context-specific resources are essential for business success but are also unique for each market, their development depends on substantial local learning, which is time-intensive. After identifying business opportunities in a given host market, multilatinas that pursue a resource acquisition strategy are likely to take time to plan their subsequent steps carefully, unlike firms that pursue a resource

---

[19] Meyer, Estrin, Bhaumik & Peng, 2009.
[20] See, for example Cuervo-Cazurra, A. (2008). The multinationalisation of developing country MNEs: The case of Multilatinas. *Journal of International Management*, 14, 138–54; Ghemawat, P. (2001). Distance still matters: The hard reality of global expansion. *Harvard Business Review*, 137, 147.

exploitation strategy. The availability of local partners can accelerate this learning process. On the other hand, multilatinas that make foreign investments to build new context-specific resources benefit from entry modes that allow them to control the resources needed. If they have a choice and are not forced into a joint venture by the host regulators,[21] multilatinas are likely to prefer controlling their operations in the host market rather than sharing ownership with a partner because misalignment of goals between the different parties might limit access to the resources required to build market advantages.[22] It is a well-known fact that joint ventures are very difficult to manage because of the structural complexity they exhibit.[23] Resource acquisitive multilatinas need to decide between entering a market through acquisition or through greenfield investment, which has the disadvantage that it does not readily provide much-needed context-specific resources.

Briefly, the resource acquisition strategy is conceptually positively related to the selection of countries with high levels of institutional uncertainty (where), negatively related to the speed of FDI (when) and positively related to the acquisition entry mode (how) because of the readily available and valuable context-specificity of the resources in the host market.

Non-market resources and the internationalisation of multilatinas

The approach to internationalisation also depends on how multilatinas deal with the non-market forces entrenched in the social, political and legal structures that impact on their relationships with relevant stakeholders in both home and host countries.[24] To deal effectively with these environmental pressures, multilatinas develop non-market

---

[21] Meyer, Estrin, Bhaumik & Peng, 2009.
[22] Yu, T., Subramaniam, M. & Canella, A. (2009). Rivalry deterrence in international markets: Contingencies governing the mutual forbearance hypothesis. *Academy of Management Journal*, 52(1), 127–47.
[23] Shenkar, O. (1990). International joint ventures' problems in China: Risk and remedies. *Long Range Planning*, 23(3), 82–90.
[24] Baron, D. (1995). The nonmarket strategy system. *Sloan Management Review*, 37(1), 73–85.

resources and competences in order to reconcile them with the companies' objectives. Sometimes the use of a specific kind of resource is not motivated by the desire to align a company's strategy or structure with the environment but to align the external context with the firm's objectives.[25] For instance, firms have reportedly used favours or political connections to improve their efficiency, unlock markets, influence regulation, handicap rivals and obtain competitive advantage at home and in foreign markets.[26]

Non-market forces differ widely across countries.[27] The non-market environment in developed markets is characterised by highly structured and stable social, political and legal frameworks. These features reduce the uncertainty of firms operating in these environments because the rules of game are highly predictable. Non-market forces in emerging markets, on the other hand, are highly unstable. The uncertainty and unpredictability of these environments are especially critical because they significantly increase the difficulty of doing business.[28] For example, in China and Brazil trust and reciprocity are seen as the rules of game that support business activities[29] and they sometimes function as substitutes for strong formal institutions like legal systems or enforceable contracts.

[25] Baron, D. & Diermeier, D. (2007). Introduction to the special issue on nonmarket strategy and social responsibility. *Journal of Economics & Management Strategy*, 16(3), 539–45, p. 540.

[26] See, for example Baron & Diermeier, 2007; Holburn, G. L. F. & Vanden Bergh, R. G. (2014). Integrated market and nonmarket strategies: Political campaign contributions around merger and acquisition events in the energy sector. *Strategic Management Journal*, 35(3), 450–60; and Bandeira-de-Mello, R., Arreola, M. F. & Marcon, R. (2012). The importance of nurturing political connections for emerging multinationals: Evidence from Brazil. In A. Hadjikhani, U. Elg & P. Ghauri (eds). *Business, society, and politics: Multinationals in emerging markets* (pp. 155–71), p. 158. Emerald Group Publishing.

[27] Baron, D. (1995b). Integrated strategy: Market and nonmarket components. *California Management Review*, 37(2), 47–65.

[28] Khanna, T., Palepu, K. & Sinha, J. (2005). Strategies that fit in emerging markets. *Harvard Business Review*, 63–75.

[29] See, for example, Amado, G. & Vinagre H. (1991). Organizational behaviors and cultural context: The Brazilian "Jeitinho". *International Studies of Management & Organization*, 21(3), 38–61; and Wong, Y. & Chin, R. (1999). Relationship marketing in China: Guanxi, favouritism and adaptation. *Journal of Business Ethics*, 22, 107–18.

Because multilatinas face volatile non-market environments at home, they have developed non-market resources and competences rooted in the informal and cultural-cognitive frameworks of their home countries to survive and prosper.[30] Non-market resources are tangible and intangible assets and competences that firms develop to shape the external forces that surround their business activities. As such these resources are highly context-specific because their development and use by multilatinas are the result of deep understanding of the non-market context at home and of a careful identification of the appropriate mechanisms to shape the social, political or legal pressures that act on them.[31]

Multilatinas can benefit from the availability of non-market resources when investing abroad for two main reasons. First, theoretical and empirical analyses suggest that emerging multinationals use both legal (e.g. negotiation) and illegal (e.g. bribery) non-market resources to shape their home market environments. Developing an extraordinarily rich repertoire of context-specific, even illegal, resources means multilatinas have great internal flexibility and the capacity to adapt to the local environment. Competitors that come from less institutionally uncertain places do not need to develop the same level of sensitivity.

Second, firms have a natural drive to replicate abroad ways of doing business that are successful in their home markets. The ability to use non-market resources, together with this tendency, can give multilatinas one more competitive lever in other highly uncertain institutional contexts. The use of non-market resources abroad will therefore depend on the level of institutional uncertainty in the host country, turning non-market resources into a prospective competitive tool. A multilatina's decision to enter a market with a high level of institutional uncertainty leverages the value of existing non-market resources, while entering a market with higher level of institutional certainty does not affect the value of any context-specific assets. In other words, multilatinas' choice of host markets with higher institutional

---

[30] Puffer, Sh., McCarthy, D., Jaeger, A. & Dunlap, D. (2013). The use of favors by emerging market managers: Facilitator or inhibitor of international expansion? *Asia Pacific Journal of Management*, 30(2): 327–49.

[31] Cuervo-Cazurra, A. & Genc, M. (2011b). Obligating, pressuring, and supporting dimensions of the environment and the nonmarket advantages of developing country multinational companies. *Journal of Management Studies*, 48(2), 441–55.

uncertainty is positively related to their use of non-market resources at home.

Although it might seem intuitive that strong regulatory mechanisms will reduce the feasibility of using some non-market resources (e.g. bribery) in markets with strong institutions, there is another important reason why multilatinas are deterred from using them when entering institutionally and economically developed markets and that is the need to gain legitimacy in the eyes of important stakeholders in the host market.[32] The use of resources that are considered inappropriate in these contexts reduces the chances of emerging multinationals being perceived as legitimate and reaching their long-term goals. Additionally, although non-market resources could probably be used everywhere (after all, corruption is present to a greater or lesser degree in all countries), multilatinas have to recognise the context-specific nature of non-market resources.

Measuring the where, when and how of internationalisation

We developed a questionnaire to test our observations about the behaviour of multilatinas (Table 11.1). This was an iterative process, from conception through development to discussions with executives and experts and vice versa. After identifying the key constructs for the study, validated measurements used in previous research were selected. When such measures were not available, a set of items were developed to captured the essence of the constructs. By following this procedure multi-item scales with content validity were created.[33]

When the first draft of the questionnaire was finalised, four experts in internationalisation and questionnaire development reviewed the draft.[34] After four rounds of discussions, a pilot study was performed, giving the questionnaire to a group of twenty-five executives enrolled

[32] Rodriguez, P., Uhlenbruck, K. & Eden, L. (2005). Government corruption and the entry strategies of multinationals. *Academy of Management Review*, 30(2), 383–96.

[33] Churchill, G. (1979). A paradigm for developing better measures of marketing constructs. *Journal of Marketing Research*, 16, 64–73.

[34] We are grateful to professors Lourdes Casanova, Javier Gimeno and Hubert Gatignon for discussions on several versions of the questionnaire. Discussions with Sarah Witman, Jorge Quiroga and Alvaro Sanmartín led to additional improvements.

Table 11.1 *Indicators of the measurement model*

Resources acquisition strategy: By investing in the host country (thereafter p1) your company was looking for (1= strongly disagree; 7 = strongly agree):

Acq_1	Acquire complementary physical, human and organisational resources to improve its competitive ability.
Acq_2	Access quickly newly physical, human and organisational resources to compete at par with competitors.
Acq_3	Acquire new physical, human and organisational resources to create advantage over competitors.

Resources exploitation strategy: Investing in p1 your company was looking for (1= strongly disagree; 7 = strongly agree):

Exp_1	By investing in p1 your company was looking for ways to compete in a similar way that it did at home.
Exp_2	The physical, human and organisational resources that your company used to create advantages at (p1) were transferred from the country of origin to the host country.
Exp_3	The physical, human and organisational resources that your company used to create advantages at (p1) were very similar to the resources used at home.

Technological resources: To what extent each of the following resources and competences was source of competitive advantage over competitors at your home country when your company decided to invest in (selected host country) (1 = not at all 7 = completely)

Tec_1	Advanced production technologies
Tec_2	Own research and development (R&D)
Tec_3	Patents obtained or acquired by your company

Context specific resources: To what extent each of the following resources and competences was source of competitive advantage over competitors in your home country when your company decided to invest in (p1) (1 = not at all 7 = completely)

Loc_1	Managerial knowledge of global markets
Loc_2	Brands
Loc_3	Supply chain networks developed by your company
Loc_4	Low cost of labour
Loc_5	Access to raw material related to natural resources
Loc_6	Market knowledge
Loc_7	Qualified labour in your home country

Institutional uncertainty at home: When your company decided to invest in (selected host country), in the home country (1= strongly disagree; 7 = strongly agree):

IUH_1	The government regulated the prices that affect the industry.
IUH_2	The risk of imitation was high because of low protection of property rights in your country.
IUH_3	The government regulated the ownership in your industry.
IUH_4	The corruption in the public sector was low.
IUH_5	The political instability was high.
IUH_6	The laws of protection to property rights were applied rigorously.
IUH_7	Was easy to get illegal copies of your products.

Institutional uncertainty in the host country: When your company decided to invest in (selected country), the government of (selected country) (1= strongly disagree; 7 = strongly agree):

IDH_1	… required from foreign investors to transfer technology to national companies.
IDH_2	… limited the foreign ownership in the industry.
IDH_3	… regulated the prices that affect the industry.
IDH_4	….(selected country) was a country with high political stability.

Non-market resources: Do you think that investors in p1 (1= never; 7 = very frequently)…?

NMR_1	Ask favours from influential decision-makers in the host country to achieve the business objectives of their companies.
NMR_2	Engage in negotiations with the regulatory agencies of (p1) to obtain favourable conditions for their business.
NMR_3	Offer money to government employees or regulators to obtain favourable conditions for business.
NMR_4	Offer gifts to influential decision-makers in p1 to obtain favourable conditions for business.
NMR_5	Respect the legal norms of the host country despite the negative effect on the business goals of their company.
Speed of investment	(a) In which month and year did your company discover the investment opportunity in the host country? (b) In which month and year did your company start the legal procedures to initiate the investment in the host country?

(continued)

Table 11.1 (*cont.*)

Entry mode	Your company invested in (selected host country) through (a) acquisition; (b) joint venture with another company; (c) greenfield.
Market choice	Name of the host country in which your company invested.
Size	What was the number of employees of your company in the year of the investment decision.
Experience	Number of years since the first FDI of the company.

in a top regional EMBA program. The draft was revised and updated at every stage of the development process.

Main variables

Our measurement model has thirty-four items that account for three exogenous and six endogenous constructs. All exogenous constructs are represented by multi-item measures: competitive advantage built on context-specific resources (seven items); competitive advantage built on technological resources (three items); and institutional uncertainty at home (seven items). Likewise, multi-item scales are applied for four endogenous constructs: resource exploitation strategy (three items); resource acquisition strategy (three items); and non-market resources (five items).

Host market choice is a special case of multi-item variable. Although research takes into account numerous aspects of a country (e.g. market size and competition), of specific interested is the institutional uncertainty of host markets. Managerial perceptions of institutional features determine whether or not a country is attractive to companies looking to exploit their technological resources or acquire new context-specific resources.[35] Items of institutional uncertainty at home and

---

[35] See, for example, Peng, M. W., Wang, D. Y. L. & Jiang, Y. (2008). An institution-based view of international business strategy: A focus on emerging economies. *Journal of International Business Studies*, 39, 920–36; and Volchek, D., Jantunen, A. & Saarenko, S. (2013). The institutional environment for international entrepreneurship in Russia: Reflections on growth decisions and performance in SMEs. *Journal of International Entrepreneurship*, 11(4), 320–50.

in the host country differ; while institutional uncertainty at home is related to threats to resources as a source of advantage, institutional uncertainty in the host country is related to the threats to the FDI process.

It is easier to achieve high levels of predictive validity by using multi-item measures.[36] For example, resource acquisition strategy gives firms speedy access to complementary resources to increase their competitive abilities.[37] In Table 11.1, these three elements are captured independently by Acq-1, Acq-2 and Acq-3, and jointly reflect the reliance of multilatinas on a resource acquisition strategy. The same reasons guided the development of the remaining constructs of interest. Two simple endogenous constructs (speed of investment and entry mode) are measured by a single item.

We use a measure based on the kinds of resources that constitute the base of competitive advantage to assess competitiveness derived from technological and context-specific resources. In this way, a common criticism of the resource-based view that resources are defined too broadly was overcome. Because of the scarcity of analysis to identify specific resources involved in the internationalisation of multilatinas,[38] a list of ten tangible and intangible resources was created based on previous research.[39] The logic behind this was to capture the degree to which multilatinas are involved in competition at home based on technological or context-specific resources (see Tec_1, Tec_2, Tec_3, Loc_1, Loc_2, Loc_3, Loc_4, Loc_5, Loc_6 and Loc_7 in Table 11.1).

Competitive strategies based on context-specific and technological resources are measured with a seven-point Likert scale. High scores for reliance on a specific resource suggest that it is perceived as a source of competitive advantage for the firm. Responses related to institutional

---

[36] See, for example, Diamantopoulos, A. & Riefler, P. (2011). Using formative measures in international marketing models: A cautionary tale using consumer animosity as an example. *Advances in International Marketing*, 10(22), 11–30; and Diamantopoulos, A. & Siguaw, J. A. (2006) Formative versus reflective indicators in organisational measure development: A comparison and empirical illustration. *British Journal of Management*. 17, 263–82.

[37] Dunning, J. H. (2009). Location and the multinational enterprise: A neglected factor? *Journal of International Business Studies*, 40, 5–19.

[38] Lockett, A. & Thompson, S. (2001). The resource-based view and economics. *Journal of Management*, 27, 723–54 (p. 742).

[39] Especially case studies by Casanova, L. (2009b). *Global Latinas: Latin America's emerging multinationals*. Palgrave Macmillan.

uncertainty at home and in the host country are measured in the same way. High scores for a specific item indicate that managers perceived that item to be a strong indicator of institutional (un)certainty at home or in the host market.

Resource exploitation and resource acquisition strategies are also measured with seven-point Likert scales. Higher scores indicate greater reliance on a specific strategy. Information about non-market resources was collected in the same way. Items with higher scores are the most common non-market resources.

Speed of investment is measured by the number of days between two points in time[40]: the month and year in which the firm undertook legal steps related to investment in the host country *minus* the month and year of the discovery of the investment opportunity. The higher the value of this variable, the less speedy the internationalisation process is.

Entry mode is measured using a categorical variable indicating whether the firm entered a selected host market through an acquisition, a joint venture or a greenfield investment.

Control variables

Besides these main variables, information about three control variables that are widely recognised in the literature as relevant factors in the internationalisation process were incorporated: size of the firm, experience in foreign markets and the cultural distance between home and host markets.

There is empirical evidence that small firms are less prone to invest abroad through cooperative ventures than large firms because they are highly vulnerable to losing their technical core.[41] Besides entry mode, small and large firms also differ in speed of investment. For instance, large firms might have a resource base (e.g. knowledge, a management team experienced in international markets and new technologies) that facilitates faster decision-making.[42] In the same vein, firms with no

---

[40] Forbes, D. (2005). Managerial determinants of decision speed in new ventures. *Strategic Management Journal*, 26, 355–66.

[41] Park, S. H. & Ungson, G. (1997). The effect of national culture, organizational complementarity, and economic motivation on joint venture dissolution. *Academy of Management Journal*, 40(2), 279–307, p. 287.

[42] Bloodgood, Sapienza & Almeida, 1996.

international experience are more likely to choose entry modes with low or shared risks (e.g. joint venture). Conversely, firms with greater international experience might prefer acquisition or greenfield investment.[43] Experience in international markets also provides firms with superior knowledge that could accelerate decision-making and implementation during internationalisation.

Finally, cultural proximity is an important driver of market choice. When they choose familiar settings, organisations limit costs they would otherwise incur by moving into unfamiliar territory.[44] There appears to be a strong relationship between perceived risk and entry mode.[45] In fact, cultural distance between home and host market is a factor that increases perceived risk:[46] when distance increases, firms are more prone to choose entry modes that reduce perceived risk and slow down the decision-making investment process. For instance, when faced with high cultural distance firms might prefer to acquire targets with established routines and networks to reduce the risk of failure. Similarly, firms might prefer to form joint ventures to bypass the risk in the host market.[47] Alternatively, where there is low cultural distance firms might prefer greenfield investment to ease the design of global strategies and speed up the decision-making process. The survey items and the scale used to measure main and control variables are reported in Table 11.1. Chapter 12 presents the empirical results involving the variables described here.

[43] See, for example, Agarwal, S. & Ramaswami, S. (1998). Choice of foreign market entry mode: Impact of ownership, location and internalisation factors. *Journal of International Business Studies*, 23, 1–27, 175; and Hennart,J. & Reddy, S. (1997). The choice between mergers, acquisitions and joint ventures: The case of Japanese investors in the United States. *Strategic Management Journal*, 18, 1–12, p. 11.

[44] Gomes, L. & Ramaswamy, K. (1998). An empirical examination of the form of the relationship between multinationality and performance. *Journal of International Business Studies*, 30(1), 173–87.

[45] Brouthers K. D. (1995). The influence of international risk on entry mode strategy in the Computer Software Industry. *Management International Review*, 35(1), 728.

[46] Kogut, B. & Singh, H. (1988). The effect of national culture on the choice of entry mode. *Journal of International Business Studies*, 411–32, p. 414.

[47] Demirbag, M., McGuinness, M. & Altay H. (2010). Perceptions of institutional environment and entry mode: FDI from an emerging country. *Management International Review*, 50, 207–40, p. 230.

12 | *Where, when and how? empirical results*

MAURICIO LOSADA-OTÁLORA AND
VENETA ANDONOVA

We use structural equation modelling (SEM) to estimate structural coefficients that reflect relationships between the constructs described in Chapter 11 rather than between directly observable variables.[1] This technique offers two main advantages: first, SEM allows the simultaneous estimation of multiple dependent and independent variables. In particular, we analyse simultaneously the strategy followed by multilatinas (resource exploitation or resource acquisition), specific strategic decisions (where, when and how) and their reliance on non-market resources. Second, SEM allows us to use multiple indicators of latent constructs to improve the content validity of the scales. These advantages have been widely acknowledged in the literature on international business.[2]

Common bias variance

As with all self-reported data, there is a risk of method variance in the use of SEM,[3] that is, variance attributable to the method of measurement rather than to the constructs themselves. The fact that we collected independent and dependent variables from the same executive could create bias in the respondent that might provide alternative explanations for the observed relationships among the constructs.[4]

[1] Isobe, T., Makino, Sh. & Montgomery, D. (2000). Resource commitment, entry timing, and market performance of foreign direct investments in emerging economies: The case of Japanese international joint ventures in China. *Academy of Management Journal*, 43(3), 468–84.

[2] Tomas, G., Hult, D., Cui, A. Sc., Prud'homme, A. M., Seggie, S. H., Stanko, M. A., Xu, A. Sh. & Cavusgil, T. (2006). An assessment of the use of structural equation modeling in international business research. *Research Methodology in Strategy and Management*, 3, 385–415.

[3] Podsakoff, P. M. & Organ, D. W. (1986). Self-reports in organizational research – problems and prospects. *Journal of Management*. 12, 531–44.

[4] Podsakoff, P. M., MacKenzie, S. B, Lee J. Y. & Podsakoff, N. P. (2003). Common method biases in behavioral research: A critical review of the

To guard against this risk we built two procedural remedies into the design of the questionnaire. First, we guaranteed the anonymity of the respondents; and second, the questionnaire was tested and adjusted to reduce the risk of bias of complicated syntax or misunderstanding.

We also conducted a Harmon one-factor test.[5] In this test all variables of interest are studied using the factor analysis method and the unrotated factor solution is examined to determine the number of factors necessary to account for the data variance. The basic assumption of this technique is that if a substantial amount of common method variance is present, either (a) a single factor will emerge from the factor analysis, or (b) one general factor will account for the majority of the covariance among the measures.[6] The results of this test show the presence of seven factors with eigenvalues greater than 1, explaining 90.3% of the variance, which implies that common method effects are not a likely contaminant of the results observed in our research.

Non-response bias

We used three tests to analyse if there were differences between multilatinas that participated in the study and those that did not. First, we compared sales and net income in 2011 and did not find significant differences between the two groups of firms in relation to either variable. Second, we tested for a relationship between the country of origin and the decision to participate in the study. A chi-square test showed that this relationship does not exist ($X^2 = 10.468$; p = 0.234). We obtained a weaker result when we analysed the relationship between the economic sector of the firms and participation in the study but we rejected the existence of bias at the generally accepted level ($X^2 = 46.867$; p = 0.087). This evidence shows that participation in the study was random and without a systematic bias.

---

literature and recommended remedies. *Journal of Applied Psychology*, 88, 879–903.
[5] Podsakoff & Organ, 1986.
[6] Podsakoff, MacKenzie, Lee & Podsakoff, 2003, p. 889.

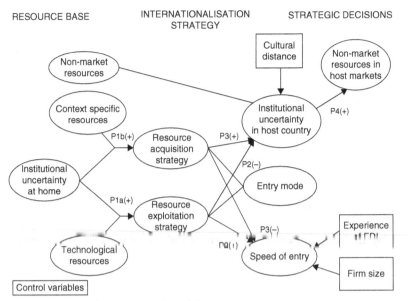

Figure 12.1 Baseline structural model.

The where, when and how model

Our baseline structural model is presented in Figure 12.1. According to this model, we expect that the interaction between context-specific resources and institutional uncertainty at home relate positively to a resource acquisition strategy. Similarly, a resource acquisition strategy is positively related to investment in countries with high institutional uncertainty and negatively related to speed of investment. We expect that companies that follow a resource acquisition strategy for internationalisation will choose acquisition as their preferred mode of entry as it will provide them with context-specific resources without the complications associated with joint ventures. According to the model, the interaction between institutional uncertainty at home and reliance on technological resources is positively related to a resource exploitation strategy. This strategy is negatively related to investment in countries with high institutional uncertainty and positively related to speed of investment. We expect multilatinas that follow a resource exploitation strategy to prefer greenfield as an entry mode but also to undertake acquisitions in order to speed up the internationalisation process. The data reveal the dominant rationale that multilatinas follow. Investment in countries with high institutional uncertainty is related to the use of non-market resources. Finally, and following previous studies, firm size and experience with foreign direct investment (FDI) are related to speed of investment and included as control variables. Cultural distance is related to the selection of countries with low institutional development as an additional control variable.

Data analysis

There were two stages to our data analysis. First, we analysed the structural relationships between the main constructs (except for entry mode) as described in Figure 12.1, using partial least squares path modelling (PLS-SEM). We then estimated a separate multinomial logistic model to study the relationship between firm strategies and entry mode. This model was needed because in its basic form PLS-SEM requires metric data and the use of dummy variables (such as entry modes) distorts the basis of the method.[7]

PLS-SEM path modelling

PLS path modelling (PLS-SEM) is a variance-based structural equation technique that differs from covariance-based structural equation modelling (CB-SEM) in its objectives and method of estimation.[8] First, while PLS-SEM seeks to minimise the unexplained variance of constructs, CB-SEM is a confirmatory approach that aims to minimise the difference between the covariance matrix implied by the model and the sample covariance matrix. Second, while PLS-SEM makes estimations based on ordinary least squares (OLS) regressions, CB-SEM makes estimations based on maximum likelihood. Third, unlike CB-SEM, PLS-SEM does not use a specific factor analytic technique (e.g. exploratory or confirmatory) because PLS-SEM relies on predetermined networks of relationships between constructs as well as between constructs and their measures.[9] The choice of method depends on the

---

[7] Hair, J. F., Hult, G. T. M., Ringle, C. M. & Sarstedt, M. (2013). *A primer on partial least squares structural equation modeling (PLS-SEM)*. Sage, p. 2.

[8] Hair, J. F., Ringle, C. M., Sarstedt, M. (2012). Partial least squares: the better approach to structural equation modeling? *Long Range Planning*, 45(5–6), 312–19.

[9] Hair, Hult, Ringle & Sarstedt, 2013, p. 15.

characteristics of the research, especially the research aim (prediction or theory testing) and model complexity (e.g. number of relationships and recursive or non-recursive relationships).

We have theoretical and practical reasons to prefer PLS-SEM. At the theoretical level, our aim is to predict and explore a set of relationships between variables in an under-analysed context (multilatinas' internationalisation strategies). Second, we analyse a complex set of relationships among variables in order to understand the strategic internationalisation decisions made by multilatinas. The nature of this research, added to the complexity of the model, make PLS-SEM a more suitable method than traditional CB-SEM methods, which are limited by theoretical and methodological assumptions.

There are also practical reasons for using PLS-SEM instead of CB-SEM. First, like many studies in social sciences, we have a relatively small sample (sixty-two observations). Although this sample size is way off the 150–400 range required to apply maximum likelihood estimation methods in a CB-SEM,[10] it is large enough to predict R^2 between 0.25 and 0.50 with a statistical power of 80%.[11]

Additional practical reasons to choose PLS are that we mix single and multi-item measures making no distributional assumptions, although in the data there are no major problems of skewedness or kurtosis. Simultaneously, recursive models (single loops) and reflective measures are used. Finally, no additional model specifications such as co-variation between error terms are applied. For these theoretical and practical reasons, PLS path modelling is the most appropriate technique for data analysis in our case.[12]

Multinomial logit model

We used a multinomial logit model (MLM) to test our theoretical predictions about the relationship between multilatinas' internationalisation

[10] Götz, O., Liehr-Gobbers, K. & Krafft, M. (2010). Evaluation of structural equation models using the partial least squares (PLS) approach. In V. Esposito Vinzi (ed.). *Handbook of partial least squares: Concepts, methods and applications*. Springer, Heidelberg, Dordrecht, London, New York, pp. 691–711, p. 692.

[11] Hair, Hult, Ringle & Sarstedt, 2013, p. 21.

[12] Barclay, D., Higgins, C. & Thompson, R. (1995). The partial least squares (PLS) approach to causal modeling: Personal computer adoption and use as an illustration. *Technology Studies*, 2(2), 285–309.

strategies and their preferred entry mode. MLM is widely used because it lends itself to the analysis of dichotomous choices while testing the significance of each variable leading to the choice.[13]

An MLM assumes independence from irrelevant alternatives (IIA), which means that the relative probability of choosing two alternatives does not depend on the availability or characteristics of other alternatives. This represents the main difference between MLM and multinomial probit models.[14] To test this assumption, we performed Hausman and Small-Hsiao tests, which support the distinction (independence) between the three entry modes and justify the use of MLM over a multinomial probit model.[15] In order to estimate the equation system required to calculate MLM, we arbitrarily made greenfield entry mode the reference option.[16] We then estimated the relative probability of a choice compared to the greenfield option. The parameter vectors, β, were estimated by maximum likelihood function using the STATA 12 software package.

Results

In this section, we present the results of the PLS-SEM model and discuss the characteristics of MLM. Table 12.1 displays the correlation matrix, which shows that some variables have correlations greater than 0.709; however, because these cases involve items measuring the same construct, it is not considered to be a problem. Table 12.2 contains a detailed description of the sample.

---

[13] McFadden, D. (1974). Conditional logit analysis of quantitative choice behavior. In P. Zarembka (ed.). *Frontiers in econometrics* (pp. 105–42). Academic Press.

[14] See, for example, Haussman, J. & McFadden, D. (1984). Specification tests for the multinomial logit model. *Econometrica*, 52(5), 1219–40; Long, J. S. & Freese, J. (2001). *Regression models for categorical dependent variables using Stata*. Stata Press; and Dow, J. & Endersby, J. (2004). Multinomial probit and multinomial logit: A comparison of choice models for voting research. *Electoral Studies*, 23, 107–22, p.108.

[15] Parmigiani, A. (2007) Why do firms both make and buy? An investigation of concurrent sourcing. *Strategic Management Journal*, 28, 285–311, p. 301.

[16] Chang, S.-J. & Rosenzweig, P. M. (2001). The choice of entry mode in sequential foreign direct investment. *Strategic Management Journal*, 22, 747–76, p. 762.

Table 12.1 Correlations

	Tec_1	Tec_2	Loc_1	Loc_2	Loc_3	Loc_4	Loc_5	Acq_1	Acq_2	Acq_3	Exp_1	Exp_2	Exp_3	IUH_1	IUH_2	IUH_3	NMR_1	NMR_2	NMR_3	IDH_1	IDH_2	IDH_3	Speed	Cul_Dis	ExpFDI	Size
Tec_1	1																									
Tec_2	0.636**	1																								
Loc_1	0.414**	0.293*	1																							
Loc_2	0.431**	0.386**	0.076	1																						
Loc_3	0.461**	0.252*	0.772**	0.181	1																					
Loc_4	0.338**	0.327**	0.19	-0.018	0.204	1																				
Loc_5	0.1630	0.251*	0.034	0.064	0.048	0.667**	1																			
Acq_1	0.460**	0.338**	0.254*	0.430**	0.278*	0.268*	0.201	1																		
Acq_2	0.403**	0.144	0.16	0.321*	0.211	-0.025	-0.121	0.168	1																	
Acq_3	0.457**	0.281*	0.121	0.421**	0.169	0.175	0.130	0.739**	0.294*	1																
Exp_1	0.127	0.155	-0.002	-0.010	0.011	-0.098	-0.029	0.040	-0.044	0.007	1															
Exp_2	0.241	0.213	0.276*	-0.013	0.146	0.172	0.218	0.118	-0.127	-0.034	0.383**	1														
Exp_3	0.142	0.201	0.147	0.008	0.104	-0.148	-0.169	-0.016	0.157	-0.076	0.741**	0.218	1													
IUH_1	0.204	0.056	0.103	-0.123	0.025	0.038	0.008	0.042	0.050	0.005	0.194	0.134	0.328**	1												
IUH_2	0.106	-0.092	0.017	-0.106	-0.064	-0.030	-0.081	-0.001	0.009	-0.002	0.146	0.230	0.246	0.683**	1											
IUH_3	0.194	0.120	0.01	0.163	-0.096	0.082	0.093	0.101	0.049	0.167	0.160	0.372**	0.210	0.440**	0.736**	1										
NMR_1	0.038	0.029	0.187	-0.082	0.102	0.030	-0.043	0.317*	-0.019	0.120	0.275*	0.160	0.259*	0.209	0.286*		1									
NMR_2	0.274*	0.230	-0.016	0.140	0.043	0.127	0.126	0.274*	0.183	0.256*	0.353**	0.078	0.274*	0.191	0.056		0.243	1								
NMR_3	0.013	0.034	-0.06	-0.070	-0.058	0.199	0.114	0.159	-0.035	0.090	0.110	-0.073	-0.036	-0.018	-0.069		0.35**	0.629**	1							
IDH_1	0.200	0.166	0.225	0.179	0.188	0.202	0.184	0.671**	-0.032	0.029	0.103	0.213	0.093	0.100	0.067		0.391**	0.169	0.17	1						
IDH_2	0.065	0.109	0.23	0.077	0.185	-0.010	-0.022	0.292*	-0.031	0.072	0.273*	0.072	0.279*	0.086	0.085		0.606**	0.100	-0.032	0.386**	1					
IDH_3	0.293*	0.279*	0.145	0.198	0.176	0.038	0.072	0.195	0.076	0.153	0.241	0.146	0.256*	0.271*	0.198		0.656**	0.161	0.221	0.270*	0.143	1				
Speed	0.239	0.079	0.073	0.178	0.265*	0.189	0.086	0.270*	0.259*	0.171	-0.221	-0.092	-0.202	0.126	0.130		0.015	0.137	0.013	0.015	0.056	0.168	1			
Cul_Dis	0.193	0.181	-0.020	0.044	0.014	0.220	0.162	0.096	0.021	0.232	-0.005	0.034	-0.073	0.044	-0.064		-0.127	0.221	0.143	-0.079	0.053	0.258*	0.087	1		
ExpFDI	0.352**	0.278*	0.086	0.21	0.090	0.223	0.091	0.101	-0.026	0.046	-0.046	0.196	-0.022	0.090	-0.056		-0.08	0.219	0.227	0.072	-0.101	0.139	0.274*	0.086	1	
Size	0.131	0.159	0.106	-0.068	0.105	0.301*	0.083	-0.012	0.008	0.097	-0.110	0.006	-0.178	-0.267**	-0.325**		-0.022	0.073	-0.017	-0.151	-0.014	-0.212	0.094	0.195	0.094	1

Table 12.2 *Descriptive statistics (N = 62)*

Variable	Mean	Std dev.	Min	Max
Tec_1	4.806452	1.772640	1	7
Tec_2	5.322581	1.989927	1	7
Loc_1	5.161290	1.538506	1	7
Loc_2	4.822581	2.336624	1	7
Loc_3	4.935484	1.871888	1	7
Loc_4	3.290323	1.464186	1	6
Loc_5	3.661290	2.318447	1	7
Acq_1	3.612903	1.334963	1	6
Acq_2	4.838710	1.839401	1	7
Acq_3	4.725806	1.917729	1	7
Exp_1	5.032258	1.773833	1	7
Exp_2	4.516129	1.808377	1	7
Exp_3	4.790323	1.527208	1	7
IUH_1	3.000000	1.764867	1	7
IUH_2	2.451613	1.522266	1	7
IUH_3	2.500000	1.097688	1	5
NMR_1	2.403226	1.419532	1	6
NMR_2	3.887097	1.942660	1	7
NMR_3	2.677419	1.565763	1	6
IDH_1	2.177419	1.760441	1	7
IDH_2	3.000000	2.268819	1	7
IDH_3	4.064516	2.296619	1	7
Speed	5.161290	1.074191	3	8
Cul_Dis	2.720048	1.459097	−0.5259	4.5985
ExpFDI	2.679097	0.837856	0	4.4188
lnemplead	8.535660	1.367483	5.2983	11.8845

Quality assessment of the PLS-SEM model

Following our analysis of the relationships between exogenous and endogenous constructs, we took a two-step analytical approach, assessing the outer model first, then the inner model.[17] The inner model specifies the relationships between unobserved or latent variables, while the outer model specifies relationships between a latent variable and

---

[17] Hulland, J. (1999). Use of partial least squares (PLS) in strategic management research: A review of four recent studies. *Strategic Management Journal*, 20(2), 195–204.

its observed or manifested components. In CB-SEM these are referred to as measurement and structural models, respectively.[18] The reason for this two-step approach is that the quality of the measures (e.g. the reliability and validity of the measurement model) is required to guarantee that the results of the structural model can be used to draw valid conclusions.

We use a number of indicators to analyse the reliability, internal consistency, discriminant validity and predictive power of the model. To assess the quality of these measures and to estimate the relationships between latent constructs we use SmartPLS 2.0 software.[19] This has recently been used in several management, strategy and marketing studies that apply PLS-SEM.[20]

Analysis of the indicators' reliability and the internal consistency of the scales shows that ten indicators did not reach the threshold of loads and statistical significance. This first analytical stage allowed us to eliminate two items related to non-market resources, one item related to institutional uncertainty in the host country, four items related to institutional uncertainty at home, two items related to context-specific resources and one item related to technological resources. The process of item elimination at this stage did not affect content validity.

The reliability and internal consistency of the indicators was studied again for the variables retained in the analysis. All the scales showed internal consistency and all the indicators reached the loads and required threshold significance. The only exception was the scale of context-specific resources, which showed relatively low levels of internal consistency, with two items showing statistically non-significant loads.

Further analysis of this result revealed that context-specific resources could be divided into two groups: created and endowed

[18] Henseler, J., Ringle, Ch. & Sinkovics, R. R. (2009). The use of partial least squares path modeling in international marketing. *Advances in International Marketing*, 20, 277–319, p. 284.

[19] Ringle, C.M., Wende, S. & Will, A. (2005). SmartPLS, vol. 2011. SmartPLS, Hamburg, Germany.

[20] Lew, K. & Sinkovics, R. R. (2013). Crossing borders and industry sectors: Behavioral governance in strategic alliances and product innovation for competitive advantage. *Long Range Planning*, 46, 13–38. Landau, Ch. & Bock, C. (2013). Value creation through vertical intervention of corporate centres in single business units of unrelated diversified portfolios: The case of private equity firms. *Long Range Planning*, 46, 97–24.

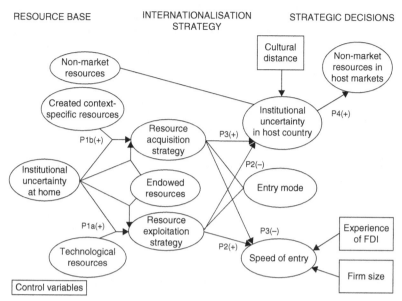

RESOURCE BASE INTERNATIONALISATION STRATEGY STRATEGIC DECISIONS

Figure 12.2 Revised model with endowed and created context-specific resources.

location-specific resources.[21] Created resources require human intervention at the firm level; in our case, they relate to brands, networks, market knowledge or managerial teams. Endowed resources do not require any human intervention and include abundant low-cost labour and access to raw materials and other natural resources. Consequently, the original model was revised to accommodate these two groups. Because we had made no theoretical predictions about a finer taxonomy of resources, we performed an exploratory analysis to study the relation between endowed resources and the strategy multilatinas follow abroad. Specifically, we introduced a new interaction between endowed resources and institutional uncertainty at home to analyse the relationship with both a resources acquisition strategy and a resources exploitation strategy. The relationships of created resources were explored only for the case of resource acquisition because these resources are context-specific and their characteristics make them difficult to exploit abroad. The revised model is shown in Figure 12.2.

[21] Dunning, J. & Lundan, S. M. (2008). *Multinational enterprises and the global economy*. Edward Elgar.

Table 12.3 *Internal reliability of the structural model*

Scale	Composite reliability	Cronbach's alpha
Acquisition strategy	0.8173	0.6669
Created resources	0.7665	0.6105
Cultural distance	1	1
Endowed resources	0.9047	0.8002
Experience of FDI	1	1
Exploitation strategy	0.8408	0.7083
Institutional development in host country	0.7717	0.5576
Institutional uncertainty in home country	0.8987	0.8302
Non-market resources	0.8	0.6747
Firm size	1	1
Speed of investment	1	1
Technological resources	0.8995	0.7776

The internal reliability of the model was examined by inspecting the Cronbach's alphas and composite reliability (CR). All constructs had alpha values above 0.6 except institutional uncertainty at home. The alpha value of this scale was $\alpha = 0.55$, which is slightly lower than 0.6. However, the CR values of this scale (CR = 0.8987) show that the three items measured the perceived institutional uncertainty at home country sufficiently well. Similarly, the CR values of the rest of the constructs were between 0.7665 and 0.904, confidently surpassing the threshold of 0.7.[22] These results confirmed that the internal consistency of the applied scales was acceptable (see Table 12.3).

Indicator reliability was examined by measuring the outer loadings on all items in the model. The absolute standardised outer loadings ranged from 0.449 to 0.950 (see Table 12.4). There are four items with scores below 0.7: $X_{min} = 0.449$ for the resource acquisition strategy; $X_{min} = 0.594$ for the resource exploitation strategy; $X_{min} = 0.670$ for institutional uncertainty at home, and $X_{min} = 0.661$ for created resources. The items with low loads were not deleted because they form part of multi-item scales: their deletion would not improve the composite reliability of the scales but would harm the content validity

---

[22] Bagozzi, R., Yi, Y. & Phillips, L. (1991). Assessing construct validity in organizational research. *Administrative Science Quarterly*, 36, 421–58.

Table 12.4 *Indicators of reliability of the structural model*

Constructs	Indicators	Outer weights	p-value
Acquisition strategy	Acq_1	0.919	0.000
	Acq_2	0.449	0.047
	Acq_3	0.898	0.000
Exploitation strategy	Exp_1	0.915	0.000
	Exp_2	0.594	0.000
	Exp_3	0.863	0.000
Institutional development in host market	IDH_1	0.670	0.000
	IDH_2	0.783	0.000
	IDH_3	0.729	0.000
Institutional uncertainty in home country	IUH_1	0.813	0.000
	IUH_2	0.925	0.000
	IUH_3	0.853	0.000
Created resources	Loc_1	0.661	0.003
	Loc_2	0.761	0.000
	Loc_3	0.745	0.001
Endowed resources	Loc_4	0.950	0.000
	Loc_5	0.866	0.000
Non-market resources	NMR_1	0.802	0.000
	NMR_2	0.762	0.003
	NMR_3	0.702	0.002
Technological resources	Tec_1	0.890	0.000
	Tec_2	0.918	0.000
Speed	Speed (Ln)	1.000	1.000
Firm size	No. Emplead (Ln)	1.000	1.000
Cultural distance	Cul_Dis (Ln)	1.000	1.000
Experience of FDI	ExpFDI (Ln)	1.000	1.000

of the measures. Generally, these results confirmed the reliability of the measurements used to study the internationalisation of multilatinas.

We also assessed convergent validity by measuring the average variance extracted (AVE).[23] All constructs show AVE values greater than the 0.5 threshold (AVEmin = 0.52 for competition based on created

[23] Fornell, C. & Larcker, D. (1981). Evaluating structural equation models with unobservable variables and measurement errors. *Journal of Marketing Research*, 18, 39–50.

Table 12.5 *Convergent validity and predictive power of the structural model*

Scale	AVE[a]	R square
Acquisition strategy	0.6175	0.3342
Created resources	0.5234	
Cultural distance	1	
Endowed resources	0.8263	
Experience of FDI	1	
Exploitation strategy	0.645	0.3533
Institutional development in host country	0.5308	0.2438
Institutional uncertainty in home country	0.7479	
Non-market resources	0.5722	0.3541
Firm size	1	
Speed of investment	1	0.2989
Technological resources	0.8174	

[a] Average variance extracted.

resources). These results indicate that all constructs, on average, explain more than half of the variance of their indicators. This implies the existence of sufficient convergent validity of all the measures (see Table 12.5).

Table 12.5 also contains details about the predictive power of the model. This aspect is analysed using R^2. Using the PLS Algorithm function in SmartPLS 2.0, we computed the R^2 statistics of the five endogenous constructs in the model. The R^2 values of resource exploitation strategy, resource acquisition strategy, institutional uncertainty in the host country, non-market resources and speed of investment were 0.35, 0.33, 0.24, 0.35 and 0.30, respectively These values are greater than the acceptable threshold of 0.1.[24]

Finally, we examined discriminant validity using the square root of AVE and cross-loadings. As shown in Table 12.6, the values of the square root of AVE for each construct are greater than the highest correlation between that construct and the others.[25] Furthermore, we

[24] Falk, R. F. & Miller, N. B. (1992). *A primer for soft modeling.* University of Akron Press.
[25] Fornell, C. & Larcker, D. (1981). Evaluating structural equation models with unobservable variables and measurement errors. *Journal of Marketing Research*, 18, 39–50.

Table 12.6 *Path coefficients in the structural model*

Variables	Acquisition strategy	Exploitation strategy	Institutional uncertainty in host country	Speed of investment	Non-market resources
Created resources	0.4732*** (4.4262)				
Created resources x Institutional uncertainty at home	-0.1789 (0.7573)				
Endowed resources x Institutional uncertainty in home country	-0.0942 (0.5652)	0.2355** (2.3089)			
Technological resources x Institutional uncertainty in home country		0.285** (2.447)			
Acquisition strategy			0.3394*** (2.9171)	0.2781** (1.9942)	
Cultural distance			0.0862 (0.6518)		
Exploitation strategy			0.3111*** (2.7862)	-0.2779** (2.3698)	
Size			-0.098 (0.9234)	-0.3208*** (3.3804)	
Experience of FDI				0.3256*** (3.097)	
Institutional uncertainty in host country					0.5951*** (10.5661)

Note: N = 62; t values in parentheses; ** $p < 0.05$; *** $p < 0.01$.

assessed discriminant validity by comparing the loading values of each indicator with the cross-loadings with other reflective indicators. The indicator loadings were all higher than the cross-loadings, suggesting satisfactory discriminant validity in the model.

Testing predictions of where and when

We introduced the interaction between institutional uncertainty at home and technological, created and endowed resources in PLS-SEM as a product term.[26] To test our predictions, we examined the significance of the path coefficient estimates for the twelve paths in the model, including three related to control variables and two to exploratory relationships. We use a bootstrap technique, which produces more reasonable standard error estimates[27] and we performed 5,000 re-samplings with sixty-two observations in each. Table 12.6 contains the estimates of the path coefficients of the structural model.

Figure 12.3 contains the results of the hypotheses testing. The path coefficient from the product term of technological resources and institutional uncertainty at home to resources exploitation strategy is 0.285 and it is statistically significant at standard levels (t = 2.447, p < 0.05). This supports our prediction that multilatinas that rely on technological resources in their home markets, and perceive high institutional uncertainty at home, follow a resource exploitation strategy for internationalisation (see Chapter 11). The path coefficients from the resource exploitation strategy to the speed of investment and institutional uncertainty in the host country are –0.2779 (t = 2.3698; p < 0.05) and 0.3111 (t = 2.7862; p < 0.05), respectively. These results show that multilatinas that invest abroad to exploit their resources spend less time between discovering an investment opportunity and beginning legal procedures to invest. Also, these multilatinas invest in countries that have high institutional uncertainty. This result is consistent with the conjecture that a resource exploitation strategy is positively related to investments in countries with low institutional uncertainty, speedy FDI and the choice of acquisition as an entry mode

---

[26] Hair, Hult, Ringle & Sarstedt, 2013.
[27] Tenenhaus, M., Vinzi, V. E., Chatelin, Y. & Lauro, C. (2005). PLS path modeling. *Computational Statistics & Data Analysis*, 48, 159–205.

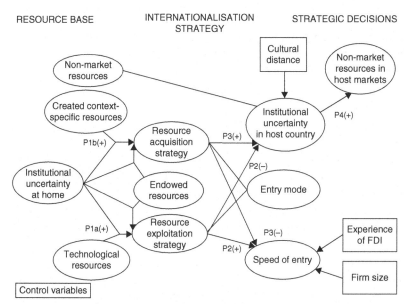

Figure 12.3 Prediction testing and statistical significance.

(see Chapter 11). This evidence also shows that when following a resource exploitation strategy, multilatinas are driven more by available opportunities abroad and less by the desire to keep resources better protected in a more predictable institutional environment. This means that the conjecture related to the choice of host markets does not find empirical support, raising important questions about the rationale behind the internationalisation of multilatinas relying on technological resources. Certainly, the nature of these resources and (above all) their redeployability make them less vulnerable to institutional threats, which opens many host market opportunities for multilatinas that follow this particular internationalisation approach.

The path coefficient from the resource acquisition strategy to the speed of investment and the selection of countries with high institutional uncertainty are 0.2781 (t = 1.9942; p < 0.05) and 0.3394 (t = 2.9171; p < 0.05), respectively. This result supports the conjecture, that a resource acquisition strategy is positively related to the selection of countries with high levels of institutional uncertainty, negatively related to speed of FDI and positively related to the acquisition entry mode (see Chapter 11).

The path coefficient from institutional uncertainty in the host country to the use of non-market resources is 0.5951 (t = 10.5661; p < 0.000). This result supports the idea that multilatinas' choice of host markets with higher institutional uncertainty is positively related to their use of non-market resources at home (see Chapter 11).

To test the robustness of these results, we also estimated the model using POLCON,[28] an objective measure of political constraints to political changes (or limitations to political discretion) based on the number and preferences of political actors with veto power within the political structure of a country. We did not find a statistically significant relationship between this new objective proxy of institutional quality and the strategies of resource exploitation and acquisition. Neither did we find a statistically significant relationship between this variable and the use of non market resources. These results also suggest that there is no correlation between the objective (POLCON) and subjective (self-reported perceptions of top managers in multilatinas) measures of institutional uncertainty. The lack of correlation between objective and subjective measures of institutional and environmental variables is not new in the field of social studies.[29] In our view, the result also corroborates the appropriateness of using managerial cognitive representations as measures of institutional uncertainty to analyse the internationalisation strategies of multilatinas.

We also tested the emergent relations between variables. The coefficient path from the product term of endowed resources and institutional uncertainty at home is −0.0942 (t = 0.5652; p < 0.574) to resource acquisition strategy and 0.2355 (t = 2.3089, p < 0.05) to resource exploitation strategy. These findings suggest that multilatinas that compete on the basis of endowed resources in markets with high institutional uncertainty invest abroad following the logic of resource exploitation. Apparently, the fungibility of endowed natural resources creates opportunities for companies to undertake internationalisation strategies that rely on resource exploitation.

---

[28] Henisz, W. J. (2000). The institutional environment for economic growth. *Economics and Politics*, 12(1), 1–31.
[29] Wills-Herrera, E., Orozco, L. E., Forero-Pineda, C., Pardo, J. & Andonova, V. (2011). The relationship between perceptions of insecurity, social capital and subjective well-being: Empirical evidences from areas of rural conflict in Colombia. *The Journal of Socio-Economics*, 40, 88–96.

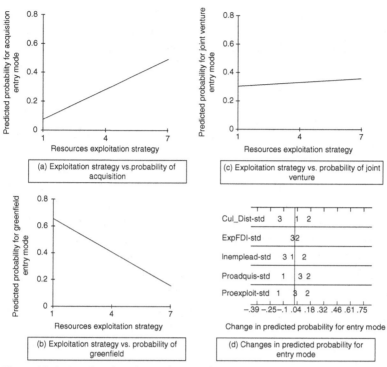

Figure 12.4 Graphical analysis of MLM for entry mode (full sample, resource exploitation strategy).

On the other hand, the coefficient path from the product term of created context-specific resources and institutional uncertainty at home to resource acquisition strategy is -0.1789 ($t = 0.7573$; $p < 0.452$), implying a statistically non-significant relationship between these constructs. However, the coefficient from created resources to resource acquisition strategy is 0.4732 ($t = 4.4262$; $p < 0.000$), suggesting that multilatinas that build their advantage on created context-specific resources go abroad to acquire new resources irrespective of the uncertainty of the institutional environment at home. The statistically significant relationships are shown graphically in Figure 12.4.

Considering control variables, firm size shows a positive relationship with speed of investment ($\beta = -0.3208$; $t = 3.3804$; $p < 0.001$). In other words, larger multilatinas are quicker to invest abroad. The experience of multilatinas on international markets, however, shows a negative relationship with speed of investment. For our sample, greater international experience (more years) correlates with an increase in the time (number of days) between the discovery of an investment opportunity and investment abroad ($\beta = 0.3256$; $t = 3.097$; $p < 0.005$). Cultural distance does not show any relationship to the selection of a host market ($\beta = 0.0862$; $t = 0.6518$; $p < 0.517$).

The final finding might seem surprising because the literature recognises cultural proximity as an important driver of market choice. For instance, Gomes and Ramaswamy assert that by choosing familiar settings organisations limit the costs they would otherwise incur if they move into unfamiliar territories.[30] The absence of a statistically significant relationship could occur for at least two reasons. First, the dimensions of cultural distance that we use in our research, following Hofstede[31] and Kogut and Singh,[32] sometimes have the opposite effect on the FDI process. For instance, Tang shows that some dimensions used by Hofstede, such as differences in individualism, encourage FDI flows between two countries while other dimensions, such as differences in power distance, impede bilateral FDI flows.[33] Because we focus on the aggregate cultural distance such effects are not accounted for and their opposite effects cancel out. Second, it is possible that market choice is influenced by aspects beyond cultural dissimilarities. For instance, the literature states that geographical distance and differences in administrative and economic frameworks are more significant than cultural dissimilarity for the success of international market entry.[34] To test for this possibility we substituted cultural distance by the CAGE distance, accounting for the cultural (C), administrative (A), geographic (G) and economic (E) distances between each pair of home-host countries, and re-ran the model.

The result of this estimation was a positive relation between the CAGE distance and the choice of host markets with high perceived

---

[30] Gomes, L. & Ramaswamy, K. (1998). An empirical examination of the form of the relationship between multinationality and performance. *Journal of International Business Studies*, 30(1),173–87.

[31] Hofstede, G. (1980). *Culture's consequences: International differences in work-related values*. Sage Publications.

[32] Kogut & Singh, 1988.

[33] Tang, L. (2012). The direction of cultural distance on FDI: Attractiveness or incongruity? *Cross Cultural Management*, 19(2), 233–56.

[34] Ghemawat, P. (2001). Distance still matters: The hard reality of global expansion. *Harvard Business Review*, 137, 147.

institutional uncertainty. That is, the perception of high institutional uncertainty in the host market relates positively to geographical distance, cultural and administrative differences and the absence of economic or commercial links between the home and host countries. The strongest effect is exhibited by geographical distance, which is at the core of the powerful gravity models of cross-country trade flows.[35] When we inspected the joint effect of the cultural, administrative and economic factors, we confirmed the initial result of no correlation between these distances and the perceived institutional uncertainty of the host market.

Testing predictions of how: a multinomial logit model

To analyse the relationship between multilatinas' internationalisation strategies in foreign markets and choice of entry mode, we computed a single score for each latent construct – one for the resource acquisition strategy and one for the exploitation strategy. Because both strategies are measured with three indicators we estimated an unweighted average of the original variables that define each one.[36] There are several reasons why this is a suitable approach. First, because the indicator variables are measured with the same continuous scale and are highly correlated, their use could create collinearity problems in the regression analysis. Second, the use of highly correlated indicators does not increase the variance of the dependent variable. Finally, this approach has been used in strategic management research.[37]

In the MLM the dependent variable is measured by a nominal variable that has a value of 1 = greenfield entry mode, 2 = acquisition entry mode, and 3 = joint venture entry mode. As well as the independent variables resource acquisition and exploitation strategies, we use three control variables: firm size, firm experience in foreign markets and cultural distance between home and host country. The results of the model estimation are shown in Table 12.7.

[35] Ghemawat, P. (2003). *World 3.0: Global prosperity and how to achieve it.* Harvard Business School Press, p. 386.

[36] Berry, W. & Feldman, Sh. (1985). *Multiple regression in practice.* Series: quantitative application in social sciences: SAGE University Papers.

[37] Agarwal, S. & Ramaswami, S. (1998). Choice of foreign market entry mode: Impact of ownership, location and internalization factors. *Journal of International Business Studies*, 23, 1–27.

Table 12.7 *Multinomial logit model of entry mode*

Variable	Acquisition entry mode	Joint venture entry mode
Cultural distance	0.268	−0.225
	(0.267)	(0.222)
Experience of FDI	0.393	0.232
	(0.429)	(0.382)
Size (Ln employees)	0.345	−0.081
	(0.261)	(−0.249)
Acquisition strategy	−0.119	−0.247
	(0.268)	(0.50)
Exploitation strategy	0.568**	0.241
	(0.275)	(0.246)
Log-likelihood		− 60.842
Nagelkerke's pseudo R^2		0.235

Note: N = 62; standard errors in parentheses; ** $p < 0.05$.

The results of the MLM (Table 12.7) do not support the suggested positive relationship between exploitation strategy and choice of greenfield entry mode. Also, the results do not show a statistically significant relationship between resource exploitation strategy and joint venture as entry mode. The results show that multilatinas that follow a resource exploitation strategy are more likely to select acquisition as an entry mode rather than greenfield (β =0.647; $p < 0.05$). In our sample, multilatinas do not exhibit a preferred entry mode when they follow a strategy of resource acquisition, as the coefficients show no statistical significance at the accepted levels. The control variables are also non-significant.

In Table 12.7, Nagelkerke's pseudo R^2 is reported as a goodness-of-fit measure, reflecting the cumulative strength of the model. It can be interpreted similarly to the R^2 in linear regression and as such it provides an estimate of the model's substantive significance.[38] In general, pseudo R^2 such as Nagelkerke's R^2 tend to be lower than real R^2 values, where values between 0.2 and 0.4 are considered acceptable.[39]

[38] Fehrenbacher, D. (2013). *Design of incentive systems: An experimental investigation of incentive and sorting effects.* Springer.
[39] Hox, J. (2010). *Multilevel analysis: Techniques and applications.* Routledge.

In our case, Nagelkerke's Pseudo R^2 is 0.235, suggesting a moderate relationship between the predictors and the dependent variable.

Figure 12.4 contains a more detailed analysis of these results. A close look at graph 4a in Figure 12.4 shows that reliance on the resource exploitation strategy increases the probability of choosing acquisition as an entry mode. Similarly, graph 4b shows that reliance on exploitation strategy reduces the likelihood of choosing greenfield entry mode. Finally, graph 4c shows that reliance on a resource exploitation strategy is not related to changes in the likelihood of choosing a joint venture as entry mode. Graph 4d presents the marginal effect of the variables on each of the three entry modes, greenfield, acquisition and joint venture. If the marginal effects are small, the entry modes will be bundled very close together. The greater the effect of a particular entry mode, the farther the option will be from the origin of the coordinate system.[40] In our case, graph 4d quantifies changes in the likelihood of choosing a specific entry mode if the measure of resource exploitation strategy changes by one standard deviation. Specifically, the graph shows that increasing the measure of exploitation strategy by one standard deviation increases the likelihood of choosing acquisition as an entry mode by 11%, while the likelihood of choosing greenfield falls by 10%, and joint venture by 1%.

The MLM results, on the other hand, do not offer evidence for a statistically significant relationship between resource acquisition strategy and any kind of entry mode. This finding suggests that there is no preference for acquisition over other entry modes.

Following this line of argument, we investigated statistically the interaction effect of business group affiliation on the relation between a resources acquisition strategy and entry mode. Business groups own 53% of the firms included in our sample. The results of the MLM, including the moderator effect, are summarised in Table 12.8. The interaction effect of a resource acquisition strategy and belonging to a business group is negatively and significantly correlated to acquisition entry mode ($\beta = -1.930$, $p < 0.05$) and joint venture entry mode ($\beta = -1.746$, $p < 0.05$). These findings show a strong preference for greenfield entry over acquisition and joint venture among multilatinas that invest abroad following a resources acquisition strategy.

---

[40] Parmigiani, A. (2007) Why do firms both make and buy? An investigation of concurrent sourcing. *Strategic Management Journal*, 28, 285–311.

Table 12.8 *MLM of entry mode with business group effect*

Variable	Acquisition entry mode	Joint venture entry mode
Cultural distance	0.271	–0.280
	(0.295)	(0.241)
Experience of FDI	0.557	0.358
	(0.471)	(0.412)
Size (Ln employees)	0.332	–0.089
	(0.295)	(0.287)
Acquisition strategy	0.526	0.369
	(0.394)	(0.341)
Exploitation strategy	0.535*	0.207
	(0.305)	(0.303)
Business group	6.53	6.41
	(2.52)	(2.618)
Resource acquisition strategy x Business group	–1.563**	–1.457**
	(0.640)	(0.580)
Log-likelihood	–55.537	
Nagelkerke's pseudo R^2	0.375	

Note: N = 62; standard error in parentheses; * $p < 0.1$; ** $p < 0.05$.

Nagelkerke's Pseudo R^2 is 0.375, which shows a moderate relationship between the independent and dependent variables.

We further explore the statistical significance of the relationship between greenfield entry mode and the interaction term between a resource acquisition strategy and business group affiliation following the procedure described in this chapter.[41] We converted the model into a dichotomous model (greenfield = 1; 0 = otherwise) and computed the algorithm of Norton, Wang and Ai.[42] This algorithm computes the correct marginal effect of a change in the predicted probability that y = 1 (entry mode = greenfield) for a change in the independent variables involved in the interaction. We also included the control variables.

[41] Parmigiani, 2007, p. 303.
[42] Norton, E., Wang, H. & Ai, Ch. (2004). Computing interaction effects and standard errors in logit and probit models. *The Stata Journal*, 4(2), 154–67, p. 161.

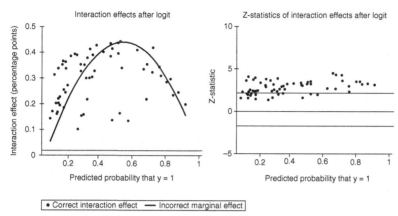

Figure 12.5 Greenfield entry mode, resource acquisition strategy and business group affiliation.

The empirical results confirm a statistically significant relationship between greenfield entry mode and the interaction term of resource acquisition strategy and business group affiliation. The x-axis of graph 5a in Figure 12.5 shows the predicted probabilities and the y-axis the interaction effect. Figure 12.5 also shows the marginal effect computed by the linear method and the corrected interaction effect computed by the applied algorithm.

Our evidence implies that multilatinas that follow a resources acquisition strategy and are affiliated to a business group are more likely to use greenfield entry mode than acquisition or joint venture. The selection of greenfield could be feasible in these cases owing to the longer timespan over which resource acquisition strategy develops. Also, business groups provide their affiliates with the tangible and intangible resources needed to internationalise. In our sample, the preference for greenfield is reinforced by the fact that multilatinas invest in their natural markets at short geographical distances,[43] environments in which context-specific resources share a substantial degree of similarity.[44] As a result of investment in proximate markets, there might

[43] Nocke, V. & Yeaple, S. (2008). An assignment theory of Foreign Direct Investment. *Review of Economic Studies*, 75, 529–57, p. 552.
[44] See, for example, Casanova, L. (2009a). From multilatinas to Global Latinas: The new Latin American multinationals (Compilation case studies). Interamerican Development Bank; and Casanova, L. (2009b). *Global Latinas: Latin America's emerging multinationals*. Palgrave Macmillan.

not be radical differences in the characteristics of the resources that firms or their business groups control at home and the resources that multilatinas can acquire abroad.[45]

If they have the time and the resources, multilatinas might actually prefer to spend time and effort building a new set of tangible and/or intangible assets in the host country instead of buying them. Acquisition means that multilatinas frequently have to buy more resources than they require. This makes internal development more attractive than buying or sharing resources with partners abroad. Internal development assures that firms' resources fit their own needs perfectly. This is especially relevant when a greenfield investment is an extension of a previous entry in the same market. In our sample, the FDI 72% of the companies were undertaking was reinvestment in the same country. Internal development of resources also allows firms to consolidate and optimise the investments associated with their international strategies.

Figure 12.6 shows a detailed graphical analysis of entry modes for multilatinas following a resource acquisition strategy of internationalisation. Graph 6a implies that an increasing reliance on resource acquisition reduces the likelihood that multilatinas owned by business groups will opt for acquisition as an entry mode. At the same time, increasing reliance on resource acquisition increases the likelihood that stand-alone firms will enter through acquisitions. Stand-alone firms have fewer restrictions and fewer opportunities to create synergies across foreign markets than firms affiliated to business groups. The strategic decisions about internationalisation made by stand-alone multilatinas are not under the control of a higher-order entity that shapes the decision-making process, but neither can they rely on a large pool of internal resources. As graph 6b in Figure 12.6 shows, the more focused on a resource acquisition strategy stand-alone multilatinas become, the less likely they are to use a greenfield entry mode. For firms affiliated to business groups, increased focus on resource acquisition is positively related to an increase in the likelihood of using greenfield entry mode. The absence of economies of scope or synergies that characterise stand-alone multilatinas could explain why this relationship is reversed in their case. Finally, graph 6d illustrates changes

[45] Lee, G. & Lieberman, M. (2010). Acquisition vs. Internal development as modes of market entry. *Strategic Management Journal*, 31, 140–58, p.145.

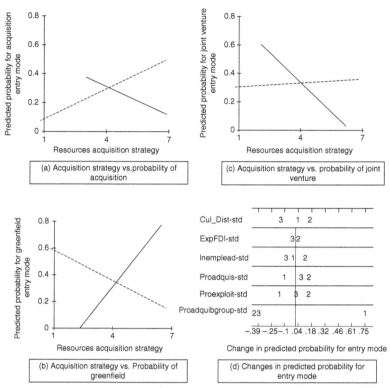

Figure 12.6 Graphical analysis of the MLM estimation for entry mode and belonging to a business group (resource acquisition strategy, full sample).

in the likelihood of choosing a specific entry mode if the interaction of a resource acquisition strategy and business group affiliation changes by one standard deviation. The graph shows that in this case the likelihood of choosing a greenfield entry mode increases by 75%, the likelihood of choosing acquisition diminishes by 39% and the likelihood of choosing joint venture diminishes by 38%.

In sum, there seems to be a pattern of internationalisation of multilatinas that is shaped by the nature of their organisational assets as well as the conditions of the home and host countries' institutional environment. This pattern is consistent with ideas and predictions offered by the existing literature on international business but it has never been characterised as fully as we have done in this book. Chapter 13 examines the lessons that emerge from the careful data analysis presented so far.

13 | Multilatinas – strategies for internationalisation

VENETA ANDONOVA AND MAURICIO
LOSADA-OTÁLORA

The natures of the resources that make multilatinas successful at home affect the approach these companies follow in their internationalisation strategies. The fact that multilatinas come from institutionally uncertain environments affects their behaviour abroad.

Multilatinas and resource exploitation strategy

Multilatinas that compete on the basis of their technological resources invest abroad to exploit those resources when managers perceive high institutional uncertainty at home. In particular, multilatinas that have advanced production and R&D technologies at home and perceive high risks of imitation, governmental intervention in prices and threats to ownership rights invest abroad to exploit the technologies that have been successful at home. In this way these multilatinas use their technological resources abroad to create similar advantages to those that they had at home and diversify the risk related to domestic institutional uncertainty.

For example, economic and political uncertainty led many Brazilian companies to increase their investments abroad during the early 2000s.[1] One of these firms was Marcopolo, the bus body builder, which opened high added value operations in several locations around the world, including China and India. The purpose of these investments was to compensate for the loss of competitiveness of the Brazilian economy and the associated threats of political and electoral crises.[2]

---

[1] ECLAC. (2006). *Foreign investment in Latin America and the Caribbean 2005*. Santiago, Chile: United Nations Publications, p. 73.
[2] Cardim de Carvalho, F. & Pires de Souza, F. (2011). Brazil in the 2000's: Financial regulation and macroeconomic stability, available at www.itf .org.ar/pdf/documentos/75–2011.pdf.

236

Investments in foreign markets allowed Marcopolo to exploit its technological knowledge by building new production facilities, gaining access to new markets while increasing its size.[3]

The transfer of technological resources abroad can create advantages because these resources are highly redeployable and fungible across markets.[4] Firms that use their technological resources to create market advantages in one specific Latin American country can use the same resources abroad to obtain similar market advantages.[5] The resource exploitation strategy of internationalisation has at least two advantages for multilatinas. First, having redeployable resources means the time required to install operations in foreign markets is reduced, as firms have experience of using a specific combination of technological resources to support their main competitive advantage.[6] Replication reduces the cost of learning about what does and does not work. Second, multilatinas that compete on the basis of highly standardised production processes can improve their efficiency by investing abroad in a similar or related business activity.[7] Our data indicate that institutional uncertainty at home correlates with a resource exploitation internationalisation strategy, but that multilatinas also internationalise in environments that have substantial institutional uncertainty. Although these host countries cannot necessarily assure better protection of technological resources, they do allow for risk diversification and offer opportunities to create advantage based on increased efficiency, scale or market structure.

Multilatinas that rely on endowed resources, like abundant labour and access to natural resources, share some similarities with companies that

---

[3] Fleury, A. & Fleury. M. T. (2011). *Brazilian multinationals: Competences for internationalization.* Cambridge University Press, p.383.

[4] Anand, J. & Delios, D. (1997b). Location specificity and the transferability of downstream assets to foreign subsidiaries. *Journal of International Business Studies*, 28(3), 579–603.

[5] Cuervo-Cazurra, A. & Genc, M. (2008). Transforming disadvantages into advantages: Developing-country MNEs in the least developed countries. *Journal of International Business Studies*, 39, 957–79.

[6] Szulansky, G. & Jensen, P. (2009). Growing through copying: The negative consequences of innovation on franchise network growth. *Research Policy*, 37, 1732–41, p. 1740.

[7] Dunning, J. H, Kim C. & Park D. (2008). Old wine in new bottles: A comparison of emerging-market TNCs today and developed-country TNCs thirty years ago. In K. Sauvant (ed.). *The rise of transnational corporations from emerging markets: Threat or opportunity?* Edward Elgar.

rely on technological resources in their approach to internationalisation. For one thing, both types of resources are fungible. Our evidence suggests that the combination of advantages based on endowed resources and institutional uncertainty at home creates incentives for multilatinas to invest abroad. Competitive advantage built on endowed resources can be very sensitive to aspects of institutional uncertainty, such as price controls, protection of property or usage rights. For instance, the regulation of the labour market can affect dramatically the operational costs of companies and force firms to internationalise to compensate for the reduction of their advantages at home.[8] Similarly, the substantial cash flow that can be generated by some natural resources (e.g. oil and gas) could make firms that exploit these resources the target of government intervention in countries where the rules of the game are not clearly established or stable.[9] Institutional uncertainty at home forces companies that compete on the basis of endowed resources to relocate some of their operations in foreign countries.[10]

Strategic decisions of resource exploiters

Market choice

Our evidence indicates that companies that exploit their technological or endowed resources abroad prefer to invest in countries with significant institutional uncertainty rather than countries with low institutional uncertainty. This finding suggests that the exploitation strategy of multilatinas relies heavily on risk normalisation through market diversification. By investing abroad multilatinas balance the risk of imitation, intervention in prices and changes in property rights regulation at home. The market choice also fits the aim of these firms to find new markets in which they can redeploy key resources and competences from home. Multilatinas know how to manage their

---

[8] See, for example, Yamamura, E., Sonobe, T. & Otsuka, K. (2003). Human capital, cluster formation, and international relocation: The case of the garment industry in Japan, 1968–98. *Journal of Economic Geography*, 3, 37–56, p. 45; and Witt, M. & Lewin, A. (2007). Outward foreign direct investment as escape response to home country institutional constraints. *Journal of International Business Studies*, 34, 579–94.

[9] Sinnott, A., Nash, J. & de la Torre, A. (2010). *Natural resources in Latin America and the Caribbean: Beyond booms and busts?* The World Bank.

[10] Lypsey, R. E. (2004). Home and host country effects of foreign direct investment. In R. Baldwin and A. Winters (eds). *Challenges to globalization*, (pp. 333–82), University of Chicago Press, p. 336.

operations in markets with high levels of institutional uncertainty. For instance, multilatinas can use non-market resources to tackle the uncertainty in these environments and diminish threats to their sources of advantage.[11] The evidence also suggests that multilatinas are entering markets that are neither completely open nor completely developed.[12] Institutional knowledge and business experience can still be key advantages in these host countries.[13] In fact, the evidence shows that the host markets of multilatinas are mainly other Latin American countries (56% of the sample). Latin American markets are natural markets for Latin American firms because home and host countries are at a relatively short distance, but in many cases they also share language, religion and a colonial history. Investments in natural markets diminish the risk of a misfit between multilatinas' resources and host market conditions. For example, the replication on large scale of the prepay cards business across Latin American countries has been one of the keys of the success of América Móvil.

Speed of investment

The evidence suggests that multilatinas that go abroad to exploit their resources do so rapidly. This result is consistent with previous research claiming that emerging multinationals internationalise fast.[14] For multilatinas that follow a resource exploitation strategy, the redeployability of resources facilitates the investment process, which can also be accelerated by firms' prior knowledge of the host market. In some cases investment abroad is simply a matter of increasing resource commitment in markets already receiving exports or previous rounds of foreign direct investment (FDI).[15] The nature of their

---

[11] Arruda, M. (1997) Ethic business in Latin America. *Journal of Business Ethics*, 16(14), 1597–603.

[12] Franco, A. & De Lombaerde, Ph. (2003). Latin American multinationals: A historical and theoretical approach. *Global Economic Review: Perspectives on East Asian Economies and Industries*, 32(1), 81–102, p. 96.

[13] Casanova, L. (2009b). *Global Latinas: Latin America's emerging multinationals*. Palgrave Macmillan.

[14] Bonaglia, F., Goldstein, A. & Mathews, J. A. (2007). Accelerated internationalization by emerging markets' multinationals: The case of the white goods sector. *Journal of World Business*, 42, 369–83.

[15] See, for example, Franco & De Lombaerde, 2003; and Johanson, J. & Vahlne, J.-E. (1977). The internationalization process of the firm: A model of

assets, together with proximity along several dimensions (e.g. physical distance, language, religion, culture), significantly reduces the amount of time that firms require to operate abroad and accelerates the investment process.

Entry mode

Multilatinas that follow a strategy of resource exploitation choose their natural markets, proceed rapidly with investment and select an entry mode that provides a consistent advantage, given the redeployability of resources. Greenfield investment is an opportunity to create a new organisation that can exploit available resources;[16] however, greenfield takes considerable time to gain market, size and efficiency.[17] Joint ventures, on the other hand, can allow multilatinas speed up the internationalisation; however, this entry mode involves sharing advanced resources with partners[18] and frequently generates difficulties owing to the asymmetry of the participants' objectives.[19] Our empirical evidence suggests that acquisition is the preferred entry mode to reach new markets rapidly while exploiting resources. Beyond meeting the requirement for speed, acquisition gives multilatinas sufficient control over their valuable technological resources, avoiding their transfer to real or potential competitors. Our data show that multilatinas looking to exploit their R&D and production technology abroad prefer acquisitions. It is easier to exploit resources abroad by acquiring an existing company with a knowledgeable workforce and good connections in the local market, than to set up a new subsidiary from zero.[20]

knowledge development and increasing foreign market commitments. *Journal of International Business Studies*, 8(1), 23–32.

[16] Meyer, K. E. & Estrin, S. (2001). Brownfield entry in emerging markets. *Journal of International Business Studies*, 32(3), 575–84, p. 576.

[17] Demirbag, M., Tatoglu, E. & Glaister, K. (2008). Factors affecting perceptions of the choice between acquisition and greenfield entry: The case of Western FDI in an emerging market. *Management International Review*, 48(1), 5–38.

[18] Demirbag, M., Tatoglu, E. & Glaister, K. (2009). Equity-based entry modes of emerging country multinationals: Lessons from Turkey. *Journal of World Business*, 44, 445–62, p. 450.

[19] Bartlett, C. A. & Ghoshal, S. (2000). Going global: Lessons from late movers. *Harvard Business Review*, 78(2), 132–42.

[20] Harzing, A.-W. (2002) Acquisitions versus greenfield investments: International strategy and management of entry modes. *Strategic Management Journal*, 23, 211–27, p. 213.

Moreover, starting a new wholly owned (greenfield) operation abroad requires establishing a net of relationships with several new key stakeholders and damaging the industry attractiveness by adding one more competitor.

Multilatinas and resource acquisition strategy

In the case of multilatinas that build their competitive advantage by relying on context-specific resources, institutional uncertainty at home does not appear to shape their internationalisation strategy. However, reliance on created context-specific resources, such as brands, is positively associated with a resource acquisition strategy. This finding suggests that regardless of institutional strengths or weaknesses at home, multilatinas that compete based on created context-specific resources show a strong trend towards a resource acquisition strategy when they invest in foreign markets.

The relationship between created context-specific resources and resource acquisition strategy is highlighted by the fact that much of the value of these resources is limited to the context in which they were developed.[21] For example, brands are difficult assets to transfer across markets because they are highly intangible.[22] Also, brands are often tied to the routines, systems and cultures of specific firms, which increase the difficulty of transferring them across countries.[23] Similarly, the entrenched nature of business networks makes them hard to transfer across countries.

The non-transferable nature of context-specific resources obliges multilatinas that use them as sources of advantage to acquire or build valuable intangible assets abroad, even if they invest in their natural markets.[24] In these cases, companies invest abroad to strengthen

---

[21] Anand & Delios, 1997b.

[22] Meyer, K. E., Estrin, S., Bhaumik, S. K. & Peng, M. W. (2009). Institutions, resources, and entry strategies in emerging economies. *Strategic Management Journal*, 30, 61–80.

[23] Capron, L. & Hulland, J. (1999). Redeployment of brands, sales forces, and general marketing management expertise following horizontal acquisitions: A resource based view. *Journal of Marketing*, 63, 41–54, p. 43.

[24] Chitoor, R., Sarkar, M., Ray, S. & Aulakh, P. (2009). Third-world copycats to emerging multinationals: Institutional changes and organizational

their ownership advantages and enable them to compete globally. For instance, in 2011 Mexican Grupo Bimbo acquired Sara Lee Corporation Spain and Portugal to access the market knowledge, distribution networks and brands controlled by its target firm on the Iberian Peninsula and so strengthen its international position.

Strategic decisions of resource acquirers

Market choice

Our evidence shows that a resource acquisition strategy is positively related to the selection of countries with high institutional uncertainty. Multilatinas that acquire resources abroad tend to invest close to their home country and in countries with which they trade or have ethnic and cultural ties. In this respect the behaviour of multilatinas with a resource acquisition strategy is similar to the behaviour of those that invest abroad to exploit their resources. In both cases the preference for developing host countries can be partly explained by the embeddedness of the resources and routines in the cultural and political structure of the selected markets.[25] By selecting neighbouring countries, multilatinas avoid higher costs of adapting to their economic, political or cultural realities, a phenomenon that has a long history. In the 1980s, 90% of the investment made by Argentine companies abroad was in Latin America, especially Brazil, Peru and Uruguay.[26] Similarly, 97% of Chilean FDI went to Latin America between 1990 and 1998.[27] Forty-seven per cent of all mergers and acquisitions concluded by Latin American companies in 2010 took place in a country in the region.[28] Apparently, familiarity complements previous experiences of doing business in a proximate market and helps multilatinas

transformation in the Indian pharmaceutical industry. *Organization Science*, 20(1), 187–205, p. 190.

[25] Henisz, W. & Delios, A. (2004). Information or influence? The benefits of experience for managing political uncertainty. *Strategic Organization*, 2(4), 389–421, p. 389.

[26] Agarwal, J. (1984). Intra-LDCs foreign direct investment: A comparative analysis of third world multinationals. Kiel Working Papers, No. 198.

[27] Del Sol, P. (2010). Chilean regional strategies in response to economic liberalization. *Universia Business Review*, 112–31, p. 119.

[28] ECLAC. (2011). *Foreign Investment in Latin America and the Caribbean 2010*. United Nations Publications.

overcome the liability of foreignness.[29] Multilatinas are also able to exploit the institutional convergence between countries of the Latin American region[30] to exploit and acquire resources to compete successfully in the global market.

Speed of investment

Our results suggest that there is a negative and significant relationship between the strategy of resource acquisition and the speed of FDI. Multilatinas that rely on created context-specific resources spend a long of time making decisions about investment after identifying an opportunity to invest abroad. Although the literature on strategy suggests that moving fast and first brings advantages for firms (e.g. a positive attitude from consumers of pioneering brands[31]), multilatinas are not in a hurry. On the global stage, multilatinas are late movers. As a consequence, it is very difficult for these firms to gain first-mover advantages. However, some last-mover advantages might be available.[32] These exist, for example, in the case of the merger and acquisition waves of privately held Colombian companies.[33] There are at least three reasons for multilatinas to be patient. First, they can choose to invest resources, especially time, in identifying high-value market segments in host countries. Second, investment delays could be used by Latin American latecomers to develop an appropriate benchmark strategy by observing the market leaders in the selected market. Third, delaying investment decisions could enable firms to learn about their

[29] Barkema, H. & Vermeulen, F. (1998). International expansion through start-up or acquisition: A learning perspective. *Academy of Management Journal*, 41(1), 7–26.

[30] Ross, J. (2012). Institutional and policy convergence with growth divergence in Latin America. CEPAL, 139.

[31] See, for example, Kardes, F., Kalyanaram, G., Chandrashekaran, M. & Dornoff, R. (1993). Brand retrieval, consideration set composition, consumer choice, and the pioneering advantage. *Journal of Consumer Research*, 20(1), 62–75; and Alpert, F. & Kamins, M. (1995). An empirical investigation of consumer memory, attitude, and perceptions towards pioneer and follower brands. *Journal of Marketing*, 59, 34–45.

[32] Bartlett, C. A. & Ghoshal, S. (2000). Going global: Lessons from late movers. *Harvard Business Review*, 78(2), 132–42.

[33] Andonova, V., Rodriguez, Y. and Sanchez, I. (2013). When waiting is strategic: Evidence from Colombian M&As 1995–2008. *Journal of Business Research*, 66(10), 1736–42.

competitors' operations and resolve many of the information asymmetries that characterise the host environment.

Entry mode

Although theoretically the acquisition entry mode could ensure access to context-specific resources, the relationship between resource acquisition strategy and acquisition entry mode is more complex. There is not a systematic preference for a single type of entry mode in our sample. More importantly, business groups are pervasive organisational forms in contexts with high institutional uncertainty and their role is significant. First, business groups offer affiliated firms enough tangible and intangible resources to act as internal markets for them. Second, entering host countries where the business group has previous investments puts within the reach of the entering multilatina a set of tangible and intangible assets that could be used to operate in the host country. When parent or related firms have previously invested in a specific country, a new entrant has available resources (i.e. reputation, experience and market knowledge) that can be used to operate in the host market. Under these circumstances, an affiliated firm could enter easily via a greenfield project making use of their own resources and using the resources available to the business group.

Institutions, resources and the decision to internationalise

The empirical evidence presented here shows that executives in multilatinas perceive institutional uncertainty as a substantial problem and that their companies' internationalisation strategies are affected by it.

First, institutional uncertainty erodes the ability of some resources to create market advantages and is positively related to internationalisation. This is the case for R&D, advanced production technologies and endowed resources that are vulnerable to government interventions like price controls or governments' inability to protect property rights. In many emerging markets, advantages gained from the control of natural resources that create high cash flows can be lost to regimes that expropriate them to gain control of financial sources. Similarly, institutional and political upheavals in emerging markets may create economic turbulence that threatens firms' advantages, especially when these are based on the cost of wages or capital (e.g. through minimum wages or interest rates).

Second, institutional uncertainty facilitates the development of specialised resources that may create advantages during the internationalisation process. Uncertain institutional environments force businesses to learn how to manage hostile external conditions. In doing so, managers develop a deep understanding of the institutional environment, which they use to develop specialised non-market resources. The non-market resources common among multilatinas at home are the ability to bargain with local authorities and a deep understanding of how use favours and bribery for business purposes. Their exploitation abroad is eased by the process of institutional convergence of Latin American countries. These non-market resources correlate positively with a higher level of institutional uncertainty in the host markets, suggesting that they might facilitate internationalisation in such environments.

Third, a special case of resource exploitation occurs when firms deploy abroad their knowledge of the institutional environment at home to face threats stemming from institutional uncertainty in different host markets. Like investments based on technological or endowed resources, the logic behind this strategy is using the same kinds of resources exploited at home to become successful abroad. Here the technological resource is dealing with institutional uncertainty.

Fourth, in the case of context-specific created resources, the interaction between these resources and the level of institutional uncertainty at home is not related to the decision of multilatinas to invest abroad. This situation occurs when firms build their competitive advantage at home by relying on brands, supply networks and managerial knowledge. In these cases the internationalisation process consists of procuring context-specific resources in the host markets without much consideration of drivers of institutional uncertainty at home.

Institutions, resources and strategic decisions

The evidence shows that multilatinas follow clear patterns of FDI. First, multilatinas appear to defy the institutional uncertainty in host markets by transferring valuable technological resources and accompanying business practices to them. The use of non-market resources is clearly associated with a choice of a host market with a higher level of institutional uncertainty. The executives of multilatinas identify the use of favours, bargaining abilities and bribery as mechanisms to obtain favourable conditions in the host markets in which they choose to operate.

In the case of firms that follow a resource acquisition strategy, the strategic market choice decision accords with previous research. In this case, multilatinas invest in countries with a level of institutional development similar to their home markets. The rationale behind this choice is to take advantage of their existing knowledge of volatile institutional environments.

Additionally, multilatinas that rely on exploiting their technological resources abroad internationalise rapidly through acquisition. This finding contradicts previous claims in the literature that suggest that firms use greenfield entry to exploit their valuable resources and avoid paying premium prices for established firms. For multilatinas, host market acquisitions provide the right balance of control and speed of internationalisation.

The entry mode of multilatinas that follow a resource acquisition strategy depends on being part of a business group. Firms that are affiliated to a business group enter foreign markets via greenfield, taking advantage of the resources controlled by the group. Stand-alone firms, on the other hand, rely on acquisition. Finally, contrary to firms that invest rapidly to exploit their resources, firms that acquire resources abroad invest slowly, which is consistent with the idea that multilatinas are looking for last-mover advantages in their foreign markets.

Overall, the behaviour patterns of multilatinas indicate that there is no need for new theories to understand their internationalisation decisions. The coherence of the process of internationalisation followed by multilatinas, as the results in the preceeding chapters show, suggests that a critical new perspective on the process should focus on institutional uncertainty at home and the vulnerability of firms' competitive advantage to its effects. These insights suggest that contextualising existing theories by adding details to the analysed context could contribute to building more useful models and knowledge about the internationalisation of emerging multinationals.

Future research

Our research is based on cross-sectional data that do not allow longitudinal analysis of the relation between institutions and resources.

Overcoming this limitation in future research is important because institutions tend to be stable and their effects on internationalisation can span long periods of time. Second, because of the lack of a complete and well-defined population, we used a non-probabilistic sample of multilatinas. Although our sampling method could limit the generalisation of our findings, we do not have theoretical or empirical evidence to suppose that unidentified firms are very different from firms included in the study, in terms of the key variables used in our research. Future efforts could increase the sample size or even identify all multilatinas.

Third, because of sample size we treated all multilatinas as a unified body of companies. However, within the Latin American region there are subtle variations within institutional frameworks and firms' resource endowments. Future research could compare Latin American sub-regions around the variables included in this study. For instance, Brazilian firms could be directly compared to Mexican firms and to firms from other countries in the region, for example Peru, of which we have only two in our sample. This would help academic analysts and practitioners gain more specific knowledge about the behaviour of multinationals in specific countries.

We were also unable to control for several variables because of the limitation of our sample. For example, we did not control for the ownership structure of multilatinas (e.g. family versus non-family business), which could influence strategy and decision-making during internationalisation.[34] Similarly, we did not control for the intensity of competition at home[35] or the effect of multilatinas' financial resources on their internationalisation process. The literature shows that this variable is important because managers are predisposed to expand their markets when they have slack financial resources or to defer investment if they do not have enough financial resources

---

[34] See, for example, Bhaumik, S. K., Driffield, N. & Pal, S. (2010). Does ownership structure of emerging-market firms affect their outward FDI? The case of the Indian automotive and pharmaceutical sectors. *Journal of International Business Studies*, 41, 437–50; and Douma, S., George, R. & Kabir, R. (2006). Foreign and domestic ownership, business groups, and firm performance: Evidence from a large emerging market. *Strategic Management Journal*, 27(7), 637–57.

[35] Deng, P. (2004). Outward investment by Chinese MNCs: Motivations and implications. *Business Horizons*, 47(3), 8–16.

to acquire or exploit opportunities in foreign markets.[36] Likewise, we did not control for managers' individual characteristics. For example, empirical evidence suggests that managers who have developed a global mindset are better equipped to deal with the complexity of internationalisation created by multiple organisational environments, structural indeterminacy and cultural heterogeneity.[37] This characteristic could affect, for example, speed of investment, market choice or the strategy followed by multilatinas abroad. Finally, we did not control for economic activity or industry because the use of categorical variables is not recommended with PLS-SEM. However, we recognise that institutional uncertainty could affect service and manufacturing firms in different ways. Future research could explore and extend our research agenda in all these directions. As a first step in this direction, Part IV of this book contains a selection of chapters that expand our understanding of multilatinas and enrich the discussion presented in the chapters in Part III.

---

[36] Tseng, Ch., Tansuhaj, P., Hallagan, W. & McCullough, J. (2007). Effects of firm resources on growth in multinationality. *Journal of International Business Studies*, 38, 961–74.

[37] Levy, O., Beechler, S., Taylor, S. & Boyacigiller, N. A. (2007). What we talk about when we talk about 'global mindset': Managerial cognition in multinational corporations. *Journal of International Business Studies*, 38, 231–58.

An introductory note by Veneta Andonova

Part IV of this book is intended to span the boundaries of the framework outlined in the preceding chapters. Four ideas appear to be especially promising: managing relationships with key political stakeholders in respect of social and ethical standards in an era of increasing technological connectivity and information transparency; engaging in shared social value creation; participating in human capital development and labour market sophistication; and boosting local innovation and knowledge creation by attending to both the highest aspirations and basic needs of prospective internationalisation champions.

Seven leading experts and researchers share their views and make recommendations in each of these areas.

In Chapter 14 Lourdes Casanova and Julian Kassum take a close look at emerging multinational companies in Brazil. As one of the most visible aspects of a country's economic power, Brazilian multilatinas are self-made players that historically have received very little government support of the kind that Spanish or Chinese multinationals have enjoyed. Moreover, weaknesses in the Brazilian political system are taking a high toll on the most internationalised Brazilian companies and contributing directly to the weakening of the country's economy. In an era of increased technological connectivity that facilitates transparency, how much government help should multilatinas get in the light of their contribution to the national economy and country brand recognition, given the institutional uncertainty and political corruption scandals that are very destructive and possibly on the rise? The authors argue for more government support for Brazilian multilatinas as they currently bear the full burden of political uncertainty and benefit from none of the support programmes devised for successful multinational companies in other developing countries. New ethical standards for both the political and business classes are needed to boost the competitiveness of the best and most internationalised Brazilian companies.

In Chapter 15, Jorge Ramírez-Vallejo and Ernesto Cuéllar-Urbano focus on the challenges in emerging countries' environments to show how the concept of shared value can help multilatinas turn challenges into business opportunities. Shared value is understood as building new business models by taking advantage of social, environmental and economic opportunities. It implies a significant change in firm behaviour, in that social and environmental problems become opportunities of which companies can take advantage. The authors suggest multiple directions for multilatinas to build competitive advantage as they are forced to adopt novel business models to tackle significant social, environmental and economic challenges in both their home and host markets. The range of issues includes reformulating food products to help fight child malnourishment and mortality; efficient resource use and supporting sustainable initiatives for natural resources; and facilitating the acquisition of construction materials and training for self-builders. Shared value is presented as a natural opportunity to upgrade the competitiveness of multilatinas during the internationalisation process and facilitate embeddedness within the local context. In shared value, multilatinas find not only an additional driver of their competitive advantage but frequently their very reason to exist.

In Chapter 16 Anabella Davila explores the challenges that underdeveloped institutions and labour markets in Latin America present to multilatinas as they restrict the pool of available human capital and impose limitations on companies' competitiveness. Related to the concept of shared value, successful human resource practices in multilatinas are associated with meeting the needs of a broader group of stakeholders associated with employees. Illustrated by the case of ALFA, a highly diversified Mexican conglomerate, this chapter highlights how the company supports the human development not only of its workers but also of their families and communities across the many Latin American countries in which ALFA is present. This example of an HR management system demonstrates a remarkable fit with the institutional voids of local labour markets and how they can be turned into a sustainable competitive advantage.

In Chapter 17 Fernanda Ribeiro Cahen and Moacir Miranda de Oliveira Jr look into the export-orientation of new high-tech ventures in Brazil and confirm that qualified human capital represents a critical bottleneck for the internationalisation process of technology-intensive companies that aspire to become international. Comparing the behaviour of new high-tech ventures with and without export activity, the authors find that the broader institutional barriers and organisational limitations, both of which are discussed extensively in this book, are the most important deterrents to internationalisation, followed by inadequate human resources. Surprisingly, basic skills such as proficiency in English emerge as a key concern for undertaking internationalisation efforts even among the new high-tech ventures in Brazil.

The competitiveness of multilatinas is inseparable from the progress of Latin American societies and the constraints and opportunities these economies offer. Building human capital emerges as one of the most significant challenges along the way. Both the state capacity to address existing shortcomings in the political, social and economic arenas and companies' abilities to deal with environmental pressures shape the competitiveness of multilatinas. The following chapters advance some of the key questions and directions for the development for multilatinas, which are increasingly compared with emerging multinationals from other regions and symbolise the economic prowess and attractiveness of a region that is home to more than 500 million people.

14 | *Are Brazilian multinationals competitive enough?*

LOURDES CASANOVA AND
JULIAN KASSUM

This chapter examines Brazil's multinational companies, which constitute one of the most visible aspects of a country's economic power. While in China and in other emerging markets like South Korea the local private sector has grown with the economy, we argue that in Brazil the expansion of local firms has been much more limited. In the face of the current economic crisis, and unless there is a major turnaround, Brazilian companies will become easy targets for international investors from countries with hard currencies. The current turmoil in the Brazilian political system is taking a high toll on the global Brazilian companies and contributing to the weakening of the country's economy.

Are Brazilian companies truly multinational?

Because of the large size of their domestic market and the immediate availability of natural resources at home, Brazilian executives often claim to have had little incentive to expand their activities globally.

The boom in outward investment from 2002 to 2009 and subsequent decline (see Figure 14.4) marked an important shift in Brazil's corporate attitude towards global markets. In just a few years, meatpackers JBS and Marfrig propelled the country to a dominant force in the global beef industry. In 2016, the jet manufacturer Embraer continues to be cited as a prominent example of an emerging market company that has taken the lead in a technology-intensive sector. Brazilian fashion

This chapter draws on previous published work: Casanova, L. & Kassum, J. (2013b). *Brazilian emerging multinationals, in search of a second wind.* INSEAD. Working papers. 2013. http://research.insead.edu/2013/05/CasanovaKassum_30.html http://ssrn.com/abstract=2712662; Casanova, L. & Kassum, J. (2014). *The political economy of an emerging global power: In search of the Brazil Dream.* Palgrave Macmillan.

and consumer brands have started to spread internationally, such as Havaianas, whose flip-flops make a fashion statement worldwide.

Which are the most active Brazilian players in the global market and how 'multi-national' are they? What are their motives for expanding globally, and what are the remaining challenges they need to overcome in order to keep conquering new markets? The answer to these questions requires a deep structural and historical analysis of Brazilian multilatinas' performance in the past few years. We begin by presenting a panorama of the current standing of Brazil's multinational companies based on the most recent corporate rankings. We then look at the main driving forces behind their globalisation, as well as the various obstacles they face on the long road to becoming world-class players or consolidating their position as such. In this, the role of the Brazilian government cannot be ignored.

Why is it important for a country to have multinational companies? While small and medium-sized enterprises constitute the backbone of any economy and are responsible for creating jobs, the presence of large companies that operate globally provides an invaluable source of research, growth, knowledge and innovation for their home countries. Not only do multinational companies bring significant tax revenues and create jobs, they also help local suppliers connect with global production chains and contribute to improving their 'country brand', which ultimately benefits all sectors of the economy.

Large companies also have the deep pockets needed to invest in research and development. Furthermore, a country's multinationals often represent one of the most visible aspects of its economic power. The active operations of Brazilian companies on a worldwide scale provide a source of economic leverage and prestige through which the country can acquire and wield power in international relations.

Are Brazilian multinationals big enough?

Brazil's companies lag behind other emerging multinationals

'It is time for Brazilian businessmen to abandon their fear of becoming multinational businessmen,' urged former Brazilian President Lula da Silva while addressing the Portuguese Industrial Association in 2003.[1]

---

[1] http://unctad.org/en/docs/webiteiia200416_en.pdf [Accessed: 6 July 2016].

Table 14.1 *Largest Latin American firms according to the* Fortune
Global 500 ranking (2016)

RANK 2016	Corporations	Countries	2015 revenue ($ billions)	% change from 2014
58	Petrobras	Brazil	97.3	(32.3)
98	Pemex	Mexico	73.5	(38.3)
115	Banco do Brasil	Brazil	67.1	(5.8)
154	América Móvil	Mexico	56.4	(11.6)
159	Itaú Unibanco Holding	Brazil	55.1	(28.4)
185	JBS	Brazil	48.9	(4.5)
209	Banco Bradesco	Brazil	43.7	(21.4)
417	Vale	Brazil	25.6	(31.8)
474	Ultrapar Holdings	Brazil	22.7	(21.1)

Source: Authors, based on data from *Fortune* Global 500 (2016).

Sixteen years later, looking at the current standing of Brazilian firms
in the annual *Fortune* Global 500 ranking, Lula's vision seems not to
have been fulfilled. On the one hand, Brazil has made an important
breakthrough with a total of seven firms among the world's top 500
companies by revenues in the *Fortune* Global 500, compared to only
three in 2005. It is well ahead of Mexico (two firms), stands equal to
India (seven firms) and stands well below South Korea (fifteen firms).
Closer to home, Brazil outshines its Latin American neighbours with
countries such as Venezuela, Colombia and Chile failing to even make
it to the Global Fortune 500 in 2016 (see Table 14.1 and Figure 14.1).

On the other hand, Brazil's performance pales by comparison with
the spectacular incursion of Chinese firms, whose total number in the
Fortune Global 500 ranking increased six-fold between 2005 and
2016 to reach 103. When compared with other countries of similar
economic weight, Brazil also lags behind (see Figure 14.2). Brazil was
the world's seventh-largest economy in 2015, according to the World
Bank.[2] However, with seven companies among the 500 largest companies in the world, it ranks only fourteenth in terms of the total number
of companies ranked per country. With a nominal GDP 25% smaller

---

[2] The Brazilian real was one of the currencies that revaluated the most with
respect to the US$ in 2011–12 and Brazil's economy became at some point
during 2012 the sixth largest in the world in nominal GDP.

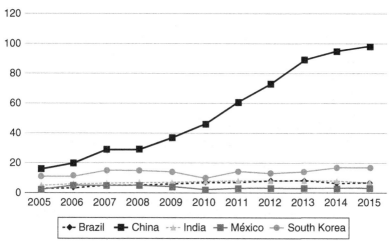

Figure 14.1 Year-on-year evolution of the number of companies listed in the annual *Fortune* Global 500 ranking (2016).
Source: Authors, based on data from *Fortune* Global 500 (2016).

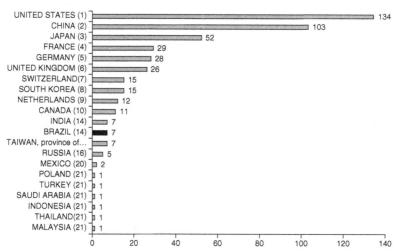

Figure 14.2 Number of companies listed in the *Fortune* Global 500 ranking (2016).
Source: Authors, based on data from *Fortune* Global 500 (2016 edition). http://money
.cnn.com/magazines/fortune/global500/2015/full_list/ [Accessed: 25 May 2016].

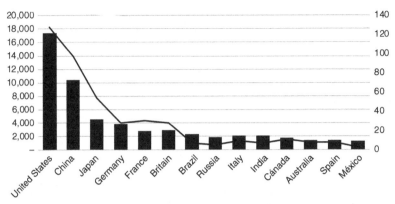

Figure 14.3 Nominal GDP and number of *Fortune* Global 500 per country.
Source: Casanova with data from World Bank and *Fortune* Global 500 (2016).

than that of Brazil, India is already on a par with the Latin American giant, with a total of seven companies in the ranking (Figure 14.3).

Not only does Brazil have a relatively small pool of large companies compared to other economies of similar size, but those companies tend to concentrate a disproportionately large share of revenues with respect to the 100 largest. Specifically, the 10 largest Brazilian companies accounted for 40% of the accumulated revenues of the country's top 100 firms. At the world level, the 10 largest companies accounted for only 25% of the top 100 corporate revenues (see Figure 14.4). In other words, the performance in global corporate rankings of a handful of very large firms, such as Petrobras and Vale, should not hide the relatively slighter presence of average-sized Brazilian multinational companies.

This concentration of power has been signalled in other studies. The Brazilian NGOs *Instituto Mais Democracia* and *Cooperativa EITA* have looked at the control of the 2,000 largest Brazilian companies. A study published in March 2013 confirmed that twelve corporations represented more than 50% of the total wealth generated by all listed companies.

The largest Brazilian firms are not the most global

The demographics of leading Brazilian companies broadly mirror the relative strengths of the Brazilian economy. Among the seven Brazilian firms listed in the *Fortune* Global 500 ranking, three are

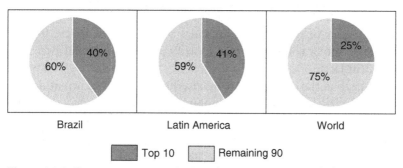

Brazil   Latin America   World

Top 10   Remaining 90

Figure 14.4 Corporate revenues in Brazil, Latin America and the world: 10 largest with respect to the 100 largest.
Source: Authors' based on data from Revista Exame, América Economía, *Fortune Global 500* (2015 editions).

financial institutions (Banco Itaú-Unibanco, Banco do Brasil and Banco Bradesco), two are from the extractive sector (Petrobras and Vale), one is a food processing company (JBS) and the latest entrant is a holding (Ultrapar). This make-up largely echoes Brazil's economic aspiration to become a regional financial centre, a natural resource powerhouse, a large-scale food exporter and a booming domestic consumer market.

As this chapter is going to print, many Brazilian companies are also under investigation in various political corruption and money launder-ing cases. Following allegations of fraud, the Dow Jones Sustainability World Index (DJSI World) decided to remove Petrobras from its pres-tigious index in March 2015, after the company had been a member for ten years. Petrobras is the biggest company in Latin America; it has been considered the best Latin American brand and an example to the world of combining shareholder value and societal interests. The upheaval began in 2014 when some of its employees participated in a corruption scandal known as *Operação Lava Jato* (Operation Car Wash), in which a group of high-profile individuals routed illegal money to Brazilian political parties and Petrobras employees via money-laundering companies. As a result, nearly forty Brazilian poli-ticians, including the leaders of both chambers, and business moguls have been jailed, including Odebrecht's CEO Marcelo Odebrecht and André Esteves, founder and leader of the Brazilian investment bank BTG Pactual, among many others. They all are under investiga-tion linked to 'suspicious' contracts worth US$22 billion with these 'Car Wash' companies. The allegations are that as much as 3% of

Petrobras's budget was diverted to finance political campaigns. The consequences of the Petrobras scandal continue to be severe for the company, the Brazilian economy, Brazil's political class and Brazilian society at large.

But beyond the corruption scandals, the cause of the current downturn in Brazil has been the economy's heavy reliance on commodities, Brazil's chief exports. Brazil has been hit hard by the plummeting prices of natural resources, such as oil and iron ore, which is Brazil's main export, coupled with lower demand from China owing to the economic slowdown there. China's economic power is sensed in Brazil, because China has become its main trade partner and in 2015 was its main investor. Whatever happens to the middle kingdom affects Latin America, especially countries like Brazil, Peru, Chile and Colombia, whose livelihoods depend on commodities. The Brazilian economy is in recession with projections of negative economic growth of –3.8% into 2016 after having contracted –3.6% in 2015, its worst crisis since the 1930s.

Corporate rankings come in many forms. Some evaluate companies on the basis of their revenues or sales, others on their market capitalisation. Whatever criteria are chosen, the Brazilian leader for a very long time was the semi-public energy giant Petrobras. Brazilian banks make up almost half of the country's large companies. While the current economic downturn is affecting most companies in the manufacturing and service sectors, the financial sector is thriving. With high interest rates at as much as 14.25% (and inflation of about 10%) and high levels of Brazilian government debt, the private Banco Itaú-Unibanco has returns on assets of about 25%, well greater than the world average, while another private bank, Banco Bradesco, continues to acquire the subsidiaries of major western banks that are leaving the country, such as HSBC.

Nevertheless, the examination of corporate rakings should come with an important caveat. Not all large companies qualify as multinational companies to the same extent. Some of the firms listed in the *Fortune* Global 500 ranking may be very large in terms of revenues and number of employees but have a limited presence in overseas markets. This is the case for several financial service providers and insurance institutions whose activities focus predominantly on their domestic markets. Therefore, for an accurate picture of the rise of Brazilian firms in the global marketplace – and of their capacity to

Table 14.2 *Ranking of Brazilian multinationals by transnationality index (TNI) (FDC, 2014)*

Position	Company	Index
1	Construtora Noberto Odebrecht	54.9%
2	Gerdau	54.7%
3	InterCement	53.9%
4	Stefanini	53.7%
5	Metalfrio	53%
6	Magnesita	52.7%
7	Marfrig	52.2%
8	JBS	49.9%
9	Artecola	39.7%
10	Ibope	39%

Note: The transnationality index (TNI) was developed by the United Nations Conference on Trade and Development (UNCTAD) and assesses the level of internationalisation of firms based on three indicators: percentage of revenues of foreign subsidiaries with respect to total revenues; percentage of foreign assets with respect to total assets; and percentage of foreign employees with respect to the total number of employees. To establish its ranking, FDC uses this index and focuses on corporations with 'physical presence abroad', using the following criteria: commercial offices, distribution centres, production and assembly unit, services, R&D with constant personnel abroad and banking agencies.

compete internationally – it is important to complement the analysis with rankings and indices that integrate the global footprint of firms in their overall evaluation.

In the latest available ranking of the most internationalised Brazilian companies published by the Brazilian business school Fundaçao Dom Cabral (FDC) in 2014, first place is held by the construction company Construtora Norberto Odebrecht, with an internationalisation index of 54.9% (see Table 14.2). CNO is followed closely by Gerdau (54.7%), the largest producer of long steel in the Americas with steel mills in fourteen countries. Third position is held by InterCement (53.9%). In fourth place is the software company Stefanini, which offers IT solutions and is present in thirty-two countries, followed by WEG (31) and Vale (27).

InterCement has the highest proportion of employees working abroad (65.6%), ahead of Marfrig (52.1%) and JBS (47.6%). We then find a mixture of large and medium-sized companies, such as the adhesive company Artecola from Rio Grande do Sul. For Artecola, as for many other companies from emerging markets, the international presence has been a 'natural hedge' against the volatility of the Brazilian market.

How do these results compare with the most internationalised companies in the world? According to the World Investment Report (2016) the British mining company Rio Tinto PLC is ranked the highest with 99.2%, followed by two Dutch companies, the telecoms Altice NV with 97.0% and the brewing company Heineken NV with 96.6%. Although classified officially as a Belgian company, the beverage company Anheuser-Busch InBev, is in fifth position (93.1%). This company grew from AMBEV S.A. and was originally a Brazilian company; its top management and main stakeholders are still Brazilian. The company represents a clear success story of Brazilian talent management, ambition, know-how and financial agility. As of 2016, Anheuser-Busch InBev was the biggest company in market capitalisation in the Brazilian stock exchange (Bovespa).

Brazilian companies have invested outside their natural markets

The years 2003–12 have become known as a golden decade for Brazil, during which many milestones were reached and 2006 marked a turning point. For the first time, total outflows of foreign direct investment (FDI) outweighed total inflows into Brazil, which themselves reached record levels in the mid-2000s. From 2000 to 2003, outward FDI from Brazil averaged less than US$1 billion a year. Over the four-year period 2004–08, this average jumped to nearly US$14 billion. Such prowess was largely seen as evidence of the take-off of Brazilian multinational companies and their increasingly active presence in global markets. Until 2009, Brazil had the largest stock of outward FDI from all emerging countries. Its FDI outflows started going down in 2009, most likely in response to the worldwide economic and financial crisis. Total outflows have been negative every year since then, with the exception of 2010, which saw a positive high, and 2011, the latter attributed to the repatriation of capital, mainly through intra-firm lending by foreign affiliates of Brazilian multinational enterprises (MNEs) to their parent firms (see Figure 14.4).

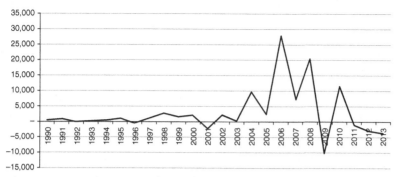

Figure 14.5 Brazilian outward FDI (flows), 1990–2015.
Source: Authors, based on data from http://unctadstat.unctad.org/EN/ using the latest data available at the time of writing this chapter.

What are the main destinations of Brazil's outward FDI? Numerous studies have highlighted the strong Latin American focus of Brazilian firms' international activities. Before expanding to industrialised or other emerging markets, Brazilian companies have traditionally begun by establishing operations in their natural markets, countries from their immediate geographical neighbourhood. This is a far cry, however, from saying that Brazilian companies dominate Latin American markets. For example, only a handful of Brazilian multinationals (e.g. Gerdau, Odebrecht, Samot) have established a major presence in Mexico, the second biggest economy on the continent. In the meantime, several Mexican companies (e.g. Grupo Carso, Telmex, América Móvil, Bimbo, Homex, Cinépolis) have made significant investments in Brazil. It is interesting to note that between 2005 and 2010 Mexico's FDI in Brazil represented US$4.7 billion, while over the same period Brazil invested only US$684 million in Mexico.[3] While Brazil is double the size of the Mexican economy, its investments in Mexico are only 15% of those of Mexico in Brazil.

Figure 14.5 compares outward FDI from the BRIC countries. In 2004, Russia's outflows were a bit higher than those of Brazil, which was in second place. Two years later, Russia and Brazil were at the

---

[3] ECLAC. (2015). Economic Commission for Latin America and the Caribbean (ECLAC). Foreign Direct Investment in the Latin America and the Caribbean, 2011, United Nations, Santiago, Chile. Available at http://repositorio.cepal.org/bitstream/handle/11362/38215/4/S1500534_en.pdf.

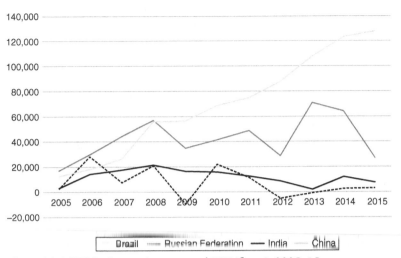

Figure 14.6 BRIC: Comparing outward FDI (flows), 2005–15.
Source: Authors, based on data from http://unctadstat.unctad.org/EN/ using the latest data available at the time of writing this chapter.

same leading position but the tide turned at that point and China took a leading position after the global financial crisis of 2008–09 while Brazil fell to last position, below India.

According to data from the Central Bank of Brazil and UNCTAD published in 2015 and referring to data from 2013 (see Figure 14.6), Europe was the main destination of Brazilian outward FDI, with 53% of the total figure, followed by the Americas, which represented 47% of all the stock. The past few years have witnessed a relative decline in outward FDI stock in Latin America and the Caribbean, coupled with expansion in Europe and the United States (Figure 14.7).

It is worth noting, however, that the top destinations of Brazilian FDI are jurisdictions in the Caribbean that are generally known as tax havens, such as the Cayman Islands (18%), the British Virgin Islands (10%) and the Bahamas (6%). Brazilian companies have also used some European countries, such as Austria (25%), the Netherlands (13%) and Luxembourg (6%), to settle subsidiaries or special purpose entities through which they channel their outward investments. This practice has been widely construed as a way for Brazilian firms to reduce their tax burden and bypass domestic regulations. As a consequence, the exact geographic distribution of Brazilian outward FDI is difficult to assess, since Brazilian companies often use intermediary

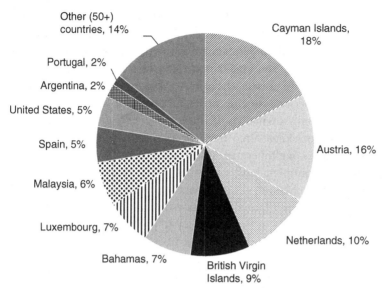

Figure 14.7 Brazil outward FDI (stock), 2014.
Note: This is the latest data available at the moment of writing this chapter.
Source: Authors based on data from http://unctadstat.unctad.org/EN/ using the latest data available at the time of writing this chapter.

vehicles located in deregulated jurisdictions to make their investments in third countries.

Leaving these and tax havens aside, the United States (10%) was the first destination of outward FDI stock from Brazil.

New markets, resources and technology: push factors for internationalisation

Why have Brazilian companies expanded their operations outside their home country, and what strengths and weaknesses they have displayed in doing so? This section looks at the trajectories of Brazilian companies and examine the main drivers and characteristics of their internationalisation.

From national champions to global players

To capture the particularities of Brazilian multinational companies, it is essential to understand the continent-wide context from which these companies have emerged. High tariffs, underdeveloped capital markets, inadequate levels of research and development, market domination by family-owned conglomerates with risk-averse cultures and a volatile political and economic climate have historically frustrated the emergence of globally oriented Latin American firms.[4] These factors, combined with periods of state protection, have fostered the growth of large-scale family-owned companies, which favoured expansion in their domestic markets, often through sector diversification, leading them to become conglomerates. When not family-controlled, companies from the continent have often been state-owned and based on primary resources like oil, gas and metals.

This state of affairs largely applies to the Brazilian context, with the added particularity of Brazil's policy to promote national champions, which prevailed until the economic liberalisation era in the 1990s. National champions can be described as state-backed firms protected from competition that benefit from government export subsidies, tax exemptions or favoured loans and are designated vehicles for national industrial policy objectives such as employment, economic growth and international prestige.[5] Brazil's policy of nurturing national champions is still deeply interwoven with its former broader economic policy of import substitution industrialisation during the 1960s and 1970s.

More than forty years later, many of yesterday's national champions feature among Brazil's most prominent global companies. During its long years as a state-owned enterprise (1969–94), the aircraft manufacturer Embraer was largely shielded from competition and developed a market niche in the supply of small jet planes for the civilian and military markets, in both Brazil and the region as a whole. Because of the conjunction of adverse internal and external factors, Embraer faced heavy losses and was privatised in 1994, with foreign ownership limited to 40%. The company's operations were rationalised and sales abroad boosted its growth. Today Embraer is the world's third-largest manufacturer of commercial aircraft, competing with the Canadian Bombardier, and has established operational units in the United States,

---

[4] Sinha, J. (2005) *Global champions from emerging markets.* McKinsey Quarterly. No 2. May 2005. Pages 27–35; Ramamurti, R. (2012). What is really different about emerging market multinationals? *Global Strategy Journal*, 2, 41–47.

[5] Casanova, L. (2009b). *Global Latinas: Latin America's emerging multinationals.* Palgrave Macmillan.

Portugal, France, Singapore and China.[6] The company is now looking to extend its presence in Africa's rising aviation sector.[7] Embraer is one of the few companies that is doing well despite the current economic downturn. The devaluation of the Brazilian real (R$), which lost 100% of its value in just three years and is at its lowest level since 2002, has worked in favour of exporting companies. Because of that, labour costs have become quite competitive and sales in dollars help the balance sheet.

Vale is another example of a former state-owned giant. The company grew in isolation from 1942 to 1995 before taking off as publicly traded company. The Companhia Vale do Rio Doce (CVRD), as it was known until 2007, first developed as an industrial conglomerate with wide interests in shipping, railroads, forestry and mining. Its privatisation took place in several phases during the period 1995–2002. Vale is now publicly listed in the São Paulo, New York, Hong Kong and Madrid stock markets. Following a series of joint ventures and acquisitions, the company strengthened its hold on the domestic market and built capacity at the global level to meet the booming demand for commodities from rapidly growing emerging countries. The boldest move of all took place in 2006, when Vale made a US$17.8 billion all-cash acquisition of the Canadian nickel producer Inco (this acquisition is behind the peak in Brazil's outward FDI in 2006, visible in Figure 14.5). With operations in thirty countries, Vale is now present on all continents and the world's largest iron and nickel producer.[8] Because of the drop in iron ore prices, caused in part by lower demand from China, revenues fell to US$38 billion in 2014, a slump of almost 40% from the high of US$62 billion in 2011. Although the company is now publicly traded, the Brazilian government still has a direct stake of 5.3% through BNDES, the national development bank, while PREVI, the pension fund of the state-controlled Banco do Brasil, holds 14.85% of the company's shares.[9]

---

[6] www.embraer.com/en-US/ConhecaEmbraer/EmbraerNumeros/Pages/Home
.aspx [Accessed: 30 December 2015].

[7] www.standardmedia.co.ke/?articleID=2000068698&story_title=Kenya-
Embraer-seeks-to-grow-sales-in-Africa [Accessed: 28 April 2013].

[8] http://assets.vale.com/docs/Documents/en/investors/Company/Fact-sheet/
factsheeti.pdf [Accessed: 28 April 2013].

[9] www.previ.com.br/pv_obj_cache/pv_obj_id_
83B93DF47954C1960407555004F120642EE62300/filename/previ-
report2012en.pdf [Accessed: 28 April 2013].

The jewel in the crown of Brazilian companies used to be Petrobras, which was founded in 1953 and benefitted from a state monopoly on oil until 1997. Unlike Embraer and Vale, Petrobras is only partially privatised and remains under government control. In September 2010, it became the Brazilian company with the largest market capitalisation, and fourth-largest in the world, after a world-record initial public offering (IPO) of US$72.8 billion in São Paulo to fund its offshore development plans. The company still retains significant advantages from state support, which has proved particularly helpful when negotiating with foreign governments for exploration rights. Today, it has operations in twenty-seven countries outside Brazil, including Angola, Argentina, Benin, Bolivia, Ecuador, Gabon, Namibia, Nigeria, and the United States. With 80,497 employees, revenues of US$137.3 billion and profits of US$10.3 billion in 2013, Petrobras trades on the stock exchanges of São Paulo, New York, Madrid and Buenos Aires. Although Petrobras maintains its leadership by revenues, the company is experiencing a double crisis. On the one hand, the price of oil at less than $40 a barrel makes the drilling of the pre-salt area in the middle of the Atlantic Ocean much less attractive. On the other hand, Operation Car Wash, the federal police investigation into money laundering and corruption, reached into the heart of the company. In March 2014 the police exposed a major scheme to embezzle assets (estimates vary between US$2 and US$4 billion) in the favour of the company's directors and politicians, with the far-reaching results described earlier in this chapter.

Phases in the internationalisation of Brazilian companies

The expansion of Brazilian companies is not a new phenomenon. Similarly to companies from other Latin American countries, the internationalisation process of Brazilian firms occurred in four successive phases.[10] The first two phases – in the 1970s and 1980s – witnessed modest signs of internationalisation, with some companies starting to export to and establish operations in their so-called 'natural markets' in countries with a cultural affinity. Target markets included Latin

---

[10] Casanova, L. (2009a). *From multilatinas to Global Latinas: The new Latin American multinationals (Compilation case studies)*. Interamerican Development Bank.

American countries but also Spain and Portugal, as well as Portuguese-speaking African countries.

It was during this period that many family-owned companies started their first business operations abroad. They included engineering and construction services firm Odebrecht, the family-owned conglomerates Votorantim, Camargo Corrêa and Andrade Gutierrez, the construction company Tigre and electrical devices producer WEG. Following its 'economic miracle' in the 1960s and early 1970s, Brazil suffered a long period of economic stagnation triggered by the debt crisis in the 1980s. Hard-pressed by falling sales at home, internationalisation became the only viable option for these companies to keep growing. Construction firms faced with falling public investment increasingly looked to foreign markets to stay afloat. For example, Odebrecht began its international operations in 1979 with infrastructure projects in Chile and Peru. In 1984, the company first set foot in Africa with the construction of a hydroelectric power plant in Angola.

The third phase broadly corresponds to the 'Washington Consensus' years (1990–2002), during which Latin American governments, encouraged (and to a certain extent obliged) by the International Monetary Fund and the World Bank, abandoned their import-substitution policies and adopted pro-market strategies, including the privatisation of state-owned enterprises in telecommunications, mining, energy, transportation and infrastructure. In Brazil, the impact of this 'competitive shock' was two-fold.[11] First, it forced the best-positioned Brazilian companies to restructure their operations to survive in the face of heightened competition from local subsidiaries of foreign multinationals. Firms sought to consolidate their positions domestically by pursuing efficiencies, comparative advantages and foreign financing, and, inevitably, accelerating their international expansion. Second, it exposed the most fragile companies to acquisition by foreign firms and ultimately meant that weaker companies faced extinction.

A fourth phase can be identified, beginning around 2002, a golden decade for emerging markets. Soaring commodity prices and high growth rates facilitated a more aggressive global expansion of

[11] Cyrino, A. B. & Tanure, B. (2009), Trajectories of Brazilian multinationals: Coping with obstacles, challenges and opportunities in the internationalization process. In *The rise of Brazilian multinationals* (pp. 13–14), Elsevier-Campus.

Brazilian firms, notably through the acquisition of foreign firms and assets.[12] This phase particularly benefitted resource-based companies, whose strong cash position permitted large-scale acquisitions in both advanced and emerging markets. It was during the 2000s that Vale, Petrobras and several other companies experienced their most intensive internationalisation phases.

The fall of Lehman Brothers in September 2008 and the global financial crisis that ensued marked the start of a fifth phase, with global investments moving from the 'North' (i.e. Europe and the United States) to the 'South' (i.e. emerging markets). The investment risk then seemed to have switched to the developed world while, thanks to their growth drivers, emerging markets became attractive again. As a region, Latin America recorded the highest percentage increase in FDI inflows, which brought its share of global inward FDI to 10%.[13] For Brazilian companies this meant that new sources of growth were located in other emerging markets. As the U.S. central bank, the 'Fed', began to raise interest rates, capital flows started to leave emerging markets and uncertain times returned. For Brazil, this crisis was worsened by the country's political and ethical crisis and turned into a perfect storm in 2015 and 2016.

Besides the broad macro-economic factors, a number of firm-specific objectives stimulated the international expansion of Brazilian firms. In the case of Petrobras and Vale, investments abroad were chiefly motivated by the desire to secure access to natural resources in foreign markets. Other companies, such as the bus manufacturer Marcopolo and Embraer, have 'followed the client' by focusing on opening commercial offices abroad to serve local markets better and become more responsive to customers' needs. Circumventing tariff and non-tariff barriers has been another major motive for investing abroad. By opening production units in key markets instead of limiting themselves to exports, Brazilian companies, like Gerdau in the steel industry, and Cutrale, the orange juice producer, were able to jump trade barriers and break into the protected markets of developed countries. Finally, several Brazilian firms have used the internationalisation process as a way to learn and acquire new skills by

---

[12] Casanova, 2009b.
[13] ECLAC, 2015.

competing in sophisticated markets with demanding consumers.[14] The cosmetics company Natura Cosméticos opened a retail store in Paris, through which it was able to connect with the latest consumer trends while disseminating its brand name in the world's most iconic perfume and cosmetics marketplace.

How to survive in a high interest rate environment

One decisive and distinctive factor behind the global expansion of Brazilian companies is the instrumental role played by BNDES, Brazil's national development bank, as a financing agent and investment partner for the country's corporate sector. In addition to more traditional forms of export financing, BNDES has fostered domestic mergers and acquisitions and the cross-border expansion of Brazilian companies through two main support mechanisms. First, the bank operates a credit line with favourable interest rates (usually at half the official rate) dedicated to investments and projects to be performed abroad. Both local and multinational companies operating in Brazil have access to these perks. Second, it has participated directly in several Brazilian companies through its investment arm BNDESPar. *The Washington Post* reported that in the period 2010–13 the bank loaned Brazilian companies twice what the World Bank had loaned to its 100 member countries.[15]

BNDESPar controlled 21% of the shares of the pulp and paper company Fibria for the first four years following its launch in 2009 (although its share later dropped to 11%). It also owned 19.85% of JBS[16] and 5.3% of Vale,[17] among others. In the period 2007–12, BNDES offered financing totalling about US$10 billion (at current rates, R$40.8 billion) to six companies, JBS, Marfrig, Oi, BRF, Fibria and Ambev.[18] The backing of BNDES proved instrumental in driving consolidation in the meat, pulp, ethanol,

---

[14] Cyrino & Tanure, 2009.
[15] *Washington Post*, A bank that may be too big for Brazil. 14 December 2013. www.washingtonpost.com/world/the_americas/a-bank-that-may-be-too-big-for-brazil/2013/12/14/5fa136d8-5c4f-11e3-8d24-31c016b976b2_story .html [Accessed: 25 May 2016].
[16] www.jbs.com.br/ri/ [Accessed: 25 May 2016].
[17] www.vale.com/EN/investors/company/shareholding-structure/Pages/default .aspx [Accessed: 25 May 2016].
[18] ECLAC 2012, p. 55.

telecommunications and banking industries. Financing from BNDES, whether in the form of loans or equity participation, facilitated the merger of domestic firms and accelerated the creation of new Brazilian champions such as Brasil Foods, created from the merger of Sadia and Perdigão; Fibria, from the merger of Aracruz Celulosa and Votorantim Celulose e Papel; and Banco Itaú Unibanco, from the merger of Banco Itaú and Unibanco. Additionally, companies that received loans or equity from BNDES benefitted from improved credit ratings and therefore greater access to international capital markets. By helping these companies to reach the necessary size to compete in global markets, BNDES has played a key, albeit indirect, role in promoting the internationalisation of Brazilian businesses.

The support of BNDES is especially crucial given that the cost of credit has been a recurring obstacle for Brazilian companies wanting to go global. From 1999 to 2012, Brazil's interest rates averaged 16.27%[19] and in 2015 were at 14.25%, compared to a very low interest rate environment in the United States and Europe. Long-term loans by private commercial banks remain prohibitively expensive.

The issue of 'affordable' financing may, however, reappear on the agenda of emerging Brazilian companies, since the president of BNDES, Luciano Coutinho, announced that the bank would focus its efforts on supporting more innovation-based sectors such as health and pharmaceuticals, where Brazilian companies continue to suffer from a lack of competitiveness. The Brazilian private sector needs to think long term and invest more in innovation, which until now has been mainly supported by public sector investments.[20] Unfortunately, the credibility of the very source of such investments has been shaken by allegations that Coutinho pressured businesses to make contributions to political campaigns in exchange of loans for overseas work.[21]

The ability to navigate in turbulent waters

Another distinctive feature of emerging Brazilian multinational companies relates to their specific experience of doing business in Brazil.

---

[19] www.tradingeconomics.com/brazil/interest-rate [Accessed: 25 May 2016].
[20] Casanova, L., F. Castellani, J. Dayton-Johnson, S. Dutta, N. Fonstad & C. Paunov (2011). *InnovaLatino: Fostering innovation in Latin America*. INSEAD/OECD; Ariel/Fundación Telefónica. Available at www.innovalatino.org/.
[21] www.reuters.com/article/us-brazil-corruption-odebrecht-bndes-idUSKCN0XZ0S8.

For decades these firms have thrived in a domestic context marked by unstable economic conditions as well as complex regulatory frameworks, infrastructure challenges and a very diverse business environment. While these factors may have impeded their long-term growth and development, the ability to deal with limited infrastructure and financial instability has become one of the major competitive advantages of Brazilian firms, especially when doing business in other geographies with similar constraints. It is important to note that Brazilian managers, like professionals from other emerging countries, have learnt to work in turbulent waters,[22] which can become another competitive advantage in driving the internationalisation process.

For example, Brasil Foods was able to develop a unique logistics expertise by building a world-class distribution network for its frozen and refrigerated products. Through its Sadia brand, Brasil Foods enjoys a strong foothold in the Middle East. Its shipments to the region account for 32% of its total exports with products sold in the United Arab Emirates, Saudi Arabia, Egypt, Kuwait, Qatar, Bahrain, Iran, Iraq, Jordan and Lebanon.[23]

Another example is Vale, which had to create vast transport networks integrating mines, railroads, ports and ships to transport and export its mineral resources. The company operates approximately 10,000 kilometres of railroad network and claims to have the largest mineral vessels in the world. The reputation of the company, however, suffered substantially following Brazil's greatest natural disaster, caused by the collapse of a dam in the state of Minas Gerais.[24] Despite the apocalyptic scale of the damage the case was rapidly settled by the attorney general for R$10 billion. A new civil lawsuit is under way demanding R$155 billion (US$44 billion) in damages.

The long road to becoming world-class players

Brazilian firms continue to face daunting challenges because they did not take full advantage of the 'golden decade' to grow both in size and

---

[22] Cuervo-Cazurra, A. (2012). Extending theory by analyzing developing Country multinational companies: Solving the goldilocks debate. *Global Strategy Journal*, 2, 153–67.

[23] www.brasilfoods.com/ri/siteri/web/conteudo_en.asp?idioma=1&conta=44& tipo=32276 [Accessed: 25 May 2016].

[24] www.ft.com/cms/s/0/f771c230-1182-11e6-bb40-c30e3bfcf63b .html#axzz4Dii2NWDi.

in competitiveness. The tide has turned and the business environment is much more challenging. It is common for Brazilian entrepreneurs to complain about the '*custo Brasil*' or 'Brazil cost', an expression used to describe the operational complications and added costs associated with doing business in Brazil. These include excessive bureaucracy, a byzantine tax system, high labour costs, the underdevelopment of infrastructure and corruption.

Beyond these home-grown factors, Brazilian companies also face a number of challenges that derive from the prevailing global economic competition. The promotion of outward investment has never been a high priority for Brazilian policy-makers. The internationalisation process of Brazilian multinationals has been largely driven by companies themselves, unlike in Spain, where the banking sector played a key role, or in China, where the government is a key driving force for the global expansion of Chinese companies.[25] Apart from the financial support of BNDES and some stand-alone programmes to support the internationalisation of Brazilian companies, there is no holistic approach to strengthening their position in global markets. This contrasts with the more aggressive stance adopted by several Asian countries, most notably South Korea and China, to increase the global competitiveness of 'strategic' industries.[26]

In addition, Brazil is at risk of remaining a bystander to the dramatic reconfiguration of the global trading system that may unfold as the result of the new generation of mega-trade agreements currently being discussed, such as the Trans-Pacific Partnership (TTP), which groups economies from the Pacific Rim and was launched in October 2015 after seven years of negotiations. As a member of the MERCOSUR trading bloc, Brazil cannot sign trade agreements with other countries on its own. The long-term risk of this looming economic isolation is that Brazilian companies will become increasingly sidelined from global value chains and production networks, as has been noted by experts and covered in the media in recent years.[27]

[25] Fleury A. & Fleury M.T. (2011). *Brazilian multinationals: Competences for internationalization*, Cambridge University Press.

[26] Cyrino & Tanure, 2009.

[27] www.estadao.com.br/noticias/impresso,o-brasil-fora-das-cadeias-produtivas-globais,1001501,0.html [Accessed: 25 May 2016].

Returning home?

For many years, Brazilian firms have been shy about going global. Brazil's corporate sector still lags behind those of equivalent economies and fails to impress when compared with the dynamism of Chinese, South Korean and Indian companies. Although the boom years witnessed an important catching up, and several Brazilian corporations started to be recognised as global leaders in their respective sectors, many qualify as global companies in the making. The expansion of Brazilian multinational companies first started in neighbouring Latin American countries and then extended to the rest of the world. Brazil's size and wealth of natural resources nourished some of the domestic conglomerates that later went global. Furthermore, the role of government has been instrumental through policies to protect and promote the development of national champions and the use of development loans by the public development bank BNDES to foster the competitive development of Brazilian companies in strategic sectors and support their international expansion.

The literature on Brazilian multinational companies provides extensive insights into their internationalisation strategies, entry modes, success factors and remaining obstacles to their further global expansion. International and national corporate rankings established by the financial press and research institutes also give a clear view of the hierarchy of Brazilian firms, in terms of size, revenues or presence abroad. What is less clear is how the globalisation of Brazilian companies will continue in the future. Is there room for continuous expansion? How many of them are consistently winning global market shares and have entered the top ten in their respective industries? How does their performance compare to those of their Chinese, Indian, Mexican or South African counterparts?

Finally, a question remains over the commitment of Brazilian companies – and of the Brazilian government – to internationalisation and supporting a competitive and innovative private sector. In 2011, the replacement of Roger Agnelli by Murilo Ferreira as Vale's chief executive was widely interpreted as a sign of the government's intention to favour domestic investments over the expansion of the company's global activities. Because of a number of factors – the recession, high interest rates, loss of investment grade by the country and some companies – Petrobras is divesting from the United States and Argentina as part of a worldwide asset-selling plan to fund the development of its deep-water oil discoveries off the coast of Brazil.

While the mood in Brazil is gloomy, with cuts everywhere and inflation kicking in, business goes on. Brazilian companies are focusing on the domestic market and exports but less on their international investments. Strangely enough, it was the larger international Brazilian companies, such as Petrobras, Odebrecht, Camargo Correa and the investment bank BTG Pactual, that were hit by the corruption scandal uncovered by *Operação Lava Jato*. Brazil needs to put political life and public institutions in order before the excellent companies it creates can stand firmly in the international arena. The largest Brazilian corruption scandal in the country's history has demonstrated that today investor confidence and economic prosperity hinge on higher ethical standards and transparency.

Hopefully, the recession will be short-lived, and – as in the past – the Brazilian economy will recover and the mood will change. It is too early to tell whether the 'renationalisation' of globally active companies will become a generalised trend, although it is clear that the promotion of home-grown multinational enterprises still does not feature among the government's highest priorities. We strongly believe that promoting Brazilian emerging multinationals will be important for the country in the long run for it to become more competitive; it will also help learning from other markets and diversify revenues and risks. Big economies pride themselves on big companies that contribute to the sustainable development of their countries. Brazil should be one of them.

15 | *Shared value – opportunities for multilatinas*

JORGE RAMÍREZ-VALLEJO AND
ERNESTO CUÉLLAR-URBANO

Multilatinas, companies of Latin American origin that have expanded regionally and globally, have grown significantly in the past two decades. However, many have failed in their approach as a result of not being able to read the advantages of various locations around the world and to gain the competitive advantages needed to succeed. Shared value, a concept introduced recently,[1] is a powerful framework for multilatinas to achieve competitive advantage and sustainability in the process of entering foreign markets. This chapter introduces the concept and different ways of generating shared value, and show how this framework allows companies to obtain competitive advantage by acting in the value chain and improving the location advantages of host and foreign business environments. Several shared value opportunities to improve regional and country competitiveness are identified, as are a collection of initiatives in specific industries (extractive, agriculture, housing, construction, healthcare and financial services) that provide levers for successful internationalisation.

The shared value concept

Shared value is defined as corporate policies and practices that enhance the competitiveness of the company while simultaneously advancing social, environmental and economic conditions in the communities in which it sells and operates.[2] It is about creating economic value by creating societal value, by using capitalism to address social problems. Therefore, all profits are not equal and the one that involves shared value enables society to advance and companies to grow faster.

[1] Porter, Michael E. & Kramer, Mark R. (2011. January–February). Creating shared value. *Harvard Business Review*, 89(1, 2).

[2] Porter & Kramer, 2011.

It is a concept that contrasts with the other ways in which companies relate to society, such as philanthropy and corporate social responsibility (CSR). While philanthropy indicates contributions to social causes, and CSR is about being a good corporate citizen, shared value integrates societal improvement into economic value creation.

Another way to understand the shared value concept is to imagine building new business models by taking advantage of social, environmental and economic opportunities. It represents a significant change in the behaviour of firms, in that social and environmental problems become opportunities that the company can take advantage of to form new business models.

Moreover, a company can become active and help improve the business environment of a foreign location, improving the social, economic and/or environmental conditions of a host country or it upgrades the possibility of generating increased profits.

Shared value is a concept that recognises that there is a disconnection between business and society. This gap is particularly evident when foreign companies penetrate new markets with poor knowledge of the environment because of information asymmetries. Often, companies try to meet conventional needs of conventional customers in foreign markets and fail to innovate with new products and services for underserved population segments.

Ways of generating shared value

There are three ways in which a company can generate shared value.[3]

The first is to reconceive products, needs and customers. For this, a company needs to redefine the business around unsolved customer problems or concerns, not traditional product definitions. This opens up new opportunities for customer segmentation, marketing, innovation and growth. Companies identify customer groups that have been poorly served or overlooked by the industry's products, and they need to think in terms of improving lives, not just meeting customer needs. Companies need to start with no preconceived constraints about product attributes, channel configuration or the economic model of the business (e.g. small loans are unprofitable).[4] The strength of this

---

[3] Porter & Kramer, 2011.
[4] Porter & Kramer, 2011.

approach is that businesses have the potential to be more effective than governments and NGOs in creating and marketing solutions to community problems. It is also replicable and scalable. When a new business model generates shared value, there are incentives to replicate it in different locations or for other customers. Therefore, the shared value approach generates scalable and self-sustaining solutions to social problems.

The second way to generate shared value is by redefining the way the organisation uses the resources in the value chain to improve productivity. Companies need to find out which resources are the more important, whether they are used efficiently, what type of waste is generated and how it could be eliminated or reduced. Other sources of shared value include reducing complex logistics and the associated environmental cost and improving the productivity of employees, which leads to higher wages and increases retention.

The third way to generate shared value is by enabling local cluster development. A cluster is a geographic concentration of interconnected businesses, suppliers and associated institutions in a particular field. Clusters increase productivity and operational efficiency, so that companies can compete nationally and globally.[5] Clusters allow access to specialised inputs, services, employees, information, institutions, training programmes and other local advantages, such as specialised local outsourcing, which enhances the overall performance of the firms within the cluster. They also facilitate the rapid diffusion of best practices. The proximity of rivals also encourages strategic differentiation.[6] Clusters stimulate and enable innovations owing to better recognition of opportunities as well as the presence of multiple suppliers and institutions that assist in knowledge creation. Finally, because of the availability of skills and suppliers, clusters create opportunities for new companies, diversification of established businesses and the commercialisation of new products.

Cluster participation is an important contributor to competitiveness. Companies generate shared value when they help upgrade the business environment for their own benefit, while helping other companies and

---

[5] Porter, Michael E. (1990). *The competitive advantage of nations*. The Free Press.

[6] Porter, M. E. (1998). Clusters and the new economics of competition. *Harvard Business Review*, Nov/Dec 1998, 76(6), p. 77.

the people in a particular location. There will be central aspects of the social environment (e.g. human resources, demand, rules/competition) that differ for each firm. Improving available skills, suppliers and supporting institutions in the region becomes a priority for firm's competitiveness. For all these reasons cluster development has become even more important as the basis of global competition has moved from low input costs to superior productivity.

Shared value and the global success of multilatinas

The value chain and the internationalisation process

Companies perform many different activities. The collection of these activities is what is called the value chain.[7] Every company is a value chain and can be shaped by shared value initiatives. Strategy, according to Porter, is the unique arrangement of activities that defines the unique positioning of a business. The competitive advantage arises in the value chain, from the price and/or cost side of the process. What companies do in the value chain is what makes customers increase their willingness to pay for a product or a service, or what reduces the cost, these being the only sources of competitive advantage. Companies generate a superior position by configuring each individual activity and the complete set of activities. Therefore, having new activities in the value chain as a result of shared value initiatives provides a good platform to upgrade the business and corporate strategy.

Companies distribute value chain activities during an internationalisation process. According to Porter, an international strategy answers two questions: first, where to locate each activity in the value chain; and second, how to coordinate dispersed activities. Value chain activities are dispersed in an internationalisation process in order to access inputs, secure or improve access to foreign markets and to exploit selectively capabilities or particular technologies available in other countries.[8] Therefore, a global strategy combines global and location advantages. In terms of strategic positioning, the internationalisation of a company implies deepening rather than widening its strategic positioning. What can the company do to elevate its market penetration

---

[7] Porter, 1998.
[8] Porter & Kramer, 2011.

in a selected category or an extension of the market in a unique way? It is recommended to extend the same positioning to new segments that imply a minimum of trade-offs, or to grow geographically to take advantage of new markets where the same positioning works well. Shared value initiatives that both upgrade the business environment and improve the set of activities of the value chain are powerful levers to improve the competitiveness of a multilatina in its internationalisation process.

Shared value approach creates new markets, new opportunities for growth and new ways to improve productivity.[9] Opportunities for disruptive innovations certainly proliferate but capturing them requires new thinking about market and customer segmentation, supply chain management, human resource management and other disciplines. Those multilatinas that fail to align their strategic positioning with shared value principles are left at a competitive disadvantage.

Improving the location in host and home markets

Multilatinas, working individually and collaboratively with other companies in the home and host markets, can catalyse significant improvements in the local business environment in the regions where they have major operations. By bringing social value to the location, multilatinas improve their competitiveness as well as the competitiveness of other collocated companies by generating shared value. They can focus on improving the availability of skills and suppliers, and supporting institutions, infrastructure and the regulatory framework in home and foreign markets.

To identify opportunities, multilatinas can use the 'diamond framework' (Figure 15.1) to analyse the multiple dimensions of microeconomic competitiveness and reflect on the interrelated nature of business.[10] The framework is a tool for systemic understanding of the business environment, in particular its main weaknesses and strengths, in order to leverage competitive advantage.

Companies need the right inputs to be competitive (Figure 15.1: Factor conditions). Therefore, for multilatinas access to these inputs is important: not only access to the right inputs in their home market, where the main activities of the value chain are located, but also access

---

[9] Porter & Kramer, 2011.
[10] Porter, Michael E. (2008). *On competition*. Harvard Business Review Press.

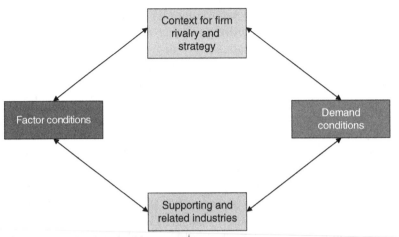

Figure 15.1 The diamond framework
Source: Porter (1990).

in their host market where some key activities of the value chain support the internationalisation process (e.g. distribution). In this process, multilatinas need to question how these inputs compare to inputs in other locations.

Multilatinas can also participate actively in helping improve the rules of the game in each location. They will benefit from a place where competition is vibrant, as this environment provides incentives for innovation and opportunities for positive spill-over effects (Figure 15.1: Context). If they do not have to compete at home, they will most likely fail abroad. Multilatinas can also help improve the sophistication of home and host country customers and turn this into an important driver of competitiveness (Figure 15.1: Demand). By helping to eliminate information asymmetries as well as by contributing to setting the right standards and environmental norms, customers grow more sophisticated. In addition, the relevance of suppliers cannot be overstated. Multilatinas can engage in supplier development programmes in the host and home markets to build up suppliers that are in close proximity (Figure 15.1: Related industries) and follow improved business practices, thus boosting the competitiveness of the host economy. In fact, building a strong local cluster in their field improves company productivity while raising regional competitiveness. This strengthens the link between company and community success.

Shared value opportunities to improve regional and country competitiveness

Creating shared value requires each multilatina to go beyond its traditional methods to identify attractive business opportunities. It requires multilatinas to understand the link between their operations and the social issues surrounding them and engage in innovation that turns challenges into opportunities.

Regional and country competitiveness represent an intersection point where social issues reflect on the company's revenue and cost structure. This holistic approach allows for a systematic review of social issues with key stakeholders and goes beyond traditional market potential and regulatory considerations. In fact, this framework allows stakeholder relationships to be audited with a new set of priorities in mind.

For example, when exploring shared value opportunities, a multilatina may consider examining social issues across several countries. A starting point might be their CSR activity; however, business units should also engage actively and deeply in conversation with key stakeholders. Factors to consider when identifying shared value opportunities include potentially affected population, incidence rates, government investment in related issues, local partners, local interest in the identified problem and alignment with local priorities. Based on preliminary research, multilatinas can create shortlists of potential shared value opportunities before visiting sites and building a business case. Establishing possible financial and social outcomes and metrics will be the key factor in pursuing investments that trigger shared value.[11]

Considering their origin, multilatinas have more experience dealing with significant social and environmental issues that generate unrest. Latin America and the Caribbean offer multiple business test grounds and different levels of social progress to create shared value.

To quantify the impact of opportunities, multilatinas could screen locally available data or international indexes. One such index to consider is the Social Progress Index (SPI), which measures several indicators that lead to the identification of social priorities[12]

[11] Hills, G., Russell, P., Borgonovi, V., Doty, A. & Iyer, L. (2012). Shared value in emerging markets, *FSG*. www.fsg.org/publications/shared-value-emerging-markets [Accessed 24 July 2015].

[12] Porter, Michael E., Stern, S. & Green, M. (2015). Social Progress Index 2015 Report. *Social Progress Imperative*. www.socialprogressimperative.org/global-index/ [Accessed 24 July 2015].

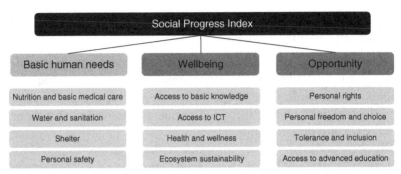

Figure 15.2 The Social Progress Index.
Source: socialprogressimperative.org (2015). www.socialprogressimperative.org/
system/resources/W1siZiIsIjIwMTUvMDUvMDcvMTcvMjkvMzEvMzI4LzIwMTV
fU09DSUFMMX1BST0dSRVNTX0lOREVYX0ZJTkFMMLnBkZiJdXQ/2015%20
~~SOCIAL%20PROGRESS%20INDEX~~ FINAL pdf [Accessed 27 May 2016].

(see Figure 15.2). Multilatinas could critically evaluate the SPI data, looking for opportunities that leverage the company's value proposition to create shared value. According to the SPI, Latin American countries rank between twenty-fourth (Uruguay) and eighty-seventh (Guyana) in a sample of 133 countries.

Once the opportunity has been identified, multilatinas are recommended to put interdisciplinary teams, including business units, in touch with divisions engaged in current CSR or philanthropic efforts.[13] The team members establish active communication channels with external stakeholders to build a pilot project that will identify and quantify possible business opportunities, challenges and intended outcomes. To incubate the initiative, multilatinas are advised to consider partnering with local governments, universities, NGOs and other companies to take advantage of expertise and resources for the pilot to gain commercial viability.[14]

Given their similar institutional, cultural and market conditions, and their focus on regional growth, multilatinas enjoy the potential benefit of replicating opportunities across borders when multiple host countries have the same social priorities. By leveraging successful shared

[13] Pol Longo, M., Smith, D., Murray, M. & Grindle, A. (2015). Shared value in Chile: Increasing private sector competitiveness by solving social problems', *Shared Value Initiative*. www.sharedvalue.org/sites/default/files/resource-files/svinchile_report_english.pdf [Accessed 27 May 2016].

[14] Pol Longo et al., 2015.

value initiatives, multilatinas can improve implementation, accelerate learning by doing and reinforce corporate strategic alignment in host countries.

By loosely following this suggested process, shared value opportunities for multilatinas have substantial potential to address successfully key social issues such as health and wellbeing, mobility and transportation, education and work-related skills development, resource efficiency and waste reduction. All of these can be dealt with by putting together a cluster development approach to increase community-level competitiveness. The following section develops and enumerates opportunities for multilatinas to create shared value by considering the specificities of the context in which multilatinas operate.

Enhancing health and wellbeing

Positive changes in health conditions and healthy lifestyles increase labour productivity and reduce overall medical costs, which creates more family income and ultimately a more prosperous society. Multilatinas that understand the opportunities to lower costs and increase revenue by reducing health-related risks can find promising shared value opportunities. The SPI recognises the challenges of undernourishment and food security, maternal and child mortality, infectious diseases, sanitation facilities, obesity, air pollution, non-communicable (non-infectious or non-transmissible) diseases and suicide, some of which are particularly relevant for the region. For example, sanitation facilities and obesity represent a clear opportunity for multilatinas. The percentage of the population with only limited access to improved sanitation facilities represents a critical health problem for some Latin American countries, such as Bolivia (46.4%) and Nicaragua (52.1%). Another important issue for Latin American countries is obesity, which generates high costs to the healthcare system and has a negative impact on productivity. Obesity rates are high in some Latin American countries, such as Mexico (32.8%), Venezuela (30.8%), Argentina (29.4%) and Chile (29.1%).

Businesses that participate in health-related industries such as pharmaceuticals, health insurance and healthcare companies would be expected to have more opportunities in this field, but food and nutrition play an important role in overall health conditions. Agribusiness, food processing companies, supermarkets and restaurant chains could also implement shared value strategies to enhance healthy conditions. Other industries, such as fitness and sports, find a rich set of opportunities to contribute to the wellbeing of a host and foreign country, by improving the business environment and generating competitive advantage.

Potential examples of shared value strategies to enhance health and wellbeing by multilatinas include:

New products and markets
- New or reformulated healthier food products with fewer calories, less fat, salt or sugar and smaller portions that help fight obesity.
- New or reformulated food products that help in the treatment of illness, with targeted benefits for patients with cardiovascular disease or early-stage diabetes.
- Easy-to-access new or reformulated food products with higher nutritional value to help fight child mortality and undernourishment.
- New healthcare services for early treatment and integral care.
- Medical insurance that rewards healthy lifestyles.

Value chain productivity
- Lowering air pollution across the entire value chain.
- Reducing food waste or implementing food donation programmes for below-standard quality produce.
- Health tracking systems to offer early health treatment and counselling to employees.
- Creating new distribution channels that facilitate access to underserved and rural populations.

Cluster and framework development
- Food and health-related companies can create networks of gyms, supermarkets, parks and other institutions and companies that promote healthy lifestyles. They can also create benefit plans to reward customers with healthy lifestyles, generating positive network effects.
- Partnering educational institutions and food-related industry professionals to boost consumer awareness after childhood.
- Educating government officials in health-related regulation and practices to enhance the local regulatory framework.

Enhancing mobility and transportation

Major Latin American cities experience congestion and capacity constraints because of poor infrastructure and urban planning. This results in low productivity of logistics and transportation services, which undermines local competitiveness. Lack of efficient transportation not only produces higher costs but also affects the environment and the wellbeing of the local population. New and innovative business models have the potential to create greater efficiencies for local transportation and freight systems and create a clear opportunity for multilatinas. At the same time, rural centres represent underserved markets and create additional opportunities for shared value strategies. Multilatinas that have experience in serving rural populations could take advantage of these business models and implement them across countries to improve competitiveness.

The World Bank's Logistics Performance Index (LPI) can be a useful indicator to identify shared value activities in this area. The index ranks 160 countries according to six dimensions, including transport-related infrastructure, customs efficiency, international shipments pricing, competence of local logistics, ability to track shipments and accordance to expected delivery time. Latin American countries rank from 42nd (Chile) to 152nd (Cuba) in the 2014 LPI survey.[15]

Potential shared value strategies to enhance mobility and transportation by multilatinas include:

New products and markets
- Creating or redefining business models to optimise or share resources and warehousing facilities.
- Reconceiving public transportation and shipping systems to include underserved populations.

Value chain productivity
- Innovating in distribution channels to serve rural populations.
- Incorporating vehicles that minimise their environmental impact across the value chain.

---

[15] World Bank, Logistics Performance Index: Quality of trade and transport-related infrastructure. http://data.worldbank.org/indicator/LP.LPI.INFR.XQ [Accessed 24 July 2015].

- Optimising capacities, routes and timing of shipments to avoid traffic congestion.
- Building corporate-sponsored employee commuter shuttle services on environmentally friendly vehicles.

Cluster and framework development
- Enhancing supplier and customer integration to minimise transportation costs.
- Partnering similar companies to share logistics and facilities in congested city centres.
- Creating education programmes for supplier and customer logistics management.

Enhancing education and work-related skills

A global society demands workers with the skills needed to improve firm competitiveness. Balancing the supply and demand of talent results in increased prosperity and reduced inequality. Multilatinas that support local communities to close these gaps not only improve the quality of their workforce but take advantage of better job market conditions and increased purchasing power.

Enhancing education and work-related skills has a spill-over effect on the local industry's innovation and productivity. Although most companies have skills development programmes, few really understand and evaluate their talent needs according to industry standards and future trends. Shared value strategies require multilatinas to understand their labour needs and career paths to fix skill gaps accordingly. Multilatinas could work with local education and training institutions to adjust curricula and obtain a better fit between the supply of human talent and the real needs of the industry. A cluster development approach supports this purpose. Properly trained and skilled workers are not only more efficient in performing their tasks but can also be part of in-house innovation and improvement programmes to generate innovative products and services.

Effective collaboration with suppliers, customers and competitors will identify common grounds that help improve and achieve industry standards and certification to the benefit of both the businesses and the community. Companies can also work with local governments and industry associations to build custom-made training agendas.

Education and training centres can be natural partners in the development of initial shared value approaches to closing the skills gap. Adopting a shared value approach helps develop new products and services that generate new and unique education and organisational capabilities within the company. IT firms partnering with multilatinas could also play an important role in delivering training programmes to remote populations and improving the learning experience.

Potential examples of shared value strategies to enhance education and work-related skills by multilatinas include:

New products and markets
- Creating and developing new business models that offer industry-wide, work-related skills training of employees, suppliers, contractors and retailers.
- Developing industry-wide employee skills databases to increase worker employability.
- Developing new business models to facilitate worker employability and career development.

Value chain productivity
- Fostering company and industry-wide innovation programmes for the most skilled workers.
- Leveraging employee knowledge to identify best practices to increase productivity and reduce costs.
- Monitoring future industry needs to develop adequate education and skill programmes and new career opportunities.

Cluster and framework development
- Working with local education institutions to align programme curricula with company and industry needs.
- Working across the industry with competitors and education institutions to achieve cross-industry certification mechanisms.
- Working with competitors and local governments to develop institutions for collaboration that focus on training and work-related skills programmes.
- Working with local governments to identify basic education gaps that undermine employee performance and optimise the use of public funds spent on education and training.

Increase resource efficiency and reduce waste

A global society demands increasingly efficient activities, products and services that generate less impact on the environment and local communities. Pollution restrictions do not only come from local regulations; markets and consumers are increasingly demanding new products and processes that incorporate cleaner interactions. Products that achieve higher levels of efficiency will have a clear competitive advantage over their competitors.

Latin American countries, the origin of multilatinas, do not have the strictest environmental regulation compared to developed countries. This creates an important opportunity for generating shared value. One of these opportunities is to work towards optimising internal processes and generating environmentally friendly products and services. Multilatinas could contribute to the protection of local ecosystems and the reduction of their carbon footprint, while increasing their environmental standards and adopting waste reduction practices.

Potential examples of shared value strategies to increase resource efficiency and reduce waste include:

New products and markets

- Creating new products that incorporate cleaner manufacturing processes.
- Creating new products that reduce emissions and waste.
- Reconceiving existing products and services, taking into account the environmental impact across the whole product cycle, from the procurement of raw materials to potential recycling after use.
- Optimising product packaging to reduce waste or offering an alternative use after consumption.
- Developing new products to monitor resource use and waste production.

Value chain productivity

- Reducing the use of water and electricity in company processes.
- Fostering greener labour environments across the company and promoting cleaner production processes.
- Working with local suppliers, distributors and retailers to achieve higher efficiencies across the value chain.
- Optimising procurement and outbound logistics.

Cluster and framework development

- Partnering with local institutions and communities to protect local ecosystems that can be affected by company operations.
- Working with local governments to enhance local environmental policies and regulations.
- Partnering with suppliers, contractors and retailers to innovate in process efficiency and productivity.
- Partnering with other actors in their clusters to innovate in recycling and waste management.

Developing clusters to increase MSME competitiveness

In the majority of countries, micro-, small- and medium-sized enterprises (MSMEs) account for the largest share of employment. These companies are usually customers, retailers or suppliers that have a direct impact on the competitiveness of the business environment and the efficiency of the value chain. A shared value approach implies working with MSMEs beyond the usual trade relation in the development of new products and services, strengthening interactions in the value chain and building lasting relationships with local communities.

Multilatinas can work on reducing productivity gaps between suppliers and distributors as size-related differences may limit the ability to solve business challenges, improve efficiency and develop innovation capacity. Multilatinas have the resources, knowledge and access to markets that MSMEs need; they can work with MSMEs to decrease logistics costs, discover new revenue streams and secure supply and distribution channels.

Conservative approaches might be sharing best practices across suppliers and distributors, but more sophisticated initiatives require multilatinas to identify specific shared value opportunities and determine which MSMEs are suitable to fulfil the strategic needs of the company. Multilatinas then need to develop close partnerships to address challenges jointly, set mutual goals and encourage shared investment. Relevant indicators should be measured to verify progress towards established goals and multilatinas should be ready to adapt and redefine any internal processes that limit their progress.

A common case is when a multilatina finds that international suppliers are unfamiliar with local challenges and their response times are slower than those of local suppliers. Foreign suppliers may also be unwilling to customise products and services for local conditions. The multilatina can then launch a supplier development programme, sharing best practices and requesting standardised solutions adapted to the local market. In a shared value initiative, the multilatina will challenge local suppliers to develop new approaches to solve the problem and take advantage of local conditions: the MSMEs engaged in the process are given access to valuable senior-level advice to improve their innovation processes. This ensures greater alignment with the multilatina's needs and a more efficient use of resources. One common local solution is for the company to enhance its internal processes to take advantage of new ways of doing things; the result is a joint programme of improvement that generates greater productivity for both the multilatina and MSMEs.

Multilatinas integrate both sides of the value chain and can foster teamwork, labour standards, integral processes and responsible procurement. Shared value initiatives aim to increase the performance of the multilatina and strengthen the whole regional value system. Multilatinas can develop new products tailored to MSMEs' needs. For example, in Latin America venture capital is scarce or non-existent. By providing financial services to entrepreneurs with no business history, limited access to the financial system or facing the closure of their business, this new market could open the door for MSMEs' improvement. Multilatinas in the financial industry can partner local institutions and related industries to create networks and offer other non-financial services to improve planning and management capacity, technology infrastructure and access to markets, which MSMEs need to improve their performance and meet their financial commitments. Further shared value can be created by supporting entrepreneurs who employ minority groups or people with limited access to the labour market, like the elderly and people with disabilities.

Once the cluster effect is created and the local environment supports the creation of specialised local firms, inputs, services, employees, information, institutions and training programmes, MSMEs will have the appropriate business environment to create shared value by themselves, addressing social and environmental challenges with their own innovative solutions, reinforcing the positive effects initiated by the multilatina and enhancing the overall business environment in which the multilatina will thrive.

Potential examples of shared value strategies to develop clusters to increase MSME competitiveness by multilatinas include:

New products and markets

- Creating new products and services tailored to MSMEs' special needs, taking into account timing, scope, scale and value.
- Developing new products or processes that increase MSME collaboration.
- Partnering with industries related to the main operation to generate new business.
- Finding alternative uses of existing products to meet the needs of underserved MSMEs.
- Addressing entrepreneurship problems with new or redesigned products or related services.
- Dealing with financial problems by redefining payment options and facilitating alternative payment schemes.
- Developing new products and services designed to alleviate or help the productivity of MSMEs.
- Creating new business models that reduce the total cost of financial or technology products for MSMEs.
- Designing alternative business models to facilitate MSMEs' procurement.
- Redefining products that address neglected clients, like entrepreneurs with no business history, limited access to the financial system or those facing the closure of their business.

Value chain productivity

- Challenging local suppliers to provide better solutions and help them to achieve goals with constant feedback and shared investments.
- Collaborating with local suppliers to find new ways to dispose of waste products and reduce environmental impact.
- Working with suppliers and local communities for resource efficiency and value chain sustainability programmes.
- Working with local MSMEs to adopt efficient resource use practices and support sustainable initiatives for natural resources.
- Innovating with logistics and transportation MSMEs to reduce the carbon footprint.
- Developing management training programmes for MSMEs.

- Innovating with MSMEs about the way products and services are distributed to reach underserved populations.
- Enhancing distribution systems and sales schemes with MSMEs to serve rural or hard-to-reach populations.

Cluster and framework development

- Working with local firms and institutions to create a cluster of reliable top-tier suppliers.
- Working on removing restrictions that limit MSMEs' and company operations.
- Working on improving labour and local suppliers to maximise the productivity of MSMEs and company operations.
- Improving the conditions of MSMEs through programmes designed to increase productivity, business knowledge, access to inputs and technical assistance and enhance social security and working conditions.
- Creating support programmes for MSMEs to facilitate the improvement of infrastructure, education and local economic development.
- Partnering local governments to implement joint infrastructure projects.
- Investing in local MSMEs to promote the employment of minorities or vulnerable members of the population.
- Supporting local MSME associations that provide market knowledge and information.
- Working with local governments and institutions to foster entrepreneurship and improve national regulatory frameworks and innovation ecosystems.

Industry-specific shared value opportunities for multilatinas

This section presents specific strategies from an industry perspective to help clarify the opportunities multilatinas face in the shared value creation process.

Possible shared value strategies can be identified from three perspectives: company strategy, regional and industry-specific. The intersection of these three perspectives determines much of the potential impact of the shared value initiative.

The industry-specific approach can supply the characterisation of stakeholders and specific opportunities for social and environmental work, facilitating the identification of the most viable shared value strategies for the company. The following examples are business cases studied by the consulting company FSG,[16] with the implications transposed to the specific circumstances of multilatinas. This approach is valuable as many of the examples may not be unique to a specific sector and can be replicated in other sectors. For example, the penetration of mobile phones can be harnessed by the banking industry to provide mobile banking, just as it can be used to improve consumer information in the food industry. Multilatinas can consider lessons from multiple sectors as potential inspiration to create shared value.

Extractive resources

Many successful multilatinas work in oil, gas, mining and renewable natural resources sectors such as timber. These tend to be large companies that generate most of their income in local communities, employing local people. They create significant operational footprints and have a substantial local influence. These companies often face environmental challenges and work with poor communities in difficult conditions.

Companies in these sectors tend to have extensive experience in dealing with local communities through CSR initiatives and public relations efforts. Some develop health, education and local infrastructure projects to gain the approval of the local community. Shared value initiatives, however, open up a new set of opportunities to take advantage of their size and influence to benefit the local business environment at the same time as they increase the profitability of the company.

Multilatinas in these industries can use by-products to generate new products or use them in a different way to reduce the environmental impact or reduce disposal costs. Environmental projects have greater shared value potential because they benefit local populations. For example, companies in the timber industry can generate electricity and steam from biomass, often becoming self-sufficient and selling the excess back to the regional power grid.

Multilatinas can also work to reduce local restrictions that limit labour productivity and have a direct impact on company operations. They can work with local governments to eradicate infectious diseases

---

[16] www.fsg.org/about.

and educate local health providers to improve diagnosis and treatment. This reduces worker morbidity and raises productivity levels.

Suppliers and local workforces may also represent a shared value opportunity in this context. Companies can offer skills training and supplier development programmes to support extractive operations. Multilatinas can create joint ventures with local suppliers to replace engineering or construction services contracted abroad, using the local workforce to procure specialised equipment locally. They may also offer technical assistance and credit lines to increase yields and outputs and supplier productivity and scale.

Examples of shared value opportunities in the extractive industries include:

New products and markets
- Use of by-products from the main operation to generate new business.
- Finding alternative uses for by-products to meet the needs of the community or the environment.

Value chain productivity
- Finding new ways to dispose of by-products to reduce environmental impact.
- Working with suppliers and local communities on resource efficiency and value chain sustainability programmes.

Cluster and framework development
- Working on removing restrictions that limit local company operations.
- Working on improving labour and local suppliers to maximise the productivity of extractive operations

Agriculture, food and beverages

Companies in these industries face environmental problems related to soil characteristics, the use of pesticides and the scarcity of arable land. They are also co-responsible for the prosperity of people in rural areas but are often criticised for the lack of fair compensation for farmers. Some products also generate obesity and related problems and do not contribute to the health of vulnerable communities.

As these industries provide a source of nutrition for local communities, multilatinas in these sectors can help meet food demand and provide a balanced diet rich in vitamins, minerals and essential fatty acids, vital for the treatment of malnourishment and other eating-related health problems. These fortified products can be tailored by geography to specific nutritional needs, with targeted distribution and marketing strategies to increase company differentiation. Multilatinas can partner local governments to create awareness of diseases like anaemia, which have no visible symptoms, and improve successful diagnosis and treatment.

Rural areas also represent possible shared value opportunities as they often suffer from a lack of transport, irrigation, power and communication infrastructure. Multilatinas can improve their competitive positioning by providing the infrastructure and co-creating solutions with local companies and institutions.

Distributing knowledge and technical assistance to increase yields can also benefit local farmers' incomes. Additional efforts include credit lines and providing access to fertilisers and livestock. Such initiatives help improve the quality of life of farmers while enhancing the quality and stability of the supply chain.

A good number of shared value opportunities are present in the manufacturing of low-calorie products, business models that enhance nutrition and the development of clusters within farming communities. Multilatinas with this approach have the potential to generate higher levels of productivity while contributing to general rural prosperity.

Examples of shared value opportunities in these industries include:

New products and markets
- Addressing obesity problems with new or redesigned products low in fat and sodium.
- Dealing with nutrition problems by adding supplements to accessible products in vulnerable communities.
- Developing new foodstuffs designed to alleviate or aid in the treatment of diseases.

Value chain productivity
- Working with farmers to adopt efficient land use practices and sustainable initiatives for natural resources.
- Innovating in logistics and transportation systems to reduce the carbon footprint.

Cluster and framework development

• Improving the conditions of farmers through programmes of increased productivity, business knowledge, access to inputs, technical assistance and enhanced social security and working conditions.
• Creating support programmes for rural communities to facilitate the improvement of infrastructure, education and local economic development.

Housing and construction

The construction sector is characterised by the employment of unskilled and low-income workers. Construction companies can create shared value with education and technical and life skills development programmes (for example, communication, time management and conflict resolution) that help prepare workers for employment. With these investments companies can address possible labour shortages and gain long-term workforce competitiveness that will encourage the creation of career development programmes with higher levels of training.

Self-building and incremental building are important ways of providing housing for communities around the world. Multilatinas can offer formal construction training to self-builders as well as financial services to increase access to affordable construction materials. Multilatinas that sell directly to self-builders or employ community members as retailers will generate network effects and additional income for locals while cutting costs. Companies can partner local financial institutions to offer micro-credits for people with informal jobs or irregular incomes and facilitate access to quality construction materials. Additional services and mobile applications can complement the shared value strategy by offering structural design and a list of materials to purchase.

Another constraint that can become a real opportunity for shared value in the housing and construction industry is access to financial resources for low-income citizens. Companies in this industry need to partner financial institutions to create new products that will penetrate the underserved population. The flow of repayments and the collateral requirements need to be adjusted to the cash flow of different models of working families. Labour associations and unions can act as large volume intermediaries to offer their members access to credit. Innovative interpretation of evidence of collateral can constitute consistent proof of income that allows independent or self-employed workers to access the housing market. Multilatinas can create new credit models consistent with the risks associated with serving these segments.

Housing projects can also be used to provide security, quality of life and access to basic services. Nevertheless, affordable housing supply remains a challenge in many countries owing to rapid urbanisation. Many cities face housing deficits that create higher prices and social tension. Rental options are also limited and promote poor living conditions for low-income residents. Shared value strategies include the creation of new business models that lower the cost of housing units and use alternative materials, such as plastics, and construction techniques, such as modular and prefabricated designs. Multilatinas can also work with local governments and hire local workforces to reduce costs and develop local suppliers, increasing productivity across the value chain.

Infrastructure projects not only bring basic services to underserved populations but also improve economic development and the interconnectedness of various communities to facilitate trade. Multilatinas can engage with affected communities and beneficiaries to include solutions that result in the best interests of all parties.

Potential examples of shared value strategies for multilatinas in the housing and construction industry include:

New products and markets
- Creating new business models that reduce the total cost of housing.
- Creating new financing schemes enabling low-income families to purchase a new home.
- Designing alternative business models to facilitate materials acquisition and training for self-builders.

Value chain productivity
- Developing training programmes for low-income families that want to start a construction business.

Cluster and framework development
- Partnering local governments to implement joint infrastructure projects.

Healthcare

Shared value is a tool multilatinas could use to grow in emerging markets while helping to generate a solution to a major social problem. Companies in the healthcare industry have the opportunity to explore underserved populations while working with local authorities to upgrade their health systems.

Healthcare challenges in emerging markets include inefficient regulation, poor facilities, lack of insurance and payment, unhealthy behaviour, crime-related injuries and counterfeit drugs. These challenges represent a significant opportunity for multilatinas in the sector to develop innovative ways to implement solutions in countries and regions experiencing rapid market growth.

Serving new markets requires accessible and affordable products adapted to local demographics and health issues. Multilatinas can develop prevention, diagnosis and treatment programmes with local governments and institutions, customise products at lower costs, address challenges like counterfeit drugs to improve patient safety, or treat neglected diseases that are not common in other parts of the world. Multilatinas can adopt a shared value strategy to maximise access to vaccines or develop a rich portfolio based on volume growth rather than margin. This approach requires innovative business models that save on costs, distribution and packaging to reduce transaction costs, especially in remote or rural areas. It involves distribution and sales schemes that reduce the risk of stock-outs and increase patient trust, creating a competitive advantage that the company can use to trigger future business opportunities. For example, programmes that bring physicians into rural areas can become a new sales channel to improve market intelligence, access and demand for treatment.

Companies can benefit from R&D programmes in one country to expand their portfolio and approved drugs in other markets. Multilatinas can also implement strategies to work with local authorities and NGOs to improve healthcare infrastructure and guidelines that allow for increased productivity and access to health services.

Multilatinas can also invest in local competitiveness, working with local factories and developing local clusters to respond more quickly to local or regional demands. They can improve research centres and increase the knowledge of local healthcare professionals and scientists. They can also create awareness about the importance of healthy habits and hygiene-oriented behaviour, like hand washing, to reduce the incidence of infectious or tropical diseases, partnering local governments for implementation and follow-up programmes that increase the sophistication of healthcare demand.

Examples of potential shared value initiatives in the health sector include:

New products and markets
* Creating or redefining products that address local health problems.
* Redefining products that address neglected diseases.

Value chain productivity
* Innovating the way drugs are distributed to reach underserved populations.
* Improving the education of local healthcare workers and professionals who serve rural populations.
* Redefining distribution and sales schemes to supply hard-to-reach populations.

Cluster and framework development
* Investing in local efforts to promote healthy habits among the most vulnerable population.
* Creating health promotion campaigns that increase patient awareness, diagnosis and demand for treatment.
* Supporting local health centres and research facilities that provide market insight.
* Working with local governments and healthcare institutions to implement health campaigns and improve national guidelines for prevention, diagnosis and treatment.

Financial services

Communities generally do not associate banks and financial services with improving local social conditions. However, their role as depositories for savings and issuers of loans is very important for economic development. Lending to sectors like agriculture and construction provides cash flow stability and access to goods needed by local communities. Financial services also protect against economic vulnerability in the event of unemployment, accidents and tragedies.

Multilatinas in this industry face challenges serving clients with low financial capabilities and increased transaction costs owing to the isolation of rural areas and lack of documentary proof of viable incomes for a huge share of the population. A series of new financial products designed to tackle the specific needs of vulnerable sectors and communities has been introduced in recent years.

Moreover, financial service companies can offer products to manage their assets and create investment services based on crowdfunding, which allows hundreds or even thousands of investors to participate in large projects by making small investments. Depending on the local regulatory environment, even retailers have started to offer micro-insurance products, to protect families in the event of unemployment, death of a wage-earning family member and motorcycle insurance. Another important strategy in this industry concerns remittance-related products. As many family members migrate to economically developed countries and begin to send money to their families, financial service companies can offer wealth-building products that capitalise on the money sent home.

Multilatinas in the financial services industry are a vital tool in the process of formalising small and medium enterprises, and their shared value experiences in home markets can be adapted to host markets. MSMEs account for more than 50% of the economy in developing nations. A credit product that meets MSMEs' needs for credit and working capital not only benefits from a wider customer base also increases the productivity of its clients. More advanced shared value approaches include a partnership between the financial company and the MSME to distribute financial products such as micro insurance and credit cards, which the MSME can offer to its customers. Small retailers are becoming natural partners for financial institutions that want to reach low-income populations.

Mobile technologies have also matured to offer inexpensive mobile banking and make financial services more accessible. Multilatinas in this industry can use mobile technology to educate customers, increase their level of financial capability, help them make sound spending decisions and take advantage of financial products.

Cross-sector integration with financial services also creates new opportunities for shared value strategies. Businesses in the retail, transportation, healthcare and construction sectors frequently interact with unbanked customers, and experience first-hand how the lack of access to credit creates restrictions for these industries. Shared value opportunities for multilatinas to innovate and build solutions by partnering with companies in other sectors include:

New products and markets
- Creating or redefining existing products to meet the needs of underserved populations.
- Creating new business models with different collateral or proof of income.
- Creating new business models to serve rural areas and nontraditional businesses.
- Developing new products that help track income and expenses to encourage financial discipline.
- Developing new products that help low-income families to pay for education, housing and health.
- Partnering local non-financial businesses to create new product and service opportunities.
- Developing new investment and asset management products for populations with low or irregular incomes.
- Developing specific financial products with local clusters.

Value chain productivity
- Creating new ways for consumers to access financial services through easy-to-use and inexpensive technologies.
- Enhancing energy efficiencies across IT banking platforms and data centres.
- Promoting digital and paperless banking and financial services.

Cluster and framework development
- Generating financial education programmes to improve financial capabilities in local communities.
- Partnering mobile phone companies to offer mobile banking solutions.
- Working with local government to improve banking regulation and accountability.
- Supporting local financial consumer associations that provide market insight.
- Partnering local IT companies to develop customised cross-industry banking platforms.

- Promoting funding for sound environmental and renewable energy projects.

Final observations

The examples presented in this chapter are illustrative rather than comprehensive but nevertheless show the great potential of the shared value framework to increase the competitiveness of multilatinas. It is clear that when exploring shared value opportunities a multilatina may consider examining social issues across several countries. In this, multilatinas can use the 'diamond framework' to analyse the multiple dimensions of microeconomic competitiveness. Possible shared value strategies can be identified from three perspectives, company strategy, regional opportunities and industrial opportunities.

Creating shared value requires intentionality to identify social problems and business models that enhance social and environmental conditions. Shared value opportunities may represent significant long-term potential but may be limited by levels of risk tolerance and innovation constraints within the company. Local institutions can provide resources and knowledge of local issues to help support shared value strategies; for example, cross-sector partnerships have the potential to create multiple opportunities for these strategies.

The three approaches to creating shared value need not be implemented in isolation. Leading firms have designed multi-pronged approaches to provide holistic solutions or mutually reinforcing schemes to solve social and environmental problems. What is important is that by creating shared value each multilatina goes beyond its traditional methods to identify attractive business opportunities.

Shared value then becomes an interesting opportunity to upgrade the competitiveness of a multilatina company when approaching the internationalisation process. It generates the right innovation incentive for the company to come up with a distinctive business model to exploit a societal and environmental opportunity. This is why shared value has the potential to become the next innovation wave for multilatinas within complex and competitive global markets.

16 | Exploring HRM systems in the multilatina enterprise

ANABELLA DAVILA

Multilatinas that started operations before and after the opening of the Latin American economies have accumulated valuable local knowledge in the context of emerging markets throughout their history.[1] Many multilatinas evolve from a business group structure that coordinates internally unrelated business units or the entire supply chain.[2] Scholars argue that many businesses in the region adopt this type of structure because of market failures, poor-quality legal and regulatory institutions[3] and to develop protection against unreliable trading partners.[4] Deficiencies in the institutional and physical infrastructure of emerging markets prevent them from functioning effectively, giving rise to institutional voids. Although institutional voids have been defined in several ways, the general notion is that emerging market economies have weak institutions for the protection or development of businesses and an absence of market intermediaries, so informal mechanisms are used to fill those gaps or roles.[5] These mechanisms could be personal relationships,[6] social

[1] Casanova, L. (2009). *Global Latinas: Latin America's emerging multinationals.* Palgrave Macmillan; Guillén, M. F. & Garcia-Canal, E. (2009). The American model of the multinational firm and the new multinationals from emerging economies. *Academy of Management Perspectives*, 23(2), 23–35.

[2] Fleury, A., Fleury, M. T. L. & Reis, G. G. (2010). El camino se hace al andar: La trayectoria de las multinacionales brasileñas. *Universia Business Review*, 25, 34–55; Sargent, J. (2001). Getting to know the neighbors: Grupos in Mexico. *Business Horizons*, 44(6), 16–24.

[3] Granovetter, M. (2005). Business groups and social organisation. In N. J. Smelser & R. Swedberg (eds). *The handbook of economic sociology* (2nd ed.) (pp. 429–50). Princeton University Press.

[4] Khanna, T. & Palepu, K. (1997). Why focused strategies may be wrong for emerging markets. *Harvard Business Review*, 75(4), 41–51.

[5] Khanna, T. & Palepu, K.G. (2010). *Winning in emerging markets: A road map for strategy and execution.* Harvard Business Press.

[6] Sargent, J. (2005). Large firms and business groups in Latin America: Towards a theory based contextually relevant research agenda. *Latin American Business Review*, 6(2), 39–66.

networks[7] or informal businesses.[8] Thus, the general conclusion is that businesses operating in emerging markets often determine that they must perform basic institutional functions themselves.[9]

An important implication of the institutional voids framework for multinational enterprises (MNEs) concerns the analysis of labour markets. Emerging markets are characterised by small pools of skilled or semi-skilled individuals and large pools of unskilled labour. Given this characteristic it is natural to argue that educational institutions fail to develop human capital adequately or to offer quality certifications.[10] In addition, employment contracts and labour regulations tend to protect disproportionately the interests of one of the contractual parties. Specifically, labour regulations in Latin America have been characterised as rigid and costly because they impose expensive restrictions on the hiring and dismissal of workers. Moreover, high dismissal costs generally prevent firms from downsizing during cyclical downturns and from hiring at optimal levels during upswings. Workers also might avoid looking for more productive jobs because of the risk of losing severance pay. Therefore, low turnover rates reduce workers' incentives to train and acquire new skills.[11] In general, effective labour markets depend on numerous country-specific factors, including education infrastructure, the availability of technical and managerial training, job mobility opportunities, the existence of a pay-for-performance culture, protection of workers' rights and enforcement of labour regulations during economic crises.[12]

Human resource management (HRM) research in the context of multilatinas has been overlooked in the literature, with the exception of a recent study[13] that attributes the successful international growth of large Latin American companies to the availability and retention

[7] Granovetter, 2005.

[8] Khanna & Palepu, 2010.

[9] Khanna & Palepu, 2010.

[10] Khanna & Palepu, 2010.

[11] Phillips, S., Mehrez, G. & Moissinac, V. (2006). *Mexico: Selected issues*. Country Report. International Monetary Fund. Retrieved on 9 November 2015 through www.imf.org/external/pubs/ft/scr/2006/cr06351.pdf.

[12] Khanna & Palepu, 2010.

[13] Deloitte (2014). Latin America rising how Latin American companies become global leaders. Retrieved 14 May 2015 through: www2.deloitte.com/content/dam/Deloitte/global/Documents/Strategy/dttl-latin%20america-rising-english.pdf.

of top executives qualified to lead international expansion and operations. There is a lack of knowledge about how multilatinas have overcome the institutional voids of local labour markets and what HRM practices multilatinas use to operate internationally. However, it is known that the leading companies in the region think fundamentally differently from the traditional strategic approach to HRM in more advanced markets.[14] The HRM models identified in the region include all stakeholders involved or affected by the employment relationship.[15] This implies that companies think about their workers in a comprehensive way and develop different types of employment relationships. This chapter explores this gap in the literature through a longitudinal in-depth analysis of the sustainability reports of ALFA, an emblematic diversified Mexican business group that today operates in eighteen countries in three different regions of the world. ALFA was ranked twenty-first in the 2015 *América Economía* multilatinas ranking and fourth among the most global Mexican companies. This chapter aims to shed some light on how multilatinas fill the inefficiencies of the labour markets and the innovative means they use to make HRM practices a source of international competitive advantage.

Competitiveness indicators of labour markets in Latin America

One of the institutional dimensions that scholars propose for the study of emerging markets is the analysis of labour markets.[16] Although most of the emerging markets recently opened their economies, following the recommendations of the Washington Consensus, development is different in each country. Emerging markets are defined as markets that fall short in providing the institutions needed to support basic business operations.[17] The absence of market intermediaries is an important deficiency that characterises these markets.

[14] Davila, A. & Elvira, M. M. (2009). Theoretical approaches to best HRM in Latin America. In A. Davila & M. M. Elvira (eds) *Best human resource management practices in Latin America* (pp. 180–88). Routledge; Davila, A. & Elvira, M. M. (2012). Latin American HRM model. In C. Brewster & W. Mayrhofer (eds) *Handbook of research in comparative human resource management* (pp. 479–93). Edward Elgar Publishing.

[15] Davila & Elvira, 2012.

[16] Khanna & Palepu, 2010.

[17] Khanna & Palepu, 2010.

In terms of labour markets, those intermediaries are educational institutions, placement agencies, unions or government agencies that enforce employment contracts and labour regulations and protect the unemployed.[18] In emerging markets, these intermediaries tend to be absent or underdeveloped.

Filling in the voids in labour markets in Latin America presents important challenges for MNEs, although it is not difficult to identify what those voids are. Multiple comparative studies and technical reports describe the economic and labour profiles of the countries in the region. For example, the World Economic Forum (WEF)'s Global Competitiveness Report assesses the competitiveness landscape of 144 economies, providing insights into the drivers of their productivity and prosperity. In this context, competitiveness is defined as the set of institutions, policies and factors that determine a country's level of productivity. Indicators of competitiveness are expressed in scores on a 1–7 scale, with 7 the best possible outcome.[19]

The WEF's 2014–15 report highlights the need to build economic resilience capabilities in the region and become less vulnerable to external fluctuations by strengthening the fundamentals of competitiveness. The report concludes that the region's low productivity is attributed to insufficient investment in growth-enhancing areas, such as infrastructure and skills development.[20] Three pillars of the report relate to the efficiency of labour markets: health and primary education, quality of higher education and training and drivers of labour market efficiency. MNEs need to understand these well when designing their HRM practices. Regarding health and primary education, businesses have to consider investing in the provision of health services in countries where workers have poor health or where there are deficient health services. This pillar measures the impact on business of diseases like malaria and tuberculosis, as well as infant mortality and life expectancy. It also reflects the provision and quality of basic education in a given country. Businesses in countries with little or low workforce education are limited; the preponderance of low-skilled technical jobs prevents companies from moving up the supply chain to produce more value-intensive products. Costa Rica obtains the highest score for health and primary education in the region (6.1) and Paraguay the lowest (4.8).

---

[18] Khanna & Palepu, 2010.
[19] World Economic Forum [WEF] (2014). *The global competitiveness report 2014–2015*. Retrieved 23 January 2016 through http://reports.weforum.org/global-competitiveness-report-2015–2016/downloads/.
[20] WEF, 2014.

Another key HRM pillar for MNEs is enrolment in secondary and tertiary education. Business leaders' evaluation of the quality of higher education is also important. The extent of staff training is taken into consideration because of the importance of vocational and continuous on-the-job training – which is neglected altogether in many economies or reduced during downturns – for ensuring a constant upgrading of workers' skills. Enhancing business competitiveness requires the availability of pools of well-educated workers who are able to perform complex tasks and adapt rapidly to their changing environment and the evolving needs of the production system. This pillar also captures the quality of maths and science education, management schools and the availability of research and training services, among others. Chile scores the highest among the Latin American countries (5.1) and Nicaragua the lowest (3.2).

The pillar related to labour market efficiency encompasses critical factors for ensuring that workers are allocated to their most effective job in the economy and provided with incentives to make their best effort. Labour markets should be flexible and facilitate workers' rapid, low-cost mobility from one economic activity to another. In efficient labour markets wage fluctuations should occur without major social disruption, for example, youth unemployment.

In addition, the attractiveness of a country in terms of its talent depends on incentives for employees, a culture of meritocracy in the workplace and business policies geared towards gender equality. The labour market efficiency pillar measures factors such as cooperation in employee-employer relations, hiring and firing practices, pay and productivity and the capacity of the country to attract and retain talent. Chile scores the highest along this dimension (4.4) and Venezuela the lowest (2.6). See Table 16.1 for the ranks and scores of the Latin American countries assessed in the WEF report.

An alternative source of data to assess the labour market realities in which multilatinas thrive is INSEAD's Global Talent Competitiveness Index (GTCI), which measures the ability of countries to compete for talent.[21] The GTCI ranks more than 100 economies according to their ability to develop, attract and retain talent. (See Table 16.2 for the ranking of Latin American countries according to the 2015–16

[21] Lanvin, B. & Evans, P. (eds). (2015). *The global talent competitiveness index 2015–2016*. INSEAD, ADECCO & HCLI. Retrieved 23 January 2016 through http://global-indices.insead.edu/gtci/gtci-2015-16-report.cfm.

Table 16.1 *Country profile on the three pillars of
competitiveness related to labour markets*

Pillars Country	Health and basic education		Higher education and training		Labour market efficiency	
	Rank (out of 144)	Score (1–7)	Rank (out of 144)	Score (1–7)	Rank (out of 144)	Score (1–7)
1 Argentina	67	5.8	45	4.8	143	3.0
2 Bolivia	109	4.9	97	3.7	127	3.6
3 Brazil	77	5.7	41	4.9	109	3.8
4 Chile	70	5.7	32	5.1	50	4.4
5 Colombia	105	5.2	60	4.4	84	4.1
6 Costa Rica	48	6.1	37	5.0	57	4.3
7 Ecuador[a]	54	5.9	71	4.2	111	4.0
8 El Salvador	80	5.6	94	3.9	125	3.6
9 Guatemala	100	5.3	103	3.6	85	4.1
10 Honduras	85	5.5	100	3.6	130	3.5
11 Mexico	71	5.7	87	4.0	121	3.7
12 Nicaragua	95	5.4	114	3.2	108	3.8
13 Panama	79	5.6	66	4.4	87	4.1
14 Paraguay	111	4.8	112	3.3	115	3.8
15 Peru	94	5.4	83	4.1	51	4.3
16 Uruguay	58	5.9	49	4.7	134	3.4
17 Venezuela	87	5.5	70	4.3	144	2.6

[a] The 2014–15 report (p. 11) records that the competitiveness profile for
Ecuador is not included in this period because of data availability issues.
The data reported in this table for Ecuador come from the 2013–14
report.

Source: Adapted from the Global Competitiveness Index 2014–15, World
Economic Forum. WEF, 2014.

GTCI report.) The GTCI is based on an input-output model. The
input sub-index is composed of four pillars that assess the policies,
resources and actions that a particular country uses to foster its talent
competitiveness. Pillar 1 (Enable) assesses factors that enable a given
country to develop the regulatory, market and business environments
favourable for talent development. Chile has the highest score (62.91)
and Venezuela the lowest (25.61) out of 100 points. Pillar 2 (Attract)

Table 16.2 *Country profile on the Global Talent Competitiveness Index 2015–16*

Country	GTCI Rank (out of 100)	GTCI Overall Score	Enable Rank (out of 100)	Enable Score	Attract Rank (out of 100)	Attract Score	Grow Rank (out of 100)	Grow Score	Retain Rank (out of 100)	Retain Score	LV[a] Skills Rank (out of 100)	LV[a] Skills Score	GK[b] Skills Rank (out of 100)	GK[b] Skills Score
1 Argentina	65	41.489	85	47.57	50	49.61	39	46.94	78	42.95	63	38.54	72	23.33
2 Brazil	67	41.368	65	52.79	39	52.79	60	40.82	68	45.65	75	33.66	74	22.50
3 Bolivia	94	33.167	107	34.73	73	45.09	75	37.37	94	31.68	93	28.01	75	22.13
4 Chile	34	52.587	30	62.91	34	53.68	20	53.68	45	58.39	36	47.46	41	36.80
5 Colombia	62	42.420	48	57.59	48	50.07	38	47.19	83	40.50	77	33.39	68	25.78
6 Costa Rica	40	51.225	36	60.64	15	64.42	23	54.77	53	52.27	57	40.40	43	34.87
7 Dominican Republic	76	39.215	58	54.74	51	49.32	84	35.12	90	37.25	67	37.06	76	21.78
8 Ecuador	78	38.345	86	47.18	56	48.18	63	39.66	69	45.45	91	29.04	80	20.56
9 El Salvador	84	37.043	70	51.70	85	43.39	70	38.23	84	39.05	68	37.05	98	12.84
10 Guatemala	75	39.215	69	52.04	42	52.06	53	43.32	87	38.14	82	31.28	85	18.45

[a] Labour and vocational skills.

[b] Global knowledge skills.

Source: Adapted from the INSEAD Global Talent Competitiveness Index 2015–16. Lanvin, Evans & Rodrigues-Montemayor, 2015.

measures the factors associated with attracting talent in the context of national competitiveness. Within the Attract pillar, the GTCI includes the external and internal openness of the country. External openness refers to aspects like business attraction, while an example of internal openness is the elimination of barriers to accept a diverse talent pool and under-represented groups. Costa Rica scores the highest (64.42) and Venezuela the lowest (33.83). Pillar 3 (Grow) considers the means for growing talent and takes into account diverse mechanisms such as apprenticeships, training and continuous education as well as access to growth opportunities. Costa Rica has the highest score (54.77) and Nicaragua the lowest (32.11). Pillar 4 (Retain) refers to retaining talent and the GTCI identifies quality of life as its main component. Uruguay has the highest score (59.06) and Honduras the lowest (31.48). The four input pillars of the GTCI model – Enable, Attract, Grow and Retain[22] – are the essential prerequisites of a system that conceives human capital as the base on which national and company competitiveness is built.

The output sub-index of the GTCI model identifies the quality of talent in a country as a result of its policies, resources and actions. It consists of two pillars: labour and vocational skills (Pillar 5) and global knowledge (Pillar 6). The labour and vocational skills pillar combines employable skills and labour productivity. Chile has the highest score (47.46) and Bolivia the lowest (28.01). Global knowledge is determined by level of education, professional and scientific skills and the impact these skills have on business outputs.[23] Chile has the highest score (36.80) and Honduras the lowest (11.71).

Both the Global Competitiveness Report and the GTCI represent a glance at the macro and labour market environments. Against this backdrop, another study examines key management practices, organisational competencies and growth factors that have proved successful for Latin American companies in the global arena.[24] This study analyses the Latin Trade Top 500 companies in the six biggest Latin American economies featured in this book: Argentina, Brazil, Chile,

---

[22] Lanvin, B., Evans, P. & Rodriguez-Montemayor, E. (2015). Attracting and mobilising talent globally and locally. In *The global talent competitiveness index 2015–2016*. INSEAD, ADECCO & HCLI, pp. 19–59. Retrieved 23 January 2016 at http://global-indices.insead.edu/gtci/gtci-2015-16-report.cfm.

[23] Lanvin, Evans & Rodriguez-Montemayor, 2015.

[24] Deloitte, 2014.

Colombia, Mexico and Peru. The companies analysed in the Deloitte report share five key characteristics and competencies that appear to be relevant to the capacity of Latin American companies to expand globally: (1) attract and retain top executives who are qualified to lead international expansion and operations; (2) access to capital markets and financing; (3) a position of market leadership at home; (4) the ability to execute international acquisitions; and (5) use of advanced corporate governance practices. While executives from Brazil, Mexico and Argentina were recognised by the INSEAD-HBR's 2013 list of top-performing CEOs in Latin America, with five CEOs listed, the Deloitte study highlights strong similarities in the challenges the six countries face.[25] Latin American countries need to improve technical and scientific training as well as basic education. The result of this deficiency is an extremely limited talent pool of skilled workers as companies encounter a large mass of unskilled workers who can perform only low-level technical jobs. This also hampers innovation because workers lack appropriate training in science and technology. In addition, the inefficiencies of the labour market are aggravated by unequal access to labour opportunities for women and minorities, as well as by inadequate pension plans. In the case of Mexico, the study indicates that labour regulation is a major barrier to business, owing to the difficulties of hiring and dismissing workers.

Moreover, the Latin American Economic Outlook 2015[26] emphasises that productivity growth remains modest compared to that of the OECD countries and other emerging economies and, despite recent improvements, Latin America remains the world's most unequal region. Currently, Latin American firms in the formal economy are three times more likely than Southeast Asian firms and thirteen times more likely than Asia-Pacific firms to face serious operational problems owing to a shortage of competitive human capital. This problem is attributed to the high informality among workers and in the business community. A number of practical steps in both education and technical training are advised in order to improve job skills. One immediate priority is to invest in improving education programmes and technical and professional training. A second step is to develop general or soft skills that help workers to access labour markets and update their skills. A third

[25] Deloitte 2014.
[26] www.latameconomy.org [accessed 1 June 2016].

course of action is to obtain coordinated public-private sector cooperation to achieve the required educational goals. Education should be seen as a driver not only of economic growth but also of social inclusion and greater equality.[27]

In Latin America, labour market analysis through the lenses of competitiveness indicators shows only weak intermediaries or no intermediaries at all. However, even weak intermediaries are urgently needed to improve the efficiency of the labour market and have a long-term impact on business productivity. Although the mechanisms that act as labour market intermediaries are crucial for correcting institutional voids, they seem to respond only to private business needs and remain unresponsive to the societal structure and cultural traditions in which labour markets are embedded.[28] Because institutional development is highly influenced by each country's history and its political, social and cultural specificities, the analysis of Latin American labour markets needs to include contextual elements such as the stakeholders that are involved or affected by the employment relationship.[29] Research indicates that as well as employees themselves, the stakeholders involved in the employment relationship include their families and local communities. Effective HRM practices, therefore, comprise actions that support stakeholders' wellbeing and social and economic development.[30] Work plays a central role in Latin American life, providing much more than a mere means of sustenance, which creates an intricate implicit social contract between workers and their employers. Thus, successful HRM must be responsive to workers' and other related stakeholders' expectations.[31]

[27] OECD (2014). Executive summary. OECD/CAF/ECLAC, *Latin American Economic Outlook 2015: Education, Skills and Innovation for Development*. Paris: OECD Publishing. DOI: http://dx.doi.org/10.1787/leo-2015-4-en.

[28] Davila, A. & Elvira, M. (2015). Human resources management in a kinship society: The case of Latin America. In F. Horwitz & P. Budhwar (eds) *Handbook of human resource management in emerging markets* (pp. 372–92). Edward Elgar.

[29] Davila & Elvira, 2009; Davila & Elvira, 2012.

[30] Davila & Elvira, 2012; Davila, A. & Elvira, M. M. (Forthcoming). Revisiting the Latin American HRM model. In C. Brewster, W. Mayrhofer & E. Farndale (eds) *Handbook of research in comparative human resource management*, 2nd. ed. Edward Elgar Publishing.

[31] Elvira, M. M. & Davila, A. (2005). Emergent directions for human resource management research in Latin America. *International Journal of Human Resource Management*, 16(12), 2265–82.

Multilatinas and HRM

Despite the accumulated years of business experience and academic knowledge about the behaviour of multilatinas in various local markets and under diverse institutional arrangements,[32] research has overlooked HRM practices and their role in companies' internationalisation processes. A notable exception is Fleury and Fleury's study on Brazilian multinationals and HRM.[33] The authors interviewed Brazilian managers to establish a hierarchical set of organisational competencies that are instrumental for domestic competition. Out of nine competencies, HRM was ranked last. However, when the same question was asked in relation to the entry phase of internationalisation, HRM was ranked third. The authors conclude that managers understood the challenges of developing efficient operations abroad, the transfer of management models to integrate international units and the expatriation of employees.[34] With respect to the international expansion stage, managers ranked the HRM competency as eighth in importance. From the subsidiary perspective, local managers felt that they had superior HRM competencies compared with managers at headquarters, perhaps because of their strong knowledge of local market specificities.[35] Because it is expected that Brazilian and other multilatinas will continue to expand into international markets, HRM challenges are going to make it into the list of their biggest challenges.

Towers Watson, a U.S.-based HRM consulting company, has surveyed the HRM practices of multilatinas in diverse economic circumstances, industrial sectors and countries since 2007, to identify the main challenges for managing talent. According to their findings multilatinas systematically base their recruitment and selection strategies on looking for talent in the local market when recruiting technical staff, specialists and professionals. This implies that multilatinas

---

[32] Fleury, A. & Fleury, M.T.L. (2014). Country of origin effects on internationalisation: Insights from Brazil. In A. Cuervo-Cazurra & R. Ramamurti (eds). *Understanding multinationals from emerging markets* (pp. 242–67). Cambridge University Press.

[33] Fleury, A. & Fleury, M.T.L. (2011). *Brazilian multinationals: Competences for internationalisation.* Cambridge University Press.

[34] Fleury & Fleury, 2011.

[35] Fleury & Fleury, 2011.

are not yet competing for top talent at the global level.[36] To enter the global competition for talent, multilatinas need to understand the labour market dynamics of foreign countries and require in-depth knowledge of both local employment practices and regulations. Furthermore, this challenge entails finding qualified people who are willing to work for a company from an emerging market, which requires overcoming the *liability of 'emergingness'*.[37] According to the Towers Watson report, multilatinas seek to adapt and develop the majority of their talent to match their firms' needs through in-house and on-the-job training, instead of looking for specialised talent within their industry or among their competitors' workforce. This might indicate that multilatinas prefer to use the untapped local talent pools,[38] as local workers seem easier to find and to retain, in particular when highly skilled workers are found in these markets. The active adoption of the in-house training programmes that multilatinas offer is also symptomatic of the need to fill in the educational or vocational voids in the region.

Retention is another challenge multilatinas have learned to manage, in particular during economic crises. According to the Towers Watson report, multilatinas adjust their HRM systems during economic downturns in an attempt to retain top-performing employees. However, turnover is a significant challenge and is mainly attributed to the issue of basic pay and the lack of career development opportunities. The report fails to specify what employees' expectations of career development are because they cover such a large set of instances, such as obtaining high-level executive or technical training, promotion or an international assignment.

Complementing the picture of multilatinas' HRM practices is the MetLife study (2013), which identifies trends in employees' benefits

[36] Towers Watson. (2010). *Multilatinas human capital practices survey*. Retrieved 18 January 2016 from www.google.com.mx/search?q=Multilatinas+Human+Capital+Practices+survey&ie=utf-8&oe=utf-8&gws_rd=cr&ei=686dVu6NJZP OjwPOqpnQAg.

[37] Madhok, A. & Keyhani, M. (2012). Acquisitions as entrepreneurship: Asymmetries, opportunities, and the internationalisation of multinationals from emerging economies. *Global Strategy Journal*, 2(1), 26–40.

[38] Lluberas, R. (2007). *The untapped skilled labor of Latin America*. Towers Watson Technical Paper No. DEC2007. Retrieved 19 January 2016 through SSRN: http://ssrn.com/abstract=1261978 or http://dx.doi.org/10.2139/ssrn.1261978.

in Brazil, Mexico and Chile. The U.S.-based insurance company and international provider of employee benefit services reports that Latin American companies strive to improve productivity and job satisfaction through employee benefits.[39] Although the report was compiled in the context of large Latin American firms and not necessarily multilatinas, it provides important information for identifying HRM challenges. For instance, benefits tend to be used as a major factor in attracting and retaining talent and some multinationals offer their executive teams exclusive benefits. Companies share the cost of certain benefits such as financial, health and employment protection (e.g. medical insurance and pension plans) with employees. The main insight of the report is that the provision of employee benefits generates a strong feeling of loyalty to the employer. In Mexico and Chile, company loyalty tends to decrease among workers who do not receive benefits. It is acknowledged, however, that strong loyalty to the company does not mean that employees are completely satisfied with their benefit levels, especially in contexts characterised by tight labour markets and in times of rising worker expectations.[40] Additionally, employees express anxiety about personal financial issues, including retirement planning, loss of income, children's educational expenses, healthcare, job security and the capacity to purchase a house. Employers need to be aware of the increasing financial-, health- and education-related expenses among middle-class groups.[41] This could translate into a more educated workforce that would value more non-monetary rewards when looking for a job. Finally, health and wellness benefits are increasing, whether paid by the company or the employee.[42] This is a significant trend considering the deficient provision of health services in these countries as identified in the INSEAD Global Competitiveness Report, 2014–15.

The MetLife report pictures Latin America as a region in which employment benefits are becoming central to HRM practices because of their impact on attraction and retention. In particular, benefits in this region target employee health and wellness. However, the report

[39] MetLife (2013). Latin America employee benefits trends study: Brazil | Chile | Mexico. Retrieved 13 March 2015 through: www.metlife.com/assets/institutional/products/benefits-products/LATAM-Study.pdf.
[40] MetLife, 2013.
[41] MetLife, 2013.
[42] MetLife, 2013.

assumes an organisational perspective and pays little attention to the specific needs and demands of employees and other relevant stakeholders affected by the employment relationship.

the rest of this chapter presents a case study of the Mexican multilatina ALFA, describing the emerging themes that result from an analysis of the evolution over time of the company's reported HRM practices.

Case study methodology

This chapter reviews the strategies that multilatinas undertake to fill institutional voids in the context of labour markets through HRM systems. These include (1) an HRM philosophy, stipulating the values, roles or approaches that the organisation should use to manage people; (2) HRM policies, the guidelines that an organisation should use to define the behaviours of employees and their relationship to the employer; (3) HRM practices, the tools that organisations use to implement HR philosophies and policies; and (4) the associated technological and social processes that are needed to implement HRM systems effectively.[43]

HRM data for this chapter were obtained from the employees' section of ALFA's annual sustainability reports 2007–14. ALFA is a company that manages a portfolio of diversified businesses: Nemak is a leading provider of light-weight components for the automotive industry, specialising in the development and manufacture of aluminum components for powertrain and body structure; Alpek is one of the world's largest producers of polyester and also leads the Mexican market in petrochemicals; Sigma Alimentos manufactures and distributes processed meats, dairy products and prepared meals; Alestra is a leading provider of information technology and telecommunications services for the Mexican corporate market; and Newpek is ALFA's most recent investment in the hydrocarbons industry in Mexico and the United States. See Table 16.3 for a description of ALFA and its investments.

---

[43] Jackson, S. E., Schuler, R. S. & Jiang, K. (2014). An aspirational framework for strategic human resource management. *Academy of Management Annals*, 8(1), 1–56; Schuler, R. S. (1992). Strategic human resource management: Linking the people with the strategic needs of the business. *Organisational Dynamics*, 21(1), 18–32.

Table 16.3 *ALFA and social investment*

Year of report	Employees	% Women	International regions (continents)[a]	International operations (countries)	International facilities (plants)	Direct economic value distributed (millions)
2007	50,695	26	3	16	72	NA[b]
2008	50,000[c]	34	3	17	77	NA
2009	52,000	31	3	16	74	NA
2010	56,300	31	3	16	82	$10,146[d]
2011	57,000	24	3	17	82	$ 3,608
2012	59,847	22	3	18	88	$15,196
2013	61,085	22	3	18	91	Ps 24,459[e]
2014	70,453	29	3	24	118	Ps 28,328[e]

[a] Main regions: Americas, Europe and Asia.
[b] Not available in the report.
[c] Approximate amount of employees reported.
[d] This figure includes: cost of sales + salaries + social benefits to employees + other expenses + payment of taxes + dividends + interest payments + investment in the community.
[e] Ps: Mexican Pesos. Employee benefit expenses, salaries, wages and benefits, contributions to social security, employees' benefits and other contributions.

Source: ALFA annual social responsibility and sustainability reports.

The analysis of multiple sustainability reports from a single company facilitates the analysis of the evolution in time of what the company reports as HRM systems. Using this analytical strategy I trace the lines of change and innovation that the company reports over a period of seven years to integrate or respond to particular pressures or demands. One of the benefits of using an evolutionary approach for data analysis is that it takes into account the parameters that define the initial activity and follows its trends over time. The description of the reports is summarised in Table 16.4.

The analysis includes the search for internal consistency across the years for each individual HRM component of the system and consistency between the components themselves. This strategy allows the emergence of key themes that best describe the components of HRM systems. The use of annual reports is a sound data-gathering strategy in times when it is difficult to obtain longitudinal data that will enable

Table 16.4 *Description of the sustainability reports*

	2007	2008	2009	2010	2011	2012	2013	2014
Title of report	Social responsibility report 2007[a]	Social responsibility report 2008[b]	2009 Social responsibility report[c]	Sustainability report 2010[d]	Sustainability report[e]	Sustainability report[f]	2013 Social responsibility report[g]	Corporate social responsibility report[h]
Language of the report	Spanish	Spanish	English	English	English	English	English	English
No of pages	40	48	40	30	38	39	52	61
No of sections	10	8	9	11	17	9	8	9
Employees section	Yes	Yes	Yes	Yes	Yes	Yes	Yes	Yes
No of pages of employees' section	8	11	7	4	8	6	7	8
GRI index	No	No	No	Yes	Yes	Yes	Yes	Yes
Global compact principles	No	No	No	Yes	Yes	Yes	Yes	Yes
External verification	No	No	No	No	Yes	Yes	Yes	No

[a] Report in Spanish and translated by the author for analysis. ALFA (2007). *Informe de Responsabilidad Social 2007* [Social Responsibility Report 2007]. Mexico: ALFA. Retrieved 15 June 2015 through: www.alfa.com.mx/down/ALFA_Rsoc07_e.pdf

[b] Report in Spanish and translated by the author for analysis. ALFA (2008). *Informe de Responsabilidad Social 2008* [Social Responsibility Report 2008]. Mexico: ALFA. Retrieved 15 June 2015 through: www.alfa.com.mx/down/ALFA_Rsoc08_e.pdf

[c] ALFA (2009). *2009 Social Responsibility Report*. Retrieved 15 June 2015 through: www.alfa.com.mx/down/ALFA_Rsoc09_i.pdf.

[d] ALFA (2010). *Sustainability Report 2010*. Retrieved 15 June 2015 through: www.alfa.com.mx/down/ALFA_Rsoc09_i.pdf.

[e] ALFA (2011). *2011 Sustainability Report*. Retrieved 15 June 2015 through: www.alfa.com.mx/down/ALFA_Rsoc11_i.pdf.

[f] ALFA (2012). *2012 Sustainability Report*. Retrieved 15 June 2015 through: www.alfa.com.mx/down/ALFA_Rsoc12_i.pdf.

[g] ALFA (2013). *2013 Social Responsibility Report*. Retrieved 15 June 2015 through:www.alfa.com.mx/down/ALFA_Rsoc13_i.pdf.

[h] ALFA (2014). *2014 Corporate Social Responsibility Report*. Retrieved 15 June 2015 through: www.alfa.com.mx/down/ALFA_Rsoc14_i.pdf.

us to understand the evolution of a specific managerial practice such as HRM. My findings narrate supporting evidence for the emerging themes to explore what ALFA reports as HRM practices. When the practice is consistent over time or is implemented in several geographic sites, it is described in general terms and as ongoing practice. When the practice is introduced in one of the reports for the first time, the narrative includes the specific year.

ALFA's HRM systems

The ALFA Group is a Mexican business group whose origin can be traced back to the final decade of the nineteenth century.[44] As a business group, however, it was constituted in 1974. The ALFA Group has always been family managed and has followed an approach of non-related diversification as its characteristic corporate-level strategy.[45] Systematic analysis of the employees' section in the company's annual sustainability reports, the content of ALFA's HRM philosophy, its policies and practices revealed themes that enable the definition of its HRM system.

HRM philosophy

ALFA's philosophy towards its employees is identified in the Letter from the Chairman of the Board and the President's section of the sustainability reports. In the context of HRM, the two leaders establish the company's vision and the analysis reveals two distinctive components: one refers to the generation of economic value and the simultaneous fulfilment of the company's social responsibilities; the other refers to the development of the company's employees, their families and host communities. Three main themes emerge regarding the approaches to the latter: (1) contribution to employees' and their families' wellbeing; (2) development of highly qualified human capital; and (3) promotion of economic growth through job creation.

---

[44] Hoshino, T. (1993). The ALFA Group: The decline and resurgence of a large-scale indigenous business group in Mexico. *The Developing Economies*, 31, 511–34.

[45] Davila, A. & Santillan, R. J. (2007). *M-form response in times of disorder: The case of a Mexican conglomerate (1974–1994)*. International Conference on Strategic Management in Latin America, Chile.

The reports highlight how the company maintains the tradition of providing its employees with training, health services and savings plans. The company states that the philosophy of providing for the wellbeing of its employees can be traced back to the early years of the Group; in 2015 this philosophy remained the foundation of its approach towards its employees. For ALFA, social responsibility starts with creating safer and healthier labour conditions for its employees and fostering opportunities for individual and family development.

Over the years, the company has added new concepts or terms to its HRM philosophy. One recurrent statement identified in the reports is that the company offers training to its employees because training promotes individual growth and foments personal and family development. Additionally, in 2008 the company reported how it provided for industrial safety and quality of life to promote individual and family development. In 2009 the company reported that it was striving to be recognised as a company that met the highest standards of social responsibility. In 2010, the company used the Global Reporting Initiative (GRI) to present the sustainability report for the first time. In 2012, ALFA added to the definition of the wellbeing of employees and their families the value of nutrition and a healthy balance between work and family life and declared its intention to strengthen such programmes. In 2013, ALFA committed to maintaining a safe, inclusive and participative workplace environment. In 2014, it was operating in line with the TEN principles in favour of human rights and social and economic development recognised by the UN Global Compact agreement, which it subscribed to in 2006. Since 2010 the company has dedicated a section to this agreement in the sustainability reports.

Developing and promoting highly qualified human capital relates both to working conditions and the environment. In the 2010 report, this understanding about the business purpose was translated into a source of pride for workers and shareholders by exceeding their expectations. In 2011 this pledge materialised as transforming ALFA into a great place to work, for attracting and developing the best talent and motivating employees to achieve their full potential.

ALFA's commitment to growth, as well as to financial investment, includes the creation of job opportunities. ALFA's philosophy of job creation consists of offering equal employment opportunities and participating in business initiatives that promote the creation of employment opportunities for people with disabilities. Thus, ALFA encourages a culture of diversity among its employees and tracks its performance by the number of reports of discriminatory actions in any of the companies in the Group. In addition, in 2013 ALFA established that all employees should demonstrate a personal commitment to improving company performance.

HRM policies

For the purpose of this study, ALFA's HRM policies are defined as the guidelines the company uses for decision-making regarding employee matters. Two major themes emerged as central to ALFA's HRM policies: (1) specially designed programmes supporting the company's employees and related stakeholders; and (2) job design and management.

Complying with the philosophy of providing opportunities for its employees and their families, ALFA has declared a firm commitment to the provision of health, educational and social development programmes. For example, the company promotes healthy eating habits among its employees by providing nutrition coaching services, including weight-loss programmes.

In 2007, the company published an extensive statement about its social responsibility programmes, understood to cover workers' families through diverse activities aiming to promote the integral development of all family members. These activities include sporting, cultural and social events and all aim to promote the identification of the family with the company.

ALFA's HRM policies also recognise that the company should adopt a lean structure and become technology-intensive, while enabling employees to fulfil their personal goals. A repeated remark in company policy has been that ALFA should provide dignifying work at a competitive salary. In this regard the company's responsibilities towards its workers extend to providing safe workplace training, motivating their professional growth and promoting personal and family development. Additionally, ALFA has sought to offer an inclusive work environment, acknowledging the value of each individual's contribution to the company. Because the company considers diversity one of its strengths, it aims to offer opportunities to workers with deficient professional backgrounds and relative inexperience. ALFA's policies subscribe to the principles of equal opportunity, development, gender equality and respect for all its employees. Regarding gender equality, the reports state that there is no difference in the basic salary for men and women, since salaries are determined by position and not by gender. It is emphasised that the resulting work environment should promote trust and cooperation.

In 2011, for the first time, the company provided an international view of its HRM policies. The report states that ALFA employs local personnel in the companies it acquires. Likewise, ALFA retains the workforce of the companies incorporated in its business portfolio and as a result a high proportion of the companies in the Group are operated and managed by local personnel.

ALFA's compensation plans are designed to offer a competitive salary and benefits package based on the labour market, job profile and responsibility, making no distinctions and observing the employment laws of the countries in which it operates. The benefits provided to ALFA's employees should exceed those established and required by local law in the countries where the company operates; this make ALFA an attractive employer for top talent. Pension plans, support for education and medical assistance are available for all employees on a permanent contract. The company also awards its employees with scholarships for all school-level academic programmes.

The company elaborated its labour relations policy in 2011. ALFA grants freedom of association and adherence to collective working agreements or contracts to its employees. In 2012 the company developed its first code of ethics outlining the behaviour and moral judgement expected from employees.

HRM practices

HRM practices are communicated in the employees' or collaborators' section of the annual reports and are conveyed through programmes, activities and outputs designed to include employees and their families, as well as members of the local community. HRM practices at ALFA are delivered in three ways: (1) through programmes and activities focused on individuals' personal development; (2) through volunteer programmes instrumental in employees' engagement with the social strategy of the company; and (3) practices relevant to the company's global labour agenda.

All the reports in the period studied highlight safety programmes and their respective monitoring mechanism, such as informing about the number of accidents and investment in protective equipment. Before joining the company, every employee undergoes a health and safety training programme. Healthcare is of special importance for the company and it offers diverse programmes and activities such as vaccination campaigns and annual check-ups. In Nemak Brazil, the health programme covers employees' spouses during pregnancy. In 2011, the company added health fairs and workshops, nutritional consulting and fitness programmes in the workplace. In addition, ALFA conducts ergonomic assessments measuring diverse healthy and safety hazards, such as levels of noise and lighting in the workplace. The impact of the health programme is measured by the number of people that benefit from the service or participate in any of the programme formats.

Regarding training, Sigma Alimentos, ALFA's subsidiary in the food sector, has a corporate university that offers technical as well as general human capital training programmes. The reports highlight the special attention paid to training programmes for developing female talent. In Mexico the spouses of company's executives volunteer to participate as instructors in such programmes and the format is extended to the Central American, Caribbean and U.S. branches of the subsidiary. In 2014, Sigma Alimentos's corporate university became a Leadership School. Over time, it has gradually incorporated other areas of knowledge in order to support Sigma's growth better. Today, the university has eleven schools offering courses in commercial, operations, marketing and leadership skills.

ALFA offers all its employees an extensive scholarship programme that includes technical workshops and short courses as well as school or university degree programmes. For this, the company has collaboration agreements with several universities. In 2010 and 2011, ALFA highlighted a programme for developing leadership skills, targeting young employees. The impact of the training programmes is assessed in terms of workable hours of training and the number of courses offered. Employees also receive regular performance and career development reviews. The company reports the percentage of employees that participate in the annual assessment.

For families, the company offers diverse programmes and recreational activities. One of these is the annual open house programme when workers' families are invited to the company's facilities and manufacturing plants. The programme includes training on diverse topics for workers' families. Variants of this programme are offered in several subsidiaries of Nemak and Alestra and sometimes include outdoor activities (e.g. in Nemak Poland). In Nemak Dillingen (Germany) there is a professional counselling service for workers and their families that provides advice on managing difficult personal situations, such as family relations. In Nemak Monterrey (Mexico), there is a youth development programme in which workers' teenage children participate in talks and visit museums and orphanages. A similar programme is offered in Nemak Brazil. Nemak Monterrey also has a development centre for employees' spouses, offering two workshops that promote moral values and family integration: My Value as an Individual and School for Parents. The impact of these programmes is measured by the number of participants.

Until 2011, ALFA did not have a programme for supporting continued relationships with people leaving the company because of retirement or layoffs. However, in 2013, the company instituted the Employee Assistance Programme for this purpose.

The company also launched the Goose Community programme to strengthen its role as a 'family-responsible employer'. The programme started with 38 active volunteers among its employees; by 2009 these had increased to 170. The impact of this programme is measured in terms of changes in HRM policies and practices, such as hiring people with disabilities, flexible work schedules and teleworking for working mothers. The company also offers monetary support for school supplies for workers' school-age children. When employees are affected by natural disasters, Goose Community volunteers organise groups to help their co-workers.

Although the company reported in 2006 that it had signed the United Nations Global Compact agreement, in 2010 it recognised for the first time that all the company's staff in security areas had received specific training in safety policies and procedures, as well as awareness of human rights. In particular, the report highlighted the importance of this topic in its relationships with suppliers and contractors. The company reported that there was no forced or compulsory labour or child labour in any of its work centres. In 2013, the company reported for the first time that employees were trained in the organisation's anti-corruption policies and procedures.

Discussion and conclusions

The purpose of this chapter is to demonstrate how multilatinas fill institutional voids in labour markets and to highlight the innovative ways in which their HRM practices might be a source of international competitive advantage. The case of ALFA is used to illustrate how an emblematic diversified business group accomplishes this. The longitudinal case study presented here draws from a systematic analysis of the company's sustainability reports during the period 2007–14.

The analysis of labour market competitiveness indicators clearly shows the extent to which Latin America presents diverse challenges to enhance business competitiveness. On the one hand, there are structural macro challenges, such as the quality of basic and tertiary education, health coverage and services, dynamic schemes for workers' allocation and provision of job incentives.[46] On the other, there are micro factors underlying the attractiveness of the labour markets. These factors include the countries' regulations concerning job protection, equality, inclusion and professional growth.[47]

Designing HRM systems solely on the basis of competitiveness indicators will provide only partial solutions to the competition for global talent, given the complexity of labour markets in Latin America. There is also a need to respond to social expectations and for sensitivity to the cultural traditions in which labour markets are embedded. This implies that attending to the broad employment relationship is much more important than has traditionally been recognised in HRM research. In this vein, the stakeholder perspective has been used to identify HRM models in Latin America.[48] In particular, HRM research seeks to identify stakeholders that are involved or affected by the employment relationship and how HRM systems contribute to stakeholders' wellbeing and social and economic development.[49]

The case of ALFA illustrates the attention one company pays to its diverse stakeholders and the substantial level of organisational commitment it makes, accompanied by efforts to measure impact. In

---

[46] World Economic Forum [WEF] (2014). *The global competitiveness report 2014–2015*. Retrieved 23 January 2016 through http://reports.weforum.org/global-competitiveness-report-2015–2016/downloads/.
[47] Lanvin & Evans, 2015.
[48] Davila & Elvira, 2009; Davila & Elvira, 2012.
[49] Davila & Elvira, 2009; Davila & Elvira, 2012.

particular, in its sustainability reports the company defines five major
stakeholder groups based on their relationship with the company and
the degree to which they are affected by its operations. These groups
are employees, shareholders, clients, suppliers and the community. The
analysis of the company's reports in the context of HRM reveals, however, that the main stakeholders in the employment relationship are a
broad group consisting of employees, their families and the communities to which they belong. Targeted efforts have been increasingly
undertaken to address the needs of these constituencies.

ALFA's HRM systems tend to be based on local traditions and
responsive to the realities in its host countries. Across the board, the
HRM systems at ALFA engage with local stakeholders by supporting the personal development of their employees, their families and
members of the local community. The analysis of the case also reveals
internal consistency over the years for each HRM system component
and between the components themselves. This consistency might be
because of the company's management style, which is reflected in its
philosophy towards its employees, rather than by external pressures.
A few instances were identified in which one HRM component clearly
changed in response to external factors.

The evidence provided by the sustainability reports assigns the
company a specific role. That is, its leaders define the company as a
provider, developer and promoter of structural and social labour conditions, such as individual and family development, commitment to
human capital growth and job creation. The evidence also presents a
clear alignment of the company's philosophy with the dimensions of
human development defined by the United Nations: education, health
and living conditions. In other words, ALFA's philosophy towards its
employees is a credible commitment to creating conditions that will
facilitate their development. HRM policies and practices follow this
framework.

ALFA's HRM systems seem a good fit with the institutional voids
of local labour markets. The company takes care of its workforce,
providing them with appropriate training, offering health and other
personal services and extending these practices to employees' families and members of the local community. Moreover, this case suggests that the role of HR departments is crucial when institutions are
unable or lack the resources to provide the physical or educational
infrastructure needed for business competitiveness. This might add a

social dimension to the HRM role, contributing to the development of the company's social capability.

ALFA's understanding of the dynamics of local labour markets in Latin America might be a source of international competitive advantage vis-à-vis other MNEs. The inclusion of relevant contextual elements in the design and implementation of HRM systems adds an important element to the company's local knowledge. The case of ALFA illustrates how, viewed from the stakeholder perspective, HRM systems have proved to be responsive to workers' and other related stakeholders' expectations, compensating for institutional voids.

17 The internationalisation of high-tech new ventures from Latin America – the Brazilian experience

FERNANDA RIBEIRO CAHEN AND
MOACIR MIRANDA DE OLIVEIRA JR.

Introduction

'Brazil is not for beginners', said Tom Jobim, one of the greatest Brazilian composers of the twentieth century. This observation indeed seems to apply to many cases of entrepreneurial Brazilian high-tech new ventures (HTNVs) attempting to conduct business in international markets. This chapter examines the remarkable progress of Brazilian HTNVs in some aspects of international entrepreneurship, in sharp contrast to the difficulties or even barriers that constrain their expansion overseas.

Despite different descriptions of the same phenomenon, such as international new ventures[1] or born globals[2] or global start-ups,[3] there is a reasonable understanding of what these companies are. HTNVs are young companies, usually small or even micro in size, that face intense product, process and business model innovations combined with an early and rapid internationalisation process.[4] The internationalisation strategies of HTNVs demonstrated in sectors such as IT, pharmaceutics, biotechnology, electronics and auto parts frequently

---

[1] Oviatt, B. & McDougall, P. (1994). Toward a theory of international new ventures. *Journal of International Business Studies*, 25(1), 45–64.

[2] Knight, G. A. & Kim, D. (2009). International business competence and the contemporary firm. *Journal of International Business Studies*, 40(2), 255–73.

[3] Oviatt, B. M., McDougall, P. P. & Loper, M. (1995). Global start-ups: Entrepreneurs on a worldwide stage. *The Academy of Management Executive*, 9(2), 30–44.

[4] Onetti, A., Zucchella, A., Jones, M. V. & McDougall-Covin, P. P. (2010). Internationalization, innovation and entrepreneurship: Business models for new technology-based firms. *Journal of Management & Governance*, 16(3), 337–68.

follow the movements of large global companies and can be linked to global value chains.

Different criteria have been chosen to operationalise HTNVs' internationalisation strategies. The most recurrent[5] are founding date, the start of international activities following foundation, the percentage of revenues from foreign operations (ranging from 5% to 75%) and market scope (one or more international markets, in the same or in different geographical regions). The analysis of these variables suggests that the adoption of a definition is contingent upon the company's home country and on the characteristics of its business environment.[6]

A large number of HTNVs have been created in Brazil in the past fifteen years and this has been accompanied by a noticeable effort by the government and private entities to promote innovation and entrepreneurship in the country. One of the eight largest economies in the world, Brazil ranks globally among the ten most entrepreneurial countries, according to the 2014 Global Entrepreneurship Monitor (GEM). Despite a number of successful ventures, the country still has a long way to go before reaching the current levels of high-tech entrepreneurship within the world's most developed nations. There are several persistent challenges identified as key barriers to business by GEM: high tax burden, red tape, educational inadequacy and governmental policies, all of which are damaging to nascent companies.[7]

Research on the accelerated internationalisation of HTNVs in North America and Europe is abundant but studies focusing on developing countries 'are virtually absent'.[8] We have been studying the internationalisation of HTNVs in Brazil since 2008, and the results

[5] Rialp, A., Rialp, J. & Knight, G. a. (2005). The phenomenon of early internationalizing firms: What do we know after a decade (1993–2003) of scientific inquiry? *International Business Review*, 14(2), 147–66; Dib, L. A., Rocha, A. & Silva, J. F. (2010). The internationalization process of Brazilian software firms and the born global phenomenon: Examining firm, network, and entrepreneur variables. *Journal of International Entrepreneurship*, 8(3), 233–53.

[6] Dib et al., 2010.

[7] GEM (2014). Global Entrepreneurship Monitor 2014. Executive Report, London Business School, London and Babson College, Babson Park, MA.

[8] Kiss, A. N., Danis, W. M. & Cavusgil, S. T. (2012). International entrepreneurship research in emerging economies: A critical review and research agenda. *Journal of Business Venturing*, 27(2), 266–90.

of our research have appeared in both local and international journals.[9] The country, however, remains a key but understudied emerging market.[10] Our previous work includes exploratory studies using qualitative data from case studies and a broader quantitative survey to identify executives' perception of factors influencing internationalisation and barriers to internationalisation.[11] More specifically, Ribeiro (2012)[12] develops four longitudinal matched case studies: two cases of early stage internationalisation and two domestic Brazilian companies. The analysis of these four cases establishes the differences between internationalised and domestic firms and confirms some key findings of previous studies on this topic.[13] This qualitative and exploratory work forms the basis of subsequent quantitative survey-based research on the specificities of domestic and internationalised HTNVs.[14]

The firms featured in the quantitative study were selected on the basis of their involvement in developing, commercialising or manufacturing in high technology, medium-high technology or technology-intensive

[9] Ribeiro, F. F., Oliveira Jr, M. M. & Borini, F. M. (2012). Internacionalização acelerada de empresas de base tecnológica: o caso das Born Globals Brasileiras. *Revista de Administração Contemporânea*, 16(6), 866–88; Cahen, F., Lahiri, S., & Borini, F. (2016). Managerial perceptions of barriers to internationalization: An examination of Brazil's new technology-based firms. *Journal of Business Research*, 69(6), 1973–79. Cahen, F. R., Oliveira Jr., M. M. & Borini, F. M. (2017). The internationalisation of new technology-based firms from emerging markets. *International Journal of Technology Management*, 74 (1–4), 23–43.
       Ribeiro, F. F., Oliveira Jr, M. M., Borini, F. M. & Bernardes, R. (2014). Accelerated internationalization in emerging markets: Empirical evidence from Brazilian technology-based firms. *Journal of technology management & innovation*, 9(1), 1–12.
[10] Amann, E. & Figueiredo, P. Brazil. Brazil. In Amann, E. & Cantwell, J. (2012). *Innovative firms in emerging market countries* (pp. 249–98). Oxford University Press.
[11] Cahen, Lahiri & Borini, 2015; Cahen, Oliveira & Borini, 2015.
[12] Ribeiro, F. C. F. (2012). *Born Globals brasileiras: estudo da internacionalização de empresas de base tecnológica.* Tese de Doutorado, Faculdade de Economia, Administração e Contabilidade, Universidade de São Paulo, São Paulo. Recuperado em 2016-06-08, de www.teses.usp.br/teses/disponiveis/12/12139/tde-26032012-205850/.
[13] Leonidou, L. C. (1995). Export barriers: Non-exporters' perceptions. *International Marketing Review*, 12(1), 4–25; Kahiya, E. (2013). Export barriers and path to internationalization: A comparison of conventional enterprises and international new ventures. *Journal of International Entrepreneurship*, 11(3), 3–29.
[14] Cahen, Lahiri & Borini, 2015; Cahen, Oliveira & Borini, 2015.

service sectors.[15] In order to identify potential participants we relied on two sources: the National Association of Entities Promoting Advanced Technology Ventures (ANPROTEC) and the Brazilian Trade and Investment Promotion Agency (Apex-Brasil). ANPROTEC supports new ventures from high-technology sectors and is associated with about 90 technological parks and 384 incubators. Apex-Brasil maintains records of government programmes that are aimed at providing incentives for internationalisation in high technology sectors.

This chapter provides a brief overview of the Brazilian environment for high-tech entrepreneurship over the past thirty years and discuss the experience of Brazilian HTNVs entering international markets and the factors influencing their internationalisation. We look at the barriers that constrain internationalisation of HTNVs in emerging markets, using the Brazilian experience as an example. We conclude with a discussion of our main theoretical findings and managerial implications and highlight directions for future research.

Changes in the Brazilian business environment for high-tech entrepreneurship: A brief overview

Background

In its boom period of industrialisation, from the 1930s until the mid-1980s, Brazil predominantly followed import substitution policies and the Brazilian government began to take the first steps towards specific polices to support local technological capabilities. These efforts were directed at strategically important sectors, such as oil and aeronautics,

---

[15] According to OECD (2002), high technology sectors include aeronautics and aerospace, IT, pharmaceutics, biotechnology, electronics, telecommunications, optical and precision medical instruments. Medium-high technology sectors include electrical machines and equipment, automotive and auto parts, oil and chemical products. Technology-intensive service sectors include R&D services, engineering and technical services, legal services, accounting, management consulting, software/computing and electronic information services, advertising and market research, telecommunication, insurance and financial services. OECD (2002). The measurement of scientific and technical activities: proposed standard practice for surveys of research and experimental development – OECD. (2002), *Frascati Manual: Proposed Standard Practice for Surveys on Research and Experimental Development*, The Measurement of Scientific and Technological Activities, OECD Publishing, Paris.

which were supported by high governmental investment and state-ownership, as in the case of Petrobras and Embraer. The 1960s marked a turbulent period in Brazil that ended in a military coup in 1964. Surprisingly, the military governments (1964–85) sought not only to substitute imports but also to build up local technological capabilities within various sectors on an unprecedented scale.[16]

For example, the Financing of Projects and Studies (FINEP) was established in 1967 as a public agency under the Ministry of Science and Technology (MCT) to finance R&D projects, mostly directed at large capital goods companies. In 1969, the government established the National Scientific and Technological Development Fund (FNDCT) to finance the advancement of science and technology. In the 1970s, the Brazilian economy forayed into the 'Brazilian Miracle' period, during which the country grew at annual rates of roughly 7%.[17] The reach of the technology policy was augmented after 1975 with the launch of the Second Scientific and Technological Development Plan. The country took its first steps towards supporting entrepreneurship in the 1970s, with the creation of the Brazilian Micro and Small Business Support Service (SEBRAE) in 1972. This private non-profit organisation was created to promote entrepreneurship, competitiveness and the development of nascent businesses. It has been very active since its inception.

During the 1980s, Brazil suffered a period of intense economic crises with critically high inflation rates of more than 1,000% a year. During this period the country suffered from serious constraints in industrial and technological development, and public investment in scientific capabilities, construction, education and infrastructure development was cut or significantly reduced. Despite all the restrictions, the first specific public policy initiative for high-tech entrepreneurship was created in the 1980s. The National Programme of Technological Parks was created in 1984 and in the same year ParqTec – the São Carlos Technology Park – was created. ParqTec was the first technology park and the first business incubator in Brazil and is considered to be the oldest in Latin America. The National Association of Incubators and Science Parks (ANPROTEC) was established in 1987 and started to attract business incubators, technology parks, educational and

---

[16] Amann & Figueiredo, 2012.
[17] Fleury, A. & Fleury, M. T., 2011. *Brazilian multinationals: competences for internationalization*. Cambridge University Press.

research institutions, public agencies and other stakeholders linked to entrepreneurship and innovation activities.

In 1988, the new Brazilian constitution came into force, marking the start of pro-market reforms in the country and the turn towards democracy. The early 1990s was a highly turbulent period. Inflation reached more than 2,000% a year and a series of political scandals led to the impeachment of the newly elected president. In 1993, inflation was finally tamed and kept under control by the inflation-fighting Real Plan, designed by Fernando Henrique Cardoso, Brazil's finance minister, who would later become president. The government embraced a market liberalisation agenda. It eliminated the differential treatment of national and foreign capital for government loans and subsidies and initiated privatisation of state-owned companies. It also removed restrictions on patenting in high-tech areas.[18]

Before the reforms, managerial thinking and organisational practices were focused on domestic markets, avoiding the challenges of competitive international markets. This was a common characteristic of most economies considered emerging markets today.[19] The pro-market reforms stimulated competition and innovation and created the bases for an environment for high-tech entrepreneurship and internationalisation of all kinds of Brazilian companies.

Creating an environment for high-tech entrepreneurship

By the mid-1990s new institutional changes had taken place with policies aiming at the development of technological and innovative capabilities in Brazil. In the first decade of the twenty-first century incentives favoured the transfer of technological knowledge to companies and several credit and subsidy programmes were created to finance innovative companies and new ventures. Programmes were also implemented to stimulate partnerships between universities, research centres and companies. All sectors had to restructure to fit this new business dynamic and oil, information technology, pharmaceutical and aeronautical companies were among those that adapted successfully.

---

[18] Amann & Figueiredo, 2012.
[19] Khanna, T. & Palepu, K. G. (2010). *Winning in emerging markets: A road map for strategy and execution.* Harvard Business Press.

Brazil enjoyed annual average growth of 4.5% up to 2011 and a rise in living standards during the first decade of the twenty-first century. Although income inequity is still shamefully high, all socio-economic classes have benefitted from this growth. For example, according to GEM, in terms of what motivates individuals to start a business, both Brazil's economic growth since the mid-2000s and the expansion of the internal market have facilitated a sharp increase in the proportion of entrepreneurs pursuing an opportunity.[20] The number was 42.4% of the surveyed population in 2002 and this increased to about 71% in 2014.[21] These results are more dramatic when compared to the share of entrepreneurs who started a business out of necessity. The rate of necessity-driven entrepreneurs (owning a business that is 0–3 months old) in Brazil fell from 5.7% in 2002 to 3.7% in 2014. The new business ownership rate (businesses that are 3–42 months old) increased from 8.5% in 2010 to 13.8% in 2014.[22]

After the pro-market reforms collaboration between government and stakeholders like private companies, banks and sector associations also increased to the benefit of entrepreneurship in high-tech sectors. For example, the number of technology parks and incubators, which support high-tech entrepreneurship, has risen significantly. According to ANPROTEC, in Brazil in 2015 there were ninety-four technology parks (twenty-nine in operation, thirty-two being built and thirty-two at project stage). Among the technology parks in operation, there were approximately 400 incubators for new ventures and a well-developed incubation ecosystem linked to universities and other entities (see Table 17.1 and Figure 17.1). Brazil leads one of the most successful incubation movements in Latin America, through innovation and adaptation of incubator models to suit indigenous needs.[23] Although there is no official census of the number of Brazilian HTNVs, according to ANPROTEC,[24] there are approximately 4,800 companies linked to technology parks and

[20] GEM Report, 2014.
[21] The other countries in 2014 rated as follows: India 60%, Mexico 76.3%, China 65.7%, United States 81.5%, Germany 75.7%. (GEM Report, 2014).
[22] GEM Report, 2014.
[23] Chandra, A. & Fealey, T. (2009). Business incubation in the United States, China and Brazil. *International Journal of Entrepreneurship*, 13, 67–86.
[24] ANPROTEC. Associação Nacional de Entidades Promotoras de Empreendimentos Inovadores. (2011). Lista de sócios. Retrieved from: www.anprotec.org.br/listaSimples2.php.

Table 17.1 *Innovation habitats in Brazil, 2015*

94 technology parks	29 parks in operation (most of which are less than 10 years old)
	32 being built
	32 at project stage
	939 companies in operation
	32,237 jobs created so far
400 business incubators	2,640 incubated companies
	2,509 graduated companies
	1,124 associated companies
	16,934 jobs in incubated and associated companies
	29,905 jobs in graduated companies
	US$266 million in yearly revenues from incubated companies
	US$2 billion in yearly revenues from graduated companies
	According to ANPROTEC,[a] 98% of the incubated companies innovate, 28% are focused on the local level, 55% on the national level and 15% on the international level.

[a] ANPROTEC, 2011.

Source: Data adapted from Zouain, D. M., & Plonski, G. A. (2015). Science and Technology Parks: laboratories of innovation for urban development – an approach from Brazil. *Triple Helix*, 2(1), 7; ANPROTEC (2011); CDT/UnB (2013) Estudo de Projetos de Alta Complexidade: indicadores de parques tecnológicos. Study made for the Ministry of Science, Technology and Innovation. Brasilia, Brazil. Available in www.mct.gov.br/upd_blob/0228/228606.pdf.

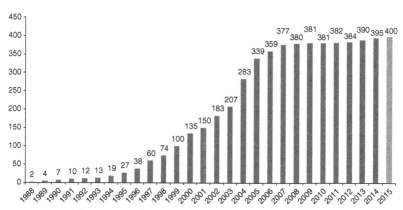

Figure 17.1 The growth of business incubators in Brazil, 1988–2015.
Source: ANPROTEC, 2011.

incubators in the country and more than 2,500 companies have passed the incubation phase (Table 17.1).

The government has played an essential role in creating and supporting innovation habitats, such as incubators and technology parks, but non-government initiatives are also common. For example, the Federation of Industries for the State of Sao Paulo (FIESP) operates a dozen incubators.[25] According to ANPROTEC,[26] funding sources for technology parks are 36% private, 22% from the federal government and 42% from state and city governments. Financial support for incubators comes from government programmes such as the National Incubation Support Programme (PNI), which is designed to support the creation of new incubators and the expansion of existing ones.

Other private stakeholders, such as ANPROTEC, are also instrumental in this process. ANPROTEC is the main articulator of the interests of its associates, including technology parks, business incubators, education and research institutions, public institutions and other entities promoting entrepreneurship and innovation in the country. It plays a linking role by supporting universities, research institutes and other bodies related to the incubators.

High-tech companies, innovation habitats and most importantly universities are mainly concentrated in the south eastern and southern states of Brazil. These are the most industrialised and richest regions of the country, responsible for approximately 75% of Brazilian GDP. The southern (43%) and south eastern (41%) states concentrate 84% of the technology parks in the country. The other regions account for 16% of parks and are spread between the northeast (7%), north (5%) and midwest (4%) of Brazil.[27]

The changes brought about by the pro-market reforms stimulated an increase in the flow of foreign direct investment (FDI) in Brazil. Multinationals from different sectors invested heavily, building new capacity and modernising existing plants. Right after the reforms, in 1998, Brazil held the eighth-largest stock of inward FDI in the world. Between 2012 and 2013 the country was the world's fourth-largest recipient of inward FDI.[28]

---

[25] Chandra & Fealey, 2009.
[26] ANPROTEC, 2011.
[27] CDT/UnB, 2013.
[28] UNCTAD (2014). World Investment Report 2014: Investing in the SDGs: An Action Plan. New York and Geneva: United Nations.

The growth of high-tech industries in Brazil has been significantly stimulated in the past ten years by the increased participation of national companies and substantial investments by large multinationals. The internationalisation strategies of Brazilian HTNVs, observed in industries such as IT, aeronautics and biotechnology, follow the pattern of large global companies. At present there is modest internationalisation and integration into global supply chains but the trend is increasing. For example, in 2013 the net sales of the Brazilian information technology and telecommunication (IT&C) sector were approximately US$150 billion.[29] In this sector, internationalisation is 'pulled' by the outsourcing of software development around the world. In the aircraft manufacturing industry, Embraer, the Brazilian aircraft manufacturer, is responsible for about 80% of the revenues from highly specialised Brazilian HTNVs,[30] but there are HTNVs in this sector looking for international routes. Biotechnology companies providing services for large pharmaceutical companies are also good examples of HTNVs. The majority of biotechnology companies (63%) in Brazil were founded in or after 2000 and are mainly micro and small companies, 56% of which have annual revenues of no more than US$1.5 million. Their operations are concentrated on vaccines and blood products for the pharmaceutical industry[31] and more than 73% of biotech companies have formal business partnerships with universities, research centres and pharmaceutical companies. These companies are increasing their technological sophistication and attempts at internationalisation.[32]

Generally the discussion about internationalisation in emerging markets focuses on low-tech sectors such as agribusiness, food, natural resources and mining.[33] Internationalisation in high-technology sectors, which are much more representative for the degree of technology development in emerging countries, have been discussed fragmentally and insufficiently in some emerging countries, such as India,[34] Costa

[29] Brasscom (2015). Brazilian Association of IT&C Companies.
[30] Amann & Figueiredo, 2012.
[31] The Brazilian pharmaceutical industry is ranked sixth globally in terms of value, with total revenues exceeding US$26 billion per year. IMS Health. (2014) Annual Report 2014. Norwalk: IMS Health.
[32] Brazilian Biotechnology Association (2011). Brazil Biotech Map. Available at: www.cebrap.org.br/v1/upload/pdf/Brazil_Biotec_Map_2011.pdf.
[33] Kahiya, 2013.
[34] Lorenzen, M. & Mudambi, R. (2013). Clusters, connectivity and catch-up: Bollywood and Bangalore in the global economy. *Journal of Economic Geography*, 13(3), 501–34.

Rica,[35] Brazil,[36] Turkey[37] and China.[38] Even though limited in number, these studies point to some singularities in the behaviour of HTNVs from emerging economies.

First, HTNVs are characterised by significant efforts in technology development.[39] In several cases, the technological and market strategies of HTNVs born in the context of emerging economies are guided by imitation and these companies often lack R&D capabilities.[40] Second, innovation typically takes place in structures other than specialised R&D departments. Third, emerging country HTNVs tend to operate in niche markets.[41] They are more efficient than larger competitors at adapting and customising their products to meet specific demands. Niche markets represent opportunities for HTNVs from emerging economies because demand is often too small or too specific to attract larger international competitors. These characteristics represent opportunities and challenges for HTNVs from emerging markets to enter and sustain their business in the international arena and to develop entirely new products to meet the demands of foreign markets.

The internationalisation of Brazilian HTNVs

How do small and nascent businesses with limited resources succeed rapidly abroad?[42] There is no consensus about the factors explaining early and accelerated internationalisation but some factors related to

[35] Ciravegna, L., Lopez, L. & Kundu, S. (2014). Country of origin and network effects on internationalization: A comparative study of SMEs from an emerging and developed economy. *Journal of Business Research*, 67(5), 916–23; Lopez, L. E., Kundu, S. K. & Ciravegna, L. (2009). Born global or born regional? Evidence from an exploratory study in the Costa Rican software industry. *Journal of International Business Studies*, 40(7), 1228–38.

[36] Dib et al., 2010.

[37] Uner, M. M., Kocak, A., Cavusgil, E. & Cavusgil, S. T. (2013). Do barriers to export vary for born globals and across stages of internationalization? An empirical inquiry in the emerging market of Turkey. *International Business Review*, 22(5), 800–13.

[38] Zou, H. & Ghauri, P. N. (2010). Internationalizing by learning: The case of Chinese high-tech new ventures. *International Marketing Review*, 27(2), 223–44.

[39] Onetti et al., 2010.

[40] Kiss et al., 2012.

[41] Dib et al., 2010.

[42] Ribeiro, Oliveira & Borini, 2012; Cahen, Oliveira & Borini, 2017; Ribeiro et al., 2014.

the entrepreneur and organisational and external factors are thought to be positively associated with the early and accelerated internationalisation of HTNVs.

Entrepreneurs are perceived as individuals who are more aware of opportunities than others.[43] Typically, entrepreneurs who run international HTNVs have a higher tolerance for risk and have developed a global mindset (thanks to an international orientation and experience or education abroad) and are often able to use their personal or professional relationships and networks to enable businesses internationally. Organisational factors, such as innovation capability combined with possession of unique assets, including brand awareness, market and product knowledge, and the orientation to meet international clients' demands, are found to be positively related to accelerated internationalisation.[44] External factors such as country size and the size of the domestic market also appear to be influential; small countries or countries with small domestic markets seem to favour accelerated internationalisation. Other factors, such as industry characteristics,[45] strategic alliances and networking may influence the likelihood of accelerated internationalisation for new ventures as well.

Based on the literature, we propose a list of internal organisational factors,[46] factors linked to the entrepreneur[47] and factors related to the business environment of the home country[48] to build a comprehensive framework for understanding the accelerated internationalisation of Brazilian HTNVs. While organisational and entrepreneurial factors are frequently mentioned in studies on accelerated internationalisation, the analysis of the external environment is less common. We call attention here to factors that are discussed in studies of born-globals, particularly those that are especially relevant to the context of emerging economies.[49] We emphasise organisational capabilities such as

[43] Oviatt & McDougall, 1994.

[44] Knight & Kim, 2009; Cavusgil, S. T. & Knight, G. (2015). The born global firm: An entrepreneurial and capabilities perspective on early and rapid internationalization. *Journal of International Business Studies*, 46(1), 3–16.

[45] Fernhaber, S. A., McDougall, P. & Oviatt, B. (2007). Exploring the role of industry structure in new venture internationalization. *Entrepreneurship Theory and Practice*, 31(4), 517–42.

[46] Knight & Kim, 2009.

[47] Oviatt & McDougall, 1994.

[48] Fernhaber et al., 2007.

[49] Kiss et al., 2012.

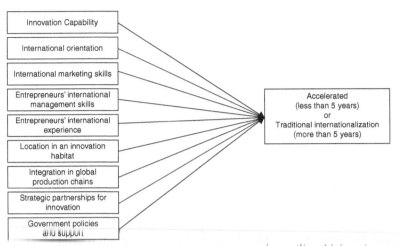

Figure 17.2 Drivers of the internationalisation of Brazilian high-tech new ventures.

international orientation, international marketing skills and innovation capabilities, the entrepreneur's international management skills and international experience. We also look at external factors such as integration into a global production chain, location in an innovation habitat, partnerships with universities, research institutes and multinational companies and government policies that support internationalisation in the home country (see Figure 17.2).

Although industry characteristics and the size of the domestic market are important external factors, they do not hold much explanatory power in this case. The influence of limited domestic markets on born-globals is a common factor studied in small European countries and is not relevant to a large market like Brazil. A study conducted in the United States identified more than twenty industry structure variables that could influence the likelihood of the early internationalisation of a new venture.[50] The complexity and variety of industry factors precludes us from analysing their effects here, especially as Brazilian HTNVs are concentrated in an extremely limited number of industries.

To study the successful internationalisation strategies of small and nascent businesses we compare HTNVs with accelerated

---

[50] Fernhaber et al., 2007.

internationalisation with HTNVs that followed a traditional, slower-paced internationalisation process. The dependent variable is binary and picks the type of internationalisation: accelerated or traditional. Accelerated internationalisation happens when the company does business in at least one international market within five years of foundation.[51] Traditional internationalisation happens when the HTNV initiates international operations more than five years after its foundation. The independent variables related to organisational factors, factors related to entrepreneurs and the external context are included in accordance with existing models.[52] The following independent variables are taken into account: innovation capability; international orientation; international marketing skills; entrepreneurs' international management skills; entrepreneurs' international experience; location in an innovation habitat; integration in global production chains; strategic partnership for innovation (in the home country) and government policies and support for internationalisation (see Figure 17.2). A logistic regression is used to estimate whether each of the independent variables correlates with the speed of entry of HTNVs in international markets.

We received responses to our survey from 214 out of a population of almost 800 firms. The precise number of HTNVs invited to take part in this research cannot be defined because in several cases we were not granted the full list of the companies present in incubators and technology parks. The invitations to answer our questionnaire were sent by the firms' managers. ANPROTEC helped advertise the research effort on its website with a direct link to the questionnaire. We could not control how many companies had exposure to this channel. Out of these 214 companies, 85 (39.7%) had some type of foreign business. However, thirty-six of these eighty-five questionnaires had missing values or several answers with no variance and were eliminated from the analysis. In total, forty-nine HTNVs were studied, of which thirty-one (63%) had experienced accelerated internationalisation and eighteen (37%) had not.

---

[51] Dib et al., 2010.
[52] Knight & Kim, 2009; Knight & Cavusgil,2004; Oviatt and McDougall, 1994; Fernhaber, S. A., Gilbert, B. A. & McDougall, P. P. (2008). International entrepreneurship and geographic location: An empirical examination of new venture internationalization. *Journal of International Business Studies*, 39(2), 267–90.

The results lend some empirical support for the construct of international management skills. In the case of Brazilian HTNVs, those with an entrepreneur or group of executives with international management skills and experience are the most likely to experience accelerated internationalisation. This result is consistent with the results in the literature on born-globals, which suggest that entrepreneurs' international management skills are essential for rapid entry into international markets. It also supports the results of other studies from emerging contexts[53] indicating that the accelerated internationalisation of HTNVs from emerging markets hinges on the international management skills of entrepreneurs.

In HTNVs from developed countries accelerated internationalisation is mainly driven by organisational capabilities such as the firm's international orientation, international marketing skills and existing technological competences.[54] In contrast to the results reported in the literature, our findings suggest that in order to establish operations in an international market, Brazilian HTNVs seem to require more time to build organisational capabilities. Moreover, Brazilian HTNVs with greater experience in the domestic market (more than five years) rely more on their innovation capability and international marketing skills during their internationalisation processes.

Among the factors related to the external environment, our results suggest that HTNVs integrated into a global production chain tend to follow an accelerated internationalisation process. The HTNVs that either become suppliers of a large multinational company or enter highly globalised sectors tend to be born-global companies. These HTNVs are in sectors where global supply chains are already configured, such as the aeronautics, biotechnology or software industries. The new ventures in our study tend to be born-globals and appear to be 'pulled' rapidly into the international domain because of the market conditions and supply needs of their foreign clients. Moreover, the more experience the HTNV has in the domestic market, the more it can benefit from certain external factors in its internationalisation process, such as being located in an innovation habitat, partnerships

---

[53] Hill, T. L. & Mudambi, R. (2010). Far from Silicon Valley: How emerging economies are re-shaping our understanding of global entrepreneurship. *Journal of International Management*, 16(4), 321–27.

[54] Knight & Kim, 2009; Cavusgil & Knight, 2015.

with universities, research institutes and multinational companies, and government policies that support internationalisation.

The results indicate that HTNVs with more experience in the domestic market have long-standing business bonds and experience in the home business environment, making it easier to use these contextual resources to enter the international market. Being located in an innovation habitat has been an efficient mechanism to facilitate access to sophisticated equipment, technological services, professional training, commercial structures for sales, and so on. Regarding partnerships, more experience in the home market benefits HTNVs in their innovation partnerships with other organisations in Brazil, compared to HTNVs that internationalised before reaching five years' activity. Given the limited organisational strength and the scarcity of resources of various types, local connections in the home country appear to be extremely important. Similarly, HTNVs that enter the international market after five years of activity are able to take significantly more advantage of government support for internationalisation than firms that follow an accelerated internationalisation process.

Barriers to internationalisation

For entrepreneurs or executives of HTNVs, it is essential to know what barriers can limit entry to international markets. This knowledge can direct internal decisions and help the realistic assessment of a firm's ability to grow and compete overseas.[55] Barriers are the constraints that hinder a firm's ability to initiate, develop or sustain business operations in overseas markets. In the context of the exporting activities of manufacturing firms, there are extensive studies focusing on barriers to entry.[56] Because we focus our attention on domestic HTNVs, as opposed to firms currently engaged in international markets, our findings are novel as we consider barriers to internationalisation, not barriers to export.

Barriers to internationalisation can be internal to the firm (e.g. lack of financial, strategic, managerial and operational resources and capabilities) or external (e.g. the institutional environment of the home country and various factors in foreign locations, such as unfamiliar

---

[55] Cahen, Lahiri & Borini, 2016.
[56] Leonidou, 1995; Uner et al., 2013.

business protocols, high tariffs and tax structures, cultural differences, etc.). Typically, domestic firms perceive barriers related to management inertia, that is, staying at home. These include the fear of non-acceptance of a product in a new market, difficulties in raising initial investment for export, lack of information about tariff and non-tariff barriers and exporting procedures, limited personal contacts in foreign markets and the lack of qualified personnel to conduct exports. Internationalised firms perceive more operational barriers, such as problems with export procedures and red tape, slow payment by foreign buyers, poor economic conditions in foreign markets, and so on.[57]

Questioned about the barriers constraining the internationalisation of HTNVs, the respondents in our survey were asked to evaluate the influence of perceived barriers to their internationalisation process on a five-point Likert scale (1 = not important and 5 = very important) (see Table 17.2).[58] The items were analysed for validation and a pretest was conducted by asking top executives of three HTNVs to review the clarity and relevance of the survey. Of the 214 responses, 114 were from companies that operated only nationally. Questionnaires with missing values were eliminated from analysis. The final sample consisted of ninety-two complete survey responses.

Our results indicate that HTNVs in Brazil perceive three major barriers to internationalisation: institutional (32.1% of the variance), organisational capabilities (22.69%) and human resources (14.87%). These difficulties create a negative attitude towards initiating internationalisation among executives in HTNVs who often decide to remain committed to their local market.[59]

Executives in Brazilian HTNVs perceive the institutional barrier as the most significant obstacle to their firms' internationalisation. Emerging markets are characterised by institutional specificities that are different from those in developed economy contexts. They can include weak or underdeveloped capital, labour and product markets,

---

[57] Leonidou, L. C. (2004). An analysis of the barriers hindering small business export development. *Journal of Small Business Management*, 42(3), 279–302; Kahiya, 2013.

[58] Knight & Kim, 2009; Da Rocha, A. D., Freitas, Y. A. & Da Silva, J. F. (2008). Do perceived export barriers change over time? A longitudinal study of Brazilian exporters of manufactured goods. *Latin American Business Review*, 9(1), 102–28.

[59] Cahen, Lahiri & Borini, 2016.

Table 17.2 *Barriers to internationalisation in Brazilian HTNVs*

Barriers	Items
Institutional	Insufficient or inadequate technological skills to compete on cost and quality
	Difficulties in offering products/services that meet the needs of international customers
	High cost of capital to start international operations (due to unfavourable government rules and regulations)
	Lack of government support (credit lines, training programmes, tax incentives)
	High logistical costs owing to the poor infrastructure of the home country
	High tax burden in the home country
	High production costs compared to competitors in international markets
	Unfavourable exchange rate
Organisational capabilities	Insufficient experience and lack of information to internationalise
	Insufficient financial resources to start an international operation
	Difficulties of access to business partners, distribution channels and/or customers in international markets
	Difficulties in offering products/services that meet the needs of international customers
	Insufficient or inadequate technological skills to compete on cost and quality
Human resources	Language barriers (for communicating with foreign clients and customers)
	Human resources unprepared for international action (lack of qualified personnel to deal with exporting procedures or to conduct exporting operations)

Sources: Da Rocha et al. (2008); Kahiya, 2013; Leonidou (1995); Uner et al. (2013); Pinho, J. C. & Martins, L. (2010). Exporting barriers: Insights from Portuguese small- and medium-sized exporters and non-exporters. *Journal of International Entrepreneurship*, 8(3), 254–72.

insufficient protection of legal and intellectual rights, and so on,[60] known as institutional voids. These voids are often reported as the main difficulties for international expansion, especially by new ventures. Embedded in the local institutional environment and deprived of institutional support, executives in Brazilian HTNVs express perceived difficulty in understanding and managing the complexities associated with entering foreign markets.[61]

Firms from emerging markets are known to be constrained. They generally lack exposure to international competition and the capabilities to access a superior knowledge base, connect with a global supply chain, create and handle reputed brands and so on. Deprived of such capabilities emerging market firms find it difficult to develop, adapt and reconfigure internal competencies that might enable them to thrive in unknown environments. This resource-based approach can explain why executives in Brazilian HTNVs perceive difficulties in offering products and services that meet the needs of international customers, possess insufficient or inadequate technological skills to compete on cost and quality bases and end up having low ratio of value to production cost relative to competitors in international markets.

In this study's context, the lack of understanding of any language other than Portuguese indicates the absence of the language skills that are essential for international expansion. Because HTNVs lack this important element of human capital they perceive it as a barrier to internationalisation, which requires proficiency in a foreign language, predominantly English, to deal with foreign partners. The second HR issue (lack of qualified personnel to deal with export procedures or to conduct export operations) reflects another important restraint on Brazilian HTNVs. These firms have not experienced any aspect of internationalisation and lack the accumulated learning necessary to enter and operate in foreign markets. Consequently, top executives in HTNVs find it difficult to consider making essential decisions about internationalisation, including choosing the appropriate entry mode and accessing valuable resources, customising products or services for foreign customers, dealing with the demands of foreign governments and suppliers and competing successfully with foreign rivals.

[60] Lahiri, S., Elango, B. & Kundu, S. (2014). Cross-border acquisition in services: Comparing ownership choice of developed and emerging economy MNEs in India. *Journal of World Business*, 49(3), 409–20.

[61] Cahen, Lahiri & Borini, 2016.

Conclusion

Our central goal in this study was to analyse the factors influencing the accelerated internationalisation of HTNVs and the barriers that limit the entry of these firms into international markets.

Our findings indicate that Brazilian HTNVs likely to experience early and accelerated internationalisation are those that have an entrepreneur or a group of executives with international management skills and are integrated into a global supply chain.[62]

Regarding the role of external factors on internationalisation, we find that the more experience a Brazilian HTNV has in the domestic market, the more it can benefit from certain external factors in its internationalisation process, such as being located in an innovation habitat, partnerships with universities, research institutes and multinational companies, and government policies that support internationalisation.[63]

While studying barriers to internationalisation, we focus only on domestic HTNVs, analysing the factors that impede the initiation of internationalisation, as opposed to firms currently engaged in international markets through exports. Much previous research on barriers to internationalisation has tended to focus on the latter. From this we know that HTNVs can perceive barriers in the form of the country's institutional environment, the level of the firm's human capital or the extent of the firm's organisational capabilities.[64]

Almost all barriers to entry in international markets identified in developed countries[65] also exist in developing countries,[66] especially organisational and human resources constraints in the case of small and nascent companies. This result gains even more relevance in the case of HTNVs from countries that do not have a consolidated position as exporters (or even producers) of high-tech products. Home country institutional barriers, which are more prominent in emerging contexts, make the challenge even greater.

---

[62] Ribeiro, Oliveira & Borini, 2012; Cahen, Oliveira & Borini, 2017; Ribeiro et al., 2014.

[63] Ribeiro, Oliveira, & Borini, 2012.

[64] Cahen, Lahiri & Borini, 2016.

[65] Leonidou, 1995, 2004.

[66] Tesfom, G. & Lutz, C. (2006). A classification of export marketing problems of small and medium sized manufacturing firms in developing countries. *International Journal of Emerging Markets*, 1(3), 262–81.

We observe that for nascent companies in high-tech sectors institutional barriers are perceived as the main obstacle to going abroad. Our results indicate that the major perceived barriers for Brazilian HTNVs are external to the company and are created by the institutional voids[67] in their home country.

Managerial implications

Our results indicate that it is essential for executives in HTNVs with accelerated internationalisation to have international management skills. At the same time, the lack of employees prepared to operate in international markets is also perceived as a significant barrier, although not the most important one, for an HTNV entering international markets.

To deal with the human resources constraint, executives in HTNVs need to invest in recruiting the right talent within the company (e.g. hiring experienced managers with high international exposure). These candidates can typically handle cultural differences, speak a second language and understand the level of international competitiveness of the company's products. The most important aspect of enhancing the human resources within the company is to provide adequate training (in-house or via consultants) to prepare top and mid-level managers for international operations. This also includes providing adequate training in foreign languages, mainly English.

Because one of the barriers associated with organisational capabilities is insufficient or inadequate technological skills to compete on cost and quality, upgrading the firm's technological skills and production methods to lower operational costs and enhance the quality of manufactured products and services is also mandatory for HTNVs. These improvements do not happen overnight; they require HTNV executives to have the proper vision and make dedicated efforts aimed at capacity and efficiency building.[68]

The barriers that HTNV executives perceive as most problematic are external to the firm. Rooted in the local institutional environment and deprived of institutional support, entrepreneurs in Brazilian HTNVs perceive difficulties in navigating the complexities associated

---

[67] Kanna & Palepu, 2010.
[68] Cahen, Lahiri & Borini, 2016.

with entering foreign markets and performing well. As a result, they develop negative attitudes towards initiating internationalisation.[69] Managers could circumvent some of these external or institutional barriers by forming strategic alliances with other companies that have expertise in overcoming such difficulties. To overcome or at least minimise institutional barriers at home, managers of HTNVs need to be on the lookout for other institutional environments that offer low capital cost to start international operations. Our results also indicate that government policies can be counterproductive for HTNVs and that entrepreneurs need to establish better relations with government institutions in order to receive important government support in the form of credits, loans, training and tax rebates and in this way overcome the main institutional constraints at home.[70]

Future research

Much work remains to be done in research into the internationalisation of high-tech new ventures from emerging markets. Early and accelerated internationalisation is still a novel approach in international expansion, according to the most recent discussions.[71] Two decades after the pioneering study by Oviatt and McDougall,[72] there are no answers to basic questions, such as, why and how these firms develop and implement their internationalisation strategies, and what makes them successful.[73] What are the advantages of internationalisation at the early stages of the life cycle of the HTNV? How do HTNVs perform after internationalisation? Why do some firms internationalise early, while others internationalise late, and some not at all?[74] Unifying and improving the contradictory operational definitions in accelerated internationalisation research is also critical for better comparative studies, and to expand theoretical explanations of the

[69] Cahen, Lahiri & Borini, 2016.
[70] Cahen, Lahiri & Borini, 2016.
[71] Cavusgil & Knight, 2015; Coviello, N. (2015). Re-thinking research on born globals. *Journal of International Business Studies*, 46(1), 17–26. http://doi.org/10.1057/jibs.2014.59; Zander, I. & Rose, E. L. (2015). Born globals and international business : Evolution of a field of research. *Journal of International Business Studies*, 46(1), 27–35.
[72] Oviatt & McDougall, 1994.
[73] Zander et al., 2015, p. 27.
[74] Cavusgil & Knight, 2015, p. 11.

phenomena. Cavusgil and Knight[75] highlight the need to bring further clarity to the definitions of early and accelerated internationalisation, born-global firms and international new ventures.

Existing studies of international entrepreneurship have focused consistently on HTNVs from developed countries, while HTNVs from emerging markets remain understudied.[76] Future research might examine consistently if the early and accelerated internationalisation of HTNVs differs in emerging economies. How do born-global firms from advanced economies perform in complex emerging markets and vice-versa? In less developed economies, how do governmental and institutional characteristics affect the international behaviour of HTNVs? Our study is an attempt to answer some of these questions, although we rely on data collected from executives in a single country. This limits the generalisability of our results. Additionally, research based on the perceptions of top executives carries an inherent bias. Future research needs to compare the international behaviour of HTNVs from various emerging markets via more case studies and quantitative approaches. The use of external measures is also critical for country comparability, such as the Global Entrepreneurship Monitor, World Bank Global Entrepreneurship Survey, OECD/Kauffman Entrepreneurship Indicators Program or the Global Competitiveness Index. These are also important sources for additional data and can facilitate longitudinal studies of HTNVs in a variety of countries. Our study took a cross-sectional approach and did not take into consideration the gradual process of the formation of managerial perceptions.

In our study we analyse external factors that feature only infrequently in studies of born-globals from developed countries, such as location in an innovation habitat, integration into global production chains, strategic partnerships for innovation in the home country and government policies.[77] Recent research has emphasised the role of these factors in the rise of HTNVs from emerging markets. Future research might investigate what differentiates these approaches and explore more deeply questions like the role played by ecosystems and industrial clusters in launching and growing born global firms. How do ecosystems advance the internationalisation goals of young firms?

---

[75] Cavusgil & Knight, 2015.
[76] Cavusgil & Knight, 2015.
[77] Ribeiro, Oliveira & Borini, 2012; Ribeiro et al., 2014.

What are the roles of government policy in supporting internationalisation of HTNVs?

Finally, the firms in this study are spread over distinctive technology-based industries that may require very different knowledge, skills, abilities and resources to internationalise. Future research needs to examine how drivers and barriers to internationalisation differ across industries. What factors, at industry and firm levels, support HTNVs' international strategies? What specific resources, capabilities, orientations and strategies enhance their performance?

Index

Printed in the United States
by Baker & Taylor Publisher Services